DATE DUE

NOV 1 3 1991	
JAN 2 1992	
NOV. 4 1994	
MAY 0 3 1995	
APR 0 8 1996	
APR 1 9 1996	
JUL 15 1996	
JAN 2 9 1997	
DEC 0 3 1997	
JAN 0 2 1998	

THE CONTEMPORARY SHAKESPEARE SERIES

VOLUME IV

King Henry The Fourth,
Part One

*

King Henry The Fourth,
Part Two

*

Love's Labour's Lost

*

Othello

*

The Winter's Tale

Edited by A. L. Rowse

Modern Text with Introduction

UNIVERSITY PRESS OF AMERICA

Copyright © 1985 by A. L. Rowse

University Press of America,® Inc.

4720 Boston Way
Lanham, MD 20706

3 Henrietta Street
London WC2E 8LU England

Distributed to the trade by The Scribner Book Companies

Library of Congress Cataloging in Publication Data
(Revised for volume 4, parts 1 and 2)

Shakespeare, William, 1564-1616.
  The contemporary Shakespeare series.

  Contents: v. 1. Hamlet. Julius Caesar. The merchant
of Venice. A Midsummer night's dream. Romeo and
Juliet. The tempest — v. 2. As you like it.
Coriolanus. King Lear. King Richard the Second.
Twelfth night —   — v. 4. Love's labours lost.
The winter's tale. Othello. King Henry the Fourth,
part I. King Henry the Fourth, part II.
  I. Rowse, A. L. (Alfred Leslie), 1903-
II. Title.
PR2754.R67   1984b   822.3'3   84-5105
ISBN 0-8191-3928-9 (v. 4)

The plays in this volume are also available individually in
paperbound editions from University Press of America.

Book design by Leon Bolognese

WHY A CONTEMPORARY SHAKESPEARE?

The starting point of my project was when I learned both from television and in education, that Shakespeare is being increasingly dropped in schools and colleges because of the difficulty of the language. In some cases, I gather, they are given just a synopsis of the play, then the teacher or professor embroiders from his notes.

This is deplorable. We do not want Shakespeare progressively dropped because of superfluous difficulties that can be removed, skilfully, conservatively, keeping to every line of the text. Nor must we look at the question statically, for this state of affairs will worsen as time goes on and we get further away from the language of 400 years ago—difficult enough in all conscience now.

We must begin by ridding our mind of prejudice, i.e. we must not pre-judge the matter. A friend of mine on New York radio said that he was 'appalled' at the very idea; but when he heard my exposition of what was proposed he found it reasonable and convincing.

Just remember, I do not need it myself: *I live in the Elizabethan age*, Shakespeare's time, and have done for years, and am familiar with its language, and his. But even for me there are still difficulties—still more for modern people, whom I am out to help.

Who, precisely?

Not only students at school and in college, but all readers of Shakespeare. Not only those, but all viewers of the plays, in the theatre, on radio and television—actors too, who increasingly find pronunciation of the words difficult, particularly obsolete ones—and there are many, besides the difficulty of accentuation.

The difficulties are naturally far greater for non-English-speaking peoples. We must remember that he is our greatest asset, and that other peoples use him a great deal in learning our language. There are no Iron Curtains for him—though, during Mao's Cultural Revolution in China, he was prohibited. Now that the ban has been lifted, I learn that the Chinese in thousands flock to his plays.

Now, a good deal that was grammatical four hundred years ago is positively ungrammatical today. We might begin by removing what is no longer good grammar.

For example: plural subjects with a verb in the singular:

'*Is* Bushy, Green and the earl of Wiltshire dead?' Any objection to replacing 'is' correctly by 'are'? Certainly not. I notice that some modern editions already correct—

These high wild hills and rough uneven ways
Draw*s* out our miles and make*s* them wearisome

to 'draw' and 'make', quite sensibly. Then, why not go further and regularise this Elizabethan usage to modern, consistently throughout?

Similarly with archaic double negatives—'Nor shall you not think neither'—and double comparatives: 'this is more worser than before.' There are hundreds of instances of what is now just bad grammar to begin with.

There must be a few thousand instances of superfluous subjunctives to reduce to simplicity and sense. Today we use the subjunctive occasionally after 'if', when we say 'if it be'. But we mostly say today 'if it is'. Now Shakespeare has hundreds of subjunctives, not only after if, but after though, although, unless, lest, whether, until, till, etc.

I see no point whatever in retaining them. They only add superfluous trouble in learning English, when the great appeal of our language as a world-language is precisely that it has less grammar to learn than almost any. Russian is unbelievably complicated. Inflected languages—German is like Latin in this respect—are really rather backward; it has been a great recommendation that English has been more progressive in this respect in simplifying itself.

Now we can go further along this line: keep a few subjunctives, if you must, but reduce them to a minimum.

Let us come to the verb. It is a great recommendation to modern English that our verbs are comparatively simple to conjugate — unlike even French, for example. In the Elizabethan age there was a great deal more of it, and some of it inconsistent in modern usage. Take Shakespeare's,

'Where is thy husband now? Where be thy brothers?'
Nothing is lost by rendering this as we should today:

Where is your husband now? Where are your brothers?

And so on.

The second and third person singular—all those shouldsts and wouldsts, wilts and shalts, haths and doths, have become completely obsolete. Here a vast simplification may be effected—with no loss as far as I can see, and with advantages from several points of view.

For example, 'st' at the end of a word is rather difficult to say, and more difficult even for us when it is succeeded by a word beginning with 'th'. Try saying, 'Why usurpedst thou this?' Foreigners have the greatest difficulty in pronouncing our 'th' anyway—many never succeed in getting it round their tongues. Many of these tongue-twisters even for us proliferate in Shakespeare, and I see no objection to getting rid of *superfluous* difficulties. Much easier for people to say, 'Why did you usurp this?'—the same number of syllables too.

This pre-supposes getting rid of almost all thous and thees and thines. I have no objection to keeping a few here and there, if needed for a rhyme—even then they are sometimes not necessary.

Some words in Shakespeare have changed their meaning into the exact opposite: we ought to remove that stumbling-block. When Hamlet says, 'By heaven, I'll make a ghost of him that *lets* me', he means *stops*; and we should replace it by stops, or holds me. Shakespeare regularly uses the word 'owe' where we should say own: the meaning has changed. Take a line like, 'Thou dost here usurp the name thou ow'st not': we should say, 'You do here usurp the name you own not', with the bonus of getting rid of two ugly 'sts'.

The word 'presently' in the Elizabethan age did not mean in a few minutes or so, but immediately—instantly has the same number of syllables. 'Prevent' then had its Latin meaning, to go before, or forestall. Shakespeare frequently uses the word 'still' for always or ever.

Let us take the case of many archaic forms of words, simple one-syllable words that can be replaced without the slightest difference to the scansion: 'sith' for since, 'wrack' for wreck, 'holp' for helped, 'writ' for wrote, 'brake' for broke, 'spake' for spoke, 'bare' for bore, etc.

These give no trouble, nor do a lot of other words that he uses: 'repeal' for recall, 'reproof' for disproof, 'decline' for incline. A few words do give more trouble. The linguistic scholar, C. T. Onions, notes that it is sometimes difficult to give the precise meaning Shakespeare attaches to the word 'conceit'; it usually means thought, or fancy, or concept. I do not know that it ever has our meaning; actually the word 'conceited' with him means ingenious or fantastic, as 'artificial' with Elizabethans meant artistic or ingenious.

There is a whole class of words that have completely gone out, of which moderns do not know the meaning. I find no harm in replacing the word 'coistrel' by rascal, which is what it means—actually it has much the same sound—or 'coil' by fuss; we find 'accite' for summon, 'indigest' for formless. Hamlet's word 'reechy', for the incestuous kisses of his mother and her brother-in-law, has gone out of use: the nearest word, I suppose, would be reeky, but filthy would be a suitable modern equivalent.

In many cases it is extraordinary how little one would need to change, how conservative one could be. Take Hamlet's famous soliloquy, 'To be or not to be.' I find only two words that moderns would not know the meaning of, and one of those we might guess:

> . . .When he himself might his *quietus* make
> With a bare bodkin? Who would *fardels* bear. . .

'Quietus' means put paid; Elizabethans wrote the Latin 'quietus est' at the bottom of a bill that was paid—when it was—to say that it was settled. So that you could replace 'quietus' by settlement, same number of syllables, though not the same accentuation; so I would prefer to use the word acquittance, which has both.

'Fardels' means burdens; I see no objection to rendering, 'Who would burdens bear'—same meaning, same number of syllables, same accent: quite simple. I expect all the ladies to know what a bodkin is: a long pin, or skewer.

Now let us take something really difficult—perhaps the most difficult passage to render in all Shakespeare. It is the virtuoso comic piece describing all the diseases that horseflesh is heir to, in *The Taming of the Shrew*. The horse is Petruchio's. President Reagan tells me that this is the one Shakespearean part that he played—and a very gallant one too. In Britain last year we saw a fine performance of his on horseback in Windsor Park alongside of Queen Elizabeth II—very familiar ground to William Shakespeare and Queen Elizabeth I, as we know from *The Merry Wives of Windsor*.

Here is a headache for us: Petruchio's horse (not President Reagan's steed) was 'possessed with the glanders, and like to mose in the chine; troubled with the lampass, infected with the fashions, full of windgalls, sped with spavins, rayed with the yellows, past cure of the fives, stark spoiled with the staggers, begnawn with the bots; swayed in the back, and shoulder-shotten; near-legged before, and with a half-cheeked bit, and a headstall of sheep's leather', etc.

What on earth are we to make of that? No doubt it raised a laugh with Elizabethans, much more familiarly acquainted with horseflesh than we are; but I doubt if Hollywood was able to produce a nag for Reagan that qualified in all these respects.

Now, even without his horsemanship, we can clear one fence at the outset: 'mose in the chine'. Pages of superfluous commentary have been devoted to that word 'mose'. There was no such Elizabethan word: it was simply a printer's misprint for 'mourn', meaning dripping or running; so it suggests a running sore. You would need to consult the *Oxford English Dictionary*, compiled on historical lines, for some of the words, others like 'glanders' country folk know and we can guess.

So I would suggest a rendering something like this: 'possessed with glanders, and with a running sore in the back; troubled in the gums, and infected in the glands; full of galls in the fetlocks and swollen in the joints; yellow with jaundice, past cure of the strangles; stark spoiled with the staggers, and gnawed by worms; swayed in the back and shoulder put out; near-legged before, and with a half-cheeked bit and headgear of sheep's leather', etc. That at least makes it intelligible.

Oddly enough, one encounters the greatest difficulty with the least important words and phrases, Elizabethan expletives and malapropisms, or salutations like God 'ild you, Godden, for God shield you, Good-even, and so on. 'God's wounds' was Elizabeth I's favourite swearword; it appears frequently enough in Victorian novels as 'Zounds'— I have never heard anyone use it. The word 'Marry!', as in the phrase 'Marry come up!' has similarly gone out, though a very old gentleman at All Souls, Sir Charles Oman, had heard the phrase in the back-streets of Oxford just after the 1914-18 war. 'Whoreson' is frequent on the lips of coarse fellows in Shakespeare: the equivalent in Britain today would be bloody, in America (I suppose) s.o.b.

Relative pronouns, who and which: today we use who for persons, which for things. In Elizabethan times the two were hardly distinguished and were interchangeable. Provokingly Shakespeare used the personal relative 'who' more frequently for impersonal objects, rivers, buildings, towns; and then he no less frequently uses 'which' for persons. This calls out to be regularised for the modern reader.

Other usages are more confusing. The word 'cousin'

was used far more widely by the Elizabethans for their kin: it included nephews, for instance. Thus it is confusing in the English History plays to find a whole lot of nephews—like Richard III's, whom he had made away with in the Tower of London—referred to and addressed as cousins. That needs regularisation today, in the interests of historical accuracy and to get the relationship clear. The word 'niece' was sometimes used of a grandchild—in fact this is the word Shakespeare used in his will for his little grand-daughter Elizabeth, his eventual heiress who ended up as Lady Barnard, leaving money to her poor relations the Hathaways at Stratford. The Latin word *neptis*, from which niece comes also meant grandchild—Shakespeare's grammar-school education at Stratford was in Latin, and this shows you that he often thought of a word in terms of its Latin derivation.

Malapropisms, misuse of words, sometimes mistaking of meanings, are frequent with uneducated people, and sometimes not only with those. Shakespeare transcribed them from lower-class life to raise a laugh, more frequently than any writer for the purpose. They are an endearing feature of the talk of Mistress Quickly, hostess of the Boar's Inn in East Cheapside, and we have no difficulty in making out what she means. But in case some of us do, and for the benefit of non-native English speakers, I propose the correct word in brackets afterwards: 'You have brought her into such a canaries [quandary]. . .and she's as fartuous [virtuous] a civil, modest wife. . .'

Abbreviations: Shakespeare's text is starred—and in my view, marred—by innumerable abbreviations, which not only look ugly on the page but are sometimes difficult to pronounce. It is not easy to pronounce 'is't', or 'in't', or 'on't', and some others: if we cannot get rid of them altogether they should be drastically reduced. Similarly with 'i'th''', 'o'th''', with which the later plays are liberally bespattered, for "in the" or "of the."

We also have a quite unnecessary spattering of apostrophes in practically all editions of the plays—''d' for the past participle, e.g. 'gather'd'. Surely it is much better to regularise the past participle 'ed', e.g. gathered; and when the last syllable is, far less frequently, to be pronounced, then accent it, gatherèd.

This leads into the technical question of scansion, where a practising poet is necessary to get the accents right, to help the reader, and still more the actor. Most people will hardly notice that, very often, the frequent ending of words in 'ion', like reputation, has to be pronounced with two syllables at the end. So I propose to accent this when necessary, e.g. reputatiòn. I have noticed the word 'ocean' as tri-syllabic, so I accent it, to help, oceàn. A number of words which to us are monosyllables were pronounced as two: hour, fire, tired; I sometimes accent or give them a dieresis, either hoùr or fïre. In New England speech words like prayèr, thëre, are apt to be pronounced as two syllables—closer to Elizabethan usage (as with words like gotten) than is modern speech in Britain.

What I notice in practically all editions of Shakespeare's plays is that the editors cannot be relied on to put the accents in the right places. One play edited by a well known Shakespearean editor had, I observed, a dozen accents placed over the wrong syllables. This is understandable, for these people don't write poetry and do not know how to scan. William Shakespeare knew all about scanning, and you need to be both familiar with Elizabethan usage and a practising traditional poet to be able to follow him.

His earlier verse was fairly regular in scansion, mostly iambic pentameter with a great deal of rhyme. As time went on he loosened out, until there are numerous irregular lines—this leaves us much freer in the matter of modernising. Our equivalents should be rhythmically as close as possible, but a strait-jacket need be no part of the equipment. A good Shakespearean scholar tells us, 'there is no necessity for Shakespeare's lines to scan absolutely. He thought of his verse as spoken rather than written and of his rhythmic units in terms of the voice rather than the page.'

There is nothing exclusive or mandatory about my project. We can all read Shakespeare in any edition we like—in the rebarbative olde Englishe spelling of the First Folio, if we wish. Any number of conventional academic editions exist, all weighed down with a burden of notes, many of them superfluous. I propose to make most of them unnecessary—only one occasionally at the foot of very few pages. Let the text be freed of superfluous difficulties, remove obstacles to let it speak for itself, while adhering conservatively to every line.

We really do not need any more editions of the Plays on conventional lines—more than enough of those exist already. But *A Contemporary Shakespeare* on these lines—both revolutionary and conservative—should be a help to everybody all round the world—though especially for younger people, increasingly with time moving away from the language of 400 years ago.

King Henry IV
Part I

INTRODUCTION

The two parts of *Henry IV* form the summit of Shakespeare's achievement in the English history plays so popular with Elizabethans. They found new inspiration in their country's past, opened up for them by the chronicles of Holinshed and Hall, of which Shakespeare made especial use. He also brought to its fullest development the mingling of history with comedy. These plays contain his greatest comic creation, the uproarious, disorderly, but verbally brilliant Falstaff (his verbal brilliance is Shakespeare's, and something of what he thought too is put into Falstaff's mouth).

This astonishing mixture of serious and sad with what is rollicking, ribald and bawdy, was the ultimate seed-bed which proliferated (via Sir Walter Scott) in the historical novel, in European and American literature. (The historically inspired novelist, William Faulkner, always carried a volume of Shakespeare in his suitcase on his journeys.) We may well regard Falstaff as the progenitor of the humorous types who abound subsequently in our literature.

As in all the English history plays we can observe the difference when Shakespeare is transcribing from the chronicle, his immediate source, plain history, and when he is writing, inspired, from his own creation—as in all the scenes whenever Falstaff appears. Sometimes the historical scenes also are inspired, when they appeal to the

dramatist's imagination—as in the affecting interviews of
the harassed King Henry IV and his errant son, Prince
Hal; or the charming scene between Hotspur and his
wife—almost the only thing that appeals to one in that
roughneck character.

Hotspur has always appealed to the public, a plain
soldierly type, very masculine, a man who lives for action:
a brave fighting fool, with no political sense. He is also
very rude to his ally, Glendower, leader of Welsh resistance,
with whom he has no patience. Glendower is faithfully
portrayed, as a very curious Celt: he was indeed something
of a magus, with an undying charisma for the Welsh
people. Shakespeare does justice to both—our sympathies
lie with the more remarkable, the strange and unique
Glendower.

Shakespeare halved the historic Hotspur's age to make
him co-eval with Prince Hal and present the two in dramatic rivalry. It is when we come to the character of this
young Prince of Wales that critics have found difficulty
and expressed least sympathy. He is too subtle for them to
understand, for he is a political type—needs must, if he is
going to be a successful ruler. We now know, as the
Victorians did not, that Prince Hal had a roistering youth—
Shakespeare was close to the tradition and sources brought
to light recently bear him out.

What did the young Prince see so much in the old
reprobate, Falstaff? Well, he was always good for a laugh—
and more, japes and jests, like the robbery on Gadshill, or
the brilliant (and realistic) scenes at the Boar's Head, with
Falstaff and Hal reversing roles and enacting an interview
between father and son, King and Prince. It is to be noticed
that the Prince is verbally a match for Falstaff: they always
have an answer for each other. And, in spite of the bad
company he keeps, the Prince's dignity is always safe-
guarded. He sees that the money robbed at Gadshill is
restored; he is courteous to the deplorable women, Mistress

Quickly and Doll Tearsheet, where Falstaff is rude to them. The Prince is chivalrous and generous about Hotspur —who is not about him. The father-son relationship, between the King with all his cares and responsibilities, and his son and heir having a good fling and adding to his worries, is true to history—and to life. Shakespeare penetrated to the heart of the matter.

Most interesting to us today is the marvellously rich and true portrait of Elizabethan social life, particularly among the lower orders who haunted the taverns like the Boar's Head in Cheapside, or that near Rochester where the highway robbery at Gadshill was planned. Mistress Quickly, hostess of the Boar's Head, is an unforgettable character—first mistress too of the malapropisms which have done such good duty in English comedy. Falstaff's whore, Doll Tearsheet—what a genius Shakespeare had for naming his creations!—is hardly less memorable, with her foul-mouthed language, her quick temper and warm-heartedness: progenitress too of the sentimental good-hearted prostitute in literature. Pistol's inflated speech—he is often drunk, or otherwise crazy—parodies the rant of the earlier Elizabethan stage, with touches from Peele and Kyd, even Marlowe.

Altogether, the Rabelaisian speech of these characters offers special difficulty to the modern reader, particularly when it is the thieves' slang, of which Robert Greene showed his mastery in his 'Conny-catching' pamphlets. Shakespeare knew his way about in it—as probably in the life itself, lodging alone in the City, away from the family at Stratford. John Aubrey noticed that both Shakespeare and Ben Jonson went about observing people's 'humours'. Theatre life and folk gave another rich opportunity. What is so remarkable is the way the dramatist responded to every challenge, with artistic decorum: from the nobility of speech proper to the King and Prince Hal when speaking to his father and as a prince, to the realistic carriers and ostlers loading their goods for Charing Cross.

A modern editor has commented on the numerous collo-
quial abbreviations in these plays, and provides a list of
them: 'a for he, an for if, an't for if it, in's for in his, on't for
on it, i'th' for in the, o'th' for of the, on's for of his, or of its,
ha' for have, 'has for he has, y'are for you are, etc. What is
the point of retaining these forms, an offence to the eye,
and a barrier to both reader and auditor? Here they are
made intelligible in their modern form, along with words
that are archaically unrecognisable. Elizabethan usage—
Shakespeare particularly so—varied greatly, making no
consistent distinction, between personal 'who' and impersonal 'which'. This has been regularised. So also the wide
contemporary use of the term 'cousin' to include uncles,
nephews, etc. apt to confuse the reader.

We catch Shakespeare in his own person, and in his
profession, both in the theatre and as writer. Mistress
Quickly is delighted by the scene put on by Falstaff and
Prince Hal at the Boar's Head: 'O Jesu, he does it as like
one of these harlotry players as ever I see!' We have references to the characters in the old morality plays so familiar
in his youth, the Vice, Iniquity, Vanity. Fun is made of the
inflated style of Lyly's *Euphues*—the platitudes expressed
in pompous antitheses: 'though the camomile, the more it
is trodden on the faster it grows, yet youth, the more it is
wasted the sooner it wears.'

Elizabethan London is all round us, with the Prince
appointing Falstaff to meet him at the Temple hall; or
Lady Percy, whom her husband reproaches for not walking further than Finsbury—where the Fields were a favourite place of recreation—or for talking like a 'comfit-maker's
wife', with her clichés 'in good sooth', and 'as true as I
live.' The speech of Puritans is caricatured: 'God give thee
the spirit of persuasion and him the ears of profiting',
prays Falstaff, who says he could take to singing psalms
like godly weavers at their work. Once more we hear of a

ring—this time a thumb-ring—on an alderman. And Warwickshire is brought to the fore, with Falstaff's march by Daintry and Sutton Co'fil, the local pronunciations for Daventry and Sutton Coldfield.

Contemporary references attest the immense popularity of the character of Falstaff, and the printings of this play were equalled in number only by *Richard III*. For Falstaff Shakespeare originally employed the name of the historic Oldcastle, the Lollard. This was objected to by Lord Cobham, into whose family earlier the Lollard martyr had married. On the first Lord Hunsdon's death in 1596, Cobham succeeded briefly as Lord Chamberlain and patron of Shakespeare's Company. He did not last long, dying next year, to be followed by Hunsdon's son, the second Lord. This must have been more congenial, for the Cobhams belonged to the Cecil grouping, opposed by Essex and Southampton—Shakespeare's affiliation. Cobham lived in Blackfriars, as did the second Lord Hunsdon—familiar ground to Shakespeare and to become more so. We see that this Elizabethan circle was not a large one, its figures known to each other.

CHARACTERS

The King's Party
KING HENRY IV, formerly Henry Bolingbroke, son of
   John of Gaunt
HENRY (or HAL), Prince of Wales, the King's eldest son
LORD JOHN OF LANCASTER, a younger son of
   King Henry IV
EARL OF WESTMORLAND
SIR WALTER BLUNT

The Rebels
HENRY PERCY, Earl of Northumberland
HARRY HOTSPUR, his son
LADY PERCY (KATE), Hotspur's wife
THOMAS PERCY, Earl of Worcester
EDMUND, LORD MORTIMER
LADY MORTIMER, Mortimer's wife, daughter of Glendower
OWEN GLENDOWER, leader of Welsh resistance
EARL OF DOUGLAS
SIR RICHARD VERNON
RICHARD SCROOP, Archbishop of York
SIR MICHAEL, a member of the household of the
   Archbishop

SIR JOHN FALSTAFF
NED POINS
BARDOLPH
PETO
MISTRESS QUICKLY, hostess of the Boar's Head in Eastcheap
FRANCIS, a drawer
GADSHILL
VINTNER, TWO CARRIERS, CHAMBERLAIN, SHERIFF
AND OFFICERS, OSTLER, MESSENGERS, TRAVELLERS,
LORDS AND ATTENDANTS, SOLDIERS

18

Act I

SCENE I
Westminster. The palace.

Enter the King, Prince John of Lancaster,
Earl of Westmorland, Sir Walter Blunt, and others

KING HENRY
So shaken as we are, so wan with care,
Find we a time for frighted peace to pant,
And breathe short-winded accents of new broils
To be commenced in strands afar remote.
No more the thirsty entrance of this soil
Shall daub her lips with her own children's blood,
No more shall trenching war channel her fields,
Nor bruise her flowerets with the armèd hoofs
Of hostile paces. Those opposèd eyes,
Which—like the meteors of a troubled heaven—
All of one nature, of one substance bred,
Did lately meet in the intestine shock
And furious close of civil butchery,
Shall now, in mutual well-beseeming ranks,
March all one way, and be no more opposed
Against acquaintance, kindred, and allies.
The edge of war, like an ill-sheathèd knife,
No more shall cut its master. Therefore friends,
As far as to the sepulchre of Christ—
Whose soldier now, under whose blessed cross
We are impressèd and engaged to fight—
Forthwith a power of English shall we levy:
Whose arms were moulded in their mother's womb

19

To chase these pagans in those holy fields
Over whose acres walked those blessèd feet,
Which fourteen hundred years ago were nailed
For our advantage on the bitter cross.
But this our purpose now is twelve month old,
And fruitless it is to tell you we will go.
Therefòr we meet not now. Then let me hear
Of you, my gentle cousin Westmorland,
What yesternight our Council did decree
In forwarding this dear expedition.

WESTMORLAND
My liege, this haste was hot in questiòn,
And many limits of the charge set down
But yesternight; when all athwart there came
A post from Wales, laden with heavy news;
Whose worst was that the noble Mortimer—
Leading the men of Herefordshire to fight
Against the irregular and wild Glendower—
Was by the rude hands of that Welshman taken,
A thousand of his people butcherèd.
Upon whose dead corpses there was such misuse,
Such beastly shameless transformatiòn
By those Welshwomen done, as may not be
Without much shame retold or spoken of.

KING HENRY
It seems then that the tidings of this strife
Broke off our business for the Holy Land.

WESTMORLAND
This matched with others did, my gracious lord.
For more uneven and unwelcome news
Came from the north, and thus it did import.
On Holy-rood day, the gallant Hotspur there,
Young Harry Percy, and brave Archibald,
That ever valiant and approvèd Scot,
At Holmedon met, where they did spend
A sad and bloody hour—

As by discharge of their artillery,
And shape of likelihood, the news was told.
For he that brought them, in the very heat
And pride of their contention did take horse,
Uncertain of the issue any way.

KING HENRY
Here is a dear, a true industrious friend,
Sir Walter Blunt, new lighted from his horse,
Stained with the variation of each soil
Betwixt that Holmedon and this seat of ours,
And he has brought us smooth and welcome news.
The Earl of Douglas is discomfited.
Ten thousand bold Scots, two-and-twenty knights,
Balked in their own blood, did Sir Walter see
On Holmedon's plains. Of prisoners Hotspur took
Mordake, Earl of Fife and eldest son
To beaten Douglas, and the Earl of Atholl,
Of Murray, Angus, and Menteith.
And is not this an honourable spoil?
A gallant prize? Ha, cousin, is it not?

WESTMORLAND   In faith,
It is a conquest for a prince to boast of.

KING HENRY
Yea, there you make me sad, and make me sin
In envy that my Lord Northumberland
Should be the father to so blest a son.
A son who is the theme of honour's tongue,
Among a grove the very straightest plant,
Who is sweet Fortune's minion and her pride.
While I by looking on the praise of him
See riot and dishonour stain the brow
Of my young Harry. O that it could be proved
That some night-tripping fairy had exchanged
In cradle-clothes our children where they lay,
And called mine Percy, his Plantagenet!
Then would I have his Harry, and he mine.

But leave him from my thoughts. What think you,
    cousin,
Of this young Percy's pride? The prisoners
Whom he in this adventure has surprised
To his own use he keeps, and sends me word
I shall have none but Mordake, Earl of Fife.

WESTMORLAND
This is his uncle's teaching. This is Worcester,
Malevolent to you in all aspècts,
Which makes him prune himself, and bristle up
The crest of youth against your dignity.

KING HENRY
But I have sent for him to answer this,
And for this cause awhile we must neglect
Our holy purpose to Jerusalem.
Cousin, on Wednesday next our Council we
Will hold at Windsor, so inform the lords.
But come yourself with speed to us again,
For more is to be said and to be done
Than out of anger can be utterèd.

WESTMORLAND
I will, my liege.

                                                        Exeunt

SCENE II
Prince Henry's house.

Falstaff asleep: Enter Prince Henry waking him

FALSTAFF Now Hal, what time of day is it, lad?

PRINCE HAL You are so fat-witted with drinking old sack,
and unbuttoning after supper, and sleeping upon benches
after noon, that you have forgotten to demand that truly
which you would truly know. What the devil have you
to do with the time of the day? Unless hours were cups

of sack, and minutes capons, and clocks the tongues of bawds, and dials the signs of brothels, and the blessed sun itself a fair hot wench in flame-coloured taffeta, I see no reason why you should be so superfluous to demand the time of the day.

FALSTAFF Indeed, you come near me now, Hal. For we that take purses go by the moon and the seven stars, and not 'by Phoebus, he, that wandering knight so fair'. And I pray you sweet wag, when you are king, as God save your grace—majesty I should say, for grace you will have none—

PRINCE HAL What, none?

FALSTAFF No, by my word, not so much as will serve to be prologue to an egg and butter.

PRINCE HAL Well, how then? Come, roundly, roundly.

FALSTAFF Well then, sweet wag, when you are king let not us that are squires of the night's body be called thieves of the day's beauty. Let us be Diana's foresters, gentlemen of the shade, minions of the moon. And let men say we are men of good government, being governed as the sea is by our noble and chaste mistress the moon, under whose countenance we steal.

PRINCE HAL You say well, and it holds well too, for the fortune of us that are the moon's men does ebb and flow like the sea, being governed as the sea is, by the moon. As for proof? Now, a purse of gold most resolutely snatched on Monday night, and most dissolutely spent on Tuesday morning, got with swearing 'Lay by!', and spent with crying 'Bring in!', now in as low an ebb as the foot of the ladder, and by and by in as high a flow as the ridge of the gallows.

FALSTAFF By the Lord, you say true, lad—and is not my hostess of the tavern a most sweet wench?

PRINCE HAL As the honey of Hybla, my old lad of the castle. And is not a buff jerkin a most sweet robe of durance?

FALSTAFF How now, how now, mad wag? What, in your quips and your quiddities? What a plague have I to do with a buff jerkin?

PRINCE HAL Why, what a pox have I to do with my hostess of the tavern?

FALSTAFF Well, you have called her to a reckoning many a time and oft.

PRINCE HAL Did I ever call for you to pay your part?

FALSTAFF No, I'll give you your due, you have paid all there.

PRINCE HAL Yea, and elsewhere, so far as my coin would stretch, and where it would not I have used my credit.

FALSTAFF Yea, and so used it that were it not here apparent that you are heir apparent—but I pray, sweet wag, shall there be gallows standing in England when you are king? And resolution thus fobbed off as it is with the rusty curb of old Father Antic the law? Do not you when you are king hang a thief.

PRINCE HAL No, you shall.

FALSTAFF Shall I? O rare! By the Lord, I'll be a brave judge!

PRINCE HAL You judge false already! I mean you shall have the hanging of the thieves, and so become a rare hangman.

FALSTAFF Well, Hal, well! And in some sort it chimes with my humour—as well as waiting in the Court, I can tell you.

PRINCE HAL For obtaining of suits?

FALSTAFF Yea, for obtaining of suits, whereof the hangman has no lean wardrobe. God, I am as melancholy as a tom cat, or a lugged bear.

PRINCE HAL Or an old lion, or a lover's lute.

FALSTAFF Yea, or the drone of a Lincolnshire bagpipe.

PRINCE HAL What say you to a hare, or the melancholy of Moorditch?

FALSTAFF You have the most unsavoury similes, and are indeed the most comparative rascalliest sweet

young prince. But Hal, I pray you trouble me no more
with vanity. I would to God you and I knew where a
commodity of good names were to be bought. An old
lord of the Council rated me the other day in the street
about you, sir. But I marked him not, and yet he talked
very wisely; but I regarded him not, and yet he talked
wisely—and in the street too.

PRINCE HAL You did well, for wisdom cries out in the
streets and no man regards it.

FALSTAFF O, you have damnable iteration, and are indeed
able to corrupt a saint. You have done much harm upon
me, Hal, God forgive you for it. Before I knew you, Hal,
I knew nothing; and now am I, if a man should speak
truly, little better than one of the wicked. I must give
over this life, and I will give it over. By the Lord, if I do
not I am a villain. I'll be damned for never a king's son
in Christendom.

PRINCE HAL Where shall we take a purse tomorrow, Jack?

FALSTAFF Zounds,[1] where you will lad, I'll make one; if
I do not, call me a villain and degrade me.

PRINCE HAL I see a good amendment of life in you, from
praying to purse-taking.

FALSTAFF Why Hal, 'tis my vocation, Hal. It is no sin for a
man to labour in his vocation.

Enter Poins

Poins! Now shall we know if Gadshill has set a match!
O, if men were to be saved by merit, what hole in hell
were hot enough for him? This is the most omnipotent
villain that ever cried 'Stand!' to a true man.

PRINCE HAL Good morrow, Ned.

POINS Good morrow, sweet Hal. What says Monsieur
Remorse? What says Sir John Sack—and Sugar? Jack!

---

[1]Short for God's wounds, Elizabeth I's usual expletive.

How agree the devil and you about your soul, that you
sold him on Good Friday last, for a cup of Madeira and
a cold capon's leg?

PRINCE HAL Sir John stands to his word, the devil shall
have his bargain; for he was never yet a breaker of
proverbs. He will give the devil his due.

POINS Then are you damned for keeping your word with
the devil.

PRINCE HAL Else he had been damned for cozening the
devil.

POINS But my lads, my lads, tomorrow morning, by four
o'clock early at Gad's Hill, there are pilgrims going to
Canterbury with rich offerings and traders riding to
London with fat purses. I have masks for you all—you
have horses for yourselves. Gadshill lies tonight in
Rochester. I have bespoken supper tomorrow night in
Eastcheap. We may do it as secure as sleep. If you will
go, I will stuff your purses full of crowns. If you will
not, tarry at home and be hanged.

FALSTAFF Hear you, Edward, if I tarry at home and go not,
I'll hang you for going.

POINS You will, chaps?

FALSTAFF Hal, will you make one?

PRINCE HAL Who I? Rob? I a thief? Not I, by my faith.

FALSTAFF There's neither honesty, manhood, nor good
fellowship in you. You came not of the blood royal, if
you dare not stand for ten shillings.

PRINCE HAL Well then, once in my days I'll be a madcap.

FALSTAFF Why, that's well said.

PRINCE HAL Well, come what will, I'll tarry at home.

FALSTAFF By the Lord, I'll be a traitor then, when you are
king.

PRINCE HAL I care not.

POINS Sir John, I pray you leave the Prince and me alone.
I will lay him down such reasons for this adventure that
he shall go.

FALSTAFF Well, God give you the spirit of persuasion, and him the ears of profiting, that what you speak may move, and what he hears may be believed: that the true prince may—for recreation sake—prove a false thief, for the poor abuses of the time want countenance. Farewell, you shall find me in Eastcheap.

PRINCE HAL Farewell, the latter spring! Farewell, Allhallows' summer!   *Exit Falstaff*

POINS Now my good sweet honey lord, ride with us tomorrow. I have a jest to execute that I cannot manage alone. Falstaff, Bardolph, Peto, and Gadshill shall rob those men that we have already waylaid—yourself and I will not be there. And when they have the booty, if you and I do not rob them—cut this head off from my shoulders.

PRINCE HAL How shall we part with them in setting forth?

POINS Why, we will set forth before or after them, and appoint them a place of meeting—wherein it is at our pleasure to fail. And then will they adventure upon the exploit themselves, which they shall have no sooner achieved but we'll set upon them.

PRINCE HAL Yea, but 'tis likely that they will know us by our horses, by our habits, and by every other appointment to be ourselves.

POINS Tut, our horses they shall not see, I'll tie them in the wood. Our masks we will change after we leave them. And, sir, I have cases of buckram for the chance, to hide our noted outward garments.

PRINCE HAL Yea, but I doubt they will be too hard for us.

POINS Well, for two of them, I know them to be as truebred cowards as ever turned back; and for the third, if he fights longer than he sees reason, I'll forswear arms. The virtue of this jest will be the incomprehensible lies that this same fat rogue will tell us when we meet at supper. How thirty at least he fought with, what wards, what

blows, what extremities he endured, and in the disproof
of this lives the jest.

PRINCE HAL Well, I'll go with you. Provide us all things
necessary and meet me tomorrow night in Eastcheap.
There I'll sup. Farewell.

POINS Farewell, my lord.   *Exit*

PRINCE HAL
I know you all, and will awhile uphold
The unyoked humour of your idleness.
Yet herein will I imitate the sun,
Which does permit the base contagious clouds
To smother up its beauty from the world,
That when it pleases again to be itself,
Being wanted, it may be more wondered at
By breaking through the foul and ugly mists
Of vapours that did seem to strangle it.
If all the year were playing holidays,
To sport would be as tedious as to work;
But when they seldom come, they wished-for come,
And nothing pleases but rare accidents.
So when this loose behaviour I throw off,
And pay the debt I never promisèd,
By how much better than my word I am,
By so much shall I falsify men's hopes.
And like bright metal on a sullen ground,
My reformation, glittering o'er my fault,
Shall show more goodly, and attract more eyes
Than that which has no foil to set it off.
I'll so offend, to make offence a skill,
Redeeming time when men think least I will.
                                                            Exit

SCENE III
Windsor Castle.

*Enter the King, Northumberland, Worcester, Hotspur,
Sir Walter Blunt, and others*

KING HENRY
My blood has been too cold and temperate,
Unapt to stir at these indignities,
And you have found me—for accordingly
You tread upon my patience. But be sure
I will from henceforth rather be myself,
Mighty, and to be feared, than my condition,
Which has been smooth as oil, soft as young down,
And therefore lost that title of respect
Which the proud soul never pays but to the proud.

WORCESTER
Our house, my sovereign liege, little deserves
The scourge of greatness to be used on it,
And that same greatness too which our own hands
Have helped to make so portly.

NORTHUMBERLAND   My lord—

KING HENRY
Worcester, get you gone, for I do see
Danger and disobedience in your eye.
O sir, your presence is too pèremptory,
And majesty might never yet endure
The moody frontier of a servant brow.
You have good leave to leave us. When we need
Your use and counsel we shall send for you.

                                        Exit Worcester
(*To Northumberland*) You were about to speak.

NORTHUMBERLAND Yea, my good lord.
Those prisoners in your highness' name demanded,
Which Harry Percy here at Holmedon took,
Were, as he says, not with such strength denied

As is delivered to your majesty.
Either envy therefore, or misunderstanding,
Is guilty of this fault, and not my son.
HOTSPUR
My liege, I did deny no prisoners.
But I remember when the fight was done,
When I was dry with rage and èxtreme toil,
Breathless and faint, leaning upon my sword,
Came there a certain lord, neat and trimly dressed,
Fresh as a bridegroom, and his chin new reaped
Showed like a stubble-land at harvest-home.
He was perfumèd like a milliner,
Between his finger and his thumb he held
A perfume-box, which ever and anon
He gave his nose, and took it away again—
Which therewith angry, when it next came there,
Took it in snuff. And still he smiled and talked.
And as the soldiers bore dead bodies by,
He called them untaught knaves, unmannerly,
To bring a slovenly unhandsome corpse
Between the wind and his nobility.
With many holiday and lady terms
He questioned me; among the rest demanded
My prisoners in your majesty's behalf.
I then, all smarting with my wounds being cold,
To be so pestered with a popinjay,
Out of my grief and my impatiènce
Answered neglectingly, I know not what—
He should, or he should not, for he made me mad
To see him shine so brisk, and smell so sweet,
And talk so like a waiting-gentlewoman
Of guns, and drums, and wounds, God save the mark!
And telling me the sovereignest thing on earth
Was parmaceti for an inward bruise,
And that it was great pity, so it was,
This villainous saltpetre should be digged

Out of the bowels of the harmless earth,
Which many a good tall fellow had destroyed
So cowardly; and but for these vile guns
He would himself have been a soldier.
This bald unjointed chat of his, my lord,
I answered indirectly, as I said,
And I beseech you, let not his report
Come current for an accusatiòn
Between my love and your high majesty.

BLUNT

The circumstance considered, good my lord,
Whatever Lord Harry Percy then had said
To such a person, and in such a place,
At such a time, with all the rest retold,
May reasonably die; and never rise
To do him wrong, or any way impeach
What then he said, so he unsays it now.

KING HENRY

Why, yet he does deny his prisoners,
But with proviso and exceptiòn,
That we at our own charge shall ransom straight
His brother-in-law, the foolish Mortimer.
Who, on my soul, has wilfully betrayed
The lives of those that he did lead to fight
Against that great magician, damned Glendower,
Whose daughter, as we hear, the Earl of March
Has lately married. Shall our coffers then
Be emptied to redeem a traitor home?
Shall we buy treason, and bargain then with fears
When they have lost and forfeited themselves?
No, on the barren mountains let him starve.
For I shall never hold that man my friend
Whose tongue shall ask me for one penny cost
To ransom home revolted Mortimer.

HOTSPUR

    Revolted Mortimer!

    He never did fall off, my sovereign liege,

    But by the chance of war. To prove that true

    Needs no more but one tongue for all those wounds—

    Those mouthèd wounds, which valiantly he took,

    When on the gentle Severn's sedgy bank,

    In single opposition hand to hand,

    He did confound the best part of an hour

    In changing hardihood with great Glendower.

    Three times they breathed, and three times did they
       drink

    Upon agreement of swift Severn's flood,

    Which then affrighted with their bloody looks

    Ran fearfully among the trembling reeds,

    And hid its crisp head in the hollow bank,

    Bloodstained with these valiant combatants.

    Never did bare and rotten policy

    Colour its working with such deadly wounds;

    And never could the noble Mortimer

    Receive so many, and all willingly.

    Then let not him be slandered with revolt.

KING HENRY

    You do belie him, Percy, you do belie him,

    He never did encounter with Glendower.

    I tell you, he durst as well have met the devil alone

    As Owen Glendower for an enemy.

    Are you not ashamed? But sir, henceforth

    Let me not hear you speak of Mortimer.

    Send me your prisoners with the speediest means—

    Or you shall hear in such a kind from me

    As will displease you. My Lord Northumberland:

    We license your departure with your son.

    Send us your prisoners, or you will hear of it.

                      Exit the King with Blunt and train

HOTSPUR

    And if the devil comes and roars for them
    I will not send them. I will after straight
    And tell him so, for I will ease my heart,
    Albeit I make a hazard of my head.

NORTHUMBERLAND

    What? Drunk with choler? Stay, and pause awhile,
    Here comes your uncle.

Enter Worcester

HOTSPUR Speak of Mortimer?

    Zounds, I will speak of him, and let my soul
    Want mercy if I do not join with him.
    Yea, on his part I'll empty all these veins
    And shed my dear blood, drop by drop in the dust,
    But I will lift the down-trodden Mortimer
    As high in the air as this unthankful King,
    As this ingrate and cankered Bolingbroke.

NORTHUMBERLAND

    Brother, the King has made your nephew mad.

WORCESTER

    Who struck this heat up after I was gone?

HOTSPUR

    He will indeed have all my prisoners,
    And when I urged the ransom once again
    Of my wife's brother, then his cheek looked pale;
    And on my face he turned an eye of death,
    Trembling even at the name of Mortimer.

WORCESTER

    I cannot blame him. Was not he proclaimed,
    By Richard that dead is, the next of blood?

NORTHUMBERLAND

    He was, I heard the proclamatiòn.
    And then it was, when the unhappy King—
    Whose wrongs in us God pardon!—did set forth

Upon his Irish expeditiòn;
From whence he, intercepted, did return
To be deposed, and shortly murderèd.

WORCESTER
And for whose death we in the world's wide mouth
Live scandalized and foully spoken of.

HOTSPUR
But soft, I pray you, did King Richard then
Proclaim my kinsman Edmund Mortimer
Heir to the crown?

NORTHUMBERLAND He did, myself did hear it.

HOTSPUR
Nay then, I cannot blame his cousin King
That wished him on the barren mountains starve.
But shall it be that you that set the crown
Upon the head of this forgetful man,
And for his sake wear the detested blot
Of murderous subornation—shall it be
That you a world of curses undergo,
Being the agents, or base second means,
The cords, the ladder, or the hangman rather?
O pardon me, that I descend so low,
To show the line and the predicament
Wherein you range under this subtle King!
Shall it for shame be spoken in these days,
Or fill up chronicles in time to come,
That men of your nobility and power
Did gage them both in an unjust behalf—
As both of you, God pardon it, have done—
To put down Richard, that sweet lovely rose,
And plant this thorn, this canker Bolingbroke?
And shall it in more shame be further spoken,
That you are fooled, discarded, shaken off
By him for whom these shames you underwent?
No, yet time serves wherein you may redeem
Your banished honours, and restore yourselves

Into the good thoughts of the world again.
Revenge the jeering and disdained contempt
Of this proud King, who studies day and night
To answer all the debt he owes to you,
Even with the bloody payment of your deaths.
Therefore, I say—

WORCESTER   Peace, cousin, say no more.
And now I will unclasp a secret book,
And to your quick-conceiving discontents
I'll read you matter deep and dangerous—
As full of peril and adventurous spirit
As to over-walk a current roaring loud
On the unsteadfast footing of a spear.

HOTSPUR
If he falls in, good night, or sink, or swim!
Send danger from the east unto the west,
So honour cross it from the north to south,
And let them grapple. O, the blood more stirs
To rouse a lion than to start a hare!

NORTHUMBERLAND
Imagination of some great exploit
Drives him beyond the bounds of patiènce.

HOTSPUR
By heaven, I think it were an easy leap
To pluck bright honour from the pale-faced moon,
Or dive into the bottom of the deep,
Where fathom-line could never touch the ground,
And pluck up drownèd honour by the locks—
So he that does redeem it thence might wear
Without corrival all its dignities.
But out upon this half-faced fellowship!

WORCESTER
He apprehends a world of figures here,
But not the form of what he should attend.
Good cousin, give me audience for a while.

HOTSPUR
  I cry you mercy.
WORCESTER   Those same noble Scots
  That are your prisoners—
HOTSPUR   I'll keep them all!
  By God he shall not have a Scot of them,
  No, if a scot would save his soul he shall not.
  I'll keep them, by this hand!
WORCESTER   You start away,
  And lend no ear unto my purposes.
  Those prisoners you shall keep—
HOTSPUR   Nay, I will. That's flat!
  He said he would not ransom Mortimer,
  Forbade my tongue to speak of Mortimer;
  But I will find him when he lies asleep,
  And in his ear I'll holla 'Mortimer!'
  Nay, I'll have a starling shall be taught to speak
  Nothing but 'Mortimer', and give it him
  To keep his anger still in motiòn.
WORCESTER
  Hear you, cousin, a word.
HOTSPUR
  All studies here I solemnly defy,
  Save how to gall and pinch this Bolingbroke.
  And that same sword-and-buckler Prince of Wales—
  But that I think his father loves him not
  And would be glad he met with some mischance—
  I would have him poisoned with a pot of ale.
WORCESTER
  Farewell, kinsman. I'll talk to you
  When you are better tempered to attend.
NORTHUMBERLAND
  Why, what a wasp-stung and impatient fool
  Are you to break into this woman's mood,
  Tying your ear to no tongue but your own!

HOTSPUR

    Why, look you, I am whipped and scourged with rods,
    Nettled, and stung with hornets, when I hear
    Of this vile politician Bolingbroke.
    In Richard's time—what do you call the place?
    A plague upon it, it is in Gloucestershire.
    'Twas where the madcap Duke his uncle kept—
    His uncle York—where I first bowed my knee
    Unto this king of smiles, this Bolingbroke—
    God, when you and he came back from Ravenspurgh—

NORTHUMBERLAND

    At Berkeley Castle.

HOTSPUR

    You say true.
    Why, what a candy deal of courtesy
    This fawning greyhound then did proffer me!
    'Look when his infant fortune came to age',
    And 'gentle Harry Percy', and 'kind cousin'.
    O, the devil take such cozeners—God forgive me!
    Good uncle, tell your tale. I have done.

WORCESTER

    Nay, if you have not, to it again,
    We will stay your leisure.

HOTSPUR   I have done, in faith.

WORCESTER

    Then once more to your Scottish prisoners.
    Deliver them up without their ransom straight,
    And make the Douglas' son your only means
    For power in Scotland. Which, for divers reasons
    Which I shall send you written, be assured
    Will easily be granted. (*To Northumberland*) You my
        lord,
    Your son in Scotland being thus employed,
    Shall secretly into the bosom creep
    Of that same noble prelate well-beloved,
    The Archbishop.

HOTSPUR   Of York, is it not?
WORCESTER   True, who bears hard
    His brother's death at Bristol, the Lord Scroop.
    I speak not this in estimatiòn,
    As what I think might be, but what I know
    Is ruminated, plotted, and set down—
    And only stays but to behold the face
    Of that occasion that shall bring it on.
HOTSPUR
    I smell it! Upon my life it will do well!
NORTHUMBERLAND
    Before the game is afoot you ever let slip.
HOTSPUR
    Why, it cannot choose but be a noble plot;
    And then the power of Scotland, and of York,
    To join with Mortimer, ha?
WORCESTER And so they shall.
HOTSPUR
    In faith it is exceedingly well aimed.
WORCESTER
    It is no little reason bids us speed,
    To save our heads by raising of a head.
    For, bear ourselves as even as we can,
    The King will always think him in our debt,
    And think we think ourselves unsatisfied,
    Till he has found a time to pay us home.
    And see already how he does begin
    To make us strangers to his looks of love.
HOTSPUR
    He does, he does, we'll be revenged on him.
WORCESTER
    Cousin, farewell. No further go in this
    Than I by letters shall direct your course.
    When time is ripe, which will be suddenly,
    I'll steal to Glendower, and Lord Mortimer,
    Where you, and Douglas, and our powers at once,

As I will fashion it, shall happily meet
To bear our fortunes in our own strong arms,
Which now we hold at much uncertainty.
NORTHUMBERLAND
Farewell, good brother. We shall thrive, I trust.
HOTSPUR
Uncle, adieu. O, let the hours be short,
Till fields, and blows, and groans applaud our sport!

Exeunt

Act II

SCENE I
Rochester. An inn yard.

Enter a Carrier with a lantern in his hand

FIRST CARRIER Heigh-ho! If it is not four by the day I'll be hanged. Charles's Wain is over the new chimney, and yet our horse not packed. What, Ostler!

OSTLER (*within*) Anon, anon.

FIRST CARRIER I pray you, Tom, beat Cut's saddle, put a few flocks in the saddle-bow; poor jade is wrung in the withers out of all bearing.

Enter another Carrier

SECOND CARRIER Peas and beans are as dank here as a dog, and that is the next way to give poor jades the worms. This house is turned upside down since Robin Ostler died.

FIRST CARRIER Poor fellow never joyed since the price of oats rose, it was the death of him.

SECOND CARRIER I think this is the most villainous house in all London road for fleas, I am stung like a tench.

FIRST CARRIER Like a tench! By the mass, there is never a king Christian could be better bit than I have been since the first cock crow.

SECOND CARRIER Why, they will allow us never a jordan, and then we leak in your chimney, and your wine breeds fleas like a lamprey.

FIRST CARRIER What, Ostler! Come away, and be hanged, come away!

SECOND CARRIER I have a gammon of bacon, and two roots of ginger, to be delivered as far as Charing Cross.

FIRST CARRIER God's body! The turkeys in my pannier are quite starved. What, Ostler! A plague on you, have you never an eye in your head? Can you not hear? If it were not as good deed as drink to break the pate on you, I am a very villain. Come, and be hanged! Have you no faith in you?

Enter Gadshill

GADSHILL Good morrow, carriers, what's o'clock?

FIRST CARRIER I think it is two o'clock.

GADSHILL I pray lend me your lantern, to see my gelding in the stable.

FIRST CARRIER Nay, by God, soft! I know a trick worth two of that, in faith.

GADSHILL I pray you lend me yours.

SECOND CARRIER Ay, when? Can tell? Lend me your lantern, says he! I'll see you hanged first.

GADSHILL Carrier, what time do you mean to come to London?

SECOND CARRIER Time enough to go to bed with a candle, I warrant you! Come, neighbour Mugs, we'll call up the gentlemen, they will along with company, for they have great charge.   *Exeunt Carriers*

GADSHILL What ho! Chamberlain!

Enter Chamberlain

CHAMBERLAIN 'At hand, says pick-purse.'

GADSHILL That's even as fair as 'At hand, says the chamberlain', for you vary no more from picking of

purses than giving direction does from labouring. You
lay the plot how.

CHAMBERLAIN Good morrow, Master Gadshill. It holds
current what I told you yesternight. There's a franklin
in the Weald of Kent has brought three hundred marks
with him in gold. I heard him tell it to one of his
company last night at supper, a kind of auditor, one
that has abundance of baggage too, God knows what.
They are up already, and call for eggs and butter. They
will away at once.

GADSHILL Sir, if they meet not with Saint Nicholas' clerks,
I'll give you this neck.

CHAMBERLAIN No, I'll none of it, I pray you keep that for
the hangman, for I know you worship Saint Nicholas,
as truly as a man of falsehood may.

GADSHILL What talk you to me of the hangman? If I
hang, I'll make a fat pair of gallows. For if I hang, old
Sir John hangs with me, and you know he is no starveling.
Tut, there are other Trojans that you dream not of,
which for sport sake are content to do the profession
some grace; that would, if matters should be looked
into, for their own credit sake make all whole. I am
joined with no footpads, no long-staff sixpenny strikers,
none of these mad mustached purple-hued drunks, but
with nobility and tranquillity, burgomasters and great
ones—such as can hold in, such as will strike sooner
than speak, and speak sooner than drink, and drink
sooner than pray. And yet, zounds, I lie; for they pray
continually to their saint the commonwealth, or rather
not pray to her, but prey on her, for they ride up and
down on her, and make her their boots.[1]

CHAMBERLAIN What, the commonwealth their boots? Will
she hold water out in foul way?

---

[1]The punning innuendo here is on boots and booty.

GADSHILL She will, she will, justice has liquored her. We steal as in a castle, cock-sure. We have the receipt of fern-seed, we walk invisible.

CHAMBERLAIN Nay, by my faith, I think you are more beholden to the night than to fern-seed for your walking invisible.

GADSHILL Give me your hand, you shall have a share in our purchase, as I am a true man.

CHAMBERLAIN Nay, rather let me have it as you are a false thief.

GADSHILL Go to, *homo* is a common name to all men. Bid the ostler bring my gelding out of the stable. Farewell, you muddy knave.   *Exeunt*

Scene II
The road by Gadshill.

Enter Prince and Poins

POINS Come, shelter, shelter! I have removed Falstaff's horse, and he frets like a gummed velvet.

PRINCE HALL Stand close!

They hide
Enter Falstaff

FALSTAFF Poins! Poins, and be hanged! Poins!

PRINCE HAL (*coming forward*) Peace, you fat-kidneyed rascal, what a brawling do you keep!

FALSTAFF Where's Poins, Hal?

PRINCE HAL He has walked up to the top of the hill. I'll go seek him.

He steps to one side

FALSTAFF I am accursed to rob in that thief's company.
The rascal has removed my horse and tied him I know
not where. If I travel but four foot by the square further
afoot, I shall break my wind. Well, I doubt not but to
die a fair death for all this, if I escape hanging for
killing that rogue. I have forsworn his company hourly
any time this two-and-twenty years, and yet I am
bewitched with the rogue's company. If the rascal has
not given me medicines to make me love him, I'll be
hanged. It could not be else. I have drunk medicines.
Poins! Hal! A plague upon you both! Bardolph! Peto! I'll
starve ere I'll rob a foot further—if it were not as good a
deed as drink to turn true man, and to leave these
rogues, I am the veriest varlet that ever chewed with a
tooth. Eight yards of uneven ground is threescore-and-
ten miles afoot with me, and the stony-hearted villains
know it well enough. A plague upon it when thieves
cannot be true one to another!

They whistle

Whew! A plague upon you all. Give me my horse,
you rogues, give me my horse and be hanged!

PRINCE HAL (*coming forward*) Peace, you fat-guts, lie
down, lay your ear close to the ground and listen if you
can hear the tread of travellers.

FALSTAFF Have you any levers to lift me up again, being
down? God, I'll not bear my own flesh so far afoot again
for all the coin in your father's exchequer. What a
plague mean you to colt [trick] me thus?

PRINCE HAL You lie, you are not colted, you are uncolted.

FALSTAFF I pray good Prince Hal, help me to my horse,
good king's son.

PRINCE HAL Out, you rogue, shall I be your ostler?

FALSTAFF Hang yourself in your own heir-apparent garters!
If I am taken, I'll peach for this. If I have not ballads

made on you all, and sung to filthy tunes, let a cup of sack be my poison. When a jest is so forward—and afoot too—I hate it!

Enter Gadshill, Bardolph, and Peto

GADSHILL Stand!

FALSTAFF So I do, against my will.

POINS O, 'tis our mate, I know his voice. Bardolph, what news?

BARDOLPH Disguise, on with your masks, there's money of the King's coming down the hill. 'Tis going to the King's exchequer.

FALSTAFF You lie, you rogue, 'tis going to the King's tavern.

GADSHILL There's enough to make us all—

FALSTAFF To be hanged.

PRINCE HAL Sirs, you four shall confront them in the narrow lane. Ned Poins and I will walk lower—if they escape from your encounter, then they light on us.

PETO How many are there of them?

GADSHILL Some eight or ten.

FALSTAFF Zounds, will they not rob us?

PRINCE HAL What, a coward, Sir John Paunch?

FALSTAFF Indeed, I am not John of Gaunt your grandfather, but yet no coward, Hal.

PRINCE HAL Well, we leave that to the proof.

POINS Sir Jack, your horse stands behind the hedge. When you need him, there you shall find him. Farewell, and stand fast!

FALSTAFF Now cannot I strike him, if I should be hanged.

PRINCE HAL (*aside to Poins*) Ned, where are our disguises?

POINS Here, hard by, stand close. *Exeunt Prince and Poins*

FALSTAFF Now, my masters, happy man be his lot, say I. Every man to his business.

Enter the Travellers

FIRST TRAVELLER Come, neighbour, the boy shall lead
   our horses down the hill. We'll walk afoot awhile and
   ease our legs.

THIEVES Stand!

SECOND TRAVELLER Jesus bless us!

FALSTAFF Strike, down with them, cut the villains' throats!
   Ah, bloody caterpillars, bacon-fed knaves, they hate us
   youth! Down with them, fleece them!

FIRST TRAVELLER O, we are undone, both we and ours for
   ever!

FALSTAFF Hang you, potbellied knaves, are you undone?
   No, you fat chuffs, I would your store were here! On,
   bacons, on! What, you knaves, young men must live!
   You are grandjurors, are you? We'll jury you, faith.

Here they rob them and bind them

Exeunt

Enter the Prince and Poins, disguised

PRINCE HAL The thieves have bound the true men. Now,
   could you and I rob the thieves, and go merrily to
   London, it would be argument for a week, laughter for a
   month, and a good jest for ever.

POINS Stand close, I hear them coming.

They hide
Enter the thieves again

FALSTAFF Come my masters, let us share, and then to
   horse before day. If the Prince and Poins are not two
   arrant cowards there's no equity stirring. There's no
   more valour in that Poins than in a wild duck.

As they are sharing the Prince and Poins set upon them

PRINCE HAL Your money!
POINS Villains!

They all run away, Falstaff too, leaving the booty
behind them

PRINCE HAL
    Got with much ease. Now merrily to horse.
    The thieves are all scattered and possessed with fear
    So strongly that they dare not meet each other.
    Each takes his fellow for an officer!
    Away, good Ned! Falstaff sweats to death,
    And lards the lean earth as he walks along.
    Were it not for laughing I should pity him.
POINS How the fat rogue roared!   *Exeunt*

SCENE III
Warkworth Castle.

Enter Hotspur reading a letter

HOTSPUR *But for my own part, my lord, I could be well*
contented to be there, in respect of the love I bear your
house.
    He could be contented! Why is he not then? In respect of
    the love he bears our house? He shows in this he loves
    his own barn better than he loves our house. Let me see
    some more.
    The purpose you undertake is dangerous,
    Why, that's certain. 'Tis dangerous to take a cold, to
    sleep, to drink. But I tell you, my lord fool, out of this
    nettle, danger, we pluck this flower, safety.
    The purpose you undertake is dangerous, the friends
    you have named uncertain, the time itself unsuitable,

and your whole plot too light, for the counterpoise of so
great an opposition.
Say you so, say you so? I say unto you again, you are a
shallow cowardly hind, and you lie. What a lack-brain
is this! By the Lord, our plot is a good plot, as ever was
laid, our friends true and constant. A good plot, good
friends, and full of expectation. An excellent plot, very
good friends. What a frosty-spirited rogue is this! Why,
my Lord of York commends the plot, and the general
course of the action. Zounds, if I were now by this rascal
I could brain him with his lady's fan. Are there not my
father, my uncle, and myself? Lord Edmund Mortimer,
my Lord of York, and Owen Glendower? Is there not
besides the Douglas? Have I not all their letters to meet
me in arms by the ninth of the next month, and are
they not some of them set forward already? What a
pagan rascal is this, an infidel! Ha! You shall see now
in very sincerity of fear and cold heart will he to the
King, and lay open all our proceedings! O, I could
divide myself, and go to buffets, for moving such a dish
of skim milk with so honourable an action! Hang him,
let him tell the King, we are prepared. I will set forward
tonight.

Enter Lady Percy

How now, Kate? I must leave you within these two
hours.
LADY PERCY
    O my good lord, why are you thus alone?
    For what offence have I this fortnight been
    A banished woman from my Harry's bed?
    Tell me, sweet lord, what is it that takes from you
    Your stomach, pleasure, and your golden sleep?
    Why do you bend your eyes upon the earth,
    And start so often when you sit alone?

Why have you lost the fresh blood in your cheeks,
And given my treasures and my rights of you
To thick-eyed musing, and curst melancholy?
In your faint slumbers I by you have watched
And heard you murmur tales of iron wars,
Speak terms of còntrol to your bounding steed,
Cry 'Courage! To the field!' And you have talked
Of sallies, and retires, of trenches, tents,
Of palisades and frontiers, parapets,
Of basilisks, of cannon, culverin,[2]
Of prisoners' ransom, and of soldiers slain,
And all the currents of a heady fight.
Your spirit within you has been so at war,
And thus has so bestirred you in your sleep,
That beads of sweat have stood upon your brow
Like bubbles in a late-disturbèd stream.
And in your face strange motions have appeared,
Such as we see when men restrain their breath
On sudden behest. O, what portènts are these?
Some heavy business has my lord in hand,
And I must know it, else he loves me not.

HOTSPUR
What ho!

Enter a Servant

            Has Gilliams with the packet gone?
SERVANT He has, my lord, an hour ago.
HOTSPUR Has Butler brought those horses from the sheriff?
SERVANT One horse, my lord, he brought even now.
HOTSPUR What horse? A roan, a crop-ear is it not?
SERVANT
    It is, my lord.
HOTSPUR   That roan shall be my throne.

---

[2]Large and small cannon.

Well, I will back him straight. O Esperance!
Bid Butler lead him forth into the park.

Exit Servant

LADY PERCY But hear you, my lord.
HOTSPUR What say you, my lady?
LADY PERCY What is it carries you away?
HOTSPUR Why, my horse, my love, my horse.
LADY PERCY
   Out, you mad-headed ape!
   A weasel has not such a deal of temper
   As you are tossed with. In faith,
   I'll know your business, Harry, that I will.
   I fear my brother Mortimer does stir
   About his title, and has sent for you
   To line his enterprise. But if you go—
HOTSPUR
   So far afoot I shall be weary, love.
LADY PERCY
   Come, come, you parakeet, now answer me
   Directly unto this question that I ask.
   In faith, I'll break your little finger, Harry,
   Now if you will not tell me all things true.
HOTSPUR
   Away,
   Away, you trifler! Love! I love you not,
   I care not for you, Kate? This is no world
   To play with puppets, and to tilt with lips.
   We must have bloody noses, and cracked crowns,
   And pass them current too. God's me! My horse!
   What say you, Kate? What would you have with me?
   What say you, Kate? What would you have with me?
LADY PERCY
   Do you not love me? Do you not indeed?
   Well, do not then, for since you love me not
   I will not love myself. Do you not love me?
   Nay, tell me if you speak in jest or no?

HOTSPUR

    Come, will you see me ride?
    And when I am a-horseback I will swear
    I love you infinitely. But hark you, Kate,
    I must not have you henceforth question me
    Whither I go, nor reason whereabout.
    Whither I must, I must. And, to conclude,
    This evening must I leave you, gentle Kate.
    I know you wise, but yet no farther wise
    Than Harry Percy's wife. Constant you are,
    But yet a woman. And for secrecy,
    No lady closer, for I well believe
    You will not utter—what you do not know.
    And so far will I trust you, gentle Kate.

LADY PERCY

    How? So far?

HOTSPUR

    Not an inch further. But hark you, Kate,
    Whither I go, thither shall you go too.
    Today will I set forth, tomorrow you.
    Will this content you, Kate?

LADY PERCY   It must, of force.   *Exeunt*

SCENE IV
East Cheap. The Boar's Head.

Enter Prince and Poins

PRINCE HAL Ned, pray come out of that fat room, and
    lend me your hand to laugh a little.

POINS Where have you been, Hal?

PRINCE HAL With three or four blockheads, among three
    or fourscore hogsheads. I have sounded the very bass
    string of humility. Man, I am sworn brother to a leash
    of drawers, and can call them all by their Christian

names, as Tom, Dick, and Francis. They take it already
upon their salvation that though I am but Prince of
Wales yet I am the king of courtesy, and tell me flatly I
am no proud Jack like Falstaff; but a Corinthian, a lad
of mettle, a good boy—by the Lord, so they call me!—and
when I am King of England I shall command all the
good lads in Eastcheap. They call drinking deep 'dyeing
scarlet', and when you breathe in your watering they cry
'Hem!' and bid you 'Play it off!' To conclude, I am so good
a proficient in one quarter of an hour that I can drink
with any tinker in his own language during my life. I
tell you, Ned, you have lost much honour that you were
not with me in this action. But, sweet Ned—to sweeten
which name of Ned I give you this pennyworth of sugar,
clapped even now into my hand by an understrapper,
one that never spoke other English in his life than
'Eight shillings and sixpence', and 'You are welcome',
with this shrill addition, 'Anon, anon, sir! Score a pint
of sherry in the Half-moon!', or so. But Ned, to drive
away the time till Falstaff comes—I pray do you stand in
some by-room while I question my puny drawer to what
end he gave me the sugar. And do you never leave
calling 'Francis!', that his tale to me may be nothing
but 'Anon'. Step aside, and I'll show you a precedent.

Exit Poins

POINS (*within*) Francis!
PRINCE HAL You art perfect.
POINS (*within*) Francis!

Enter Francis, a Drawer

FRANCIS Anon, anon, sir. Look down into the Pomegranate,
  Ralph!
PRINCE HAL Come hither, Francis.
FRANCIS My lord?
PRINCE HAL How long have you to serve, Francis?

FRANCIS Truly, five years, and as much as to—

POINS (*within*) Francis!

FRANCIS Anon, anon, sir.

PRINCE HAL Five year! By our lady, a long lease for the
clinking of pewter. But Francis, dare you be so valiant
as to play the coward with your indenture, and show it
a fair pair of heels, and run from it?

FRANCIS O Lord, sir, I'll be sworn upon all the books in
England, I could find in my heart—

POINS (*within*) Francis!

FRANCIS Anon, sir.

PRINCE HAL How old are you, Francis?

FRANCIS Let me see, about Michaelmas next I shall be—

POINS (*within*) Francis!

FRANCIS Anon, sir—pray stay a little, my lord.

PRINCE HAL Nay, but hark you, Francis, for the sugar you
gave me, it was a pennyworth, was it not?

FRANCIS O Lord, I would it had been two!

PRINCE HAL I will give you for it a thousand pound—ask
me when you will, and you shall have it.

POINS (*within*) Francis!

FRANCIS Anon, anon.

PRINCE HAL Anon, Francis? No, Francis, but tomorrow,
Francis. Or Francis, a-Thursday. Or indeed Francis, when
you will. But Francis!

FRANCIS My lord?

PRINCE HAL Will you rob this leather-jerkin, crystal-
button, crop-pated, agate-ring, puke-stocking, tape-garter,
smooth-tongue Spanish pouch?

FRANCIS O Lord, sir, who do you mean?

PRINCE HAL Why then your brown sherry is your only
drink. For look you, Francis, your white canvas doublet
will sully. In Barbary, sir, it cannot come to so much.

FRANCIS What, sir?

POINS (*within*) Francis!

PRINCE HAL Away, you rogue, do you not hear them call?

Here they both call him; the Drawer stands amazed,
not knowing which way to go
Enter Vintner

VINTNER What, stand you still and hear such a calling?
Look to the guests within. *Exit Francis*
My lord, old Sir John with half-a-dozen more are at the
door. Shall I let them in?
PRINCE HAL Let them alone awhile, and then open the
door. *Exit Vintner*
Poins!

Enter Poins

POINS Anon, anon, sir.
PRINCE HAL Falstaff and the rest of the thieves are at the
door. Shall we be merry?
POINS As merry as crickets, my lad. But hark you, what
cunning match have you made with this jest of the
drawer? Come, what's the issue?
PRINCE HAL I am now of all humours that have shown
themselves humours since the old days of goodman
Adam to the pupil age of this present twelve o'clock at
midnight.

Enter Francis

What's o'clock, Francis?
FRANCIS Anon, anon, sir. *Exit*
PRINCE HAL That ever this fellow should have fewer words
than a parrot, and yet the son of a woman! His industry
is up-stairs and down-stairs, his eloquence the parcel of
a reckoning. I am not yet of Percy's mind, the Hotspur of
the North, he that kills some six or seven dozen of Scots
at a breakfast, washes his hands, and says to his wife,
'Fie upon this quiet life, I want work.' 'O my sweet

Harry,' says she, 'how many have you killed today?'
'Give my roan horse a drench,' says he, and answers,
'Some fourteen,' an hour after, 'a trifle, a trifle'. I pray
call in Falstaff. I'll play Percy, and that damned brawn
shall play Dame Mortimer his wife. 'Right-ho!' says the
drunkard. Call in Ribs, call in Tallow!

Enter Falstaff, Gadshill, Bardolph, and Peto;
followed by Francis, with wine

POINS Welcome, Jack, where have you been?
FALSTAFF A plague of all cowards, I say, and a vengeance
too, sure and amen! Give me a cup of sack, boy. Ere I
lead this life long, I'll sew nether-stockings, and mend
them and foot them too. A plague of all cowards! Give
me a cup of sack, rogue. Is there no virtue extant?

He drinks

PRINCE HAL Did you never see Titan kiss a dish of butter—
pitiful-hearted Titan!—that melted at the sweet tale of
the sun's? If you did, then behold that compound.
FALSTAFF You rogue, here's lime in this sack too. There is
nothing but roguery to be found in villainous man, yet
a coward is worse than a cup of sack with lime in it. A
villainous coward! Go your ways, old Jack, die when you
will. If manhood, good manhood, is not forgotten upon
the face of the earth, then am I a shotten herring. There
live not three good men unhanged in England, and one of
them is fat, and grows old. God help the while, a bad
world I say. I would I were a weaver: I could sing
psalms—or anything. A plague of all cowards, I say ever.
PRINCE HAL How now, woolsack, what mutter you?
FALSTAFF A king's son! If I do not beat you out of your
kingdom with a dagger of lath, and drive all your
subjects before you like a flock of wild geese, I'll never
wear hair on my face more. You, Prince of Wales!

PRINCE HAL Why, you damned round man, what's the matter?

FALSTAFF Are not you a coward? Answer me to that—and Poins there?

POINS Zounds, you fat paunch, if you call me coward by the Lord I'll stab you.

FALSTAFF I call you coward? I'll see you damned ere I call you coward, but I would give a thousand pound I could run as fast as you can. You are straight enough in the shoulders, you care not who sees your back. Call you that backing of your friends? A plague upon such backing, give me them that will face me! Give me a cup of sack! I am a rogue if I drunk today.

PRINCE HAL O villain! Your lips are scarce wiped since you drunk last.

FALSTAFF All is one for that. (He drinks) A plague of all cowards, still say I.

PRINCE HAL What's the matter?

FALSTAFF What's the matter? There are four of us here have taken a thousand pound this day morning.

PRINCE HAL Where is it, Jack, where is it?

FALSTAFF Where is it? Taken from us it is. A hundred upon poor four of us.

PRINCE HAL What, a hundred, man?

FALSTAFF I am a rogue if I were not at half-sword with a dozen of them two hours together. I have escaped by miracle. I am eight times thrust through the doublet, four through the hose, my buckler cut through and through, my sword hacked like a handsaw—*ecce signum!*[3] I never dealt better since I was a man. All would not do. A plague of all cowards! Let them speak. If they speak more or less than truth, they are villains and the sons of darkness.

PRINCE HAL Speak, sirs, how was it?

---

[3]Here is the evidence.

GADSHILL We four set upon some dozen—

FALSTAFF Sixteen at least, my lord.

GADSHILL And bound them.

PETO No, no, they were not bound.

FALSTAFF You rogue, they were bound, every man of them, or I am a Jew else: a Hebrew Jew.

GADSHILL As we were sharing, some six or seven fresh men set upon us—

FALSTAFF And unbound the rest, and then come in the others.

PRINCE HAL What, fought you with them all?

FALSTAFF All? I know not what you call all, but if I fought not with fifty of them I am a bunch of radish. If there were not two or three and fifty upon poor old Jack, then am I no two-legged creature.

PRINCE HAL Pray God you have not murdered some of them.

FALSTAFF Nay, that's past praying for, I have peppered two of them. Two I am sure I have paid, two rogues in buckram suits. I tell you what, Hal, if I tell you a lie, spit in my face, call me horse. You know my old tactics— here I lay, and thus I bore my point. Four rogues in buckram let drive at me—

PRINCE HAL What, four? You said but two even now.

FALSTAFF Four, Hal, I told you four.

POINS Ay, ay, he said four.

FALSTAFF These four came all afront, and mainly thrust at me. I made no more ado, but took all their seven points in my buckier, thus!

PRINCE HAL Seven? Why, there were but four even now.

PRINCE HAL Seven? Why, there were but four even now.

FALSTAFF In buckram?

POINS Ay, four, in buckram suits.

FALSTAFF Seven, by these hilts, or I am a villain else.

PRINCE HAL Pray let him alone, we shall have more anon.

FALSTAFF Do you hear me, Hal?

PRINCE HAL Ay, and mark you too, Jack.

FALSTAFF Do so, for it is worth the listening to. These nine in buckram that I told you of—

PRINCE HAL So, two more already.

FALSTAFF Their points being broken—

POINS Down fell their hose.

FALSTAFF —began to give me ground. But I followed close, came in, foot and hand, and, with a thought, seven of the eleven I slew.

PRINCE HAL O monstrous! Eleven buckram men grown out of two!

FALSTAFF But as the devil would have it, three misbegotten knaves in Kendal green came at my back and let drive at me, for it was so dark, Hal, that you could not see your hand.

PRINCE HAL These lies are like their father that begets them, gross as a mountain, open, palpable. Why, you clay-brained guts, you knotty-pated fool, you obscene greasy tallow-catch—

FALSTAFF What, are you mad? Are you mad? Is not the truth the truth?

PRINCE HAL Why, how could you know these men in Kendal green when it was so dark you could not see your hand? Come, tell us your reason. What say you to this?

POINS Come, your reason, Jack, your reason!

FALSTAFF What, upon compulsion? Zounds, if I were at the torture, or all the racks in the world, I would not tell you on compulsion. Give you a reason on compulsion? If reasons were as plentiful as blackberries, I would give no man a reason upon compulsion, I.

PRINCE HAL I'll be no longer guilty of this sin. This sanguine coward, this bed-presser, this horse-back-breaker, this huge hill of flesh—

FALSTAFF God, you starveling, you eel-skin, you dried calf's-tongue, you bull's-pizzle, you cod-fish! O for breath to utter what is like you! You tailor's-yard, you sheath, you bow-case, you vile standing stick!

PRINCE HAL Well, breathe awhile, and then to it again, and when you have tired yourself in base comparisons hear me speak but this.

POINS Mark, Jack!

PRINCE HAL We two saw you four set on four, and bound them and were masters of their wealth—mark now how a plain tale shall put you down. Then did we two set on you four, and, with a word, out-faced you from your prize, and have it, yea, and can show it you here in the house. And Falstaff, you carried your guts away as nimbly, with as quick dexterity, and roared for mercy, and still ran and roared, as ever I heard bull-calf. What a slave are you to hack your sword as you have done, and then say it was in fight! What trick, what device, what starting-hole can you now find out, to hide you from this open and apparent shame?

POINS Come, let's hear Jack, what trick have you now?

FALSTAFF By the Lord, I knew you as well as he that made you. Why, hear you, my masters, was it for me to kill the heir apparent? Should I turn upon the true prince? Why, you know I am as valiant as Hercules. But beware instinct. The lion will not touch the true prince. Instinct is a great matter. I was now a coward on instinct. I shall think the better of myself, and you, during my life—I for a valiant lion, and you for a true prince. But by the Lord, lads, I am glad you have the money! Hostess, clap to the doors! Watch tonight, pray tomorrow! Gallants, lads, boys, hearts of gold, all the titles of good fellowship come to you! What, shall we be merry? Shall we have a play extempore?

PRINCE HAL Content, and the argument shall be your running away.

FALSTAFF Ah, no more of that Hal, if you love me.

Enter Hostess

HOSTESS O Jesu, my lord the Prince!

PRINCE HAL How now, my lady the Hostess, what say you
    to me?

HOSTESS Sure, my lord, there is a nobleman of the Court
    at door would speak with you. He says he comes from
    your father.

PRINCE HAL Give him as much as will make him a royal
    man and send him back again to my mother.

FALSTAFF What manner of man is he?

HOSTESS An old man.

FALSTAFF What does gravity out of his bed at midnight?
    Shall I give him his answer?

PRINCE HAL Pray do, Jack.

FALSTAFF Faith, and I'll send him packing.   *Exit*

PRINCE HAL Now, sirs, by our lady, you fought fair, so did
    you, Peto, so did you, Bardolph. You are lions too, you
    ran away upon instinct, you will not touch the true
    prince, no, fie!

BARDOLPH Faith, I ran when I saw others run.

PRINCE HAL Faith, tell me now in earnest, how came
    Falstaff's sword so hacked?

PETO Why, he hacked it with his dagger, and said he would
    swear truth out of England but he would make you
    believe it was done in fight, and persuaded us to do the
    like.

BARDOLPH Yea, and to tickle our noses with spear-grass,
    to make them bleed, and then to beslubber our garments
    with it, and swear it was the blood of true men. I did
    that I did not this seven year before: I blushed to hear
    his monstrous devices.

PRINCE HAL O villain, you stole a cup of sack eighteen
    years ago, and were taken with the manner, and ever
    since you have blushed extempore. You had fire and

sword on your side, and yet you ran away. What instinct had you for it?

BARDOLPH My lord, do you see these meteors? Do you behold these exhalations?

PRINCE HAL I do.

BARDOLPH What think you they portend?

PRINCE HAL Hot livers, and cold purses.

BARDOLPH Choler, my lord, if rightly taken.

PRINCE HAL No, if rightly taken, halter.

Enter Falstaff

Here comes lean Jack, here comes bare-bone. How now my sweet creature of bombast, how long is it ago, Jack, since you saw your own knee?

FALSTAFF My own knee? When I was about your years, Hal, I was not an eagle's talon in the waist—I could have crept into any alderman's thumb-ring. A plague of sighing and grief, it blows a man up like a bladder. There's villainous news abroad. Here was Sir John Bracy from your father. You must to the Court in the morning. That same mad fellow of the North, Percy, and he of Wales that gave Amamon the bastinado, and made Lucifer cuckold, and swore the devil his true liegeman upon the cross of a Welsh hook—what a plague call you him?

POINS O, Glendower.

FALSTAFF Owen, Owen, the same. And his son-in-law Mortimer, and old Northumberland, and that sprightly Scot of Scots, Douglas, that runs a-horseback up a hill perpendicular—

PRINCE HAL He that rides at high speed, and with his pistol kills a sparrow flying.

FALSTAFF You have hit it.

PRINCE HAL So did he never the sparrow.

FALSTAFF Well, that rascal has good mettle in him, he will not run.

PRINCE HAL Why, what a rascal are you then, to praise him so for running!

FALSTAFF A-horseback, you cuckoo, but afoot he will not budge a foot.

PRINCE HAL Yes, Jack, upon instinct.

FALSTAFF I grant you, upon instinct. Well, he is there too, and one Mordake, and a thousand Scots more. Worcester is stolen away tonight. Your father's beard is turned white with the news. You may buy land now as cheap as stinking mackerel.

PRINCE HAL Why then, it is likely if there comes a hot June, and this civil buffeting holds, we shall buy maidenheads as they buy hob-nails, by the hundreds.

FALSTAFF By the mass, lad, you say true, it is likely we shall have good trading that way. But tell me, Hal, are not you horribly afraid? You being heir apparent, could the world pick out three such enemies again, as that fiend Douglas, that spirit Percy, and that devil Glendower? Are you not horribly afraid? Does not your blood thrill at it?

PRINCE HAL Not a whit, in faith, I lack some of your instinct.

FALSTAFF Well, you will be horribly chidden tomorrow when you come to your father. If you love me, practise an answer.

PRINCE HAL Do you stand for my father and examine me upon the particulars of my life.

FALSTAFF Shall I? Content! This chair shall be my state, this dagger my sceptre, and this cushion my crown.

PRINCE HAL Your state is taken for a joint-stool, your golden sceptre for a leaden dagger, and your precious rich crown for a pitiful bald crown.

FALSTAFF Well, if the fire of grace is not quite out of you, now shall you be moved. Give me a cup of sack to make my eyes look red, that it may be thought I have wept, for

I must speak in passion, and I will do it in King
Cambyses' vein.

PRINCE HAL Well, here is my leg.

FALSTAFF And here is my speech. Stand aside, nobility.

HOSTESS O Jesu, this is excellent sport, in faith.

FALSTAFF

Weep not, sweet Queen, for trickling tears are vain.

HOSTESS O the Father, how he holds his countenance!

FALSTAFF

For God's sake, lords, convey my tristful Queen,
For tears do stop the floodgates of her eyes.

HOSTESS O Jesu, he does it as like one of these harlotry
players as ever I see!

FALSTAFF Peace, good pint-pot, peace, good ticklebrain.

(as KING*)*

Harry, I do not only marvel where you spend your time,
but also how you are accompanied. For though the
camomile, the more it is trodden on the faster it grows,
yet youth, the more it is wasted the sooner it wears. That
you are my son I have partly your mother's word, partly
my own opinion, but chiefly a villainous trick of your
eye and a foolish hanging of your nether lip that do
warrant me. If then you are son to me—here lies the
point—why, being son to me, are you so pointed at?
Shall the blessed sun of heaven prove a truant, and eat
blackberries? A question not to be asked. Shall the son
of England prove a thief, and take purses? A question to
be asked. There is a thing, Harry, which you have often
heard of, and it is known to many in our land by the
name of pitch. This pitch—as ancient writers do report—
does defile, so does the company you keep. For, Harry,
now I do not speak to you in drink, but in tears; not in
pleasure, but in passion; not in words only, but in woes

also. And yet there is a virtuous man whom I have often noted in your company, but I know not his name.

PRINCE HAL (as himself)

What manner of man, if it likes your Majesty?

FALSTAFF (as KING)

A goodly portly man, in faith, and a corpulent; of a cheerful look, a pleasing eye, and a most noble carriage; and, as I think, his age some fifty, or by our lady inclining to threescore. And now I remember, his name is Falstaff. If that man should be lewdly given, he deceives me; for, Harry, I see virtue in his looks. If then the tree may be known by the fruit, as the fruit by the tree, then peremptorily I speak it, there is virtue in that Falstaff. Him keep with, the rest banish. And tell me now, you naughty varlet, tell me where have you been this month?

PRINCE HAL Do you speak like a king? Do you stand for me, and I'll play my father.

FALSTAFF Depose me? If you do it half so gravely, so majestically, both in word and matter, hang me up by the heels for a rabbit-sucker, or a poulter's hare.

PRINCE HAL Well, here I am set.

FALSTAFF And here I stand. Judge, my masters.

PRINCE HAL (as KING)

Now, Harry, whence come you?

FALSTAFF (as HAL)

My noble lord, from Eastcheap.

PRINCE HAL (as KING)

The complaints I hear of you are grievous.

FALSTAFF (as HAL)

God's blood, my lord, they are false!

Nay, I'll tickle you for a young prince, in faith.

PRINCE HAL (as KING)

Swear you, ungracious boy? Henceforth never look on me. You are violently carried away from grace. There is a devil haunts you in the likeness of an old fat man, a

tun of man is your companion. Why do you converse
with that trunk of humours, that sifting-hutch of
beastliness, that swollen parcel of dropsies, that huge
bombard of sack, that stuffed cloak-bag of guts, that
roasted Manningtree ox with the pudding in his belly,
that reverend Vice, that grey Iniquity, that Father Ruffian,
that Vanity in years? Wherein is he good, but to taste
sack and drink it? Wherein neat and cleanly, but to carve
a capon and eat it? Wherein cunning, but in craft?
Wherein crafty, but in villainy? Wherein villainous,
but in all things? Wherein worthy, but in nothing?

FALSTAFF (*as* HAL)

I would your grace would take me with you. Whom
means your grace?

PRINCE HAL (*as* KING)

That villainous abominable misleader of youth, Falstaff,
that old white-bearded Satan.

FALSTAFF (*as* HAL)

My lord, the man I know.

PRINCE HAL (*as* KING)

I know you do.

FALSTAFF (*as* HAL)

But to say I know more harm in him than in myself
were to say more than I know. That he is old, the more
the pity, his white hairs do witness it; but that he is,
saving your reverence, a whoremaster, that I utterly
deny. If sack and sugar are a fault, God help the wicked!
If to be old and merry is a sin, then many an old host
that I know is damned. If to be fat is to be hated, then
Pharaoh's lean kine are to be loved. No, my good lord!
Banish Peto, banish Bardolph, banish Poins—but for
sweet Jack Falstaff, kind Jack Falstaff, true Jack Falstaff,
valiant Jack Falstaff—and therefore more valiant, being
as he is old Jack Falstaff—banish not him your Harry's
company, banish not him your Harry's company. Banish
plump Jack, and banish all the world.

PRINCE HAL (*as* KING)
  I do, I will.

                    Exeunt Hostess, Francis and Bardolph

              Enter Bardolph, running

BARDOLPH O my lord, my lord, the sheriff with a most
  monstrous watch is at the door.
FALSTAFF Out, you rogue! Play out the play! I have much
  to say in behalf of that Falstaff.

                    Enter the Hostess

HOSTESS O Jesu, my lord, my lord!
PRINCE HAL Heigh, heigh, the devil rides upon a fiddle-
  stick. What's the matter?
HOSTESS The sheriff and all the watch are at the door.
  They are come to search the house. Shall I let them in?
FALSTAFF Do you hear, Hal? Never call a true piece of gold
  a counterfeit. You are essentially made without seeming so.
PRINCE HAL And you a natural coward without instinct.
FALSTAFF I deny your major. If you will deny the sheriff,
  so; if not, let him enter. If I become not a cart as well as
  another man, a plague on my bringing up! I hope I
  shall as soon be strangled with a halter as another.
PRINCE HAL Go hide behind the arras. The rest, walk
  up above. Now, my masters, for a true face, and good
  conscience.
FALSTAFF Both which I have had, but their date is out,
  and therefore I'll hide.
                    Exeunt all but the Prince and Peto
PRINCE HAL Call in the Sheriff.

Enter Sheriff and the Carrier

Now, master Sheriff, what is your will with me?

SHERIFF

First, pardon me, my lord. A hue and cry
Has followed certain men unto this house.

PRINCE HAL

What men?

SHERIFF

One of them is well known my gracious lord,
A gross fat man.

CARRIER   As fat as butter.

PRINCE HAL

The man I do assure you is not here,
For I myself at this time have employed him.
And Sheriff, I will engage my word to you,
That I will by tomorrow dinner-time
Send him to answer you, or any man,
For anything he shall be chargèd with.
And so let me entreat you leave the house.

SHERIFF

I will, my lord. There are two gentlemen
Have in this robbery lost three hundred marks.

PRINCE HAL

It may be so. If he has robbed these men
He shall be answerable. And so, farewell.

SHERIFF

Good night, my noble lord.

PRINCE HAL

I think it is good morrow, is it not?

SHERIFF

Indeed, my lord, I think it is two o'clock.

Exit with Carrier

PRINCE HAL This oily rascal is known as well as Paul's.
Go call him forth.

PETO Falstaff! Fast asleep behind the arras, and snorting like a horse.

PRINCE HAL Hark how hard he fetches breath. Search his pockets.

Peto searches his pockets, and finds certain papers

What have you found?

PETO Nothing but papers, my lord.

PRINCE HAL Let's see what they are, read them.

PETO *Item a capon* . . . . *2s. 2d.*
  Item sauce . . . . *4d.*
  Item sack two gallons . . . . *5s. 8d.*
  Item anchovies and sack after supper . . . . . . *2s. 6d.*
  Item bread. . . . . *ha'penny*

PRINCE HAL O monstrous! But one halfpennyworth of bread to this intolerable deal of sack? What there is else keep close, we'll read it at more advantage. There let him sleep till day. I'll to the Court in the morning. We must all to the wars, and your place shall be honourable. I'll procure this fat rogue a charge of foot, and I know his death will be a march of twelve score. The money shall be paid back again with advantage. Be with me betimes in the morning, and so, good morrow, Peto.

PETO Good morrow, good my lord.   *Exeunt*

Act III

SCENE I
Wales. Glendower's house.

Enter Hotspur, Worcester, Mortimer, and Glendower

MORTIMER
These promises are fair, the parties sure,
And our induction full of prosperous hope.

HOTSPUR
Lord Mortimer, and cousin Glendower, will you sit
   down?
And uncle Worcester. A plague upon it!
I have forgotten the map.

GLENDOWER   No, here it is.
Sit, cousin Percy, sit—good cousin Hotspur—
For by that name as oft as Lancaster does speak of you
His cheek looks pale, and with a rising sigh
He wishes you in heaven.

HOTSPUR   And you in hell,
As oft as he hears Owen Glendower spoken of.

GLENDOWER
I cannot blame him. At my nativity
The front of heaven was full of fiery shapes,
Of burning cressets, and at my birth
The frame and huge foundation of the earth
Shook like a coward.

HOTSPUR   Why, so it would have done
At the same season if your mother's cat
Had but kittened, though yourself had never been born.

GLENDOWER
    I say the earth did shake when I was born.
HOTSPUR
    And I say the earth was not of my mind,
    If you suppose as fearing you it shook.
GLENDOWER
    The heavens were all on fire, the earth did tremble—
HOTSPUR
    O, then the earth shook to see the heavens on fire,
    And not in fear of your nativity.
    Diseasèd nature oftentimes breaks forth
    In strange eruptions, oft the teeming earth
    Is with a kind of colic pinched and vexed
    By the imprisoning of unruly wind
    Within her womb; which for enlargement striving
    Shakes the old beldam earth, and topples down
    Steeples and moss-grown towers. At your birth
    Our grandam earth, having this distemperature,
    In passion shook.
GLENDOWER   Cousin, of many men
    I do not bear these crossings. Give me leave
    To tell you once again that at my birth
    The front of heaven was full of fiery shapes,
    The goats ran from the mountains, and the herds
    Were strangely clamorous to the frighted fields.
    These signs have marked me extra-ordinary,
    And all the courses of my life do show
    I am not in the roll of common men.
    Where is he living, clipped in with the sea
    That chides the banks of England, Scotland, Wales,
    Who calls me pupil or has read to me?
    And bring him out that is but woman's son
    Can trace me in the tedious ways of art,
    And hold me pace in deep experiments.

HOTSPUR
  I think there's no man speaks better Welsh.
  I'll to dinner.
MORTIMER
  Peace, cousin Percy, you will make him mad.
GLENDOWER
  I can call spirits from the vasty deep.
HOTSPUR
  Why, so can I, or so can any man:
  But will they come when you do call for them?
GLENDOWER
  Why, I can teach you, cousin, to command the devil.
HOTSPUR
  And I can teach you, cousin, to shame the devil
  By telling truth. Tell truth, and shame the devil.
  If you have power to raise him, bring him hither,
  And I'll be sworn I have power to shame him hence.
  O, while you live, tell truth, and shame the devil!
MORTIMER
  Come, come, no more of this unprofitable chat.
GLENDOWER
  Three times has Henry Bolingbroke made head
  Against my power; thrice from the banks of Wye
  And sandy-bottomed Severn have I sent him
  Bootless [fruitless] home, and weather-beaten back.
HOTSPUR
  Home without boots, and in foul weather too!
  How escapes he agues, in the devil's name?
GLENDOWER
  Come, here is the map, shall we divide our right
  According to our threefold order taken?
MORTIMER
  The Archdeacon has divided it
  Into three limits very equally.
  England, from Trent and Severn hitherto,
  By south and east is to my part assigned.

All westward, Wales beyond the Severn shore,
And all the fertile land within that bound,
To Owen Glendower. And, dear cousin, to you
The remnant northward lying off from Trent.
And our indentures tripartite are drawn,
Which being sealèd interchangeably—
A business that this night may execute—
Tomorrow, cousin Percy, you and I
And my good Lord of Worcester will set forth
To meet your father and the Scottish power,
As is appointed us, at Shrewsbury.
My father Glendower is not ready yet,
Nor shall we need his help these fourteen days.
(*To Glendower*) Within that space you may have drawn
    together
Your tenants, friends, and neighbouring gentlemen.

GLENDOWER
A shorter time shall send me to you, lords,
And in my conduct shall your ladies come,
From whom you now must steal and take no leave;
For there will be a world of water shed
Upon the parting of your wives and you.

HOTSPUR
I think my moiety, north from Burton here,
In quantity equals not one of yours.
See how this river comes cranking in,
And cuts me from the best of all my land
A huge half-moon, a monstrous cantle out.
I'll have the current in this place dammed up,
And here the smug and silver Trent shall run
In a new channel fair and evenly.
It shall not wind with such a deep indent,
To rob me of so rich a bottom here.

GLENDOWER
Not wind? It shall, it must—you see it does.

MORTIMER
  Yes,
  But mark how it bears its course, and runs up
  With like advantage on the other side,
  Gelding the opposèd continent as much
  As on the other side it takes from you.
WORCESTER
  Yes, but a little charge will trench him here,
  And on this north side win this cape of land,
  And then he runs straight and even.
HOTSPUR
  I'll have it so, a little charge will do it.
GLENDOWER
  I'll not have it altered.
HOTSPUR   Will not you?
GLENDOWER
  No, and you shall not.
HOTSPUR   Who shall say me nay?
GLENDOWER
  Why, that will I.
HOTSPUR
  Let me not understand you then, speak it in Welsh.
GLENDOWER
  I can speak English, lord, as well as you,
  For I was trained up in the English Court;
  Where being but young I framèd to the harp
  Many an English ditty lovely well,
  And gave the tongue a helpful ornament—
  A virtue that was never seen in you.
HOTSPUR
  Indeed, and I am glad of it with all my heart!
  I had rather be a kitten and cry 'mew'
  Than one of these same metre ballad-mongers.
  I had rather hear a brazen candlestick turned,
  Or a dry wheel grate on the axle-tree;
  And that would set my teeth nothing on edge,

Nothing so much as mincing poetry.
'Tis like the forced gait of a shuffling nag.

GLENDOWER

Come, you shall have Trent turned.

HOTSPUR

I do not care, I'll give thrice so much land
To any well-deserving friend.
But in the way of bargain, mark you me,
I'll cavil on the ninth part of a hair.
Are the indentures drawn? Shall we be gone?

GLENDOWER

The moon shines fair, you may away by night.
I'll haste the writer, and with that
Break with your wives of your departure hence.
I am afraid my daughter will run mad,
So much she dotes now on her Mortimer.   *Exit*

MORTIMER

Fie, cousin Percy, how you cross my father!

HOTSPUR

I cannot choose. Sometime he angers me
With telling me of the mole and the ant indeed,
Of the dreamer Merlin and his prophecies;
And of a dragon and a finless fish,
A clip-winged griffin and a moulting raven,
A couching lion and a ramping cat;
And such a deal of skimble-skamble stuff
As puts me from my faith. I tell you what—
He held me last night at least nine hours
In reckoning up the several devils' names
That were his lackeys. I cried 'Hum', and 'Well, go to!'
But marked him not a word. O, he is as tedious
As a tirèd horse, a railing wife,
Worse than a smoky house. I had rather live
With cheese and garlic in a windmill, far,
Than feed on dainties and have him talk to me
In any summer house in Christendom.

MORTIMER
In faith, he is a worthy gentleman,
Exceedingly well read, and profited
In strange concealments; valiant as a lion,
And wondrous affable, and as bountiful
As mines of India. Shall I tell you, cousin?
He holds your temper in a high respect
And curbs himself even of his natural scope
When you come across his humour, faith he does.
I warrant you that man is not alive
Might so have tempted him as you have done
Without the taste of danger and reproof.
But do not use it oft, let me entreat you.

WORCESTER
In faith, my lord, you are too wilful-blame,
And since your coming hither have done enough
To put him quite beside his patiènce.
You must needs learn, lord, to amend this fault.
Though sometimes it shows greatness, courage, blood—
And that's the dearest grace it renders you—
Yet oftentimes it does present harsh rage,
Defect of manners, want of government,
Pride, haughtiness, opinion, and disdain:
The least of which haunting a nobleman
Loses men's hearts and leaves behind a stain
Upon the beauty of all parts besides,
Beguiling them of commendatiòn.

HOTSPUR
Well, I am schooled—good manners be your luck!
Here come our wives, and let us take our leave.

Enter Glendower with the ladies

MORTIMER
This is the deadly spite that angers me,
My wife can speak no English, I no Welsh.

GLENDOWER
  My daughter weeps, she will not part with you,
  She'll be a soldier too, she'll to the wars.
MORTIMER
  Good father, tell her that she and my aunt Percy
  Shall follow in your conduct speedily.

*Glendower speaks to her in Welsh, and she answers him
in the same*

GLENDOWER She is desperate here, a peevish, self-willed
  harlotry, one that no persuasion can do good upon.

The lady speaks in Welsh

MORTIMER
  I understand your looks, that pretty Welsh
  Which you pour down from these swelling heavens
  I am too perfect in, and but for shame
  In such a parley should I answer you.

The lady speaks again in Welsh

  I understand your kisses, and you mine,
  And that's a feeling disputatiòn.
  But I will never be a truant, love,
  Till I have learnt your language, for your tongue
  Makes Welsh as sweet as ditties highly penned,
  Sung by a fair queen in a summer's bower
  With ravishing division to her lute.
GLENDOWER
  Nay, if you melt, then will she run mad.

The lady speaks again in Welsh

MORTIMER
    O, I am ignorance itself in this!
GLENDOWER
    She bids you on the wanton rushes lay you down,
    And rest your gentle head upon her lap,
    And she will sing the song that pleases you;
    And on your eyelids crown the god of sleep,
    Charming your blood with pleasing heaviness—
    Making such difference between wake and sleep
    As is the difference betwixt day and night,
    The hour before the heavenly-harnessed team
    Begins his golden progress in the east.
MORTIMER
    With all my heart I'll sit and hear her sing,
    By that time will our book, I think, be drawn.
GLENDOWER
    Do so, and those musicians that shall play to you
    Hang in the air a thousand leagues from hence,
    And straight they shall be here. Sit, and attend.
HOTSPUR
    Come, Kate, you are perfect in lying down.
    Come, quick, quick, that I may lay my head in your lap.
LADY PERCY Go, you giddy goose.

The music plays

HOTSPUR
    Now I perceive the devil understands Welsh:
    It is no marvel he is so humorous,
    By our lady, he is a good musiciàn.
LADY PERCY
    Then should you be nothing but musical,
    For you are altogether governed by humours.
    Lie still, you thief, and hear the lady sing in Welsh.
HOTSPUR I had rather hear Lady my hound howl in Irish.
LADY PERCY Would you have your head broken?

HOTSPUR No.
LADY PERCY Then be still.
HOTSPUR Neither, 'tis a woman's fault.
LADY PERCY Now, God help you!
HOTSPUR To the Welsh lady's bed.
LADY PERCY What's that?
HOTSPUR Peace, she sings.

Here the lady sings a Welsh song

Come, Kate, I'll have your song too.
LADY PERCY Not mine, in good sooth [truth].
HOTSPUR Not yours, in good sooth! Heart, you swear like
    a comfit-maker's wife—'Not you, in good sooth!', and
    'As true as I live!', and 'As God shall mend me!', and 'As
    sure as day!'—
    And give such silken surety for your oaths
    As if you never walk further than Finsbury.
    Swear me, Kate, like a lady as you are,
    A good mouth-filling oath, and leave 'In sooth',
    And such protest of pepper-gingerbread,
    To velvet-trimmings, and Sunday citizens.
    Come, sing.
LADY PERCY I will not sing.
HOTSPUR 'Tis the next way to turn tailor, or be redbreast
    teacher. If the indentures are drawn I'll away within
    these two hours. And so, come in when you will.   *Exit*
GLENDOWER
    Come, come, Lord Mortimer, you are as slow
    As hot Lord Percy is on fire to go.
    By this our book is drawn. We'll but seal,
    And then to horse immediately.
MORTIMER   With all my heart.
                                              Exeunt

SCENE II
Westminster. The palace.

Enter the King, Prince Henry, and others

KING HENRY

Lords, give us leave. The Prince of Wales and I
Must have some private conference—but be near at
    hand,
For we shall presently have need of you.   *Exeunt Lords*
I know not whether God will have it so
For some displeasing service I have done,
That in his secret sentence out of my blood
He'll breed revengement and a scourge for me.
But you do in your passages of life
Make me believe that you are only marked
For the hot vengeance and the rod of heaven,
To punish my mistreadings. Tell me else,
Could such inordinate and low desires,
Such poor, such bare, such lewd, such mean attempts,
Such barren pleasures, rude society,
As you are matchèd with, and grafted to,
Accompany the greatness of your blood
And hold their level with your princely heart?

PRINCE HAL

So please your majesty, I would I could
Quit all offences with as clear excuse
As well as, I am doubtless, I can purge
Myself of many I am chargèd with.
Yet such extenuation let me beg
As, in reproof of many tales devised,
Which oft the ear of greatness needs must hear,
By smiling tale-tellers, and base newsmongers,
I may for some things true. Wherein my youth
Has faulty wandered and irregular,
Find pardon on my true submissiòn.

KING HENRY

God pardon you! Yet let me wonder, Harry,
At your affections, which do hold a wing
Quite from the flight of all your ancestors.
Your place in Council you have rudely lost,
Which by your younger brother is supplied,
And are almost an alien to the hearts
Of all the Court and princes of my blood.
The hope and expectation of your time
Are ruined, and the soul of every man
Prophetically does forethink your fall.
Had I so lavish of my presence been,
So common-hackneyed in the eyes of men,
So stale and cheap to vulgar company,
Opinion, that did help me to the crown,
Had still kept loyal to possessiòn,
And left me in reputeless banishment,
A fellow of no mark nor likelihood.
By being seldom seen, I could not stir
But like a comet I was wondered at,
That men would tell their children, 'This is he!'
Others would say, 'Where, which is Bolingbroke?'
And then I stole all courtesy from heaven,
And dressed myself in such humility
That I did pluck allegiance from men's hearts,
Loud shouts and salutations from their mouths,
Even in the presence of the crownèd King.
Thus did I keep my person fresh and new,
My presence, like a robe pontifical,
Never seen but wondered at, and so my state,
Seldom, but sumptuous, showed like a feast,
And won by rareness such solemnity.
The skipping King, he ambled up and down,
With shallow jesters, and rash sputtering wits,
Soon kindled and soon burnt, lowered his state,
Mingled his royalty with capering fools,

Had his great name profanèd with their scorns;
And gave his countenance against his name
To laugh at gibing boys, and stand the push
Of every beardless vain comparative:
Grew a companion to the common streets,
Enfeoffed himself to popularity,
That, being daily swallowed by men's eyes,
They surfeited with honey, and began
To loathe the taste of sweetness, whereof a little
More than a little is by much too much.
So, when he had occasion to be seen,
He was but as the cuckoo is in June,
Heard, not regarded; seen, but with such eyes
As, sick and blunted with community,
Afford no extra-ordinary gaze—
Such as is bent on sun-like majesty
When it shines seldom in admiring eyes,
But rather drowsed and hung their eyelids down;
Slept in his face, and rendered such aspèct
As cloudy men use to their adversaries,
Being with his presence glutted, gorged, and full.
And in that very line, Harry, stand you,
For you have lost your princely privilege
With vile participation. Not an eye
But is a-weary of your common sight,
Save mine, which has desired to see you more,
Which now does that I would not have it do,
Make blind itself with foolish tenderness.

PRINCE HAL
I shall hereafter, my thrice-gracious lord,
Be more myself.

KING HENRY   For all the world
As you are to this hour was Richard then
When I from France set foot at Ravenspurgh,
And even as I was then is Percy now.
Now by my sceptre, and my soul as well,

He has more worthy interest to the state
Than you the shadow of successiòn.
For of no right, nor colour like to right,
He does fill fields with harness in the realm,
Turns head against the lion's armèd jaws;
And being no more in debt to years than you
Leads ancient lords and reverend bishops on
To bloody battles, and to bruising arms.
What never-dying honour has he got
Against renownèd Douglas! Whose high deeds,
Whose hot incursions and great name in arms
Hold from all soldiers chief majority
And military title capital
Through all the kingdoms that acknowledge Christ.
Thrice has this Hotspur, Mars in swaddling clothes,
This infant warrior, in his enterprises
Discomfited great Douglas, taken him once,
Enlargèd him, and made a friend of him,
To fill the mouth of deep defiance up,
And shake the peace and safety of our throne.
And what say you to this? Percy, Northumberland,
The Archbishop's grace of York, Douglas, Mortimer,
Combine together against us and are up.
But wherefore do I tell these news to you?
Why, Harry, do I tell you of my foes,
Who are my nearest and dearest enemy?
You that are likely enough, through vassal fear,
Base inclination, and a fit of pique,
To fight against me under Percy's pay,
To dog his heels, and curtsy at his frowns,
To show how much you are degenerate.

PRINCE HAL
Do not think so, you shall not find it so;
And God forgive them that so much have swayed
Your majesty's good thoughts away from me!
I will redeem all this on Percy's head,

And in the closing of some glorious day
Be bold to tell you that I am your son;
When I will wear a garment all of blood,
And stain my features in a bloody mask,
Which, washed away, shall scour my shame with it.
And that shall be the day, whenever it lights,
That this same child of honour and renown,
This gallant Hotspur, this all-praisèd knight,
And your unthought-of Harry chance to meet.
For every honour sitting on his helm,
Would they were multitudes, and on my head
My shames redoubled. For the time will come
That I shall make this northern youth exchange
His glorious deeds for my indignities.
Percy is but my factor, good my lord,
To engross up glorious deeds on my behalf,
And I will call him to so strict account
That he shall render every glory up,
Yes, even the slightest worship of his time,
Or I will tear the reckoning from his heart.
This in the name of God I promise here,
Which if He be pleased I shall perform,
I do beseech your majesty may salve
The long-grown wounds of my intemperance.
If not, the end of life cancels all bonds,
And I will die a hundred thousand deaths
Ere break the smallest parcel of this vow.

KING HENRY
A hundred thousand rebels die in this.
You shall have charge and sovereign trust herein.

Enter Blunt

How now, good Blunt? Your looks are full of speed.

BLUNT
  So has the business that I come to speak of.
  Lord Mortimer of Scotland has sent word
  That Douglas and the English rebels met
  The eleventh of this month at Shrewsbury.
  A mighty and a fearful head they are,
  If promises be kept on every hand,
  As ever offered foul play in a state.

KING HENRY
  The Earl of Westmorland set forth today,
  With him my son, Lord John of Lancaster,
  For this advertisement is five days old.
  On Wednesday next, Harry, you shall set forward.
  On Thursday we ourselves will march.
  Our meeting is Bridgnorth and, Harry, you
  Shall march through Gloucestershire, by which account,
  Our business valued, some twelve days hence
  Our general forces at Bridgnorth shall meet.
  Our hands are full of business, let's away,
  Advantage feeds him fat while men delay.

                                     Exeunt

Scene III
The Boar's Head.

Enter Falstaff and Bardolph

FALSTAFF Bardolph, am I not fallen away vilely since this
  last action? Do I not slim? Do I not dwindle? Why, my
  skin hangs about me like an old lady's loose gown. I am
  withered like an old apple. Well, I'll repent, and that
  suddenly, while I am in some liking. I shall be out of
  heart shortly, and then I shall have no strength to
  repent. If I have not forgotten what the inside of a
  church is made of, I am a peppercorn, a brewer's horse.

The inside of a church! Company, villainous company, has been the spoil of me.

BARDOLPH Sir John, you are so fretful you cannot live long.

FALSTAFF Why, there is it. Come, sing me a bawdy song, make me merry. I was as virtuously given as a gentleman need to be. Virtuous enough. Swore little. Diced not above seven times a week. Went to a bawdy-house not above once in a quarter—of an hour. Paid money that I borrowed —three or four times. Lived well, and in good compass: and now I live out of all order, out of all compass.

BARDOLPH Why, you are so fat, Sir John, that you must needs be out of all compass, out of all reasonable compass, Sir John.

FALSTAFF Do you amend your face, and I'll amend my life. You are our admiral, you bear the lantern in the poop, but it is in the nose of you. You are the Knight of the Burning Lamp.

BARDOLPH Why, Sir John, my face does you no harm.

FALSTAFF No, I'll be sworn, I make as good use of it as many a man does of a death's-head, or a *memento mori*. I never see your face but I think upon hell-fire, and Dives that lived in purple: for there he is in his robes, burning, burning. If you were any way given to virtue, I would swear by your face. My oath should be 'By this fire, that's God's angel!' But you are altogether given over, and were indeed, but for the light in your face, the son of utter darkness. When you ran up Gad's Hill in the night to catch my horse, if I did not think you had been a will-ò-the-wisp, or a ball of wildfire, there's no purchase in money. O, you are a perpetual triumph, an everlasting bonfire-light! You have saved me a thousand marks in links and torches, walking with you in the night between tavern and tavern. But the sack that you have drunk would have bought me lights as good cheap at the dearest chandler's in Europe. I have maintained that salamander of yours with fire any time this two-and-thirty years, God reward me for it!

BARDOLPH God, I would my face were in your belly!

FALSTAFF God-a-mercy! So should I be sure to be heartburnt.

Enter Hostess

How now, dame Partlet the hen, have you enquired yet who picked my pocket?

HOSTESS Why, Sir John, what do you think, Sir John, do you think I keep thieves in my house? I have searched, I have enquired, so has my husband, man by man, boy by boy, servant by servant—the tithe of a hair was never lost in my house before.

FALSTAFF You lie, hostess. Bardolph was shaved and lost many a hair, and I'll be sworn my pocket was picked. Go to, you are a woman, go!

HOSTESS Who, I? No, I defy you! God's light, I was never called so in my own house before.

FALSTAFF Go to, I know you well enough.

HOSTESS No, Sir John, you do not know me, Sir John, I know you, Sir John, you owe me money, Sir John, and now you pick a quarrel to beguile me of it. I bought you a dozen of shirts to your back.

FALSTAFF Canvas, filthy canvas. I have given them away to bakers' wives. They have made sieves of them.

HOSTESS Now as I am a true woman, holland of eight shillings an ell! You owe money here besides, Sir John, for your diet, and by-drinkings, and money lent you, four-and-twenty pound.

FALSTAFF He had his part of it, let him pay.

HOSTESS He? Alas, he is poor, he has nothing.

FALSTAFF How? Poor? Look upon his face. What call you rich? Let them coin his nose, let them coin his cheeks, I'll not pay a penny. What, will you make a youngster of me? Shall I not take my ease in my inn but I shall have my pocket picked? I have lost a seal-ring of my grandfather's worth forty marks.

HOSTESS O Jesu, I have heard the Prince tell him I know not how oft, that that ring was copper.

FALSTAFF How? The Prince is a Jack, a sneak-up. By God, if he were here I would cudgel him like a dog if he would say so.

Enter the Prince marching, with Peto, and Falstaff meets him, playing upon his truncheon like a fife

How now, lad? Is the wind in that door, in faith, must we all march?

BARDOLPH Yea, two and two, Newgate fashion.

HOSTESS My lord, I pray you hear me.

PRINCE HAL What say you, Mistress Quickly? How does your husband? I love him well, he is an honest man.

HOSTESS Good my lord, hear me.

FALSTAFF Pray let her alone, and listen to me.

PRINCE HAL What say you, Jack?

FALSTAFF The other night I fell asleep here, behind the arras, and had my pocket picked. This house is turned bawdy-house, they pick pockets.

PRINCE HAL What did you lose, Jack?

FALSTAFF Will you believe me, Hal, three or four bonds of forty pound apiece, and a seal-ring of my grandfather's.

PRINCE HAL A trifle, some eightpenny matter.

HOSTESS So I told him, my lord, and I said I heard your grace say so. And, my lord, he speaks most vilely of you, like a foul-mouthed man as he is, and said he would cudgel you.

PRINCE HAL What! He did not?

HOSTESS There's neither faith, truth, nor womanhood in me else.

FALSTAFF There's no more faith in you than in a stewed prune, and no more truth in you than in a drawn fox—and for womanhood, Maid Marian may be the deputy's wife of the ward to you. Go, you thing, go!

HOSTESS Say, what thing, what thing?

FALSTAFF What thing? Why, a thing to thank God on.

HOSTESS I am no thing to thank God on, I would you should know it. I am an honest man's wife, and setting your knighthood aside, you are a knave to call me so.

FALSTAFF Setting your womanhood aside, you art a beast to say otherwise.

HOSTESS Say, what beast, you knave, you?

FALSTAFF What beast? Why—an otter.

PRINCE HAL An otter, Sir John? Why an otter?

FALSTAFF Why? She's neither fish nor flesh, a man knows not where to have her.

HOSTESS You are an unjust man in saying so, you or any man knows where to have me, you knave, you.

PRINCE HAL You say true, hostess, and he slanders you most grossly.

HOSTESS So he does you, my lord, and said this other day you owed him a thousand pound.

PRINCE HAL Man, do I owe you a thousand pound?

FALSTAFF A thousand pound, Hal? A million, your love is worth a million, you owe me your love.

HOSTESS Nay my lord, he called you Jack, and said he would cudgel you.

FALSTAFF Did I, Bardolph?

BARDOLPH Indeed, Sir John, you said so.

FALSTAFF Yes, if he said my ring was copper.

PRINCE HAL I say it is copper, dare you be as good as your word now?

FALSTAFF Why Hal, you know as you are but man I dare, but as you are prince, I fear you as I fear the roaring of the lion's whelp.

PRINCE HAL And why not as the lion?

FALSTAFF The King himself is to be feared as the lion. Do
    you think I'll fear you as I fear your father? Nay, if I do, I
    pray God my girdle breaks.
PRINCE HAL O, if it should, how would your guts fall
    about your knees! But there's no room for faith, truth,
    nor honesty in this bosom of yours. It is all filled up with
    guts and midriff. Charge an honest woman with picking
    your pocket? Why, you impudent swollen rascal, if there
    were anything in your pocket but tavern reckonings,
    memorandums of bawdy-houses, and one poor penny-
    worth of sugar-candy to make you long-winded, if your
    pocket were enriched with any other injuries but these,
    I am a villain. And yet you will stand to it, you will not
    pocket up wrong! Are you not ashamed?
FALSTAFF Do you hear, Hal? You know in the state of
    innocency Adam fell, and what should poor Jack Falstaff
    do in the days of villainy? You see I have more flesh
    than another man, and therefore more frailty. You confess
    then, you picked my pocket?
PRINCE HAL It appears so by the story.
FALSTAFF Hostess, I forgive you, go make ready breakfast,
    love your husband, look to your servants, cherish your
    guests, you shall find me tractable to any honest reason,
    you see I am pacified—nay, pray be gone. *Exit Hostess*
    Now, Hal, to the news at Court: for the robbery, lad,
    how is that answered?
PRINCE HAL O my sweet beef, I must still be good angel to
    you—the money is paid back again.
FALSTAFF O, I do not like that paying back, 'tis a double
    labour.
PRINCE HAL I am good friends with my father and may
    do anything.
FALSTAFF Rob me the exchequer the first thing you do,
    and do it with unwashed hands too.
BARDOLPH Do, my lord.
PRINCE HAL I have procured you, Jack, a charge of foot.

FALSTAFF I would it had been of horse. Where shall I
   find one that can steal well? O for a fine thief of the
   age of two-and-twenty or thereabouts! I am heinously
   unprovided. Well, God be thanked for these rebels, they
   offend none but the virtuous. I laud them, I praise
   them.

PRINCE HAL Bardolph!

BARDOLPH My lord?

PRINCE HAL
   Go bear this letter to Lord John of Lancaster,
   To my brother John, this to my Lord of Westmorland.

                                                Exit Bardolph

   Go, Peto, to horse, to horse, for you and I
   Have thirty miles to ride yet ere dinner-time.

                                                   Exit Peto

   Jack, meet me tomorrow in the Temple hall
   At two o'clock in the afternoon.
   There shall you know your charge, and there receive
   Money and order for their furniture.
   The land is burning, Percy stands on high,
   And either we or they must lower lie.   *Exit*

FALSTAFF
   Rare words! Brave world! Hostess, my breakfast, come!
   O, I could wish this tavern were my drum.   *Exit*

Act IV

Scene I
The rebel camp near Shrewsbury.

Enter Hotspur, Worcester, and Douglas

HOTSPUR
    Well said, my noble Scot! If speaking truth
    In this fine age were not thought flattery,
    Such attribution should the Douglas have
    As not a soldier of this season's stamp
    Should go as general current through the world.
    By God, I cannot flatter, I do defy
    The tongues of soothers, but a braver place
    In my heart's love has no man than yourself.
    Nay, task me to my word and prove me, lord.

DOUGLAS
    You are the king of honour.
    No man so potent breathes upon the ground
    But I will beard him.

HOTSPUR   Do so, and it is well.

Enter Messenger with letters

    What letters have you there?—I can but thank you.

MESSENGER
    These letters come from your father.

HOTSPUR
    Letters from him? Why comes he not himself?

MESSENGER
He cannot come, my lord, he is grievous sick.
HOTSPUR
Zounds, how has he the leisure to be sick
In such a jostling time? Who leads his army?
Under whose government come they along?
MESSENGER
His letters bear his mind, not I my mind.
WORCESTER
I pray you tell me, does he keep his bed?
MESSENGER
He did, my lord, four days ere I set forth,
And at the time of my departure thence
He was much feared for by his physiciàns.
WORCESTER
I would the state of time had first been whole
Ere he by sickness had been visited.
His health was never better worth than now.
HOTSPUR
Sick now? Droop now? This sickness does infect
The very life-blood of our enterprise.
'Tis catching hither, even to our camp.
He writes me here that inward sickness—
And that his friends by deputation could not
So soon be drawn. Nor did he think it meet
To lay so dangerous and dear a trust
On any soul not sworn, but on his own.
Yet does he give us bold advertisement
That with our small conjunction we should on,
To see how fortune is disposed to us.
For, as he writes, there is no quailing now,
Because the King is certainly informed
Of all our purposes. What say you to it?
WORCESTER
Your father's sickness is a maim to us.

HOTSPUR

    A perilous gash, a very limb lopped off—
    And yet, in faith, it is not! His present want
    Seems more than we shall find it. Were it good
    To set the exact wealth of all our states
    All at one cast? To set so rich a main
    On the fine hazard of one doubtful hour?
    It were not good, for therein should we read
    The very bottom and the soul of hope,
    The very limit, the very utmost bound
    Of all our fortunes.

DOUGLAS

    Faith, and so we should, where now remains
    A sweet reversion—we may boldly spend
    Upon the hope of what is to come in.
    A comfort of retirement lives in this.

HOTSPUR

    A rendezvous, a home to fly unto,
    If now the devil and mischance look big
    Upon the maidenhead of our affairs.

WORCESTER

    But yet I would your father had been here.
    The quality and lock of our attempt
    Brook no division. It will be thought,
    By some that know not why he is away,
    That wisdom, loyalty, and mere dislike
    Of our proceedings kept the Earl from hence.
    And think how such an apprehension
    May turn the tide of fearful faction,
    And breed a kind of question in our cause.
    For well you know we of the offering side
    Must keep aloof from strict arbitrament,
    And stop all sight-holes, every loop from whence
    The eye of reason may pry in upon us.
    This absence of your father's draws a curtain

That shows the ignorant a kind of fear
Before not dreamt of.
HOTSPUR   You strain too far.
I rather of his absence make this use.
It lends a lustre and more great opinion,
A larger dare to our great enterprise,
Than if the Earl were here. For men must think
If we without his help can make a head
To push against a kingdom, with his help
We shall o'erturn it topsy-turvy down.
Yet all goes well, yet all our joints are whole.
DOUGLAS
As heart can think. There is not such a word
Spoken in Scotland as this term of fear.

Enter Sir Richard Vernon

HOTSPUR
My cousin Vernon! Welcome, by my soul!
VERNON
Pray God my news be worth a welcome, lord.
The Earl of Westmorland seven thousand strong
Is marching hitherwards, with him Prince John.
HOTSPUR
No harm, what more?
VERNON   And further, I have learned,
The King himself in person is set forth,
Or hitherwards intended speedily,
With strong and mighty preparatiòn.
HOTSPUR
He shall be welcome too. Where is his son,
The nimble-footed madcap Prince of Wales,
And his comrades that doffed the world aside
And bid it pass?
VERNON   All furnished, all in arms,
All plumed like ostriches, that with the wind

Bated like eagles having lately bathed,
Glittering in golden coats like images,
As full of spirit as the month of May,
And gorgeous as the sun at midsummer,
Wanton as youthful goats, wild as young bulls.
I saw young Harry with his helmet on,
His armour on his thighs, gallantly armed,
Rise from the ground like feathered Mercury,
And vaulted with such ease into his seat
As if an angel dropped down from the clouds
To turn and wind a fiery Pegasus,
And witch the world with noble horsemanship.

HOTSPUR
No more, no more! Worse than the sun in March,
This praise does nourish agues. Let them come!
They come like sacrifices in their trim,
And to the fire-eyed maid of smoky war
All hot and bleeding will we offer them.
The mailèd Mars shall on his altar sit
Up to the ears in blood. I am on fire
To hear this rich reprisal is so nigh,
And yet not ours! Come, let me taste my horse,
Who is to bear me like a thunderbolt
Against the bosom of the Prince of Wales.
Harry to Harry shall, hot horse to horse,
Meet and never part till one drops down a corpse.
O that Glendower were come!

VERNON   There is more news.
I learned in Worcester as I rode along
He cannot draw his force these fourteen days.

DOUGLAS
That's the worst tidings that I hear of yet.

WORCESTER
Ay, by my faith, that bears a frosty sound.

HOTSPUR
What may the King's whole army reach unto?

VERNON
  To thirty thousand.
HOTSPUR   Forty let it be.
  My father and Glendower being both away,
  The powers of us may serve so great a day.
  Come, let us take a muster speedily.
  Doomsday is near. Die all, die merrily.
DOUGLAS
  Talk not of dying, I am out of fear
  Of death or death's hand for this one half year.

                                              Exeunt

SCENE II
A road near Coventry.

Enter Falstaff and Bardolph

FALSTAFF Bardolph, get you before to Coventry. Fill me a
  bottle of sack. Our soldiers shall march through. We'll
  to Sutton Coldfield tonight.
BARDOLPH Will you give me money, captain?
FALSTAFF Lay out, lay out.
BARDOLPH This bottle makes an angel.
FALSTAFF If it does, take it for your labour—and if it
  makes twenty, take them all, I'll answer the coinage.
  Bid my lieutenant Peto meet me at town's end.
BARDOLPH I will, captain. Farewell.   *Exit*
FALSTAFF If I am not ashamed of my soldiers, I am a
  soused gurnet. I have misused the King's press damnably.
  I have got in exchange of a hundred and fifty soldiers
  three hundred and odd pounds. I press none but good
  householders, yeomen's sons; enquire out contracted
  bachelors, such as had been asked twice on the banns;
  such a commodity of warm slaves as had as soon hear
  the devil as a drum, such as fear the report of a musket

worse than a struck fowl or a hurt wild duck. I pressed
none but such toasts-and-butter, with hearts in their
bellies no bigger than pins' heads, and they have bought
out their services. And now my whole charge consists of
ensigns, corporals, lieutenants, gentlemen of companies—
slaves as ragged as Lazarus in the painted çloth, where
the glutton's dogs licked his sores. And such as indeed
were never soldiers, but discarded dishonest serving-
men, younger sons to younger brothers, revolted tapsters,
and ostlers trade-fallen; the cankers of a calm world and
a long peace, ten times more dishonourable-ragged than
an old frayed ensign. And such have I to fill up the
rooms of them as have bought out their services, that
you would think that I had a hundred and fifty tattered
prodigals lately come from swine-keeping, from eating
swill and husks. A mad fellow met me on the way, and
told me I had unloaded all the gibbets and pressed the
dead bodies. No eye has seen such scarecrows. I'll not
march through Coventry with them, that's flat. Nay,
and the villains march wide between the legs as if they
had fetters on, for indeed I had the most of them out of
prison. There's not a shirt and a half in all my company,
and the half-shirt is two napkins tacked together and
thrown over the shoulders like a herald's coat without
sleeves. And the shirt, to say the truth, stolen from my
host at Saint Albans, or the rednosed innkeeper of
Daventry. But that's all one, they'll find linen enough
on every hedge.

Enter the Prince and Westmorland

PRINCE HAL How now, blown Jack? How now, jacket?
FALSTAFF What, Hal! How now, mad wag? What a devil
do you in Warwickshire? My good Lord of Westmorland,
I cry you mercy, I thought your honour had already
been at Shrewsbury.

WESTMORLAND Faith, Sir John, 'tis more than time that I
   were there, and you too; but my forces are there already.
   The King I can tell you looks for us all, we must away
   all night.

FALSTAFF Tut, never fear me, I am as vigilant as a cat to
   steal cream.

PRINCE HAL I think, to steal cream indeed, for your theft
   has already made you butter. But tell me, Jack, whose
   fellows are these that come after?

FALSTAFF Mine, Hal, mine.

PRINCE HAL I did never see such pitiful rascals.

FALSTAFF Tut, tut, good enough to toss, food for powder,
   food for powder, they'll fill a pit as well as better. Tush,
   man, mortal men, mortal men.

WESTMORLAND Ay, but Sir John, I think they are exceeding
   poor and bare, too beggarly.

FALSTAFF Faith, for their poverty I know not where they
   had that. And for their bareness I am sure they never
   learned that of me.

PRINCE HAL No, I'll be sworn, unless you call three fingers
   in the ribs bare. But man, make haste. Percy is already
   in the field.   *Exit*

FALSTAFF What, is the King encamped?

WESTMORLAND He is, Sir John, I fear we shall stay too
   long.   *Exit*

FALSTAFF Well,
   To the latter end of a fray, and the beginning of a feast
   Fits a dull fighter and a keen guest.   *Exit*

SCENE III
The rebel camp.

Enter Hotspur, Worcester, Douglas, Vernon

HOTSPUR
  We'll fight with him tonight.
WORCESTER   It may not be.
DOUGLAS
  You give him then advantage.
VERNON   Not a whit.
HOTSPUR
  Why say you so, looks he not for supply?
VERNON
  So do we.
HOTSPUR His is certain, ours is doubtful.
WORCESTER
  Good cousin, be advised, stir not tonight.
VERNON
  Do not, my lord.
DOUGLAS   You do not counsel well.
  You speak it out of fear and cold heart.
VERNON
  Do me no slander, Douglas. By my life,
  And I dare well maintain it with my life,
  If well-respected honour bids me on,
  I hold as little counsel with weak fear
  As you, my lord, or any Scot that this day lives.
  Let it be seen tomorrow in the battle
  Which of us fears.
DOUGLAS   Yes, or tonight.
VERNON   Content.
HOTSPUR
  Tonight, say I.
VERNON
  Come, come, it may not be. I wonder much,

Being men of such great leading as you are,
That you foresee not what impediments
Drag back our expedition. Certain horse
Of my cousin Vernon's are not yet come up,
Your uncle Worcester's horse came but today,
And now their pride and mettle are asleep,
Their courage with hard labour tame and dull,
That not a horse is half the half itself.

HOTSPUR

So are the horses of the enemy
In general journey-worn and so brought low.
The better part of ours are full of rest.

WORCESTER

The numbers of the King exceed now ours.
For God's sake, cousin, stay till all come in.

The trumpet sounds a parley
Enter Sir Walter Blunt

BLUNT

I come with gracious offers from the King,
If you permit me hearing and respect.

HOTSPUR

Welcome, Sir Walter Blunt: and would to God
You were of our determinatiòn!
Some of us love you well, and even those some
Envy your great deservings and good name,
Because you are not of our quality,
But stand against us like an enemy.

BLUNT

And God defend but ever I should stand so,
So long as out of limit and true rule
You stand against anointed majesty.
But to my charge. The King has sent to know
The nature of your griefs, and whereupon
You conjure from the breast of civil peace

Such bold hostility, teaching his duteous land
Audacious cruelty. If then the King
Has any way your good deserts forgotten.
Which he confesses to be manifold,
He bids you name your griefs. And with all speed
You shall have your desires with interest
And pardon absolute for yourself, and these
Herein misled by your suggestiòn.

HOTSPUR
The King is kind, and well we know the King
Knows at what time to promise, when to pay.
My father, and my uncle, and myself
Did give him that same royalty he wears.
And when he was not six-and-twenty strong,
Sick in the world's regard, wretched and low,
A poor unminded outlaw sneaking home,
My father gave him welcome to the shore.
And when he heard him swear and vow to God
He came but to be Duke of Lancaster,
To sue his heritage, and beg his peace
With tears of innocency and terms of zeal,
My father, in kind heart and pity moved,
Swore him assistance, and performed it too.
Now when the lords and barons of the realm
Perceived Northumberland did lean to him,
The more and less came in with cap and knee,
Met him in boroughs, cities, villages,
Attended him on bridges, stood in lanes,
Laid gifts before him, proffered him their oaths,
Gave him their heirs as pages, followed him
Even at the heels in golden multitudes.
He presently, as greatness knows itself,
Steps up a little higher than his vow
Made to my father while his blood was poor
Upon the naked shore at Ravenspurgh.
And now indeed takes on him to reform

Some certain edicts and some strait decrees
That lie too heavy on the commonwealth;
Cries out upon abuses, seems to weep
Over his country's wrongs. And by this face,
This seeming brow of justice, did he win
The hearts of all that he did angle for.
Proceeded further—then cut off the heads
Of all the favourites that the absent King
In deputation left behind him here,
When he was personal in the Irish war.

BLUNT

Tut, I came not to hear this.

HOTSPUR   Then to the point.
In short time after he deposed the King,
Soon after that deprived him of his life,
And in the neck of that taxed the whole state.
To make that worse, suffered his kinsman March—
Who is, if every owner were well placed,
Indeed his King—to be engaged in Wales,
There without ransom to lie forfeited.
Disgraced me in my happy victories,
Sought to entrap me by espìonage,
Berated my uncle from the Council-board,
In rage dismissed my father from the Court,
Broke oath on oath, committed wrong on wrong;
And in conclusion drove us to seek out
This head of safety, and with that to pry
Into his title, which we do find
Too indirect for long continuance.

BLUNT

Shall I return this answer to the King?

HOTSPUR

Not so, Sir Walter. We'll withdraw awhile.
Go to the King, and let there be impawned
Some surety for a safe return again.

And in the morning early shall my uncle
  Bring him our purposes. And so, farewell.
BLUNT
  I would you would accept of grace and love.
HOTSPUR
  And may be so we shall.
BLUNT   Pray God you do.   *Exeunt*

SCENE IV
York. The Archbishop's palace.

Enter the Archbishop of York and Sir Michael

ARCHBISHOP
  Hie, good Sir Michael, bear this sealèd brief
  With wingèd haste to the Lord Marshàl,
  This to my cousin Scroop, and all the rest
  To whom they are directed. If you knew
  How much they do import you would make haste.
SIR MICHAEL
  My good lord,
  I guess their tenor.
ARCHBISHOP   Like enough you do.
  Tomorrow, good Sir Michael, is a day
  Wherein the fortune of ten thousand men
  Must bide the touch. For, sir, at Shrewsbury,
  As I am truly given to understand,
  The King with mighty and quick-raisèd power
  Meets with Lord Harry. And I fear, Sir Michael,
  What with the sickness of Northumberland,
  Whose power was in the first proportiòn,
  And what with Owen Glendower's absence thence—
  Who with them was a valued sinew too,
  And comes not in, o'er-ruled by prophecies—

I fear the power of Percy is too weak
To wage an instant trial with the King.

SIR MICHAEL

Why, my good lord, you need not fear,
There are Douglas and Lord Mortimer.

ARCHBISHOP

No, Mortimer is not there.

SIR MICHAEL

But there are Mordake, Vernon, Lord Harry Percy,
And there is my Lord of Worcester, and a head
Of gallant warriors, noble gentlemen.

ARCHBISHOP

And so there is. But yet the King has drawn
The special head of all the land together.
The Prince of Wales, Lord John of Lancaster,
The noble Westmorland, and warlike Blunt,
And many more associates and dear men
Of estimation and command in arms.

SIR MICHAEL

Doubt not, my lord, they shall be well opposed.

ARCHBISHOP

I hope no less, yet needful it is to fear,
And to prevent the worst, Sir Michael, speed.
For if Lord Percy thrives not, ere the King
Disbands his army he means to visit us,
For he has heard of our confederacy,
And 'tis but wisdom to make strong against him.
Therefore make haste—I must go write again
To other friends. And so, farewell, Sir Michael.

Exeunt

Act V

SCENE I
The King's camp near Shrewsbury.

Enter the King, Prince Henry, Prince John,
Sir Walter Blunt, Falstaff

KING HENRY
How bloodily the sun begins to peer
Above yon bulky hill! The day looks pale
At its distemperature.
PRINCE HAL   The southern wind
Does play the trumpet to its purposes,
And by its hollow whistling in the leaves
Foretells a tempest and a blustering day.
KING HENRY
Then with the losers let it sympathize,
For nothing can seem foul to those that win.

The trumpet sounds
Enter Worcester and Vernon

How now, my Lord of Worcester! It is not well
That you and I should meet upon such terms
As now we meet. You have deceived our trust,
And made us doff our easy robes of peace
To crush our old limbs in ungentle steel.
This is not well, my lord, this is not well.
What say you to it? Will you again unknit
The churlish knot of all-abhorrèd war,
And move in that obedient orb again

107

Where you did give a fair and natural light,
And be no more an exhaled meteor,
A prodigy of fear, and a portent
Of broachèd mischief to the unborn times?

WORCESTER

Hear me, my liege.
For my own part I could be well content
To entertain the lag end of my life
'With quiet hours. For I protest
I have not sought the day of this dislike.

KING HENRY

You have not sought it? How comes it, then?

FALSTAFF Rebellion lay in his way, and he found it.

PRINCE HAL Peace, chatterer, peace!

WORCESTER

It pleased your majesty to turn your looks
Of favour from myself, and all our house,
And yet I must remember you, my lord,
We were the first and dearest of your friends.
For you my staff of office did I break
In Richard's time, and posted day and night
To meet you on the way, and kiss your hand,
When yet you were in place and in account
Nothing so strong and fortunate as I.
It was myself, my brother, and his son,
That brought you home, and boldly did outdare
The dangers of the time. You swore to us,
And you did swear that oath at Doncaster,
That you did nothing purpose against the state,
Nor claim further than your new-fallen right,
The seat of Gaunt, dukedom of Lancaster.
To this we swore our aid. But in short space
It rained down fortune showering on your head,
And such a flood of greatness fell on you,
What with our help, what with the absent King,
What with the injuries of a wanton time,

The seeming sufferances that you had borne,
And the contrarious winds that held the King
So long in his unlucky Irish wars
That all in England did repute him dead.
And from this swarm of fair advantages
You took occasion to be quickly wooed
To grip the general sway into your hand,
Forget your oath to us at Doncaster,
And being fed by us, you used us so
As that ungentle nestling the cuckoo's bird
Uses the sparrow—did oppress our nest,
Grew by our feeding to so great a bulk
That even our love durst not come near your sight
For fear of swallowing. But with nimble wing
We were enforced for safety sake to fly
Out of your sight, and raise this present force.
Whereby we stand opposèd by such means
As you yourself have forged against yourself,
By unkind usage, dangerous countenance,
And violation of all faith and troth
Sworn to us in your younger enterprise.

KING HENRY

These things indeed you have articulated,
Proclaimed at market crosses, read in churches,
To face the garment of rebelliòn
With some fine colour that may please the eye
Of fickle changelings and poor discontents—
Which gape and rub the elbow at the news
Of hurlyburly innovatiòn.
And never yet did insurrection want
Such water-colours to impaint its cause,
Nor moody beggars starving for a time
Of pell-mell havoc and confusiòn.

PRINCE HAL

In both your armies there are many a soul
Shall pay full dearly for this encounter

If once they join in trial. Tell your nephew,
The Prince of Wales does join with all the world
In praise of Henry Percy. By my hopes—
This present enterprise set off against—
I do not think a braver gentleman,
More active-valiant or more valiant-young,
More daring or more bold, is now alive
To grace this latter age with noble deeds.
For my part, I may speak it to my shame,
I have a truant been to chivalry,
And so I hear he does account me too.
Yet this before my father's majesty—
I am content that he shall take the odds
Of his great name and estimatiòn,
And will, to save the blood on either side,
Try fortune with him in a single fight.

KING HENRY

And, Prince of Wales, so dare we venture you,
Albeit considerations infinite
Do make against it. No, good Worcester, no,
We love our people well, even those we love
That are misled upon your cousin's part.
And will they take the offer of our grace,
Both he, and they, and you, yes, every man
Shall be my friend again, and I'll be his.
So tell your cousin, and bring me word
What he will do. But if he will not yield,
Rebuke and dread correction wait on us,
And they shall do their office. So, be gone.
We will not now be troubled with reply.
We offer fair, take it advisedly.

Exeunt Worcester and Vernon

PRINCE HAL

It will not be accepted, on my life.
The Douglas and the Hotspur both together
Are confident against the world in arms.

KING HENRY
    Hence, therefore, every leader to his charge,
    For on their answer will we set on them,
    And God befriend us as our cause is just!

                    Exeunt all but the Prince and Falstaff

FALSTAFF Hal, if you see me down in the battle and bestride
    me, so. 'Tis a point of friendship.

PRINCE HAL Nothing but a Colossus can do you that
    friendship. Say your prayers, and farewell.

FALSTAFF I would it were bed-time, Hal, and all well.

PRINCE HAL Why, you owe God a death.   *Exit*

FALSTAFF 'Tis not due yet—I would be loath to pay him
    before his day. What need I be so forward with him that
    calls not on me? Well, 'tis no matter, honour pricks me
    on. Yes, but how if honour pricks me off when I come
    on, how then? Can honour set to a leg? No. Or an arm?
    No. Or take away the grief of a wound? No. Honour has
    no skill in surgery then? No. What is honour? A word.
    What is in that word honour? What is that honour?
    Air. A trim reckoning! Who has it? He that died on
    Wednesday. Does he feel it? No. Does he hear it? No.
    'Tis insensible, then? Yes, to the dead. But will it not
    live with the living? No. Why? Detraction will not
    suffer it. Therefore I'll none of it. Honour is a mere
    scutcheon. And so ends my catechism.   *Exit*

SCENE II
The rebel camp.

Enter Worcester and Vernon

WORCESTER
    O no, my nephew must not know, Sir Richard,
    The liberal and kind offer of the King.

VERNON
  It were best he did.
WORCESTER   Then are we all undone.
  It is not possible, it cannot be,
  The King should keep his word in loving us.
  He will suspect us ever, and find a time
  To punish this offence in other faults.
  Suspicion all our lives shall be stuck full of eyes,
  For treason is but trusted like the fox,
  Which never so tame, so cherished and locked up,
  Will have a wild trick of his ancestors.
  Look how we can or sad or merrily,
  Interpretation will misquote our looks,
  And we shall feed like oxen at a stall,
  The better cherished ever the nearer death.
  My nephew's trespass may be well forgotten,
  It has the excuse of youth and heat of blood,
  And an adopted name of privilege—
  A hare-brained Hotspur, governed by a pique.
  All his offences live upon my head
  And on his father's. We did train him on,
  And, his corruption being taken from us,
  We as the spring of all shall pay for all.
  Therefore, good cousin, let not Harry know
  In any case the offer of the King.
VERNON
  Deliver what you will; I'll say it is so.
  Here comes your cousin.

                    Enter Hotspur and Douglas

HOTSPUR   My uncle has returned;
  Deliver up my Lord of Westmorland.
  Uncle, what news?

WORCESTER
  The King will bid you battle presently.
DOUGLAS
  Defy him by the Lord of Westmorland.
HOTSPUR
  Lord Douglas, go you and tell him so.
DOUGLAS
  Certainly, and shall, and very willingly.   *Exit*
WORCESTER
  There is no seeming mercy in the King.
HOTSPUR
  Did you beg any? God forbid!
WORCESTER
  I told him gently of our grievances,
  Of his oath-breaking—which he mended thus,
  By now denying that he is forsworn.
  He calls us rebels, traitors, and will scourge
  With haughty arms this hateful name in us.

                  Enter Douglas

DOUGLAS
  Arm, gentlemen, to arms! For I have thrown
  A brave defiance in King Henry's teeth,
  And Westmorland that was engaged did bear it,
  Which cannot choose but bring him quickly on.
WORCESTER
  The Prince of Wales stepped forth before the King,
  And, nephew, challenged you to single fight.
HOTSPUR
  O, would the quarrel lay upon our heads,
  And that no man might draw short breath today
  But I and Harry Monmouth! Tell me, tell me,
  How showed his tasking? Seemed it in contempt?

VERNON
    No, by my soul, I never in my life
    Did hear a challenge urged more modestly,
    Unless a brother should a brother dare
    To gentle exercise and proof of arms.
    He gave you all the duties of a man,
    Trimmed up your praises with a princely tongue,
    Spoke your deserving like a chronicle,
    Making you ever better than his praise
    By still dispraising praise valued with you.
    And, what became him like a prince indeed,
    He made a blushing recital of himself,
    And chid his truant youth with such a grace
    As if he mastered there a double spirit
    Of teaching and of learning instantly.
    There did he pause. But let me tell the world—
    If he outlives the envy of this day,
    England did never own so sweet a hope
    So much miscònstrued in his wantonness.
HOTSPUR
    Cousin, I think you are enamourèd
    On his follies! Never did I hear
    Of any prince so wild a liberty.
    But be he as he will, yet once ere night
    I will embrace him with a soldier's arm,
    That he shall shrink under my courtesy.
    Arm, arm with speed! And fellows, soldiers, friends,
    Better consider what you have to do
    Than I that have not well the gift of tongue
    Can lift your blood up with persuasiòn.

Enter a Messenger

FIRST MESSENGER My lord, here are letters for you.

HOTSPUR I cannot read them now.
   O gentlemen, the time of life is short!
   To spend that shortness basely were too long
   If life did ride upon a dial's point,
   Still ending at the arrival of an hour.
   And if we live, we live to tread on kings,
   If die, brave death when princes die with us!
   Now, for our consciences, the arms are fair
   When the intent of bearing them is just.

Enter another Messenger

SECOND MESSENGER
   My lord, prepare, the King comes on apace.
HOTSPUR
   I thank him that he cuts me from my tale,
   For I profess not talking. Only this—
   Let each man do his best. And here draw I
   A sword whose temper I intend to stain
   With the best blood that I can meet with now
   In the adventure of this perilous day.
   Now, Esperance! Percy! and set on!
   Sound all the lofty instruments of war,
   And by that music let us all embrace,
   For, heaven to earth, some of us never shall
   A second time do such a courtesy.

Here they embrace, the trumpets sound

Exeunt

SCENE III
Plain between the camps.

The King enters with his army. Alarum. Then enter
Douglas, and Blunt, disguised as the King

BLUNT

What is your name that in the battle thus
You cross me? What honour do you seek
Upon my head?

DOUGLAS   Know then my name is Douglas,
And I do haunt you in the battle thus
Because some tell me that you are a king.

BLUNT

They tell you true.

DOUGLAS

The Lord of Stafford dear today has bought
Your likeness, for instead of you, King Harry,
This sword has ended him. So shall it you
Unless you yield you as my prisoner.

BLUNT

I was not born a yielder, you proud Scot,
And you shall find a king that will revenge
Lord Stafford's death.

They fight; Douglas kills Blunt
Then enter Hotspur

HOTSPUR

O Douglas, had you fought at Holmedon thus
I never had triumphed upon a Scot.

DOUGLAS

All's done, all's won. Here breathless lies the King.

HOTSPUR Where?

DOUGLAS Here.

HOTSPUR

    This, Douglas? No, I know this face full well.
    A gallant knight he was, his name was Blunt,
    Semblably furnished like the King himself.

DOUGLAS

    Ah fool, go with your soul, whither it goes!
    A borrowed title have you bought too dear.
    Why did you tell me that you were a king?

HOTSPUR

    The King has many marching in his coats.

DOUGLAS

    Now, by my sword, I will kill all his coats!
    I'll murder all his wardrobe, piece by piece,
    Until I meet the King.

HOTSPUR   Up and away!

    Our soldiers stand full fairly for the day.   *Exeunt*

Alarum. Enter Falstaff alone

FALSTAFF Though I could escape shot-free at London, I
    fear the shot here: here's no scoring but upon the pate.
    Soft! Who are you? Sir Walter Blunt—there's honour for
    you! Here's no vanity! I am as hot as molten lead, and as
    heavy too. God keep lead out of me, I need no more
    weight than my own bowels. I have led my ragamuffins
    where they are peppered. There's not three of my hundred-
    and-fifty left alive—and they are for the town's end, to
    beg during life. But who comes here?

Enter the Prince

PRINCE HAL

    What, stand you idle here? Lend me your sword.
    Many a nobleman lies stark and stiff
    Under the hoofs of vaunting enemies,

Whose deaths are yet unrevenged. I pray you
Lend me your sword.

FALSTAFF O Hal, I pray, give me leave to breathe awhile.
Turk Gregory never did such deeds in arms as I have
done this day. I have killed Percy, I have made him sure.

PRINCE HAL
He is indeed, and living to kill you.
I pray you, lend me your sword.

FALSTAFF Nay, before God, Hal, if Percy is alive you get
not my sword, but take my pistol if you will.

PRINCE HAL Give it me. What, is it in the case?

FALSTAFF Ay, Hal, 'tis hot, 'tis hot. There's that will sack a
city.

The Prince draws it out, and finds it to be a bottle of sack

PRINCE HAL
What, is it a time to jest and dally now?

He throws the bottle at him   *Exit*

FALSTAFF Well, if Percy is alive, I'll pierce him. If he does
come in my way, so. If he does not, if I come in his
willingly, let him make a grilled rasher of me. I like not
such grinning honour as Sir Walter has. Give me life,
which if I can save, so. If not, honour comes unlooked
for, and there's an end.   *Exit*

SCENE IV
The same.

Alarum. Excursions. Enter the King, Prince Henry,
Prince John, and Westmorland

KING HENRY
I pray, Harry, withdraw yourself, you bleed too much.
Lord John of Lancaster, go you with him.

LANCASTER
Not I, my lord, unless I did bleed too.

PRINCE HAL
I beseech your majesty, make up,
Lest your retirement does amaze your friends.

KING HENRY
I will do so. My Lord of Westmorland,
Lead him to his tent.

WESTMORLAND
Come, my lord, I'll lead you to your tent.

PRINCE HAL
Lead me, my lord? I do not need your help,
And God forbid a shallow scratch should drive
The Prince of Wales from such a field as this,
Where stained nobility lies trodden on,
And rebels' arms triumph in massacres!

LANCASTER
We breathe too long: come, cousin Westmorland,
Our duty this way lies: for God's sake, come.
                        Exeunt Lancaster and Westmorland

PRINCE HAL
By God, you have deceived me, Lancaster,
I did not think you lord of such a spirit.
Before, I loved you as a brother, John,
But now I do respect you as my soul.

KING HENRY

   I saw him hold Lord Percy at the point
   With lustier maintenance than I did look for
   Of such an ungrown warrior.

PRINCE HAL   O, this boy

   Lends mettle to us all!   *Exit*

Enter Douglas

DOUGLAS

   Another king! They grow like Hydra's heads.
   I am the Douglas, fatal to all those
   That wear those colours on them. What are you
   That counterfeit the person of a king?

KING HENRY

   The King himself, who, Douglas, grieves at heart
   So many of his shadows you have met,
   And not the very King. I have two boys
   Seek Percy and yourself about the field,
   But seeing you fall on me so luckily
   I will assay you—and defend yourself.

DOUGLAS

   I fear you are another counterfeit,
   And yet, in faith, you bear you like a king—
   But mine I am sure you are, whoever you are,
   And thus I win you.

They fight, the King being in danger; enter Prince Henry

PRINCE HAL

   Hold up your head, vile Scot, or you are like
   Never to hold it up again! The spirits
   Of valiant Shirley, Stafford, Blunt are in my arms.
   It is the Prince of Wales that threatens you,
   Who never promises but he means to pay.

They fight; Douglas flees

Cheerily, my lord, how fares your grace?
Sir Nicholas Gawsey has for succour sent,
And so has Clifton—I'll to Clifton straight.

KING HENRY
Stay and breathe a while.
You have redeemed your lost opiniòn,
And showed you make tender care of my life
In this fair rescue you have brought to me.

PRINCE HAL
O God, they did me too much injury
That ever said I hearkened for your death.
If it were so, I might have let alone
The insulting hand of Douglas over you:
Which would have been as speedy in your end
As all the poisonous potions in the world,
And saved the treacherous labour of your son.

KING HENRY
Make up to Clifton, I'll to Sir Nicholas Gawsey.   *Exit*

Enter Hotspur

HOTSPUR
If I mistake not, you are Harry Monmouth.

PRINCE HAL
You speak as if I would deny my name.

HOTSPUR
My name is Harry Percy.

PRINCE HAL   Why then I see
A very valiant rebel of the name.
I am the Prince of Wales, and think not, Percy,
To share with me in glory any more.
Two stars keep not their motion in one sphere,
Nor can one England brook a double reign
Of Harry Percy and the Prince of Wales.

HOTSPUR
> Nor shall it, Harry, for the hour is come
> To end the one of us; and would to God
> Your name in arms were now as great as mine.

PRINCE HAL
> I'll make it greater ere I part from you,
> And all the budding honours on your crest
> I'll crop to make a garland for my head.

HOTSPUR
> I can no longer brook your vanities.

They fight
Enter Falstaff

FALSTAFF Well said, Hal! To it, Hal! Nay, you shall find no boy's play here, I can tell you.

Enter Douglas; he fights with Falstaff, who falls
down as if he were dead

Exit Douglas

The Prince mortally wounds Hotspur

HOTSPUR
> O Harry, you have robbed me of my youth!
> I better brook the loss of brittle life
> Than those proud titles you have won of me.
> They wound my thoughts worse than your sword my
>   flesh.
> But thoughts, the slaves of life, and life, time's fool,
> And time, that takes survèy of all the world,
> Must have a stop. O, I could prophesy,
> But that the earthy and cold hand of death
> Lies on my tongue. No, Percy, you are dust,

And food for—

He dies

PRINCE HAL
   For worms, brave Percy. Fare you well, great heart!
   Ill-weaved ambition, how much are you shrunk.
   When this body did contain a spirit,
   A kingdom for it was too small a bound.
   But now two paces of the vilest earth
   Are room enough. This earth that bears you dead
   Bears not alive so stout a gentleman.
   If you were sensible of courtesy
   I should not make so dear a show of zeal,
   But let my favours hide your mangled face,
   And even in your behalf I'll thank myself
   For doing these fair rites of tenderness.
   Adieu, and take your praise with you to heaven!
   Your ignominy sleep with you in the grave,
   But not remembered in your epitaph.

He spies Falstaff on the ground

   What, old acquaintance, could not all this flesh
   Keep in a little life? Poor Jack, farewell!
   I could have better spared a better man.
   O, I should have a heavy miss of you
   If I were much in love with vanity.
   Death has not struck so fat a deer today,
   Though many dearer, in this bloody fray.
   Disbowelled will I see thee by and by,
   Till then in blood by noble Percy lie.   *Exit*

Falstaff rises

FALSTAFF Disbowelled? If you disbowel me today, I'll give
   you leave to powder me and eat me too tomorrow. God's
   blood, it was time to counterfeit, or that hot termagant

Scot had paid me, scot and lot too. Counterfeit? I lie, I am no counterfeit. To die is to be a counterfeit, for he is but the counterfeit of a man who has not the life of a man. But to counterfeit dying, when a man thereby lives, is to be no counterfeit, but the true and perfect image of life indeed. The better part of valour is discretion, in which better part I have saved my life. Zounds, I am afraid of this gunpowder Percy, though he is dead. How if he should counterfeit too and rise? By my faith, I am afraid he would prove the better counterfeit. Therefore I'll make him sure, yea, and I'll swear I killed him. Why may not he rise as well as I? Nothing confutes me but eyes, and nobody sees me. Therefore, man (*stabbing him*), with a new wound in your thigh, come you along with me.

He takes up Hotspur on his back. Enter Prince Henry and Prince John

PRINCE HAL
   Come, brother John, full bravely have you fleshed
   Your maiden sword.
LANCASTER   But soft, whom have we here?
   Did you not tell me this fat man was dead?
PRINCE HAL
   I did, I saw him dead,
   Breathless and bleeding on the ground. Are you alive?
   Or is it fantasy that plays upon our eyesight?
   I pray you, speak, we will not trust our eyes
   Without our ears. You are not what you seem.
FALSTAFF No, that's certain, I am not a double-man. But if
   I am not Jack Falstaff, then am I a Jack. There is Percy!

He throws the body down

If your father will do me any honour, so. If not, let him
kill the next Percy himself. I look to be either earl or
duke, I can assure you.

PRINCE HAL Why, Percy I killed myself, and saw you
dead.

FALSTAFF Did you? Lord, Lord, how this world is given to
lying! I grant you I was down, and out of breath, and so
was he; but we rose both at an instant, and fought a
long hour by Shrewsbury clock. If I may be believed, so.
If not, let them that should reward valour bear the sin
upon their own heads. I'll take it upon my death, I gave
him this wound in the thigh. If the man were alive, and
would deny it, zounds, I would make him eat a piece of
my sword.

LANCASTER This is the strangest tale that ever I heard.

PRINCE HAL This is the strangest fellow, brother John.
Come, bring your luggage nobly on your back.
(*Aside to Falstaff*) For my part, if a lie may do you grace,
I'll gild it with the happiest terms I have.

A retreat is sounded

The trumpet sounds retreat, the day is ours.
Come, brother, let us to the highest of the field,
To see what friends are living, who are dead.

Exeunt Prince of Wales and Lancaster

FALSTAFF I'll follow, as they say, for reward. He that rewards
me, God reward him! If I do grow great, I'll grow less,
for I'll purge, and leave sack, and live cleanly as a
nobleman should do.

Exit, bearing off the body

SCENE V
The same.

The trumpets sound. Enter the King, Prince Henry, Prince John, Westmorland, with Worcester and Vernon prisoners

KING HENRY
Thus ever did rebellion find rebuke.
Ill-spirited Worcester, did not we send grace,
Pardon, and terms of love to all of you?
And would you turn our offers contrary?
Misuse the tenor of your kinsman's trust?
Three knights upon our party slain today,
A noble earl, and many a creature else
Had been alive this hour
If like a Christian you had truly borne
Between our armies true intelligence.

WORCESTER
What I have done my safety urged me to,
And I embrace this fortune patiently,
Since not to be avoided it falls on me.

KING HENRY
Bear Worcester to the death, and Vernon too;
Other offenders we will pause upon.
                    [*Exeunt Worcester and Vernon, guarded.*]
How goes the field?

PRINCE HAL
The noble Scot, Lord Douglas, when he saw
The fortune of the day quite turned from him,
The noble Percy slain, and all his men
Upon the foot of fear, fled with the rest;
And falling from a hill, he was so bruised
That the pursuers took him. At my tent
The Douglas is, and I beseech your grace
I may dispose of him.

KING HENRY   With all my heart.

PRINCE HAL

    Then, brother John of Lancaster, to you
    This honorable bounty shall belong.
    Go to the Douglas and deliver him
    Up to his pleasure, ransomless and free.
    His valors shown upon our crests to-day
    Have taught us how to cherish such high deeds,
    Even in the bosom of our adversaries.

PRINCE JOHN

    I thank your grace for this high courtesy,
    Which I shall give away immediately.

KING HENRY

    Then this remains, that we divide our power.
    You, son John, and my cousin Westmorland,
    Towards York shall bend you with your dearest speed
    To meet Northumberland and the prelate Scroop,
    Who, as we hear, are busily in arms.
    Myself and you, son Harry, will toward Wales
    To fight with Glendower and the Earl of March.
    Rebellion in this land shall lose its sway,
    Meeting the check of such another day;
    And since this business so fair is done,
    Let us not leave till all our own be won.   *Exeunt.*

King Henry IV
Part II

INTRODUCTION

It is usual to regard the *Second Part of King Henry IV* as having less dramatic interest than the *First*, largely because it has less fighting. But we can easily have too much of that. Elizabethan drama was full of it; for, with their smaller stage resources and few stage properties, what else was there but fighting and love-making as their two main staples? And for the rest—words. Hence their extraordinary richness and imaginative variety in words, compared with the impoverished vocabulary of much modern drama—Becket, for example.

The essential, and more subtle, drama of the father-son relationship between the sick and dying King, and his son, Prince Henry, is heightened, rendered more poignant and reaches a splendid climax at the end. The scene in which father and son confront the dire responsibilities of rule, the King's sense of guilt in deposing Richard II—however necessary politically—the penance Henry endured in the ceaseless troubles of his reign, his prayer that, having paid the price and now being worn out, he might hand on the succession with more acceptance:

> For all the soil of the achievement goes
> With me into the earth—

all this makes one of the most touching scenes in Shakespeare, to anyone who understands the inwardness and strains of politics—as few other dramatists did, and hardly any literary critics do. Shakespeare's extraordinary *political* understanding is again one of the most remarkable, and exceptional, things about him.

Where did he get it from? It was one of the rewards that came from his identifying himself with the governing point of view.

Prince Henry's character gets further development with this, on his way to becoming the hero-king that Henry V was to the Elizabethans. He confesses the riots of his youth, and promises that he will be a different man as king. More subtly, there was a different man in him already: Falstaff, no fool, knew that he had inherited the cold blood of his father—a prime necessity for rule—and was not for a moment taken in by the bad company he kept. He learned from it what ordinary people are like, not cut off from real life by the exalted isolation of royalty. (It was remarkable that Elizabeth I, surrounded, almost insulated, by exaltation and flattery, should have so kept her feet on the ground—a recent monarch, whose gay youth may be compared with Prince Hal, not so.)

The play ends with what has been called 'the grandest snub in literature', the rejection of Falstaff: 'I know you not, old man.' After all the fun and frolics they had had together, this action has been usually unpopular, especially with critics. But of course Falstaff had to be rejected. There was the old reprobate, who had just swindled Justice Shallow of a thousand pounds with his promises of what he could do with his Hal when he came to the throne, leering upon the young King as he came by in state from his coronation . . . to find that Henry was a new man. The newly made King was ready also to do justice to the Lord Chief Justice who had imprisoned him, very properly, renew him in office and give him his confidence. Actually,

Hal as King provides generously for Falstaff's old age—provided he reforms.

Shakespeare would not have known the fact that the day Henry IV died, the Prince spent all night alone with an anchorite in Westminster Abbey, and underwent something like a conversion. After all, the historic Henry and his father were medieval men, to whom religion and conscience were very real. Falstaff, Shakespeare's creation, was entirely Elizabethan.

Contemporary social life is even more richly rendered in this play, for in addition to the London scenes at the endearing Boar's Head in Eastcheap we have now country scenes, over countryside with which Shakespeare was very familiar, from which he came. We have Falstaff's progress through the Cotswolds to Gloucestershire, picking up the recruits Justice Shallow has impressed for service against the rebels in the North. They are a rag-tag collection—Mouldy, Shadow, Wart, Feeble, Bullcalf: Shakespeare's gift for names again! We see what they looked like. Professor C. J. Sisson—whose great qualification as a Shakespeare scholar was his familiarity with the actual documents of the age—comments: 'the court of Star Chamber has many a tale to tell of Elizabethan Falstaffs and Shallows abusing the Queen's writ in the recruiting of soldiers.' And Falstaff typically enough takes bribes for letting off those who could afford to pay.

The scenes with Justice Shallow in his Gloucestershire orchard are enchanting, not only comic but touched with nostalgia. His young 'cousin'—Elizabethan for nephew—is still at Oxford but must 'to the Inns of Court shortly.' This brings back memories of the days when the old J.P. was a lad at Clement's Inn. 'There was I, and little John Doit of Staffordshire . . . and Will Squeal, a Cotswold man.' The old boy recalls fighting with a fruiterer behind Gray's Inn, and playing Sir Dagonet in Arthur's show, and the 'little quiver fellow' at the musters at Mile End. Then, 'how a good yoke of bullocks at Stamford fair?' Or, 'O, Sir John, do you remember since we lay all night in the windmill in St. George's Field? . . . And is Jane Nightwork alive?' Falstaff: 'Old, old, Master Shallow.' 'Nay, she must be old, she cannot choose but be old, certain she's old, and had Robin Nightwork by old Nightwork before I came to Clement's Inn.'

As always Shakespeare's own profession is to the fore in the images that come to mind:

> And let this world no longer be a stage
> To feed contention in a lingering act.

The King looks back on the troubles issuing from the deposition of Richard II—'all my reign has been but a scene acting that argument.' The Vice's dagger in the old moralities occurs naturally to Falstaff.

It would seem that the Epilogue was originally spoken by the dramatist, for it has the personal ring of the writer himself: 'what I have to say is of my own making, and what I should say will, I fear, prove my own marring.' There follows a reference to a displeasing play for which he had had to apologise and to promise a better. But he hopes to win their favour by continuing the present piece with Falstaff in it. Once more he disclaims the original name he had used for the character, to meet the objections of Lord Cobham: 'for Oldcastle died a martyr, and this is not the man.' The date then is 1598—the year of *As You Like It.* What a contrast, and how ambidextrous to turn out a history play with one hand, and a pastoral comedy with the other!

At this time Shakespeare had repairs going on at New Place at Stratford, the grand new house which success in London enabled him to buy. So we have a whole verse-paragraph about building and surveying the plot, drawing the model:

> Then must we rate the cost of the erection,
> Which, if we find outweighs ability . . .

we settle for 'fewer offices'. He was, unlike his father the alderman, careful about his financial affairs.

All sorts of reflections of contemporary society occur. 'Glasses, glasses, is the only drinking'—they were just coming into fashion. 'And for your walls, a pretty slight drollery, or the story of the Prodigal . . . in waterwork' —just like the Tobit scene we still see upon the wall of the White Swan at Stratford, or the frescoed room of the Crossed Keys he knew at Oxford. We have a unique expression of contemporary snobbery—for snobbery we have always with us—in the piece of information that 'those that are kin to the king never prick their finger but they say, "There's some of the king's blood spilt".' And as usual people pretend not to understand, to elicit the ready response, 'I am the king's poor cousin, sir.'

In Pistol's extraordinary rhodomontade Shakespeare is parodying the exaggerated rhetoric of earlier Elizabethan drama, as before in the *First Part*—here, George Peele in particular, and a line from Marlowe with the 'hollow pampered jades of Asia.' Classical references come ready to mind at every turn, for such had been his education at grammar school, in which too he had fairly certainly taught earlier for a time.

The extraordinary language of Falstaff and his boon companions presents difficulties for the modern reader and hearer, and simply demands the removal of unnecessary obstacles to understanding it.

CHARACTERS

RUMOUR, the presenter
KING HENRY IV
PRINCE HENRY, afterwards King Henry V
PRINCE JOHN OF LANCASTER
Humphrey DUKE OF GLOUCESTER   } sons of Henry IV
Thomas DUKE OF CLARENCE
EARL OF WARWICK
EARL OF WESTMORLAND
EARL OF SURREY
SIR JOHN BLUNT
GOWER
HARCOURT
The LORD CHIEF JUSTICE
EARL OF NORTHUMBERLAND
The ARCHBISHOP OF YORK
LORD MOWBRAY
LORD HASTINGS
LORD BARDOLPH
TRAVERS
MORTON
SIR JOHN COLEVILE
LADY NORTHUMBERLAND
LADY PERCY
POINS
SIR JOHN FALSTAFF
BARDOLPH
PISTOL, an ensign [ancient]
PETO
HOSTESS Quickly
DOLL TEARSHEET

136

Justice SHALLOW ⎱
SILENCE   ⎰ country justices

DAVY, Shallow's servant

Ralph MOULDY ⎞
Simon SHADOW ⎟
Thomas WART ⎬ Falstaff's recruits
Francis FEEBLE ⎟
Peter BULLCALF ⎠

FANG ⎱
SNARE ⎰ sergeants

FRANCIS, WILL, and another DRAWER

EPILOGUE
Officers, musicians, a page, soldiers, a captain, lords, beadles,
servants, messenger.

INDUCTION

Before Warkworth Castle.

Enter Rumour, painted full of tongues

RUMOUR
  Open your ears, for which of you will stop
  The vent of hearing when loud Rumour speaks?
  I, from the orient to the drooping west,
  Making the wind my post-horse, ever unfold
  The acts commencèd on this ball of earth.
  Upon my tongues continual slanders ride,
  Which then in every language I pronounce,
  Stuffing the ears of men with false reports.
  I speak of peace while covert enmity,
  Under the smile of safety, wounds the world.
  And who but Rumour, who but only I,
  Make fearful musters, and prepared defence,
  While the big year, swollen with some other grief,
  Is thought with child by the stern tyrant War,
  And no such matter? Rumour is a pipe
  Blown by surmises, jealousies, conjectures,
  And of so easy and so plain a stop
  That the blunt monster with uncounted heads,
  The still-discordant wavering multitude,
  Can play upon it. But what need I thus
  My well-known body to anatomize
  Among my household? Why is Rumour here?
  I run before King Harry's victory,
  Who in a bloody field by Shrewsbury
  Has beaten down young Hotspur and his troops,

139

Quenching the flame of bold rebellìon
Even with the rebels' blood. But what mean I
To speak so true at first? My office is
To noise abroad that Harry Monmouth fell
Under the wrath of noble Hotspur's sword,
And that the King before the Douglas' rage
Stooped his anointed head as low as death.
This have I rumoured through the peasant towns
Between that royal field of Shrewsbury
And this worm-eaten hold of raggèd stone,
Where Hotspur's father, old Northumberland,
Lies crafty-sick. The posts come tiring on,
And not a man of them brings other news
Than they have learnt of me. From Rumour's tongues
They bring smooth comforts false, worse than true
    wrongs.   *Exit*

Act I

SCENE I
The same.

Enter Lord Bardolph

LORD BARDOLPH
  Who keeps the gate here, ho?

Enter the Porter

  Where is the Earl?

PORTER
  What shall I say you are?

LORD BARDOLPH   Tell you the Earl
  That the Lord Bardolph does attend him here.

PORTER
  His lordship has walked forth into the orchard.
  Please it your honour knock but at the gate,
  And he himself will answer.

Enter Northumberland

LORD BARDOLPH   Here comes the Earl.

Exit Porter

NORTHUMBERLAND
  What news, Lord Bardolph? Every minute now
  Should be the father of some stratagem.
  The times are wild; contention, like a horse
  Full of high feeding, madly has broken loose
  And bears down all before it.

LORD BARDOLPH   Noble Earl,
  I bring you certain news from Shrewsbury.
NORTHUMBERLAND
  Good, if God wills!
LORD BARDOLPH As good as heart can wish.
  The King is almost wounded to the death,
  And, in the fortune of my lord your son,
  Prince Harry slain outright; and both the Blunts
  Killed by the hand of Douglas; young Prince John
  And Westmorland and Stafford fled the field.
  And Harry Monmouth's brawn, the hulk Sir John,
  Is prisoner to your son. O, such a day,
  So fought, so followed, and so fairly won,
  Came not till now to dignify the times
  Since Caesar's fortunes!
NORTHUMBERLAND   How is this derived?
  Saw you the field? Came you from Shrewsbury?
LORD BARDOLPH
  I spoke with one, my lord, that came from thence,
  A gentleman well bred, and of good name,
  That freely rendered me these news for true.

Enter Travers

NORTHUMBERLAND
  Here comes my servant Travers, whom I sent
  On Tuesday last to listen after news.
LORD BARDOLPH
  My lord, I over-rode him on the way,
  And he is furnished with no certainties
  More than he haply may retail from me.
NORTHUMBERLAND
  Now, Travers, what good tidings come with you?
TRAVERS
  My lord, Sir John Umfrevile turned me back
  With joyful tidings and, being better horsed,

Out-rode me. After him came spurring hard
A gentleman almost exhausted with speed,
That stopped by me to breathe his bloodied horse.
He asked the way to Chester, and of him
I did demand what news from Shrewsbury.
He told me that rebellion had ill luck,
And that young Harry Percy's spur was cold.
With that he gave his able horse the head,
And bending forward struck his armèd heels
Against the panting sides of his poor jade
Up to the rowel-head. And starting so
He seemed in running to devour the way,
Staying no longer question.

NORTHUMBERLAND   Ha? Again!
Said he young Harry Percy's spur was cold?
Of Hotspur, Coldspur? That rebelliòn
Had met ill luck?

LORD BARDOLPH My lord, I'll tell you what.
If my young lord your son had not the day,
Upon my honour, for a silken point
I'll give my barony—never talk of it.

NORTHUMBERLAND
Why should that gentleman that rode by Travers
Give then such instances of loss?

LORD BARDOLPH   Who, he?
He was some wretched fellow that had stolen
The horse he rode on and, upon my life,
Spoke at a venture. Look, here comes more news.

Enter Morton

NORTHUMBERLAND
Yes, this man's brow, like to a title-leaf,
Foretells the nature of a tragic volume.
So looks the strand whereon the imperious flood

Has left a witnessed usurpatiòn.
Say, Morton, did you come from Shrewsbury?

MORTON

I ran from Shrewsbury, my noble lord,
Where hateful death put on its ugliest mask
To fright our party.

NORTHUMBERLAND How do my son and brother?
You tremble, and the whiteness in your cheek
Is apter than your tongue to tell your errand.
Even such a man, so faint, so spiritless,
So dull, so dead in look, so woe-begone,
Drew Priam's curtain in the dead of night
And would have told him half his Troy was burnt.
But Priam found the fire ere he his tongue,
And I my Percy's death ere you report it.
This you would say, 'Your son did thus and thus;
Your brother thus; so fought the noble Douglas',
Stopping my greedy ear with their bold deeds.
But in the end, to stop my ear indeed,
You have a sigh to blow away this praise,
Ending with 'Brother, son, and all are dead'.

MORTON

Douglas is living, and your brother, yet;
But, for my lord your son—

NORTHUMBERLAND   Why, he is dead!
See what a ready tongue suspicion has!
He that but fears the thing he would not know
Has by instinct knowledge from others' eyes
That what he feared has chanced. Yet speak, Morton;
Tell you an earl his divination lies,
And I will take it as a sweet disgrace
And make you rich for doing me such wrong.

MORTON

You are too great to be by me gainsaid;
Your spirit is too true, your fears too certain.

NORTHUMBERLAND
  Yet, for all this, say not that Percy's dead.
  I see a strange confession in your eye.
  You shake your head, and hold it fear or sin
  To speak a truth. If he is slain—
  The tongue offends not that reports his death;
  And he does sin that does belie the dead,
  Not he who says the dead is not alive.
  Yet the first bringer of unwelcome news
  Has but a losing office, and his tongue
  Sounds ever after as a sullen bell
  Remembered, tolling a departing friend.
LORD BARDOLPH
  I cannot think, my lord, your son is dead.
MORTON
  I am sorry I should force you to believe
  That which I would to God I had not seen.
  But these my eyes saw him in bloody state,
  Rendering faint quittance, wearied and out-breathed,
  To Harry Monmouth, whose swift wrath beat down
  The never-daunted Percy to the earth,
  From whence with life he never more sprang up.
  In short, his death, whose spirit lent a fire
  Even to the dullest peasant in his camp,
  Being rumoured once, took fire and heat away
  From the best-tempered courage in his troops.
  For from his metal was his party steeled,
  Which once in him abated, all the rest
  Turned on themselves, like dull and heavy lead.
  And as the thing that's heavy in itself
  Upon enforcement flies with greatest speed,
  So did our men, heavy in Hotspur's loss,
  Lend to this weight such lightness with their fear
  That arrows fled not swifter toward their aim
  Than did our soldiers, aiming at their safety,
  Fly from the field. Then was that noble Worcester

So soon taken prisoner, and that furious Scot,
The bloody Douglas, whose well-labouring sword
Had three times slain the appearance of the King,
Began to falter, and did grace the shame
Of those that turned their backs, and in his flight,
Stumbling in fear, was taken. The sum of all
Is that the King has won, and has sent out
A speedy power to encounter you, my lord,
Under the conduct of young Lancaster
And Westmorland. This is the news at full.

NORTHUMBERLAND
For this I shall have time enough to mourn.
In poison there is physic, and these news,
Having been well, that would have made me sick,
Being sick, have in some measure made me well.
And as the wretch whose fever-weakened joints,
Like strengthless hinges, buckle under life,
Impatient of his fit, breaks like a fire
Out of his keeper's arms, even so my limbs,
Weakened with grief, being now enraged with grief,
Are thrice themselves. Hence, therefore, you nice crutch!
A scaly gauntlet now with joints of steel
Must glove this hand. And hence, you sickly scarf!
You are a guard too wanton for the head
Which princes, fleshed with conquest, aim to hit.
Now bind my brows with iron, and approach
The raggèd hour that time and spite dare bring
To frown upon the enraged Northumberland!
Let heaven kiss earth! Now let not Nature's hand
Keep the wild flood confined! Let order die!
And let this world no longer be a stage
To feed contention in a lingering act;
But let one spirit of the first-born Cain
Reign in all bosoms, that each heart being set
On bloody courses, the rude scene may end,
And darkness be the burier of the dead!

LORD BARDOLPH
  This strainèd passion does you wrong, my lord.
MORTON
  Sweet Earl, divorce not wisdom from your honour;
  The lives of all your loving accomplices
  Lean on your health, which, if you give over
  To stormy passion, must perforce decay.
  You cast the event of war, my noble lord,
  And summed the account of chance before you said
  'Let us make head'. It was your presurmise
  That in the share of blows your son might drop.
  You knew he walked o'er perils, on an edge,
  More likely to fall in than to get over.
  You were advised his flesh was capable
  Of wounds and scars, and that his forward spirit
  Would lift him where most trade of danger ranged.
  Yet did you say 'Go forth'; and none of this,
  Though strongly apprehended, could restrain
  The stiff-borne action. What has then befallen,
  Or what has this bold enterprise brought forth,
  More than that being which was like to be?
LORD BARDOLPH
  We all that are engagèd to this loss
  Knew that we ventured on such dangerous seas
  That if we wrought out life 'twas ten to one.
  And yet we ventured, for the gain proposed
  Choked the respect of likely peril feared,
  And since we are overset, venture again.
  Come, we will all put forth, body and goods.
MORTON
  'Tis more than time. And, my most noble lord,
  I hear for certain, and dare speak the truth,
  The gentle Archbishop of York is up
  With well-appointed forces. He is a man
  Who with a double surety binds his followers.
  My lord, your son had only but the corpse,

But shadows and the shows of men, to fight;
For that same word 'rebellion' did divide
The action of their bodies from their souls.
And they did fight with queasiness, constrained,
As men drink potions, that their weapons only
Seemed on our side. But, for their spirits and souls,
This word, 'rebellion', it had frozen them up
As fish are in a pond. But now the Bishop
Turns insurrection to religiòn;
Supposed sincere and holy in his thoughts,
He's followed both with body and with mind,
And does enlarge his rising with the blood
Of fair King Richard, scraped from Pomfret stones;
Derives from heaven his quarrel and his cause;
Tells them he does bestride a bleeding land,
Gasping for life under great Bolingbroke.
And more and less do flock to follow him.

NORTHUMBERLAND

I knew of this before, but, to speak truth,
This present grief had wiped it from my mind.
Go in with me, and counsel every man
The aptest way for safety and revenge.
Get posts and letters, and make friends with speed—
Never so few, and never yet more need.

Exeunt

SCENE II
London. A street.

*Enter Sir John Falstaff, followed by his Page
bearing his sword and buckler*

FALSTAFF Young fellow, you giant, what says the doctor to
my water?

PAGE He said, sir, the water itself was a good healthy
   water; but, for the party that owned it, he might have
   more diseases than he knew of.

FALSTAFF Men of all sorts take a pride to gird at me. The
   brain of this foolish-compounded clay, man, is not able
   to invent anything that intends to laughter more than I
   invent, or is invented on me. I am not only witty in
   myself, but the cause that wit is in other men. I do here
   walk before you like a sow that has overwhelmed all her
   litter but one. If the Prince puts you into my service for
   any other reason than to put me off, why then I have no
   judgement. You little mandrake, you are fitter to be
   worn in my cap than to wait at my heels. I was never
   manned with an agate till now, but I will inset you
   neither in gold nor silver, but in vile apparel, and send
   you back again to your master for a jewel—the juvenile
   Prince your master, whose chin is not yet fledged. I will
   sooner have a beard grow in the palm of my hand than
   he shall get one of his cheek; and yet he will not stick to
   say his face is a face-royal. God may finish it when He
   wills, 'tis not a hair amiss yet. He may keep it ever at a
   face-royal, for a barber shall never earn sixpence out of
   it. And yet he'll be crowing as if he had written man
   ever since his father was a bachelor. He may keep his
   own grace, but he's almost out of mine, I can assure
   him. What said Master Dombleton about the satin for
   my short cloak and my slops?

PAGE He said, sir, you should procure him better assurance
   than Bardolph. He would not take his bond and yours;
   he liked not the security.

FALSTAFF Let him be damned like the glutton! Pray God
   his tongue be hotter! A bloody Achitophel! A rascally
   yes-forsooth knave, to bespeak a gentleman, and then
   stand upon security! The smooth-pates do now wear
   nothing but high shoes and bunches of keys at their
   girdles; and if a man is through with them in honest

bargain, then they must stand upon security. I had as soon they would put ratsbane in my mouth as offer to stop it with security. I looked he should have sent me two-and-twenty yards of satin, as I am a true knight, and he sends me 'security'! Well he may sleep in security, for he has the horn of abundance, and the lightness of his wife shines through it—and yet cannot he see, though he has his own lantern to light him. Where's Bardolph?

PAGE He's gone into Smithfield to buy your worship a horse.

FALSTAFF I bought him in Paul's, and he'll buy me a horse in Smithfield. If I could get me but a wife in the stews, I were manned, horsed, and wived.

Enter the Lord Chief Justice and his Servant

PAGE Sir, here comes the nobleman that committed the Prince for striking him about Bardolph.

FALSTAFF Wait close; I will not see him.

LORD CHIEF JUSTICE What is he that goes there?

SERVANT Falstaff, please your lordship.

LORD CHIEF JUSTICE He that was in question for the robbery?

SERVANT He, my lord—but he has since done good service at Shrewsbury and, as I hear, is now going with some charge to the Lord John of Lancaster.

LORD CHIEF JUSTICE What, to York? Call him back again.

SERVANT Sir John Falstaff!

FALSTAFF Boy, tell him I am deaf.

PAGE You must speak louder; my master is deaf.

LORD CHIEF JUSTICE I am sure he is, to the hearing of anything good. Go pluck him by the elbow; I must speak with him.

SERVANT Sir John!

FALSTAFF What! A young knave, and begging! Are there not wars? Is there not employment? Does not the King lack subjects? Do not the rebels need soldiers? Though

it is a shame to be on any side but one, it is worse shame
to beg than to be on the worst side, were it worse than
the name of rebellion can tell how to make it.

SERVANT You mistake me, sir.

FALSTAFF Why, sir, did I say you were an honest man?
Setting my knighthood and my soldiership aside, I had
lied in my throat if I had said so.

SERVANT I pray you, sir, then set your knighthood and
your soldiership aside, and give me leave to tell you you
lie in your throat if you say I am any other than an
honest man.

FALSTAFF I give you leave to tell me so? I lay aside that
which grows to me? If you get any leave of me, hang me.
If you take leave, you were better be hanged. You hunt
wrong. Hence! Away!

SERVANT Sir, my lord would speak with you.

LORD CHIEF JUSTICE Sir John Falstaff, a word with you.

FALSTAFF My good lord! God give your lordship good time
of day. I am glad to see your lordship abroad; I heard say
your lordship was sick. I hope your lordship goes abroad
by advice. Your lordship, though not clean past your
youth, have yet some smack of age in you, some relish of
the saltness of time; and I most humbly beseech your
lordship to have a reverend care of your health.

LORD CHIEF JUSTICE Sir John, I sent for you—before your
expedition to Shrewsbury.

FALSTAFF If it please your lordship, I hear his majesty has
returned with some discomfort from Wales.

LORD CHIEF JUSTICE I talk not of his majesty. You would
not come when I sent for you.

FALSTAFF And I hear, moreover, his highness is fallen into
this same miserable apoplexy.

LORD CHIEF JUSTICE Well, God mend him! I pray you let
me speak with you.

FALSTAFF This apoplexy, as I take it, is a kind of lethargy, if it please your lordship, a kind of sleeping in the blood, a wretched tingling.

LORD CHIEF JUSTICE What tell you me of it? Be it as it is.

FALSTAFF It has its original from much grief, from study, and perturbation of the brain. I have read the cause of its effects in Galen; it is a kind of deafness.

LORD CHIEF JUSTICE I think you have fallen into the disease, for you hear not what I say to you.

FALSTAFF Very well, my lord, very well. Rather, if it please you, it is the disease of not listening, the malady of not marking, that I am troubled with.

LORD CHIEF JUSTICE To punish you by the heels would amend the attention of your ears, and I care not if I do become your physician.

FALSTAFF I am as poor as Job, my lord, but not so patient. Your lordship may minister the potion of imprisonment to me in respect of poverty; but how I should be your patient to follow your prescriptions, the wise may make some dram of a scruple, or indeed a scruple itself.

LORD CHIEF JUSTICE I sent for you, when there were matters against you for your life, to come speak with me.

FALSTAFF As I was then advised by my learned counsel in the laws of this land-service, I did not come.

LORD CHIEF JUSTICE Well, the truth is, Sir John, you live in great infamy.

FALSTAFF He that buckles himself in my belt cannot live in less.

LORD CHIEF JUSTICE Your means are very slender, and your waste is great.

FALSTAFF I would it were otherwise; I would my means were greater and my waist slenderer.

LORD CHIEF JUSTICE You have misled the youthful Prince.

FALSTAFF The young Prince has misled me. I am the fellow with the great belly, and he my dog.

LORD CHIEF JUSTICE Well, I am loath to gall a new-healed wound. Your day's service at Shrewsbury has a little gilded over your night's exploit on Gadshill. You may thank the unquiet time for your quiet overposting that action.

FALSTAFF My lord!

LORD CHIEF JUSTICE But since all is well, keep it so. Wake not a sleeping wolf.

FALSTAFF To wake a wolf is as bad as smell a fox.

LORD CHIEF JUSTICE What! You are as a candle, the better part burnt out.

FALSTAFF A wassail candle, my lord, all tallow—if I did say of wax, my growth would prove the truth.

LORD CHIEF JUSTICE There is not a white hair in your face but should have its effect of gravity.

FALSTAFF Its effect of gravy, gravy, gravy.

LORD CHIEF JUSTICE You follow the young Prince up and down, like his ill angel.

FALSTAFF Not so, my lord; your ill angel is light, but I hope he that looks upon me will take me without weighing. And yet in some respects, I grant, I cannot go. I cannot tell—virtue is of so little regard in these costermongers' times that true valour is turned bearherd. Pregnancy is made a tapster, and its quick wit wasted in giving reckonings. All the other gifts appertinent to man, as the malice of this age shapes them, are not worth a gooseberry. You that are old consider not the capacities of us that are young; you do measure the heat of our livers with the bitterness of your galls; and we that are in the vanguard of our youth, I must confess, are wags too.

LORD CHIEF JUSTICE Do you set down your name in the scroll of youth, that are written down old with all the characters of age? Have you not a moist eye, a dry hand, a yellow cheek, a white beard, a decreasing leg, an increasing belly? Is not your voice broken, your wind

short, your chin double, your wit single, and every part
about you blasted with antiquity? And will you yet call
yourself young? Fie, fie, fie, Sir John!

FALSTAFF My lord, I was born about three of the clock in
the afternoon, with a white head, and something a
round belly. For my voice, I have lost it with hallooing,
and singing of anthems. To prove my youth further, I
will not. The truth is, I am only old in judgement and
understanding; and he that will caper with me for a
thousand marks, let him lend me the money, and have
at him! For the box of the ear that the Prince gave you,
he gave it like a rude prince, and you took it like a
sensible lord. I have checked him for it, and the young
lion repents — (aside) sure, not in ashes and sackcloth,
but in new silk and old sack.

LORD CHIEF JUSTICE Well, God send the Prince a better
companion!

FALSTAFF God send the companion a better prince! I cannot
rid my hands of him.

LORD CHIEF JUSTICE Well, the King has severed you
and Prince Harry. I hear you are going with Lord John
of Lancaster against the Archbishop and the Earl of
Northumberland.

FALSTAFF Yes, I thank your pretty sweet wit for it. But
look you pray, all you that kiss my lady Peace at home,
that our armies join not in a hot day; for, by the Lord,
I take but two shirts out with me, and I mean not to
sweat extraordinarily. If it is a hot day, and I brandish
anything but a bottle — I would I might never spit white
again. There is not a dangerous action can peep out its
head but I am thrust upon it. Well, I cannot last ever —
but it was always yet the trick of our English nation, if
they have a good thing, to make it too common. If you
will needs say I am an old man, you should give me
rest. I would to God my name were not so terrible to the
enemy as it is. I would better be eaten to death with

a rust than to be scoured to nothing with perpetual motion.

LORD CHIEF JUSTICE Well, be honest, be honest, and God bless your expedition!

FALSTAFF Will your lordship lend me a thousand pound to furnish me forth?

LORD CHIEF JUSTICE Not a penny, not a penny! You are too impatient to bear crosses. Fare you well. Commend me to my cousin Westmorland.

Exeunt Lord Chief Justice and Servant

FALSTAFF If I do, strike me with a three-man sledge-hammer. A man can no more separate age and covetousness than he can part young limbs and lechery. But the gout galls the one, and the pox pinches the other; and so both the degrees forestall my curses. Boy!

PAGE Sir?

FALSTAFF What money is in my purse?

PAGE Seven groats and two pence.

FALSTAFF I can get no remedy against this consumption of the purse; borrowing only lingers and lingers it out, but the disease is incurable. Go bear this letter to my lord of Lancaster; this to the Prince; this to the Earl of Westmorland—and this to old mistress Ursula, whom I have weekly sworn to marry since I perceived the first white hair of my chin. About it! You know where to find me.   *Exit Page*

A pox of this gout! Or a gout of this pox! For the one or the other plays the rogue with my great toe. 'Tis no matter if I do limp; I have the wars for my excuse, and my pension shall seem the more reasonable. A good wit will make use of anything; I will turn diseases to convenience.   *Exit*

SCENE III
York. The Archbishop's palace.

Enter the Archbishop of York, Mowbray, Hastings,
and Lord Bardolph

ARCHBISHOP
    Thus have you heard our cause and known our means,
    And, my most noble friends, I pray you all
    Speak plainly your opinions of our hopes.
    And first, Lord Marshal, what say you to it?
MOWBRAY
    I well allow the occasion of our arms,
    But gladly would be better satisfied
    How in our means we should advance ourselves
    To look with forehead bold and big enough
    Upon the power and forces of the King.
HASTINGS
    Our present musters grow upon the file
    To five-and-twenty thousand men of choice;
    And our supplies live largely in the hope
    Of great Northumberland, whose bosom burns
    With an incensèd fire of injuries.
LORD BARDOLPH
    The question then, Lord Hastings, should stand thus—
    Whether our present five-and-twenty thousand
    May hold up head without Northumberland.
HASTINGS
    With him we may.
LORD BARDOLPH Yes, indeed, there's the point;
    But if without him we are thought too feeble,
    My judgement is, we should not step too far
    Till we had his assistance by the hand.
    For in a theme so bloody-faced as this,
    Conjecture, expectation, and surmise
    Of aids uncertain should not be admitted.

ARCHBISHOP

    'Tis very true, Lord Bardolph, for indeed

    It was young Hotspur's case at Shrewsbury.

LORD BARDOLPH

    It was, my lord; who lined himself with hope,

    Eating the air, and promise of supply,

    Flattering himself in project of a power

    Much smaller than the smallest of his thoughts;

    And so, with great imaginatiòn

    Proper to madmen, led his powers to death,

    And winking leaped into destructiòn.

HASTINGS

    But, by your leave, it never yet did hurt

    To lay down likelihoods and forms of hope.

LORD BARDOLPH

    Yes, if this present quality of war,

    Indeed, the instant action, a cause on foot,

    Lives so in hope—as in an early spring

    We see the appearing buds; which to prove fruit

    Hope gives not so much warrant, as despair

    That frosts will bite them. When we mean to build,

    We first survey the plot, then draw the model,

    And when we see the figure of the house,

    Then must we rate the cost of the erection,

    Which if we find outweighs ability,

    What do we then but draw anew the model

    In fewer offices, or at least desist

    To build at all? Much more, in this great work—

    Which is almost to pluck a kingdom down

    And set another up—should we survey

    The plot of situation and the model,

    Consent upon a sure foundatiòn,

    Question surveyors, know our own estate,

    How able such a work to undergo,

    To weigh against its opposite. Or else

    We fortify in paper and in figures,

Using the names of men instead of men,
Like one that draws the model of a house
Beyond his power to build it: who, half-through,
Gives over, and leaves his part-created cost
A naked subject to the weeping clouds,
And waste for churlish winter's tyranny.

HASTINGS

Grant that our hopes, yet likely of fair birth,
Should be still-born, and that we now possessed
The utmost man of expectatiòn,
I think we are so, body strong enough,
Even as we are, to equal with the King.

LORD BARDOLPH

What, is the King but five-and-twenty thousand?

HASTINGS

To us no more, nay, not so much, Lord Bardolph;
For his divisions, as the times do brawl,
Are in three heads: one power against the French;
And one against Glendower; perforce a third
Must take up us. So is the unfirm King
In three divided, and his coffers sound
With hollow poverty and emptiness.

ARCHBISHOP

That he should draw his several strengths together
And come against us in full combination
Need not be dreaded.

HASTINGS   If he should do so,
He leaves his back unarmed, the French and Welsh
Baying him at the heels; never fear that.

LORD BARDOLPH

Who is it likely should lead his forces hither?

HASTINGS

The Duke of Lancaster, and Westmorland;
Against the Welsh, himself and Harry Monmouth;
But who is substituted against the French
I have no certain notice.

ARCHBISHOP   Let us on,
  And publish the occasion of our arms.
  The commonwealth is sick of their own choice;
  Their over-greedy love has surfeited.
  A habitation giddy and unsure
  Has he that builds so on the vulgar heart.
  O foolish many, with what loud applause
  Did you beat heaven with blessing Bolingbroke,
  Before he was what you would have him be!
  And being now trimmed in your own desires,
  You, beastly feeder, are so full of him
  That you provoke yourself to cast him up.
  So, so, you common dog, did you disgorge
  Your glutton bosom of the royal Richard—
  And now you would eat your dead vomit up,
  And howl to find it. What trust is in these times?
  They that, when Richard lived, would have him die
  Are now become enamoured on his grave.
  You that threw dust upon his goodly head,
  When through proud London he came sighing on
  After the admirèd heels of Bolingbroke,
  Cry now 'O earth, yield us that king again,
  And take you this!' O thoughts of men accursed!
  Past and to come seems best; things present, worst.
MOWBRAY
  Shall we go draw our numbers and set on?
HASTINGS
  We are time's subjects, and time bids be gone.
                                      Exeunt

Act II

SCENE I
London. Eastcheap.

Enter Hostess with two officers, Fang and Snare

HOSTESS Master Fang, have you entered the action?

FANG It is entered.

HOSTESS Where's your yeoman? Is it a lusty yeoman? Will he stand to it?

FANG Fellow—where's Snare?

HOSTESS O Lord, ay! Good Master Snare.

SNARE *(from behind them)* Here, here!

FANG Snare, we must arrest Sir John Falstaff.

HOSTESS Yea, good Master Snare, I have entered him and all.

SNARE It may chance cost some of us our lives, for he will stab.

HOSTESS Alas the day, take heed of him—he stabbed me in my own house, most beastly, in good faith. He cares not what mischief he does, if his weapon is out. He will thrust like any devil; he will spare neither man, woman, nor child.

FANG If I can close with him, I care not for his thrust.

HOSTESS No, nor I either; I'll be at your elbow.

FANG If I but fist him once, if he comes but within my view—

HOSTESS I am undone by his going, I warrant you, he's an infinitive thing upon my score. Good Master Fang, hold him sure; good Master Snare, let him not escape. He comes continuantly to Pie Corner—saving your manhoods—

to buy a saddle, and he is invited to dinner to the Lubber's Head in Lombard Street to Master Smooth's the silkman. I pray you, since my action is entered, and my case so openly known to the world, let him be brought in to his answer. A hundred marks is a long one for a poor lone woman to bear, and I have borne, and borne, and borne, and have been fobbed off, and fobbed off, and fobbed off, from this day to that day, that it is a shame to be thought on. There is no honesty in such dealing, unless a woman should be made an ass, and a beast, to bear every knave's wrong.

Enter Falstaff, Bardolph, and the Page

Yonder he comes, and that arrant malmsey-nose knave Bardolph with him. Do your offices, do your offices, Master Fang and Master Snare, do me, do me, do me your offices.

FALSTAFF How now, whose mare's dead? What's the matter?

FANG I arrest you at the suit of Mistress Quickly.

FALSTAFF Away, varlets! Draw, Bardolph! Cut off the villain's head! Throw the quean in the gutter!

HOSTESS Throw me in the gutter? I'll throw you in the gutter! Will you, will you, you bastardly rogue? Murder! Murder! Ah, you honeysuckle [homicidal] villain, will you kill God's officers and the King's? Ah, you honey-seed rogue! You art a honeyseed, a man-queller—and a woman-queller.

FALSTAFF Keep them off, Bardolph!

FANG A rescue! A rescue!

HOSTESS Good people, bring a rescue or two. You will, will you, you will, will you? Do, do, you rogue! Do, you hempseed!

PAGE Away, you scullion! You rampallian! You fustilarian! I'll tickle your catastrophe!

Enter the Lord Chief Justice and his men

LORD CHIEF JUSTICE What is the matter? Keep the peace
here, ho!

HOSTESS Good my lord, be good to me; I beseech you,
stand to me.

LORD CHIEF JUSTICE
How now, Sir John? What are you brawling here?
Does this become your place, your time, and business?
You should have been well on your way to York.
Stand from him, fellow; wherefore hang you upon him?

HOSTESS O my most worshipful lord, if it please your
grace, I am a poor widow of Eastcheap, and he is arrested
at my suit.

LORD CHIEF JUSTICE For what sum?

HOSTESS It is more than for some, my lord, it is for all I
have. He has eaten me out of house and home; he has
put all my substance into that fat belly of his—but
I will have some of it out again, or I will ride you of
nights like the mare.

FALSTAFF I think I am as like to ride the mare if I have any
vantage of ground to get up.

LORD CHIEF JUSTICE How comes this, Sir John? What
man of good temper would endure this tempest of
exclamation? Are you not ashamed to enforce a poor
widow to so rough a course to come by her own?

FALSTAFF What is the gross sum that I owe you?

HOSTESS Sure, if you were an honest man, yourself and
the money too. You did swear to me upon a parcelgilt
goblet, sitting in my Dolphin chamber, at the round
table, by a sea-coal fire, upon Wednesday in Whitsun
week, when the Prince broke your head for likening his
father to a singing-man of Windsor, you did swear to
me then, as I was washing your wound, to marry me,
and make me my lady your wife. Can you deny it? Did
not goodwife Keech the butcher's wife come in then and

call me gossip Quickly?—coming in to borrow a mess of vinegar, telling us she had a good dish of prawns; whereby you did desire to eat some, whereby I told you they were ill for a green wound? And did you not, when she was gone downstairs, desire me to be no more so familiar with such poor people, saying that ere long they should call me madam? And did you not kiss me, and bid me fetch you thirty shillings? I put you now to your book oath. Deny it if you can.

FALSTAFF My lord, this is a poor mad soul, and she says up and down the town that her eldest son is like you. She has been in good case, and the truth is, poverty has distracted her. But, for these foolish officers, I beseech you I may have redress against them.

LORD CHIEF JUSTICE Sir John, Sir John, I am well acquainted with your manner of wrenching the true cause the false way. It is not a confident brow, nor the throng of words that come with such more than impudent sauciness from you, can thrust me from a level consideration. You have, as it appears to me, practised upon the easy-yielding spirit of this woman, and made her serve your uses both in purse and in person.

HOSTESS Yes, in truth, my lord.

LORD CHIEF JUSTICE Pray you, peace. Pay her the debt you owe her, and unpay the villainy you have done with her. The one you may do with sterling money and the other with current repentance.

FALSTAFF My lord, I will not undergo this rebuke without reply. You call honourable boldness impudent sauciness; if a man will make curtsy and say nothing, he is virtuous. No, my lord, my humble duty remembered, I will not be your suitor. I say to you I do desire deliverance from these officers, being upon hasty employment in the King's affairs.

LORD CHIEF JUSTICE You speak as having power to do
   wrong; but answer in the effect of your reputation, and
   satisfy the poor woman.
FALSTAFF Come hither, hostess.

He takes her aside
Enter Gower

LORD CHIEF JUSTICE Now, Master Gower, what news?
GOWER
   The King, my lord, and Harry Prince of Wales
   Are near at hand; the rest the paper tells.

He gives him a letter

FALSTAFF As I am a gentleman!
HOSTESS Faith, you said so before.
FALSTAFF As I am a gentleman! Come, no more words of it.
HOSTESS By this heavenly ground I tread on, I must be
   fain to pawn both my plate and the tapestry of my
   dining-chambers.
FALSTAFF Glasses, glasses, is the only drinking; and for
   your walls, a pretty slight drollery, or the story of the
   Prodigal, or the German hunting, in waterwork, is worth
   a thousand of these bed-hangers and these flybitten
   tapestries. Let it be ten pound if you can. Come, if were
   not for your humours, there's not a better wench in
   England! Go, wash your face, and withdraw the action.
   Come, you must not be in this humour with me; do you
   not know me? Come, come, I know you were set on to this.
HOSTESS Pray you, Sir John, let it be but twenty crowns;
   in faith, I am loath to pawn my plate, so God save me, la!
FALSTAFF Let it alone; I'll make other shift—you'll be a
   fool ever.
HOSTESS Well, you shall have it, though I pawn my gown.
   I hope you'll come to supper. You'll pay me all together?

FALSTAFF Will I live? (*To Bardolph*) Go, with her, with her! Hook on, hook on!

HOSTESS Will you have Doll Tearsheet meet you at supper?

FALSTAFF No more words; let's have her.

Exeunt Hostess, Fang, Snare, Bardolph, and Page

LORD CHIEF JUSTICE I have heard better news.

FALSTAFF What's the news, my lord?

LORD CHIEF JUSTICE Where lay the King tonight?

GOWER At Basingstoke, my lord.

FALSTAFF I hope, my lord, all's well. What is the news, my lord?

LORD CHIEF JUSTICE Come all his forces back?

GOWER

No, fifteen hundred foot, five hundred horse

Have marched up to my lord of Lancaster,

Against Northumberland and the Archbishop.

FALSTAFF Comes the King back from Wales, my noble lord?

LORD CHIEF JUSTICE

You shall have letters of me presently.

Come, go along with me, good Master Gower.

FALSTAFF My lord!

LORD CHIEF JUSTICE What's the matter?

FALSTAFF Master Gower, shall I entreat you with me to dinner?

GOWER I must wait upon my good lord here, I thank you, good Sir John.

LORD CHIEF JUSTICE Sir John, you loiter here too long, seeing you are to take soldiers up in counties as you go.

FALSTAFF Will you sup with me, Master Gower?

LORD CHIEF JUSTICE What foolish master taught you these manners, Sir John?

FALSTAFF Master Gower, if they become me not, he was a fool that taught them me. This is the right fencing grace, my lord: tap for tap, and so part fair.

LORD CHIEF JUSTICE Now the Lord lighten you, you are a
  great fool.

Exeunt

SCENE II
Prince Henry's house.

Enter Prince Henry and Poins

PRINCE HENRY Before God, I am exceedingly weary.

POINS Is it come to that? I had thought weariness durst
  not have attached one of so high blood.

PRINCE HENRY Faith, it does me, though it discolours the
  complexion of my greatness to acknowledge it. Does it
  not show vilely in me to desire small beer?

POINS Why, a prince should not be so loosely studied as to
  remember so weak a composition.

PRINCE HENRY Perhaps then my appetite was not
  princely got, for, by my word, I do now remember the
  poor creature small beer. But indeed, these humble
  considerations make me out of love with my greatness.
  What a disgrace is it to me to remember your name! Or
  to know your face tomorrow! Or to take note how many
  pair of silk stockings you have—viz. these, and those
  that were your peach-coloured once! Or to bear the
  inventory of your shirts, as, one for superfluity, and
  another for use! But that the tennis-court keeper knows
  better than I, for it is a low ebb of linen with you when
  you keep not racket there. As you have not done a great
  while, because the rest of your low countries have made
  a shift to eat up your holland. And God knows whether
  those that bawl out the ruins of your linen shall inherit
  his kingdom. But the midwives say the children are
  not in the fault. Whereupon the world increases, and
  kindreds are mightily strengthened.

POINS How ill it follows, after you have laboured so hard, you should talk so idly! Tell me, how many good young princes would do so, their fathers being so sick as yours at this time is?

PRINCE HENRY Shall I tell you one thing, Poins?

POINS Yes, faith, and let it be an excellent good thing.

PRINCE HENRY It shall serve, among wits of no higher breeding than yours.

POINS Go to, I stand the push of your one thing that you will tell.

PRINCE HENRY Indeed, I tell you it is not meet that I should be sad now my father is sick. Albeit I could tell you, as one it pleases me for fault of a better to call my friend, I could be sad, and sad indeed too.

POINS Very hardly, upon such a subject.

PRINCE HENRY By this hand, you think me as far in the devil's book as you and Falstaff, for obduracy and persistency. Let the end try the man. But I tell you, my heart bleeds inwardly that my father is so sick; and keeping such vile company as you are has in reason taken from me all ostentation of sorrow.

POINS The reason?

PRINCE HENRY What would you think of me if I should weep?

POINS I would think you a most princely hypocrite.

PRINCE HENRY It would be every man's thought, and you are a blessed fellow, to think as every man thinks. Never a man's thought in the world keeps the roadway better than yours. Every man would think me a hypocrite indeed. And what incites your most worshipful thought to think so?

POINS Why, because you have been so lewd, and so much engrafted to Falstaff.

PRINCE HENRY And to you.

POINS By this light, I am well spoken of; I can hear it with my own ears. The worst that they can say of me is that I am a second brother, and that I am a proper fellow of my hands; and those two things I confess I cannot help. By the mass, here comes Bardolph.

Enter Bardolph and the Page

PRINCE HENRY And the boy that I gave Falstaff—he had him from me human, and look if the fat villain has not transformed him ape.

BARDOLPH God save your grace!

PRINCE HENRY And yours, most noble Bardolph!

POINS (*to Bardolph*) Come, you virtuous ass, you bashful fool, must you be blushing? Wherefore blush you now? What a maidenly man-at-arms have you become! Is it such a matter to get a pottle-pot's maidenhead?

PAGE He calls me even now, my lord, through a red lattice, and I could discern no part of his face from the window. At last I spied his eyes, and thought he had made two holes in the ale-wife's petticoat, and so peeped through.

PRINCE HENRY Has not the boy profited?

BARDOLPH Away, you upright rabbit, away!

PAGE Away, you rascally Althaea's dream, away!

PRINCE HENRY Instruct us, boy! What dream, boy?

PAGE Sure, my lord, Althaea dreamt she was delivered of a firebrand; and therefore I call him her dream.

PRINCE HENRY A crown's-worth of good interpretation! There it is, boy.

POINS O that this blossom could be kept from cankers! Well, there is sixpence to preserve you.

BARDOLPH If you do not make him be hanged among you, the gallows shall have wrong.

PRINCE HENRY And how does your master, Bardolph?

BARDOLPH Well, my lord. He heard of your grace's coming to town. There's a letter for you.

POINS Delivered with good respect. And how does the Martinmas your master?

BARDOLPH In bodily health, sir.

POINS Well, the immortal part needs a physician, but that moves not him. Though that is sick, it dies not.

PRINCE HENRY I do allow this wen to be as familiar with me as my dog, and he holds his place, for look you how he writes—

POINS (reading the letter) John Falstaff, knight—every man must know that as oft as he has occasion to name himself, even like those that are kin to the king, for they never prick their finger but they say 'There's some of the King's blood spilt.' 'How comes that?' says he that takes upon him not to know. The answer is as ready as a borrower's cap: 'I am the King's poor cousin, sir.'

PRINCE HENRY Nay, they will be kin to us, or they will fetch it from Japhet. But the letter: Sir John Falstaff, knight, to the son of the King nearest his father, Harry Prince of Wales, greeting.

POINS Why, this is a certificate!

PRINCE HENRY Peace! I will imitate the honourable Romans in brevity.

POINS He sure means brevity in breath, short-winded.

PRINCE HENRY I commend me to you, I commend you, and I leave you. Be not too familiar with Poins, for he misuses your favours so much that he swears you are to marry his sister Nell. Repent at idle times as you may, and so farewell.
    Your by yes and no—which is as much as to say, as you use him—Jack Falstaff with my familiars, John with my brothers and sisters, and Sir John with all Europe.

POINS My lord, I'll steep this letter in sack and make him eat it.

PRINCE HENRY That's to make him eat twenty of his words. But do you use me thus, Ned? Must I marry your sister?

POINS God send the wench no worse fortune! But I never said so.

PRINCE HENRY Well, thus we play the fools with the time, and the spirits of the wise sit in the clouds and mock us. —Is your master here in London?

BARDOLPH Yes, my lord.

PRINCE HENRY Where sups he? Does the old boar feed in the old sty?

BARDOLPH At the old place, my lord, in Eastcheap.

PRINCE HENRY What company?

PAGE Ephesians, my lord, of the old church.

PRINCE HENRY Sup any women with him?

PAGE None, my lord, but old Mistress Quickly, and Mistress Doll Tearsheet.

PRINCE HENRY What pagan may that be?

PAGE A proper gentlewoman, sir, and a kinswoman of my master's.

PRINCE HENRY Even such kin as the parish heifers are to the town bull. Shall we steal upon them, Ned, at supper?

POINS I am your shadow, my lord; I'll follow you.

PRINCE HENRY You boy, and Bardolph, no word to your master that I have yet come to town. There's for your silence.

BARDOLPH I have no tongue, sir.

PAGE And for mine, sir, I will govern it.

PRINCE HENRY Fare you well; go.

Exeunt Bardolph and Page

This Doll Tearsheet should be some road.

POINS I warrant you, as common as the way between St. Albans and London.

PRINCE HENRY How might we see Falstaff bestow himself tonight in his true colours, and not ourselves be seen?

POINS Put on two leather jerkins and aprons, and wait upon him at his table as drawers.

PRINCE HENRY From a god to a bull? A heavy descension! It was Jove's case. From a prince to a prentice? A low transformation, that shall be mine; for in everything the purpose must weigh with the folly. Follow me, Ned.

Exeunt

SCENE III
Before Warkworth castle.

Enter Northumberland, Lady Northumberland,
and Lady Percy

NORTHUMBERLAND
  I pray you, loving wife, and gentle daughter,
  Give even way unto my rough affairs;
  Put not you on the visage of the times
  And be like them to Percy troublesome.
LADY NORTHUMBERLAND
  I have given over; I will speak no more.
  Do what you will; your wisdom be your guide.
NORTHUMBERLAND
  Alas, sweet wife, my honour is at pawn,
  And but my going, nothing can redeem it.
LADY PERCY
  O, yet, for God's sake, go not to these wars!
  The time was, father, that you broke your word
  When you were more endeared to it than now:
  When your own Percy, when my heart's dear Harry,
  Threw many a northward look to see his father
  Bring up his forces. But he did long in vain.
  Who then persuaded you to stay at home?
  There were two honours lost, yours and your son's.
  For yours, the God of heaven brighten it!
  For his, it stuck upon him as the sun
  In the grey vault of heaven, and by his light
  Did all the chivalry of England move
  To do brave acts. He was indeed the glass
  Wherein the noble youth did dress themselves.
  He had no legs that practised not his gait;
  And speaking thick, which nature made his blemish,
  Became the accents of the valiant.
  For those that could speak low and tardily

Would turn their own perfection to abuse,
To seem like him. So that in speech, in gait,
In diet, in affections of delight,
In military rules, humours of blood,
He was the mark and glass, copy and book,
That fashioned others. And him—O wondrous him!
O miracle of men!—him did you leave,
Second to none, unseconded by you,
To look upon the hideous god of war
In disadvantage; to abide a field
Where nothing but the sound of Hotspur's name
Did seem defensible. So you left him.
Never, O never, do his ghost the wrong
To hold your honour more precise and nice
With others than with him! Let them alone.
The Marshal and the Archbishop are strong;
Had my sweet Harry had but half their numbers,
Today might I, hanging on Hotspur's neck,
Have talked of Monmouth's grave.

NORTHUMBERLAND   Bless your heart,
Fair daughter, you do draw my spirits from me
With new lamenting ancient oversights.
But I must go and meet with danger there,
Or it will seek me in another place
And find me worse provided.

LADY NORTHUMBERLAND O, fly to Scotland,
Till the nobles and the armèd commons
Have of their strength made a little taste.

LADY PERCY
If they get ground and vantage of the King,
Then join you with them like a rib of steel,
To make strength stronger; but, for all our loves,
First let them try themselves. So did your son;
He was so suffered; so came I a widow,
And never shall have length of life enough
To rain upon remembrance with my eyes,

That it may grow and sprout as high as heaven
For remembrance to my noble husband.
NORTHUMBERLAND
  Come, come, go in with me. 'Tis with my mind
  As with the tide swelled up unto its height,
  That makes a still-stand, running neither way.
  Fain would I go to meet the Archbishop,
  But many thousand reasons hold me back.
  I will resolve for Scotland. There am I,
  Till time and vantage crave my company.   *Exeunt*

SCENE IV
Eastcheap. The Boar's Head.

Enter Francis and another Drawer

FRANCIS What the devil have you brought there—apple-
  johns? You know Sir John cannot endure an apple-john.
DRAWER Mass, you say true. The Prince once set a dish of
  apple-johns before him, and told him there were five
  more Sir Johns and, putting off his hat, said 'I will now
  take my leave of these six dry, round, old, withered
  knights.' It angered him to the heart. But he has forgotten
  that.
FRANCIS Why then, lay the cloth, and set them down, and
  see if you can find out Sneak's noise. Mistress Tearsheet
  would fain hear some music.
DRAWER (*preparing to leave*) Dispatch! The room where
  they supped is too hot; they'll come in straight.

Enter Will

WILL Here will be the Prince and Master Poins anon, and
  they will put on two of our jerkins and aprons, and Sir
  John must not know of it. Bardolph has brought word.

FRANCIS By the mass, here will be a high old time. It will
   be an excellent stratagem.
DRAWER I'll see if I can find out Sneak.

                                        Exeunt Francis and Drawer

                   Enter Hostess and Doll Tearsheet

HOSTESS In faith, sweetheart, I think now you are in an
   excellent good temperality [temper]. Your pulsidge
   [pulse] beats as extraordinarily as heart would desire,
   and your colour, I warrant you, is as red as any rose, in
   good truth, la!
But, in faith, you have drunk too much canaries, and
   that's a marvellous searching wine, and it perfumes the
   blood ere one can say 'What's this?' How do you now?
DOLL Better than I was—hem!
HOSTESS Why, that's well said—a good heart's worth gold.
   Lo, here comes Sir John.

                       Enter Falstaff, singing

FALSTAFF
            When Arthur first in court—
      empty the chamber-pot—   *Exit Will*
            And was a worthy king—
      how now, Mistress Doll?
HOSTESS Sick of a qualm, yes, good faith.
FALSTAFF So is all her sect; if they are once in a qualm
   they are sick.
DOLL A pox damn you, you muddy rascal, is that all the
   comfort you give me?
FALSTAFF You make fat rascals, Mistress Doll.
DOLL I make them? Gluttony and diseases make them; I
   make them not.

FALSTAFF If the cook helps to make the gluttony, you help
to make the diseases, Doll. We catch of you, Doll, we
catch of you. Grant that, my poor virtue, grant that.

DOLL Yes, joy, *our chains and our jewels*—

FALSTAFF —*your brooches, pearls, and trinkets*—for to serve
bravely is to come halting off, you know; to come off the
breach, with his pike bent bravely; and to surgery bravely;
to venture upon the loaded chambers bravely—

DOLL Hang yourself, you muddy conger, hang yourself!

HOSTESS By my word, this is the old fashion; you two
never meet but you fall to some discord. You are both,
in good truth, as rheumatic as two dry toasts; you cannot
one bear with another's confirmities [infirmities]. What
the good-year! One must bear, and that (*to Doll*) must
be you; you are the weaker vessel, as they say, the
emptier vessel.

DOLL Can a weak empty vessel bear such a huge full
hogshead? There's a whole merchant's venture of
Bordeaux stuff in him. You have not seen a hulk better
stuffed in the hold. Come, I'll be friends with you, Jack;
you are going to the wars, and whether I shall ever see
you again or no there is nobody cares.

Enter the Drawer

DRAWER Sir, Ensign Pistol's below, and would speak with
you.

DOLL Hang him, swaggering rascal. Let him not come
hither. It is the foul-mouthedest rogue in England.

HOSTESS If he swaggers, let him not come here. No, by
my faith! I must live among my neighbours; I'll no
swaggerers. I am in good name and fame with the very
best. Shut the door. There come no swaggerers here. I
have not lived all this while to have swaggering now.
Shut the door, I pray you.

FALSTAFF Do you hear, hostess?

HOSTESS Pray you, pacify yourself, Sir John; there come no
    swaggerers here.
FALSTAFF Do you hear? It is my ancient [ensign].
HOSTESS Tilly-fally, Sir John, never tell me; if your ancient
    swaggers, he comes not in my doors. I was before Master
    Tisick the deputy the other day, and as he said to
    me—'twas no longer ago than Wednesday last, in good
    faith—'Neighbour Quickly,' says he—Master Dumb our
    minister was by then—'Neighbour Quickly,' says he,
    'receive those that are civil, for,' said he, 'you are in an
    ill name.' Now he said so, I can tell whereupon. 'For,'
    says he, 'you are an honest woman, and well thought of;
    therefore take heed what guests you receive; receive,'
    says he, 'no swaggering companions.' There comes none
    here. You would bless you to hear what he said. No, I'll
    no swaggerers.
FALSTAFF He's no swaggerer, hostess, a tame cheater,
    in faith. You may stroke him as gently as a puppy
    greyhound. He'll not swagger with a Barbary hen, if her
    feathers turn back in any show of resistance. Call him
    up, drawer.   *Exit Drawer*
HOSTESS Cheater, call you him? I will bar no honest man
    my house, and no cheater, but I do not love swaggering;
    by my word, I am the worse when one says 'swagger'.
    Feel, masters, how I shake, look you, I warrant you.
DOLL So you do, hostess.
HOSTESS Do I? Yes, in very truth, do I, as it were an aspen
    leaf. I cannot abide swaggerers.

Enter Ancient Pistol, Bardolph, and the Page

PISTOL God save you, Sir John!
FALSTAFF Welcome, Ancient [Ensign] Pistol! Here, Pistol, I
    charge you with a cup of sack—do you discharge upon
    my hostess.

PISTOL I will discharge upon her, Sir John, with two bullets.

FALSTAFF She is pistol-proof, sir; you shall not hardly offend her.

HOSTESS Come, I'll drink no proofs, and no bullets. I'll drink no more than will do me good, for any man's pleasure, I.

PISTOL Then to you, Mistress Dorothy! I will charge you.

DOLL Charge me? I scorn you, scurvy companion. What, you poor, base, rascally, cheating, lack-linen mate! Away, you mouldy rogue, away! I am meat for your master.

PISTOL I know you, Mistress Dorothy.

DOLL Away, you cutpurse rascal, you filthy thief, away! By this wine, I'll thrust my knife in your mouldy chaps if you play the saucy blade with me. Away, you bottle-ale rascal, you basket-hilt stale juggler, you! Since when, I pray you, sir? God's light, with two points on your shoulder? Much!

PISTOL God let me not live but I will murder your ruff for this.

FALSTAFF No more, Pistol! I would not have you go off here. Discharge yourself of our company, Pistol.

HOSTESS No, good Captain Pistol, not here, sweet captain!

DOLL Captain! You abominable damned cheater, are you not ashamed to be called captain? If captains were of my mind, they would truncheon you out, for taking their names upon you before you have earned them. You a captain? You slave! For what? For tearing a poor whore's ruff in a bawdy-house? He a captain! Hang him, rogue, he lives upon mouldy stewed prunes and dried cakes. A captain? God's light, these villains will make the word as odious as the word 'occupy', which was an excellent good word before it was ill-used. Therefore captains had need look to it.

BARDOLPH Pray you go down, good ensign.

FALSTAFF Hark you hither, Mistress Doll.

PISTOL Not I; I tell you what, Corporal Bardolph, I could
   tear her! I'll be revenged of her.

PAGE Pray you go down.

PISTOL I'll see her damned first! To Pluto's damnèd lake,
   by this hand, to the infernal deep, with Erebus and
   tortures vile also! Hold hook and line, say I! Down,
   down, dogs! Down, traitors! Have we not Hiren here?

He brandishes his sword

HOSTESS Good Captain Pistol, be quiet; 'tis very late, in
   faith. I beseech you now, aggravate [moderate] your choler.

PISTOL
   These are good humours indeed! Shall pack-horses,
   And hollow pampered jades of Asia,
   Which cannot go but thirty mile a day,
   Compare with Caesars and with Hannibals,
   And Trojan Greeks? Nay, rather damn them with
   King Cerberus, and let the heavens roar!
   Shall we fall foul for toys?

HOSTESS By my troth, captain, these are very bitter words.

BARDOLPH Be gone, good ensign; this will grow to a brawl
   anon.

PISTOL Die men like dogs! Give crowns like pins! Have
   we not Hiren here?

HOSTESS On my word, captain, there's none such here.
   What the goodyear, do you think I would deny her?
   For God's sake, be quiet.

PISTOL
   Then feed and be fat, my fair Calipolis!
   Come, give us some sack.
   Si fortune me tormente sperato me contento.[1]
   Fear we broadsides? No, let the fiend give fire!
   Give me some sack. And, sweetheart, lie you there!

---

[1]This mish-mash should mean, 'If fortune torments me
hope contents me.'

(He lays down his sword)

Come we to full stops here? And are etceteras nothings?

FALSTAFF Pistol, I would be quiet.

PISTOL Sweet knight, I kiss your hand. What! We have seen the seven stars!

DOLL For God's sake, thrust him downstairs; I cannot endure such a fustian rascal.

PISTOL Thrust him downstairs? Know we not Galloway nags?

FALSTAFF Chuck him down, Bardolph, like a shove-groat shilling. Nay, if he does nothing but speak nothing, he shall be nothing here.

BARDOLPH Come, get you downstairs.

PISTOL

What! Shall we have incision? Shall we imbrue?

(He snatches up his sword)

Then death rock me asleep, abridge my doleful days!
Why then, let grievous, ghastly, gaping wounds
Untwine the Sisters Three! Come, Atropos, I say!

HOSTESS Here's goodly stuff toward!

FALSTAFF Give me my rapier, boy.

DOLL I pray you, Jack, I pray you do not draw.

FALSTAFF *(drawing)* Get you downstairs.

HOSTESS Here's a goodly tumult! I'll forswear keeping house afore I'll be in these fits and frights! So!

(Falstaff thrusts at Pistol)

Murder, I warrant now! Alas, alas, put up your naked weapons, put up your naked weapons.

                              Exit Bardolph, driving Pistol out

DOLL I pray you, Jack, be quiet; the rascal's gone. Ah, you bloody little valiant villain, you!

HOSTESS Are you not hurt in the groin? I thought he made a shrewd thrust at your belly.

Enter Bardolph

FALSTAFF Have you turned him out of doors?

BARDOLPH Yes, sir, the rascal's drunk. You have hurt him, sir, in the shoulder.

FALSTAFF A rascal, to brave me!

DOLL Ah, you sweet little rogue, you! Alas, poor ape, how you sweat! Come, let me wipe your face. Come on, you bloody chaps! Ah, rogue, in faith, I love you. You are as valorous as Hector of Troy, worth five of Agamemnon, and ten times better than the Nine Worthies. Ah, villain!

FALSTAFF A rascally slave! I will toss the rogue in a blanket.

DOLL Do, if you dare for your heart. If you do, I'll canvass you between a pair of sheets.

Enter musicians

PAGE The music is come, sir.

FALSTAFF Let them play. Play, sirs!

(Music)

Sit on my knee, Doll. A rascal bragging slave! The rogue fled from me like quicksilver.

DOLL In faith, and you followed him like a church. You bloody little tidy Bartholomew boar-pig, when will you leave fighting a-days, and thrusting a-nights, and begin to patch up your old body for heaven?

Enter, behind, the Prince and Poins disguised as drawers

FALSTAFF Peace, good Doll, do not speak like a death's-head; do not bid me remember my end.

DOLL Man, what humour is the Prince of?

FALSTAFF A good shallow young fellow. He would have made a good pantryman; he would have chipped bread well.

DOLL They say Poins has a good wit.

FALSTAFF He a good wit? Hang him, baboon! His wit's as thick as Tewkesbury mustard. There's no more wit in him than is in a mallet.

DOLL Why does the Prince love him so, then?

FALSTAFF Because their legs are both of a bigness, and he plays at quoits well, and eats conger and fennel, and drinks off candles' ends for flap-dragons; and rides the wild mare with the boys, and jumps upon joint-stools; and swears with a good grace, and wears his boots very smooth like unto the sign of the leg, and loses no love with telling of discreet stories. And such other gambol faculties he has that show a weak mind and an able body, for which the Prince admits him. For the Prince himself is such another—the weight of a hair will turn the scales between their avoirdupois.

PRINCE HENRY Would not this hub of a wheel have his ears cut off?

POINS Let's beat him before his whore.

PRINCE HENRY Look whether the withered elder has not his poll clawed like a parrot.

POINS Is it not strange that desire should so many years outlive performance?

FALSTAFF Kiss me, Doll.

PRINCE HENRY Saturn and Venus this year in conjunction! What says the almanac to that?

POINS And look whether the fiery triangle his man is not lisping to his master's old tables, his note-book, his counsel-keeper.

FALSTAFF You do give me flattering kisses.

DOLL By my faith, I kiss you with a most constant heart.

FALSTAFF I am old, I am old.

DOLL I love you better than I love ever a scurvy young boy
of them all.

FALSTAFF What stuff will you have a kirtle of? I shall
receive money on Thursday; shall have a cap tomorrow.
A merry song! Come, it grows late; we'll to bed. You'll
forget me when I am gone.

DOLL By my faith, you'll set me a-weeping if you say so.
Prove that ever I dress myself handsome till your return.
Well, hearken at the end.

FALSTAFF Some sack, Francis.

PRINCE HENRY *and* POINS *(coming forward)* Anon, anon,
sir.

FALSTAFF Ha! A bastard son of the King's? And are not
you Poins' brother?

PRINCE HENRY Why, you globe of sinful continents, what
a life do you lead!

FALSTAFF A better than you—I am a gentleman; you are a
drawer.

PRINCE HENRY Very true, sir, and I come to draw you out
by the ears.

HOSTESS O, the Lord preserve your grace! By my word,
welcome to London! Now the Lord bless that sweet face
of yours! O Jesu, are you come from Wales?

FALSTAFF You mad compound of majesty, by this light—
flesh and corrupt blood *(laying his hand upon Doll)*,
you are welcome.

DOLL How! You fat fool, I scorn you.

POINS My lord, he will drive you out of your revenge and
turn all to a merriment, if you do not join in.

PRINCE HENRY You miserable candle-mine you, how vilely
did you speak of me now, before this honest, virtuous,
civil gentlewoman!

HOSTESS God's blessing of your good heart, and so she is,
by my word!

FALSTAFF Did you hear me?

PRINCE HENRY Yes, and you knew me, as you did when
   you ran away by Gadshill; you knew I was at your
   back, and spoke it on purpose to try my patience.

FALSTAFF No, no, no, not so; I did not think you were
   within hearing.

PRINCE HENRY I shall drive you then to confess the wilful
   abuse, and then I know how to handle you.

FALSTAFF No abuse, Hal, on my honour, no abuse.

PRINCE HENRY Not? To dispraise me, and call me
   pantryman, and bread-chipper, and I know not what?

FALSTAFF No abuse, Hal.

POINS No abuse?

FALSTAFF No abuse, Ned, in the world, honest Ned, none.
   I dispraised him before the wicked that the wicked
   might not fall in love with (*turning to Prince Henry*)
   you, in which doing, I have done the part of a careful
   friend and a true subject, and your father is to give me
   thanks for it. No abuse, Hal; none, Ned, none; no, faith,
   boys, none.

PRINCE HENRY See now whether pure fear and entire
   cowardice do not make you wrong this virtuous gentlewoman to side with us. Is she of the wicked? Is your
   hostess here of the wicked? Or is your boy of the wicked?
   Or honest Bardolph, whose zeal burns in his nose, of
   the wicked?

POINS Answer, you dead elm, answer.

FALSTAFF The fiend has pricked down Bardolph irre-
   coverably, and his face is Lucifer's privy-kitchen, where
   he does nothing but roast malt-worms. For the boy,
   there is a good angel about him, but the devil blinds
   him to it.

PRINCE HENRY For the women?

FALSTAFF For one of them, she's in hell already, and burns
   poor souls. For the other, I owe her money, and whether
   she is damned for that I know not.

HOSTESS No, I warrant you.

FALSTAFF No, I think you are not; I think you are quit for
    that. For sure, there is another indictment upon you, for
    suffering flesh to be eaten in your house, contrary to the
    law, for which I think you will howl.
HOSTESS All victuallers do so. What's a joint of mutton or
    two in a whole Lent?
PRINCE HENRY You, gentlewoman—
DOLL What says your grace?
FALSTAFF His grace says that which his flesh rebels against.

Knocking within

HOSTESS Who knocks so loud at door? Look to the door
    there, Francis.

Enter Peto

PRINCE HENRY
    Peto, how now, what news?
PETO
    The King your father is at Westminster,
    And there are twenty weak and wearied posts
    Come from the north. And as I came along
    I met and overtook a dozen captains,
    Bare-headed, sweating, knocking at the taverns,
    And asking every one for Sir John Falstaff.
PRINCE HENRY
    By heaven, Poins, I feel me much to blame,
    So idly to profane the precious time
    When tempest of commotion, like the south
    Borne with black vapour, does begin to melt
    And drop upon our bare unarmèd heads.
    Give me my sword and cloak. Falstaff, good night.
                                    Exeunt Prince and Poins
FALSTAFF Now comes in the sweetest morsel of the night,
    and we must hence and leave it unpicked.

Knocking within   *Exit Bardolph*

More knocking at the door?

Enter Bardolph

How now, what's the matter?

BARDOLPH
You must away to Court, sir, presently.
A dozen captains stay at door for you.

FALSTAFF *(to Page)* Pay the musicians, fellow. Farewell,
hostess; farewell, Doll. You see, my good wenches, how
men of merit are sought after; the undeserver may sleep,
when the man of action is called on. Farewell, good
wenches. If I am not sent away post, I will see you again
ere I go.

DOLL I cannot speak; if my heart is not ready to burst—
well, sweet Jack, have a care of yourself.

FALSTAFF Farewell, farewell.

Exit with Bardolph, Peto, Page, and musicians

HOSTESS Well, fare you well. I have known you these
twenty-nine years, come peascod-time, but an honester
and truer-hearted man—well, fare you well.

BARDOLPH *(at the door)* Mistress Tearsheet!

HOSTESS What's the matter?

BARDOLPH Bid Mistress Tearsheet come to my master.

HOSTESS O, run, Doll, run! Run, good Doll! Come!—She
comes blubbered.—Yes, will you come, Doll?

Exeunt

Act III

SCENE I
Westminster. The palace.

Enter the King in his nightgown, followed by a page

KING HENRY IV
  Go call the Earls of Surrey and of Warwick—
  But, ere they come, bid them o'er-read these letters
  And well consider of them. Make good speed.

Exit page

  How many thousand of my poorest subjects
  Are at this hour asleep! O sleep, O gentle sleep,
  Nature's soft nurse, how have I frighted you,
  That you no more will weigh my eyelids down
  And steep my senses in forgetfulness?
  Why rather, sleep, lie you in smoky hovels,
  Upon uneasy pallets stretching out,
  And hushed with buzzing night-flies to your slumber,
  Than in the perfumed chambers of the great,
  Under the canopies of costly state,
  And lulled with sound of sweetest melody?
  O you dull god, why lie you with the vile
  In loathsome beds, and leave the kingly couch
  A watch-case, or a common alarum-bell?
  Will you upon the high and giddy mast
  Seal up the ship-boy's eyes, and rock his brains
  In cradle of the rude imperious surge,
  And in the visitation of the winds,
  Which take the ruffian billows by the top,
  Curling their monstrous heads, and hanging them

187

With deafening clamour in the slippery clouds,
That with the tumult death itself awakes?
Can you, O partial sleep, give your repose
To the wet sea's-son in an hour so rude,
And in the calmest and most still of nights,
With all appliances and means at hand,
Deny it to a king? Then happy low, lie down!
Uneasy lies the head that wears a crown.

Enter Warwick and Surrey

WARWICK
   Many good morrows to your majesty!
KING HENRY IV
   Is it good morrow, lords?
WARWICK
   It is one o'clock, and past.
KING HENRY IV
   Why then, good morrow to you all, my lords.
   Have you read over the letters that I sent you?
WARWICK
   We have, my liege.
KING HENRY IV
   Then you perceive the body of our kingdom
   How foul it is, what rank diseases grow,
   And with what danger, near the heart of it.
WARWICK
   It is but as a body yet distempered,
   Which to its former strength may be restored
   With good advice and little medicine.
   My lord Northumberland will soon be cooled.
KING HENRY IV
   O God, that one might read the book of fate,
   And see the revolution of the times
   Make mountains level, and the continent,
   Weary of solid firmness, melt itself

Into the sea; and other times to see
The beachy girdle of the oceàn
Too wide for Neptune's hips. How chance's mocks
And changes fill the cup of alteration
With divers liquors! 'Tis not ten years gone
Since Richard and Northumberland, great friends,
Did feast together, and in two years after
Were they at wars. It is but eight years since
This Percy was the man nearest my soul;
Who like a brother toiled in my affairs
And laid his love and life under my foot;
Yes, for my sake, even to the eyes of Richard
Gave him defiance. But which of you was by—
(*To Warwick*) You, cousin Neville, as I may remember—
When Richard, with his eye brimful of tears,
Then checked and berated by Northumberland,
Did speak these words, now proved a prophecy?
'Northumberland, you ladder by which now
My cousin Bolingbroke ascends my throne'—
Though then, God knows, I had no such intent
But that necessity so bowed the state
That I and greatness were compelled to kiss—
'The time shall come'—thus did he follow it—
'The time will come that foul sin, gathering head,
Shall break into corruption'—so went on,
Foretelling this same time's conditiòn,
And the division of our amity.

WARWICK
There is a history in all men's lives
Figuring the natures of the times deceased,
Which when observed, a man may prophesy,
With a near aim, of the main chance of things
As yet not come to life, which in their seeds
And weak beginning lie intreasurèd.
Such things become the hatch and brood of time,
And by the necessary form of this

King Richard might create a perfect guess
That great Northumberland, then false to him,
Would of that seed grow to a greater falseness,
Which should not find a ground to root upon
Unless on you.

KING HENRY IV Are these things then necessities?
Then let us meet them like necessities,
And that same word even now cries out on us.
They say the Bishop and Northumberland
Are fifty thousand strong.

WARWICK   It cannot be, my lord.
Rumour does double, like the voice and echo,
The numbers of the feared. Please it your grace
To go to bed. Upon my soul, my lord,
The powers that you already have sent forth
Shall bring this prize in very easily.
To comfort you the more, I have received
A certain instance that Glendower is dead.
Your majesty has been this fortnight ill,
And these unseasoned hours perforce must add
Unto your sickness.

KING HENRY IV   I will take your counsel.
And were these inward wars once out of hand,
We would, dear lords, unto the Holy Land.   *Exeunt*

SCENE II
Before Justice Shallow's house.

Enter Justice Shallow and Justice Silence

SHALLOW Come on, come on, come on! Give me your
hand, sir, give me your hand, sir! An early stirrer, by
the rood! And how does my good cousin Silence?
SILENCE Good morrow, good cousin Shallow.

SHALLOW And how does my cousin your bedfellow? And
    your fairest daughter and mine, my god-daughter Ellen?
SILENCE Alas, a black ousel, cousin Shallow!
SHALLOW By yes and no, sir. I dare say my cousin William
    has become a good scholar—he is at Oxford still, is
    he not?
SILENCE Indeed, sir, to my cost.
SHALLOW He must then to the Inns of Court shortly. I was
    once of Clement's Inn, where I think they will talk of
    mad Shallow yet.
SILENCE You were called 'lusty Shallow' then, cousin.
SHALLOW By the mass, I was called anything, and I would
    have done anything indeed too, and roundly too. There
    was I, and little John Doit of Staffordshire, and black
    George Barnes, and Francis Pickbone, and Will Squeal,
    a Cotswold man. You had not four such swashbucklers
    in all the Inns of Court again. And I may say to you, we
    knew where the goods were, and had the best of them
    all at commandment. Then was Jack Falstaff, now Sir
    John, a boy, and page to Thomas Mowbray, Duke of
    Norfolk.
SILENCE This Sir John, cousin, that comes hither anon
    about soldiers?
SHALLOW The same Sir John, the very same. I see him
    break Scoggin's head at the Court gate, when he was a
    lad, not thus high. And the very same day did I fight
    with one Samson Stockfish, a fruiterer, behind Gray's
    Inn. Jesu, Jesu, the mad days that I have spent! And to
    see how many of my old acquaintance are dead!
SILENCE We shall all follow, cousin.
SHALLOW Certain, 'tis certain, very sure, very sure. Death,
    as the Psalmist says, is certain to all; all shall die. How
    much a good yoke of bullocks at Stamford fair?
SILENCE By my word, I was not there.
SHALLOW Death is certain. Is old Double of your town
    living yet?

SILENCE Dead, sir.

SHALLOW Jesu, Jesu, dead! He drew a good bow, and dead! He shot a fine shoot. John of Gaunt loved him well, and betted much money on his head. Dead! He would have hit the bulls-eye at twelve score, and carried you a forehand shaft a fourteen and fourteen and a half, that it would have done a man's heart good to see. How much a score of ewes now?

SILENCE Thereafter as they are; a score of good ewes may be worth ten pounds.

SHALLOW And is old Double dead?

SILENCE Here come two of Sir John Falstaff's men, as I think.

Enter Bardolph and soldier

SHALLOW Good morrow, honest gentlemen.

BARDOLPH I beseech you, which is Justice Shallow?

SHALLOW I am Robert Shallow, sir, a poor esquire of this county, and one of the King's justices of the peace. What is your good pleasure with me?

BARDOLPH My captain, sir, commends him to you, my captain Sir John Falstaff, a tall gentleman, by heaven, and a most gallant leader.

SHALLOW He greets me well, sir; I knew him a good backsword man. How does the good knight? May I ask how my lady his wife does?

BARDOLPH Sir, pardon; a soldier is better accommodated than with a wife.

SHALLOW It is well said, in faith, sir, and it is well said indeed too. 'Better accommodated'! It is good, yes indeed is it. Good phrases are surely, and ever were, very commendable. 'Accommodated': it comes of *accommodo.* Very good, a good phrase.

BARDOLPH Pardon, sir, I have heard the word—phrase call you it? By this day, I know not the phrase, but I will maintain the word with my sword to be a soldier-like word, and a word of exceeding good command, by heaven. Accommodated: that is, when a man is, as they say, accommodated, or when a man is being whereby he may be thought to be accommodated; which is an excellent thing.

SHALLOW It is very just.

Enter Falstaff

Look, here comes good Sir John. Give me your good hand, give me your worship's good hand. By my word, you like well, and bear your years very well. Welcome, good Sir John.

FALSTAFF I am glad to see you well, good Master Robert Shallow. Master Surecard, as I think?

SHALLOW No, Sir John, it is my cousin Silence, in commission with me.

FALSTAFF Good Master Silence, it well befits you should be of the peace.

SILENCE Your good worship is welcome.

FALSTAFF Fie, this is hot weather, gentlemen. Have you provided me here half a dozen sufficient men?

SHALLOW Certainly, have we, sir. Will you sit?

FALSTAFF Let me see them, I beseech you.

SHALLOW Where's the roll? Where's the roll? Where's the roll? Let me see, let me see, let me see. So, so, so, so, so, so, so. Yes, sure, sir. Rafe Mouldy! Let them appear as I call, let them do so, let them do so. Let me see—where is Mouldy?

Enter Mouldy

MOULDY Here, if it please you.

SHALLOW What think you, Sir John? A good-limbed fellow, young, strong, and of good friends.

FALSTAFF Is your name Mouldy?

MOULDY Yes, if it please you.

FALSTAFF 'Tis the more time you were used.

SHALLOW Ha, ha, ha! Most excellent, in faith! Things
    that are mouldy lack use! Very singular good, in faith,
    well said, Sir John, very well said.

FALSTAFF Prick him.

MOULDY I was pricked well enough before, if you could
    have let me alone. My old dame will be undone now for
    one to do her husbandry and her drudgery. You need not
    to have pricked me; there are other men fitter to go out
    than I.

FALSTAFF Go to! Peace, Mouldy; you shall go, Mouldy; it
    is time you were spent.

MOULDY Spent?

SHALLOW Peace, fellow, peace—stand aside. Know you
    where you are? For the others, Sir John—let me see.
    Simon Shadow!

Enter Shadow

FALSTAFF Yes, indeed, let me have him to sit under. He's
    likely to be a cold soldier.

SHALLOW Where's Shadow?

SHADOW Here, sir.

FALSTAFF Shadow, whose son are you?

SHADOW My mother's son, sir.

FALSTAFF Your mother's son! Likely enough, and your
    father's shadow. So the son of the female is the shadow
    of the male; it is often so, indeed—but much of the
    father's substance!

SHALLOW Do you like him, Sir John?

FALSTAFF Shadow will serve for summer. Prick him, for
    we have a number of shadows fill up the muster-book.

SHALLOW Thomas Wart!

Enter Wart

FALSTAFF Where's he?

WART Here, sir.

FALSTAFF Is your name Wart?

WART Yes, sir.

FALSTAFF You are a very ragged Wart.

SHALLOW Shall I prick him, Sir John?

FALSTAFF It were superfluous, for his apparel is built upon
his back, and the whole frame stands upon pins. Prick
him no more.

SHALLOW Ha, ha, ha! You can do it, sir, you can do it; I
commend you well. Francis Feeble!

Enter Feeble

FEEBLE Here, sir.

SHALLOW What trade are you, Feeble?

FEEBLE A woman's tailor, sir.

SHALLOW Shall I prick him, sir?

FALSTAFF You may; but if he had been a man's tailor he'd
have pricked you. Will you make as many holes in an
enemy's army as you have done in a woman's petticoat?

FEEBLE I will do my good will, sir; you can have no more.

FALSTAFF Well said, good woman's tailor! Well said,
courageous Feeble! You will be as valiant as the wrathful
dove, or most magnanimous mouse. Prick the woman's
tailor well, Master Shallow; deep, Master Shallow.

FEEBLE I would Wart might have gone, sir.

FALSTAFF I would you were a man's tailor, that you might
mend him and make him fit to go. I cannot put him to a
private soldier, that is the leader of so many thousands.
Let that suffice, most forcible Feeble.

FEEBLE It shall suffice, sir.

FALSTAFF I am bound to you, reverend Feeble. Who is next?

SHALLOW Peter Bullcalf of the green!

Enter Bullcalf

FALSTAFF Yes, indeed, let's see Bullcalf.

BULLCALF Here, sir.

FALSTAFF Before God, a likely fellow! Come, prick Bullcalf till he roars again.

BULLCALF O Lord, good my lord captain—

FALSTAFF What, do you roar before you are pricked?

BULLCALF O Lord, sir, I am a diseased man.

FALSTAFF What disease have you?

BULLCALF A bloody cold, sir, a cough, sir, which I caught with ringing in the King's affairs upon his coronation day, sir.

FALSTAFF Come, you shall go to the wars in a gown. We will have away your cold, and I will take such order that your friends shall ring for you. Is here all?

SHALLOW Here are two more called than your number. You must have but four here, sir; and so, I pray you, go in with me to dinner.

FALSTAFF Come, I will go drink with you, but I cannot tarry dinner. I am glad to see you, by my word, Master Shallow.

SHALLOW O, Sir John, do you remember since we lay all night in the windmill in St. George's Field?

FALSTAFF No more of that, Master Shallow.

SHALLOW Ha, 'twas a merry night! And is Jane Nightwork alive?

FALSTAFF She lives, Master Shallow.

SHALLOW She never could away with me.

FALSTAFF Never, never. She would always say she could not abide Master Shallow.

SHALLOW By the mass, I could anger her to the heart. She
 was then good stuff. Does she hold her own well?
FALSTAFF Old, old, Master Shallow.
SHALLOW Nay, she must be old, she cannot choose but be
 old, certain she's old, and had Robin Nightwork by old
 Nightwork before I came to Clement's Inn.
SILENCE That's fifty-five year ago.
SHALLOW Ha, cousin Silence, that you had seen what this
 knight and I have seen! Ha, Sir John, said I well?
FALSTAFF We have heard the chimes at midnight, Master
 Shallow.
SHALLOW That we have, that we have, that we have! In
 faith, Sir John, we have. Our watchword was 'Hem,
 boys!' Come, let's to dinner; come, let's to dinner. Jesus,
 the days that we have seen! Come, come.

                    Exeunt Falstaff, Shallow, and Silence
BULLCALF Good Master Corporate Bardolph, stand my
 friend—and here's four Harry ten shillings in French
 crowns for you. In very truth, sir, I had as soon be
 hanged, sir, as go. And yet for my own part, sir, I do not
 care, but rather because I am unwilling and, for my
 own part, have a desire to stay with my friends. Else, sir,
 I did not care, for my own part, so much.
BARDOLPH Go to; stand aside.
MOULDY And, good Master Corporal Captain, for my old
 dame's sake stand my friend. She has nobody to do
 anything about her when I am gone, and she is old and
 cannot help herself. You shall have forty, sir.
BARDOLPH Go to; stand aside.
FEEBLE By my faith, I care not; a man can die but once; we
 owe God a death. I'll never bear a base mind. If it is my
 destiny, so; if it is not, so. No man's too good to serve his
 prince; and, let it go which way it will, he that dies this
 year is quit for the next.
BARDOLPH Well said; you are a good fellow.
FEEBLE Faith, I'll bear no base mind.

Enter Falstaff and the Justices

FALSTAFF Come, sir, which men shall I have?

SHALLOW Four of which you please.

BARDOLPH *(aside to Falstaff)* Sir, a word with you. I have three pound to free Mouldy and Bullcalf.

FALSTAFF Go to, well.

SHALLOW Come, Sir John, which four will you have?

FALSTAFF Do you choose for me.

SHALLOW Certainly, then, Mouldy, Bullcalf, Feeble, and Shadow.

FALSTAFF Mouldy and Bullcalf: for you, Mouldy, stay at home till you are past service; and for your part, Bullcalf, grow till you come unto it. I will none of you.

SHALLOW Sir John, Sir John, do not yourself wrong; they are your likeliest men, and I would have you served with the best.

FALSTAFF Will you tell me, Master Shallow, how to choose a man? Care I for the limb, the sinews, the stature, bulk, and big assemblance of a man? Give me the spirit, Master Shallow. Here's Wart; you see what a ragged appearance it is. He shall charge you, and discharge you, with the motion of a pewterer's hammer; come off and on swifter than he that gibbets on the brewer's bucket. And this same half-faced fellow Shadow; give me this man; he presents no mark to the enemy—the foeman may with as great aim level at the edge of a penknife. And for a retreat, how swiftly will this Feeble the woman's tailor run off! O, give me the spare men, and spare me the great ones. Put a musket into Wart's hand, Bardolph.

BARDOLPH Hold, Wart, reverse. Thus! Thus! Thus!

FALSTAFF Come, manage your musket. So, very well! Go to, very good! Exceeding good! O, give me always a little, lean, old, chapped, bald shot. Well said, in faith! Wart, you are a good rascal. Hold, there's a sixpence for you.

SHALLOW He is not his craft's master; he does not do it
     right. I remember at Mile End Green, when I lay at
     Clement's Inn—I was then Sir Dagonet in Arthur's
     show—there was a little quiver fellow, and he would
     manage you his piece thus. And he would about, and
     about, and come you in, and come you in. 'Rah, tah,
     tah!' would he say. 'Bounce!' would he say. And away
     again would he go, and again would he come. I shall
     never see such a fellow.
FALSTAFF These fellows will do well, Master Shallow. God
     keep you, Master Silence; I will not use many words with
     you. Fare you well, gentlemen both; I thank you. I must
     a dozen mile tonight. Bardolph, give the soldiers coats.
SHALLOW Sir John, the Lord bless you! God prosper your
     affairs! God send us peace! At your return, visit my
     house; let our old acquaintance be renewed. Peradventure
     I will with you to the Court.
FALSTAFF Before God, would you would.
SHALLOW Go to; I have spoken at a word. God keep you!
FALSTAFF Fare you well, gentle gentlemen.
               Exeunt Shallow and Silence
     On, Bardolph, lead the men away.
               Exeunt Bardolph with men
     As I return, I will fetch off these justices. I do see the
     bottom of Justice Shallow. Lord, Lord, how subject we
     old men are to this vice of lying! This same starved
     Justice has done nothing but prate to me of the wildness
     of his youth, and the feats he has done about Turnbull
     Street, and every third word a lie, duer paid to the
     hearer than the Turk's tribute. I do remember him at
     Clement's Inn, like a man made after supper of a cheese-
     paring. When he was naked, he was for all the world like
     a forked radish, with a head fantastically carved upon it
     with a knife. He was so forlorn that his dimensions to
     any thick sight were invisible. He was the very genius
     of famine, yet lecherous as a monkey, and the whores

called him mandrake. He came ever in the rearward of the fashion, and sung those tunes to the overworked housewives that he heard the carmen whistle, and swore they were his fancies or his goodnights. And now is this Vice's dagger become a squire, and talks as familiarly of John of Gaunt as if he had been sworn brother to him. And I'll be sworn he never saw him but once in the tilt-yard, and then he burst his head for crowding among the marshal's men. I saw it and told John of Gaunt he beat his own name, for you might have thrust him and all his apparel into an eelskin—the case of a treble oboe was a mansion for him, a court. And now has he land and beefs. Well, I'll be acquainted with him if I return, and it shall go hard but I'll make him a philosopher's two stones to me. If the young dace is a bait for the old pike, I see no reason in the law of nature but I may snap at him. Let time shape, and there an end.   *Exit*

Act IV

SCENE I
Gaultree forest.

Enter the Archbishop of York, Mowbray, Hastings,
and others

ARCHBISHOP
What is this forest called?
HASTINGS
'Tis Gaultree Forest, if it shall please your grace.
ARCHBISHOP
Here stand, my lords, and send discoverers forth
To know the numbers of our enemies.
HASTINGS
We have sent forth already.
ARCHBISHOP   It is well done.
My friends and brethren in these great affairs,
I must acquaint you that I have received
New-dated letters from Northumberland,
Their cold intent, tenor, and substance, thus.
Here does he wish his person, with such forces
As might accord with his quality,
But which he could not levy. Whereupon
He has retired to ripen his growing fortunes
To Scotland, and concludes in hearty prayers
That your attempts may overlive the hazard
And fearful meeting of their opposite.
MOWBRAY
Thus do the hopes we have in him touch ground
And dash themselves to pieces.

Enter a Messenger

HASTINGS   Now, what news?
MESSENGER
    West of this forest, scarcely off a mile,
    In goodly form comes on the enemy,
    And, by the ground they hide, I judge their number
    Upon or near the rate of thirty thousand.
MOWBRAY
    The just proportion that we gave them out.
    Let us sway on and face them in the field.

Enter Westmorland

ARCHBISHOP
    What well-appointed leader fronts us here?
MOWBRAY
    I think it is my lord of Westmorland.
WESTMORLAND
    Health and fair greeting from our general,
    The Prince, Lord John and Duke of Lancaster.
ARCHBISHOP
    Say on, my lord of Westmorland, in peace,
    What does concern your coming.
WESTMORLAND   Then, my lord,
    Unto your grace do I in chief address
    The substance of my speech. If rebellion
    Came like itself, in base and abject routs,
    Led on by bloody youth, guarded with rage,
    And countenanced by boys and beggary;
    I say, if damned commotion so appeared
    In its true, native, and most proper shape,
    You, reverend father, and these noble lords
    Had not been here to dress the ugly form
    Of base and bloody insurrectiòn
    With your fair honours. You, Lord Archbishop,

Whose see is by a civil peace maintained,
Whose beard the silver hand of peace has touched,
Whose learning and good letters peace has tutored,
Whose white investments figure innocence,
The dove and very blessèd spirit of peace—
Wherefore do you so ill translate yourself
Out of the speech of peace that bears such grace
Into the harsh and boisterous tongue of war,
Turning your books to graves, your ink to blood,
Your pens to lances, and your tongue divine
To a loud trumpet and a point of war?

ARCHBISHOP
Wherefore do I this? So the question stands.
Briefly, to this end: we are all diseased,
And with our surfeiting and wanton hours
Have brought ourselves into a burning fever,
And we must bleed for it; of which disease
Our late King Richard being infected died.
But, my most noble lord of Westmorland,
I take not on me here as a physician,
Nor do I as an enemy to peace
Troop in the throngs of military men,
But rather show awhile like fearful war
To diet rank minds sick of happiness,
And purge the obstructions which begin to stop
Our very veins of life. Hear me more plainly.
I have in equal balance justly weighed
What wrongs our arms may do, what wrongs we suffer,
And find our griefs heavier than our offences.
We see which way the stream of time does run
And are enforced from our most quiet there
By the rough torrent of occasiòn;
And have the summary of all our griefs,
When time shall serve, to show in articles,
Which long ere this we offered to the King,
And might by no suit gain our audience.

When we are wronged, and would unfold our griefs,
We are denied access unto his person
Even by those men that most have done us wrong.
The dangers of the days but newly gone,
Whose memory is written on the earth
With yet-appearing blood, and the examples
Of every minute's instance, present now,
Have put us in these ill-beseeming arms,
Not to break peace, or any branch of it,
But to establish here a peace indeed,
Concurring both in name and quality.

WESTMORLAND

Whenever yet was your appeal denied?
Wherein have you been gallèd by the King?
What peer has been suborned to grate on you,
That you should seal this lawless bloody book
Of forged rebellion with a seal divine?

ARCHBISHOP

My brother general, the commonwealth,
I make my quarrel in particular.

WESTMORLAND

There is no need of any such redress,
Or if there were, it not belongs to you.

MOWBRAY

Why not to him in part, and to us all
That feel the bruises of the days before,
And suffer the condition of these times
To lay a heavy and unequal hand
Upon our honours?

WESTMORLAND   O, my good lord Mowbray,
Construe the times to their necessities,
And you shall say, indeed, it is the time,
And not the King, that does you injuries.
Yet for your part, it not appears to me
Either from the King or in the present time
That you should have an inch of any ground

To build a grief on. Were you not restored
To all the Duke of Norfolk's signories,
Your noble and right well-remembered father's?
MOWBRAY
What thing, in honour, had my father lost
That needs to be revived and breathed in me?
The King that loved him, as the state stood then,
Was force perforce compelled to banish him;
And then when Henry Bolingbroke and he,
Being mounted and both rousèd in their seats,
Their neighing coursers daring of the spur,
Their armèd staves in charge, their helmets down,
Their eyes of fire sparkling through sights of steel,
And the loud trumpet blowing them together—
Then, then, when there was nothing could have stayed
My father from the breast of Bolingbroke,
O, when the King did throw his baton down,
His own life hung upon the staff he threw.
Then threw he down himself and all their lives
That by indictment and by dint of sword
Have since miscarried under Bolingbroke.
WESTMORLAND
You speak, Lord Mowbray, now you know not what.
The Earl of Hereford was reputed then
In England the most valiant gentleman.
Who knows on whom fortune would then have smiled?
But if your father had been victor there,
He never had borne it out of Coventry;
For all the country, in a general voice,
Cried hate upon him, and all their prayers and love
Were set on Hereford, whom they doted on,
And blessed, and graced, and did more than the King.
But this is mere digression from my purpose.
Here come I from our princely general
To know your griefs, to tell you from his grace
That he will give you audience; and wherein

It shall appear that your demands are just,
You shall enjoy them, everything set aside
That might so much as think you enemies.

MOWBRAY
But he has forced us to compel this offer,
And it proceeds from policy, not love.

WESTMORLAND
Mowbray, you overween to take it so.
This offer comes from mercy, not from fear;
For lo, within a ken our army lies,
Upon my honour, all too confident
To give admittance to a thought of fear.
Our army is more full of names than yours,
Our men more perfect in the use of arms,
Our armour all as strong, our cause the best;
Then reason will our hearts should be as good.
Say you not then our offer is compelled.

MOWBRAY
Well, by my will we shall admit no parley.

WESTMORLAND
That argues but the shame of your offence;
A rotten case abides no handling.

HASTINGS
Has the Prince John a full commission,
In very ample virtue of his father,
To hear and absolutely to determine
Of what conditions we shall stand upon?

WESTMORLAND
That is intended in the general's name.
I muse you make so slight a question.

ARCHBISHOP
Then take, my lord of Westmorland, this schedule,
For this contains our general grievances.
Each several article herein redressed,
All members of our cause, both here and hence,
That are ensinewed to this actiòn

Acquitted by a true substantial form
And present execution of our wills—
To us and to our purposes confined
We come within our awful banks again,
And knit our forces to the arm of peace.

WESTMORLAND
This will I show the general. Please you, lords,
In sight of both our armies we may meet,
At either end in peace—which God so frame!—
Or to the place of difference call the swords
Which must decide it.

ARCHBISHOP   My lord, we will do so.

Exit Westmorland

MOWBRAY
There is a thing within my bosom tells me
That no conditions of our peace can stand.

HASTINGS
Fear you not that. If we can make our peace
Upon such large terms, and so absolute,
As our conditions shall insist upon,
Our peace shall stand as firm as rocky mountains.

MOWBRAY
Yes, but our valuation shall be such
That every slight and false-derivèd cause,
Yes, every idle, nice, and wanton reason,
Shall to the King taste of this actiòn;
That, were our royal faiths martyrs in love,
We shall be winnowed with so rough a wind
That even our corn shall seem as light as chaff,
And good from bad find no partitiòn.

ARCHBISHOP
No, no, my lord. Note this: the King is weary
Of dainty and such picking grievances,
For he has found to end one doubt by death
Revives two greater in the heirs of life.
And therefore will he wipe his tables clean,

And keep no tell-tale to his memory
That may repeat and history his loss
To new remembrance. For full well he knows
He cannot so precisely weed this land
As his misdoubts present occasiòn.
His foes are so enrooted with his friends
That, plucking to unfix an enemy,
He does unfasten so and shake a friend.
So that this land, like an offensive wife
That has enraged him on to offer strokes,
As he is striking, holds his infant up,
And hangs resolved correction in the arm
That was upreared to executiòn.

HASTINGS
Besides, the King has wasted all his rods
On late offenders, that he now does lack
The very instruments of chastisement,
So that his power, like to a fangless lion,
May offer, but not hold.

ARCHBISHOP   'Tis very true;
And therefore be assured, my good Lord Marshal,
If we do now make our atonement well,
Our peace will, like a broken limb united,
Grow stronger for the breaking.

MOWBRAY   Be it so.
Here is returned my lord of Westmorland.

Enter Westmorland

WESTMORLAND
The Prince is here at hand. Please it your lordship
To meet his grace just distance between our armies?

MOWBRAY
Your grace of York, in God's name then, set forward.

ARCHBISHOP
  Before, and greet his grace! My lord, we come.

                  They come forward

                  ## SCENE II
                  The same.

        Enter Prince John of Lancaster and his army

PRINCE JOHN
  You are well encountered here, my cousin Mowbray;
  Good day to you, gentle Lord Archbishop;
  And so to you, Lord Hastings, and to all.
  My lord of York, it better showed with you
  When ever your flock, assembled by the bell,
  Encircled you to hear with reverence
  Your exposition on the holy text,
  Than now to see you here an iron man,
  Cheering a rout of rebels with your drum,
  Turning the word to sword, and life to death.
  That man that sits within a monarch's heart
  And ripens in the sunshine of his favour,
  Would he abuse the countenance of the king?
  Alas, what mischiefs might he set abroad.
  In shadow of such greatness! With you, Lord Bishop,
  It is even so. Who has not heard it spoken
  How deep you were within the books of God?
  To us the speaker in his parliament,
  To us the imagined voice of God himself,
  The very opener and intelligencer
  Between the grace, the sanctities, of heaven
  And our dull workings. O, who shall believe
  But you misuse the reverence of your place,
  Employ the countenance and grace of heaven

As a false favourite does his prince's name,
In deeds dishonourable? You have taken up,
Under the counterfeited zeal of God,
The subjects of his substitute, my father,
And both against the peace of heaven and him
Have here up-swarmed them.

ARCHBISHOP   Good my lord of Lancaster,
I am not here against your father's peace,
But, as I told my lord of Westmorland,
The time misordered does, in common sense,
Crowd us and crush us to this monstrous form
To hold our safety up. I sent your grace
The parcels and particulars of our grief,
Which has been with scorn shoved from the Court,
Whereon this Hydra son of war is born:
Whose dangerous eyes may well be charmed asleep
With grant of our most just and right desires,
And true obedience, of this madness cured,
Stoop tamely to the foot of majesty.

MOWBRAY
If not, we ready are to try our fortunes
To the last man.

HASTINGS   And though we here fall down,
We have supplies to second our attempt.
If they miscarry, theirs shall second them,
And so success of mischief shall be born,
And heir from heir shall hold this quarrel up
While England shall have generatiòn.

PRINCE JOHN
You are too shallow, Hastings, much too shallow,
To sound the bottom of the after-times.

WESTMORLAND
Please it your grace to answer them directly
How far forth you do like their articles.

PRINCE JOHN
    I like them all, and do allow them well,
    And swear here, by the honour of my blood,
    My father's purposes have been mistaken,
    And some about him have too lavishly
    Wrested his meaning and authority.
    My lord, these griefs shall be with speed redressed,
    Upon my soul, they shall. If this may please you,
    Discharge your forces unto their several counties,
    As we will ours. And here, between the armies,
    Let's drink together friendly and embrace,
    That all their eyes may bear those tokens home
    Of our restorèd love and amity.
ARCHBISHOP
    I take your princely word for these redresses.
PRINCE JOHN
    I give it you, and will maintain my word;
    And thereupon I drink unto your grace.
HASTINGS
    Go, captain, and deliver to the army
    This news of peace. Let them have pay, and part.
    I know it will well please them. Hie you, captain!
                                        Exit a captain
ARCHBISHOP
    To you, my noble lord of Westmorland!
WESTMORLAND
    I pledge your grace—and if you knew what pains
    I have bestowed to breed this present peace
    You would drink freely; but my love to you
    Shall show itself more openly hereafter.
ARCHBISHOP
    I do not doubt you.
WESTMORLAND   I am glad of it.
    Health to my lord and gentle cousin, Mowbray.

MOWBRAY
    You wish me health in very happy season,
    For I am on the sudden something ill.
ARCHBISHOP
    Against ill chances men are ever merry,
    But heaviness foreruns the good event.
WESTMORLAND
    Therefore be merry, cousin, since sudden sorrow
    Serves to say thus, 'Some good thing comes tomorrow.'
ARCHBISHOP
    Believe me, I am passing light in spirit.
MOWBRAY
    So much the worse, if your own rule is true.

                        Shouts within

PRINCE JOHN
    The word of peace is rendered. Hark how they shout!
MOWBRAY
    This had been cheerful after victory.
ARCHBISHOP
    A peace is of the nature of a conquest,
    For then both parties nobly are subdued,
    And neither party loser.
PRINCE JOHN   Go, my lord,
    And let our army be dischargèd too.   *Exit Westmorland*
    And, good my lord, so please you, let our trains
    March by us, that we may peruse the men
    We should have coped with.
ARCHBISHOP   Go, good Lord Hastings,
    And, ere they are dismissed, let them march by.
                                        Exit Hastings

PRINCE JOHN
  I trust, lords, we shall lie tonight together.

Enter Westmorland

  Now, cousin, wherefore stands our army still?
WESTMORLAND
  The leaders, having charge from you to stand,
  Will not go off until they hear you speak.
PRINCE JOHN
  They know their duties.

Enter Hastings

HASTINGS
  My lord, our army is dispersed already.
  Like youthful steers unyoked they take their courses
  East, west, north, south; or like a school broken up,
  Each hurries toward his home and sporting-place.
WESTMORLAND
  Good tidings, my lord Hastings—and for which
  I do arrest you, traitor, of high treason;
  And you, Lord Archbishop, and you, Lord Mowbray,
  Of capital treason I attach you both.
MOWBRAY
  Is this proceeding just and honourable?
WESTMORLAND
  Is your assembly so?
ARCHBISHOP
  Will you thus break your faith?
PRINCE JOHN   I pawned you none.
  I promised you redress of these same grievances
  Whereof you did complain; which, by my honour,
  I will perform with a most Christian care.
  But, for you rebels, look to taste the due
  Meet for rebellion and such acts as yours.

Most shallowly did you these arms commence,
Fondly brought here, and foolishly sent hence.
Strike up our drums, pursue the scattered stray;
God, and not we, has safely fought today.
Some guard these traitors to the block of death,
Treason's true bed and yielder-up of breath.   *Exeunt*

SCENE III
The same.

Alarum. Excursions. Enter Falstaff and Sir John Colevile

FALSTAFF What's your name, sir? Of what condition are
  you, and of what place?
COLEVILE I am a knight, sir, and my name is Colevile of
  the Dale.
FALSTAFF Well then, Colevile is your name, a knight is
  your degree, and your place the Dale. Colevile shall be
  still your name, a traitor your degree, and the dungeon
  your place. A place deep enough; so shall you be still
  Colevile of the Dale.
COLEVILE Are not you Sir John Falstaff?
FALSTAFF As good a man as he, sir, whoever I am. Do you
  yield, sir, or shall I sweat for you? If I do sweat, they are
  the drops of your lovers, and they weep for your death.
  Therefore rouse up fear and trembling, and do observance
  to my mercy.
COLEVILE I think you are Sir John Falstaff, and in that
  thought yield me.
FALSTAFF I have a whole school of tongues in this belly of
  mine, and not a tongue of them all speaks any other word
  but my name. If I had but a belly of any indifferency,
  I were simply the most active fellow in Europe; my
  womb, my womb, my womb undoes me. Here comes
  our general.

Enter Prince John, Westmorland, and Blunt, with soldiers

PRINCE JOHN
  The heat is past; follow no further now.
  Call in the forces, good cousin Westmorland.
                                    Exit Westmorland
  Now, Falstaff, where have you been all this while?
  When everything is ended, then you come.
  These tardy tricks of yours will, on my life,
  One time or other break some gallows' back.

FALSTAFF I would be sorry, my lord, but it should be thus.
  I never knew yet but rebuke and check were the reward
  of valour. Do you think me a swallow, an arrow, or a
  bullet? Have I in my poor and old motion the expedition
  of thought? I have speeded hither with the very extremest
  inch of possibility; I have foundered nine score and odd
  posts. And here, travel-tainted as I am, have in my pure
  and immaculate valour taken Sir John Colevile of the
  Dale, a most furious knight and valorous enemy. But
  what of that? He saw me, and yielded; that I may justly
  say, with the hook-nosed fellow of Rome, three words, 'I
  came, saw, and overcame.'

PRINCE JOHN It was more of his courtesy than your
  deserving.

FALSTAFF I know not. Here he is, and here I yield him.
  And I beseech your grace, let it be booked with the rest
  of this day's deeds, or by the Lord I will have it in a
  particular ballad else, with my own picture on the top
  of it, Colevile kissing my foot. To which course if I am
  enforced, if you do not all show like gilt twopences to me,
  and I in the clear sky of fame overshine you as much as
  the full moon does the cinders of the element, which
  show like pins' heads to it, believe not the word of the
  noble. Therefore let me have right, and let desert mount.

PRINCE JOHN Yours is too heavy to mount.

FALSTAFF Let it shine, then.

PRINCE JOHN Yours is too thick to shine.

FALSTAFF Let it do something, my good lord, that may do
me good, and call it what you will.

PRINCE JOHN Is your name Colevile?

COLEVILE It is, my lord.

PRINCE JOHN A famous rebel are you, Colevile.

FALSTAFF And a famous true subject took him.

COLEVILE
I am, my lord, but as my betters are
That led me hither. Had they been ruled by me,
You should have won them dearer than you have.

FALSTAFF I know not how they sold themselves, but you
like a kind fellow gave yourself away gratis, and I thank
you for you.

Enter Westmorland

PRINCE JOHN
Now, have you left pursuit?

WESTMORLAND
Retreat is made and execution stayed.

PRINCE JOHN
Send Colevile with his confederates
To York, to present execution.
Blunt, lead him hence, and see you guard him sure.

Exit Blunt with Colevile

And now dispatch we toward the Court, my lords.
I hear the King my father is sore sick.
Our news shall go before us to his majesty,
Which, cousin, you shall bear to comfort him,
And we with sober speed will follow you.

FALSTAFF My lord, I beseech you give me leave to go
through Gloucestershire, and when you come to Court,
stand my good lord in your good report.

PRINCE JOHN
Fare you well, Falstaff. I, in my condition,
Shall better speak of you than you deserve.

Exeunt all but Falstaff

FALSTAFF I would you had the wit; it were better than your
dukedom. Good faith, this same young sober-blooded
boy does not love me, and a man cannot make him
laugh. But that's no marvel, he drinks no wine. There's
never any of these demure boys come to any proof, for
thin drink does so over-cool their blood, and making
many fish meals, that they fall into a kind of male
green-sickness; and then when they marry they get
wenches. They are generally fools and cowards—which
some of us should be too, but for inflammation. A good
sherry-sack has a twofold operation in it. It ascends into
the brain, dries there all the foolish and dull and crude
vapours which environ it; makes it apprehensive, quick,
forgetive, full of nimble, fiery, and delectable shapes,
which delivered over to the voice, the tongue, which is
the birth, becomes excellent wit. The second property of
your excellent sherry is the warming of the blood; which
before, cold and settled, left the liver white and pale,
which is the badge of pusillanimity and cowardice. But
the sherry warms it, and makes it course from the inwards
to the parts' extremes. It illumines the face, which, as a
beacon, gives warning to all the rest of this little kingdom,
man, to arm. And then the vital commoners and inner
petty spirits muster all to their captain, the heart, which,
great and puffed up with this retinue, does any deed of
courage. And this valour comes of sherry. So that skill
in the weapon is nothing without sack, for that sets it
a-work; and learning a mere hoard of gold kept by a
devil, till sack commences it and sets it in act and use.
Hereof comes it that Prince Harry is valiant; for the cold
blood he did naturally inherit of his father he has like
lean, sterile, and bare land manured, husbanded, and
tilled, with excellent endeavour of drinking good and
good store of fertile sherry, that he has become very hot
and valiant. If I had a thousand sons, the first human
principle I would teach them should be to forswear thin
potations, and to addict themselves to sack.

Enter Bardolph

How now, Bardolph?
BARDOLPH The army is discharged all and gone.
FALSTAFF Let them go. I'll through Gloucestershire, and
there will I visit Master Robert Shallow, Esquire. I have
him already softening between my finger and my
thumb, and shortly will I seal with him. Come away.

Exeunt

SCENE IV
Westminster. The Jerusalem Chamber.

Enter the King, carried in a chair, Warwick, Clarence,
Gloucester, and others

KING HENRY IV
  Now, lords, if God does give successful end
  To this debate that bleeds now at our doors,
  We will our youth lead on to higher fields,
  And draw no swords but what are sanctified.
  Our navy is addressed, our power collected,
  Our substitutes in absence well invested,
  And everything lies level to our wish.
  Only we want a little personal strength,
  And pause us till these rebels now afoot
  Come underneath the yoke of government.
WARWICK
  Both which we doubt not but your majesty
  Shall soon enjoy.
KING HENRY IV Humphrey, my son of Gloucester,
  Where is the Prince your brother?
GLOUCESTER
  I think he's gone to hunt, my lord, at Windsor.

KING HENRY IV
  And how accompanied?
GLOUCESTER   I do not know, my lord.
KING HENRY IV
  Is not his brother Thomas of Clarence with him?
GLOUCESTER
  No, my good lord, he is in presence here.
CLARENCE
  What would my lord and father?
KING HENRY IV
  Nothing but well to you, Thomas of Clarence.
  How chance you are not with the Prince your brother?
  He loves you, and you do neglect him, Thomas.
  You have a better place in his affection
  Than all your brothers. Cherish it, my boy,
  And noble offices you may effect
  Of mediation, after I am dead,
  Between his greatness and your other brethren.
  Therefore omit him not; blunt not his love,
  Nor lose the good advantage of his grace
  By seeming cold, or careless of his will.
  For he is gracious, if he is regarded;
  He has a tear for pity, and a hand
  Open as day for melting charity.
  Yet notwithstanding, being incensed, he is flint,
  As temperamental as winter, and as sudden
  As flaws congealèd in the spring of day.
  His temper therefore must be well observed.
  Chide him for faults, and do it reverently,
  When you perceive his blood inclined to mirth;
  But, being moody, give him time and scope,
  Till his passions, like a whale on ground,
  Confound themselves with working. Learn this, Thomas,
  And you shall prove a shelter to your friends,
  A hoop of gold to bind your brothers in,
  That the united vessel of their blood,

Mingled with venom of suggestiòn,
As force perforce the age will pour it in,
Shall never leak, though it does work as strong
As aconitum or rash gunpowder.

CLARENCE
I shall observe him with all care and love.

KING HENRY IV
Why are you not at Windsor with him, Thomas?

CLARENCE
He is not there today; he dines in London.

KING HENRY IV
And how accompanied? Can you tell that?

CLARENCE
With Poins, and other his continual followers.

KING HENRY IV
Most subject is the fattest soil to weeds,
And he, the noble image of my youth,
Is overspread with them; therefore my grief
Stretches itself beyond the hour of death.
The blood weeps from my heart when I do shape
In forms imaginary the unguided days
And rotten times that you shall look upon
When I am sleeping with my ancestors.
For when his headstrong riot has no curb,
When rage and hot blood are his counsellors,
When means and lavish manners meet together,
O, with what wings shall his affections fly
Towards fronting peril and opposed decay!

WARWICK
My gracious lord, you look beyond him quite.
The Prince but studies his companions
Like a strange tongue; wherein, to gain the language,
'Tis needful that the most immodest word
Is looked upon and learnt, which, once attained,
Your highness knows, comes to no further use
But to be known and hated. So, like gross terms,

The Prince will, in the perfectness of time,
Cast off his followers. And their memory
Shall as a pattern or a measure live
By which his grace must judge the lives of others,
Turning past evils to advantages.

KING HENRY IV
'Tis seldom when the bee does leave her comb
In the dead carrion.

Enter Westmorland

Who's here? Westmorland?

WESTMORLAND
Health to my sovereign, and new happiness
Added to that that I am to deliver!
Prince John your son does kiss your grace's hand.
Mowbray, the Bishop Scroop, Hastings, and all
Are brought to the correction of your law.
There is not now a rebel's sword unsheathed,
But peace puts forth its olive everywhere.
The manner how this action has been borne
Here at more leisure may your highness read,
With every course in its particular.

KING HENRY IV
O Westmorland, you are a summer bird,
Which ever in the haunch of winter sings
The lifting up of day.

Enter Harcourt

Look, here's more news.

HARCOURT
From enemies heaven keep your majesty,
And, when they stand against you, may they fall
As those that I am come to tell you of!
The Earl Northumberland and the Lord Bardolph,

With a great force of English and of Scots,
Are by the sheriff of Yorkshire overthrown.
The manner and true order of the fight
This packet, please it you, contains at large.

KING HENRY IV
    And wherefore should these good news make me sick?
    Will Fortune never come with both hands full,
    But write her fair words still in foulest letters?
    She either gives a stomach and no food—
    Such are the poor, in health—or else a feast
    And takes away the stomach—such are the rich
    That have abundance and enjoy it not.
    I should rejoice now at this happy news,
    And now my sight fails, and my brain is giddy.
    O me! Come near me. Now I am too ill.

GLOUCESTER
    Comfort, your majesty!

CLARENCE   O my royal father!

WESTMORLAND
    My sovereign lord, cheer up yourself, look up.

WARWICK
    Be patient, Princes. You do know these fits
    Are with his highness very ordinary.
    Stand from him, give him air; he'll straight be well.

CLARENCE
    No, no, he cannot long hold out these pangs.
    The incessant care and labour of his mind
    Have wrought the bond that should confine it in
    So thin that life looks through and will break out.

GLOUCESTER
    The people fear me, for they do observe
    Unfathered heirs and loathly births of nature.
    The seasons change their manners, as the year
    Had found some months asleep and leaped them over.

CLARENCE
 The river has thrice flowed, no ebb between,
 And the old folk, time's doting chronicles,
 Say it did so a little time before
 Our great-grandsire, Edward, sickened and died.
WARWICK
 Speak lower, Princes, for the King recovers.
GLOUCESTER
 This apoplexy will certainly be his end.
KING HENRY IV
 I pray you take me up, and bear me hence
 Into some other chamber. Softly, pray.

    They take up the King and lay him on a bed

SCENE V
The same.

 Let there be no noise made, my gentle friends,
 Unless some dull and favourable hand
 Will whisper music to my weary spirit.
WARWICK
 Call for the music in the other room.
KING HENRY IV
 Set me the crown upon my pillow here.
CLARENCE
 His eye is hollow, and he changes much.
WARWICK
 Less noise, less noise!

    Enter Prince Henry

PRINCE HENRY Who saw the Duke of Clarence?
CLARENCE I am here, brother, full of heaviness.

PRINCE HENRY How now, rain within doors, and none
  abroad? How does the King?

GLOUCESTER Exceeding ill.

PRINCE HENRY Heard he the good news yet? Tell it him.

GLOUCESTER
  He altered much upon hearing it.

PRINCE HENRY If he is sick with joy, he'll recover without
  physic.

WARWICK
  Not so much noise, my lords. Sweet Prince, speak low;
  The King your father is disposed to sleep.

CLARENCE
  Let us withdraw into the other room.

WARWICK
  Will it please your grace to go along with us?

PRINCE HENRY
  No, I will sit and watch here by the King.
                              Exeunt all but Prince Henry
  Why does the crown lie there upon his pillow,
  Being so troublesome a bedfellow?
  O polished perturbation! Golden care!
  That keep the ports of slumber open wide
  To many a watchful night! Sleep with it now!
  Yet not so sound, and half so deeply sweet,
  As he whose brow with homely nightcap bound
  Snores out the watch of night. O majesty!
  When you do pinch your bearer, you do sit
  Like a rich armour worn in heat of day,
  That scald with safety. By his gates of breath
  There lies a downy feather which stirs not;
  Did he suspire, that light and weightless down
  Perforce must move. My gracious lord! My father!
  This sleep is sound indeed; this is a sleep
  That from this golden circle has divorced
  So many English kings. Your due from me
  Is tears and heavy sorrows of the blood,
  Which nature, love, and filial tenderness

Shall, O dear father, pay you plenteously,
My due from you is this imperial crown,
Which, as immediate from your place and blood,
Derives itself to me.

He puts the crown on his head

              Lo where it sits,
Which God shall guard, and put the world's whole
    strength
Into one giant arm, it shall not force
This lineal honour from me. This from you
Will I to mine leave, as it is left to me.   *Exit*

KING HENRY IV
Warwick! Gloucester! Clarence!

Enter Warwick, Gloucester, Clarence, and attendant lords

CLARENCE
Does the King call?
WARWICK   What would your majesty?
KING HENRY IV
Why did you leave me here alone, my lords?
CLARENCE
We left the Prince my brother here, my liege,
Who undertook to sit and watch by you.
KING HENRY IV The Prince of Wales? Where is he?
Let me see him. He is not here.
WARWICK
This door is open; he has gone this way.
GLOUCESTER
He came not through the chamber where we stayed.
KING HENRY IV Where is the crown? Who took it from
my pillow?

WARWICK
    When we withdrew, my liege, we left it here.
KING HENRY IV
    The Prince has taken it hence. Go, seek him out.
    Is he so hasty that he does suppose
    My sleep my death?
    Find him, my lord of Warwick; chide him hither.
                                              Exit Warwick

    This part of his conjoins with my disease,
    And helps to end me. See, sons, what things you are.
    How quickly nature falls into revolt
    When gold becomes its object!
    For this the foolish over-careful fathers
    Have broken their sleep with thoughts,
    Their brains with care, their bones with industry.
    For this they have engrossed and pilèd up
    The cankered heaps of strange-achievèd gold;
    For this they have been thoughtful to invest
    Their sons with arts and martial exercises.
    When, like the bee tolling from every flower,
    Our thighs packed with wax, our mouths with honey,
    We bring it to the hive; and like the bees
    Are murdered for our pains. This bitter taste
    Yields its furthering to the ending father.

                    Enter Warwick

    Now where is he that will not stay so long
    Till his friend sickness has determined me?
WARWICK
    My lord, I found the Prince in the next room,
    Washing with kindly tears his gentle cheeks,
    With such a deep demeanour in great sorrow,
    That tyranny, which never quaffed but blood,
    Would, by beholding him, have washed its knife
    With gentle eye-drops. He is coming hither.

KING HENRY IV
>   But wherefore did he take away the crown?

>   *Enter Prince Henry*

>   Lo where he comes. Come hither to me, Harry.—
>   Depart the chamber, leave us here alone.
>   *Exeunt all except King Henry IV and Prince Henry*
PRINCE HENRY
>   I never thought to hear you speak again.
KING HENRY IV
>   Your wish was father, Harry, to that thought.
>   I stay too long by you, I weary you.
>   Do you so hunger for my empty chair
>   That you will needs invest you with my honours
>   Before your hour is ripe? O foolish youth!
>   You seek the greatness that will overwhelm you.
>   Stay but a little, for my cloud of dignity
>   Is held from falling with so weak a wind
>   That it will quickly drop; my day is dim.
>   You have stolen that which after some few hours
>   Were yours without offence, and at my death
>   You have sealed up my expectatiòn.
>   Your life did manifest you loved me not,
>   And you will have me die assured of it.
>   You hide a thousand daggers in your thoughts,
>   Which you have whetted on your stony heart,
>   To stab at half an hoùr of my life.
>   What, can you not forbear me half an hour?
>   Then get you gone, and dig my grave yourself,
>   And bid the merry bells ring to your ear
>   That you are crownèd, not that I am dead.
>   Let all the tears that should bedew my hearse
>   Be drops of balm to sanctify your head;
>   Only compound me with forgotten dust.
>   Give that which gave you life unto the worms.

Pluck down my officers, break my decrees;
For now a time is come to mock at form—
Harry the Fifth is crowned! Up, vanity!
Down, royal state! All you sage counsellors, hence!
And to the English Court assemble now,
From every region, apes of idleness!
Now, neighbour confines, purge you of your scum!
Have you a ruffian that will swear, drink, dance,
Revel the night, rob, murder, and commit
The oldest sins the newest kind of ways?
Be happy, he will trouble you no more.
England shall double gild his treble guilt;
England shall give him office, honour, might;
For the fifth Harry from curbed licence plucks
The muzzle of restraint, and the wild dog
Shall flesh his tooth on every innocent.
O my poor kingdom, sick with civil blows!
When my care could not withhold your riots,
What will you do when riot is your care?
O, you will be a wilderness again,
Peopled with wolves, your old inhabitants!

PRINCE HENRY (*kneels*)

O, pardon me, my liege! But for my tears,
The moist impediments unto my speech,
I had forestalled this dear and deep rebuke
Ere you with grief had spoken and I had heard
The course of it so far. There is your crown,
And he that wears the crown immortally
Long guard it yours! If I affect it more
Than as your honour and as your renown,
Let me no more from this obedience rise—
Which my most inward true and duteous spirit
Teaches this prostrate and exterior bending.
God witness with me, when I here came in
And found no course of breath within your majesty,
How cold it struck my heart! If I do feign,

O, let me in my present wildness die,
And never live to show the incredulous world
The noble change that I have purposèd!
Coming to look on you, thinking you dead,
And dead almost, my liege, to think you were,
I spoke unto this crown as having sense,
And thus upbraided it: 'The care on you depending
Has fed upon the body of my father;
Therefore you best of gold are worse than gold.
Other, less fine in carat, is more precious,
Preserving life in medicine potable;
But you, most fine, most honoured, most renowned,
Have eaten your bearer up.' Thus, my most royal liege,
Accusing it, I put it on my head,
To try with it, as with an enemy
That had before my face murdered my father,
The quarrel of a true inheritor.
But if it did infect my blood with joy
Or swell my thoughts to any strain of pride,
If any rebel or vain spirit of mine
Did with the least affection of a welcome
Give entertainment to the might of it,
Let God for ever keep it from my head,
And make me as the poorest vassal is
That does with awe and terror kneel to it!
KING HENRY IV
God put it in your mind to take it hence,
That you might win the more your father's love,
Pleading so wisely in excuse of it!
Come hither, Harry; sit you by my bed,
And hear, I think, the very latest counsel
That ever I shall breathe. God knows, my son,
By what by-paths and indirect crooked ways
I met this crown; and I myself know well
How troublesome it sat upon my head.
To you it shall descend with better quiet,

Better opinion, better confirmation;
For all the soil of the achievement goes
With me into the earth. It seemed in me
But as an honour snatched with boisterous hand,
And I had many living to upbraid
My gain of it by their assistances,
Who daily grew to quarrel and to bloodshed,
Wounding supposèd peace. All these bold fears
You see with peril I have answerèd,
For all my reign has been but as a scene
Acting that argument. And now my death
Changes the mood, for what in me was purchased
Falls upon you in a far fairer sort,
So you the garland wear successively.
Yet though you stand more sure than I could do,
You are not firm enough, since griefs are green;
And all my friends, which you must make your friends,
Have but their stings and teeth newly taken out,
By whose harsh working I was first advanced,
And by whose power I well might lodge a fear
To be again displaced. Which to avoid,
I cut them off, and had a purpose now
To lead out many to the Holy Land,
Lest rest and lying still might make them look
Too near unto my state. Therefore, my Harry,
Be it your course to busy giddy minds
With foreign quarrels, that action hence borne out
May waste the memory of the former days.
More would I, but my lungs are wasted so
That strength of speech is utterly denied me.
How I came by the crown, O God forgive,
And grant it may with you in true peace live!
PRINCE HENRY
    You won it, wore it, kept it, gave it me;
    Then plain and right must my possession be,

Which I with more than with a common pain
Against all the world will rightfully maintain.

Enter Prince John of Lancaster, Warwick,
and attendant lords

KING HENRY IV
Look, look, here comes my John of Lancaster.
PRINCE JOHN
Health, peace, and happiness to my royal father!
KING HENRY IV
You bring me happiness and peace, son John,
But health, alas, with youthful wings is flown
From this bare withered trunk. Upon your sight
My worldly business makes a period.
Where is my lord of Warwick?
PRINCE HENRY   My lord of Warwick!
KING HENRY IV
Does any name particular belong
Unto the lodging where I first did swoon?
WARWICK
It is called Jerusalem, my noble lord.
KING HENRY IV
Laud be to God! Even there my life must end.
It has been prophesied to me, many years,
I should not die but in Jerusalem,
Which vainly I supposed the Holy Land.
But bear me to that chamber; there I'll lie;
In that Jerusalem shall Harry die.   *Exeunt*

Act V

SCENE I
Shallow's house.

Enter Shallow, Falstaff, Bardolph, and Page

SHALLOW By cock and pie,[1] sir, you shall not away tonight. What, Davy, I say!

FALSTAFF You must excuse me, Master Robert Shallow.

SHALLOW I will not excuse you; you shall not be excused; excuses shall not be admitted; there is no excuse shall serve; you shall not be excused. Why, Davy!

Enter Davy

DAVY Here, sir.

SHALLOW Davy, Davy, Davy, Davy! Let me see, Davy; let me see, Davy; let me see—yes, for sure, William cook, bid him come hither. Sir John, you shall not be excused.

DAVY Well, sir, thus: those precepts cannot be served. And again, sir—shall we sow the head land with wheat?

SHALLOW With red wheat, Davy. But for William cook— are there no young pigeons?

DAVY Yes, sir. Here is now the smith's note for shoeing and plough-irons.

SHALLOW Let it be cast up and paid. Sir John, you shall not be excused.

DAVY Now, sir, a new link to the bucket must needs be had. And, sir, do you mean to stop any of William's wages, about the sack he lost at Hinckley fair?

---

[1] By God and the Book.

SHALLOW He shall answer it. Some pigeons, Davy, a couple
of short-legged hens, a joint of mutton, and any pretty
little tiny kickshaws, tell William cook.

DAVY Does the man of war stay all night, sir?

SHALLOW Yes, Davy. I will use him well; a friend in the
Court is better than a penny in purse. Use his men well,
Davy, for they are arrant knaves, and will backbite.

DAVY No worse than they are backbitten, sir, for they have
marvellous foul linen.

SHALLOW Well conceived, Davy. About your business,
Davy.

DAVY I beseech you, sir, to countenance William Visor of
Woncot against Clement Perkes of the Hill.

SHALLOW There are many complaints, Davy, against that
Visor; that Visor is an arrant knave, on my knowledge.

DAVY I grant your worship that he is a knave, sir; but
yet God forbid, sir, but a knave should have some
countenance at his friend's request. An honest man, sir,
is able to speak for himself, when a knave is not. I have
served your worship truly, sir, these eight years, and if I
cannot once or twice in a quarter bear out a knave
against an honest man, I have little credit with your
worship. The knave is my honest friend, sir; therefore,
I beseech you, let him be countenanced.

SHALLOW Go to; I say he shall have no wrong. Look
about, Davy.

Exit Davy

Where are you, Sir John? Come, come, come, off with
your boots. Give me your hand, Master Bardolph.

BARDOLPH I am glad to see your worship.

SHALLOW I thank you with all my heart, kind Master
Bardolph; *(to the Page)* and welcome, my tall fellow.
Come, Sir John.

FALSTAFF I'll follow you, good Master Robert Shallow.

Exit Shallow

Bardolph, look to our horses.

Exeunt Bardolph and Page

If I were sawed into quantities, I should make four dozen of such bearded hermits' staves as Master Shallow. It is a wonderful thing to see the semblable coherence of his men's spirits and his. They, by observing him, do bear themselves like foolish justices; he, by conversing with them, is turned into a justice-like servingman. Their spirits are so married in conjunction, with the participation of society, that they flock together in consent, like so many wild geese. If I had a suit to Master Shallow, I would humour his men with the imputation of being near their master; if to his men, I would curry with Master Shallow that no man could better command his servants. It is certain that either wise bearing or ignorant carriage is caught, as men take diseases, one of another; therefore let men take heed of their company. I will devise matter enough out of this Shallow to keep Prince Harry in continual laughter the wearing out of six fashions, which is four terms, or two actions, and he shall laugh without intervals. O, it is much that a lie with a slight oath, and a jest with a sad brow, will do with a fellow that never had the ache in his shoulders! O, you shall see him laugh till his face is like a wet cloak ill laid up!

SHALLOW *(within)* Sir John!

FALSTAFF I come, Master Shallow, I come, Master Shallow.

Exit

SCENE II
Westminster. The palace.

Enter Warwick and the Lord Chief Justice

WARWICK
  How now, my Lord Chief Justice, whither away?
LORD CHIEF JUSTICE
  How does the King?
WARWICK
  Exceeding well; his cares are now all ended.
LORD CHIEF JUSTICE
  I hope, not dead.
WARWICK   He has walked the way of nature,
  And to our purposes he lives no more.
LORD CHIEF JUSTICE
  I would his majesty had called me with him.
  The service that I truly did his life
  Has left me open to all injuries.
WARWICK
  Indeed I think the young King loves you not.
LORD CHIEF JUSTICE
  I know he does not, and do arm myself
  To welcome the condition of the time,
  Which cannot look more hideously upon me
  Than I have drawn it in my fantasy.

*Enter Prince John of Lancaster, Clarence, Gloucester
  and attendant lords*

WARWICK
  Here come the heavy issue of dead Harry.
  O that the living Harry had the temper
  Of him, the worst of these three gentlemen!
  How many nobles then should hold their places
  That must strike sail to spirits of vile sort!

LORD CHIEF JUSTICE
  O God, I fear all will be overturned.
PRINCE JOHN
  Good morrow, cousin Warwick, good morrow.
GLOUCESTER *and* CLARENCE
  Good morrow, cousin.
PRINCE JOHN
  We meet like men that had forgotten to speak.
WARWICK
  We do remember, but our argument
  Is all too heavy to admit much talk.
PRINCE JOHN
  Well, peace be with him that has made us heavy.
LORD CHIEF JUSTICE
  Peace be with us, lest we are heavier.
GLOUCESTER
  O, good my lord, you have lost a friend indeed,
  And I dare swear you borrow not that face
  Of seeming sorrow—it is sure your own.
PRINCE JOHN
  Though no man is assured what grace to find,
  You stand in coldest expectatiòn.
  I am the sorrier; would it were otherwise.
CLARENCE
  Well, you must now speak Sir John Falstaff fair,
  Which swims against your stream of quality.
LORD CHIEF JUSTICE
  Sweet Princes, what I did I did in honour,
  Led by the impartial conduct of my soul.
  And never shall you see that I will beg
  A raggèd and forestalled remissiòn.
  If truth and upright innocency fail me,
  I'll to the King my master that is dead,
  And tell him who has sent me after him.
WARWICK
  Here comes the Prince.

Enter King Henry V, attended by Blunt and others

LORD CHIEF JUSTICE
Good morrow, and God save your majesty!
KING HENRY V
This new and gorgeous garment, majesty,
Sits not so easy on me as you think.
Brothers, you mix your sadness with some fear.
This is the English, not the Turkish court;
Not Amurath an Amurath succeeds,
But Harry Harry. Yet be sad, good brothers,
For, by my faith, it very well becomes you.
Sorrow so royally in you appears
That I will deeply put the fashion on
And wear it in my heart. Why then, be sad;
But entertain no more of it, good brothers,
Than a joint burden laid upon us all.
For me, by heaven, I bid you be assured,
I'll be your father and your brother too.
Let me but bear your love, I'll bear your cares.
Yet weep that Harry's dead, and so will I.
But Harry lives, that shall convert those tears
By number into hours of happiness.
PRINCES
We hope no otherwise from your majesty.
KING HENRY V
You all look strangely on me—and (*to Lord Chief Justice*)
   you most;
You are, I think, assured I love you not.
LORD CHIEF JUSTICE
I am assured, if I am measured rightly,
Your majesty has no just cause to hate me.
KING HENRY V
No?
How might a prince of my great hopes forget
So great indignities you laid upon me?
What! Berate, rebuke, and roughly send to prison

The immediate heir of England? Was this easy?
May this be washed in Lethe and forgotten?
LORD CHIEF JUSTICE
   I then did use the person of your father;
   The image of his power lay then in me
   And in the administration of his law.
   While I was busy for the commonwealth,
   Your highness pleasèd to forget my place,
   The majesty and power of law and justice,
   The image of the King I represented,
   And struck me in my very seat of judgement.
   Whereon, as an offender to your father,
   I gave bold way to my authority
   And did commit you. If the deed were ill,
   Be you contented, wearing now the garland,
   To have a son set your decrees at naught?
   To pluck down justice from your awful bench?
   To trip the course of law, and blunt the sword
   That guards the peace and safety of your person?
   Nay, more, to spurn at your most royal image,
   And mock your workings in a second body?
   Question your royal thoughts, make the case yours;
   Be now the father and propose a son,
   Hear your own dignity so much profaned,
   See your most dreadful laws so loosely slighted,
   Behold yourself so by a son disdained;
   And then imagine me taking your part,
   And in your power soft silencing your son.
   After this cold considerance sentence me,
   And, as you are a king, speak in your state
   What I have done that misbecame my place,
   My person, or my liege's sovereignty.
KING HENRY V
   You are right justice, and you weigh this well.
   Therefore still bear the balance and the sword,
   And I do wish your honours may increase

Till you do live to see a son of mine
Offend you and obey you, as I did.
So shall I live to speak my father's words:
'Happy am I, that have a man so bold
That dares do justice on my very son;
And not less happy, having such a son
That would deliver up his greatness so
Into the hands of justice.' You did commit me—
For which I do commit into your hand
The unstained sword that you have used to bear,
With this remembrance: that you use the same
With the like bold, just, and impartial spirit
As you have done against me. There is my hand.
You shall be as a father to my youth;
My voice shall sound as you do prompt my ear,
And I will stoop and humble my intents
To your well-practised wise directions.
And, Princes all, believe me, I beseech you,
My father is gone wild into his grave,
For in his tomb lie my affections.
And with his spirit sadly I survive
To mock the expectation of the world,
To frustrate prophecies, and to erase
Rotten opinion, which has written me down
After my seeming. The tide of blood in me
Has proudly flowed in vanity till now.
Now does it turn, and ebb back to the sea,
Where it shall mingle with the state of floods,
And flow henceforth in formal majesty.
Now call we our high court of parliament,
And let us choose such limbs of noble counsel
That the great body of our state may go
In equal rank with the best-governed nation;
That war, or peace, or both at once, may be
As things acquainted and familiar to us;
In which you, father, shall have foremost hand.

Our coronation done, we will summon,
As I before reminded, all our state.
And, God consigning to my good intents,
No prince nor peer shall have just cause to say,
God shorten Harry's happy life one day!   *Exeunt*

SCENE III
Shallow's orchard.

Enter Falstaff, Shallow, Silence, Davy, Bardolph,
and the Page

SHALLOW Nay, you shall see my orchard, where, in an
arbour, we will eat a last year's pippin of my own
grafting, with a dish of caraways, and so forth—come,
cousin Silence—and then to bed.

FALSTAFF Before God, you have here a goodly dwelling,
and a rich.

SHALLOW Barren, barren, barren; beggars all, beggars all,
Sir John—well, good air. Spread, Davy, spread, Davy,
well said, Davy.

FALSTAFF This Davy serves you for good uses—he is your
servingman and your husbandman.

SHALLOW A good varlet, a good varlet, a very good varlet,
Sir John—by the mass, I have drunk too much sack at
supper—a good varlet. Now sit down, now sit down—
come, cousin.

SILENCE Ah, fellow! said he, we shall
(*sings*)   Do nothing but eat, and make good cheer,
            And praise God for the merry year,
            When flesh is cheap and females dear,
            And lusty lads roam here and there,
                So merrily,
            And ever among so merrily.

FALSTAFF There's a merry heart, good Master Silence!
  I'll give you a health for that anon.
SHALLOW Give Master Bardolph some wine, Davy.
DAVY Sweet sir, sit—I'll be with you anon. Most sweet sir,
  sit; master page, good master page, sit. Your health!
  What you want in meat, we'll have in drink; but you
  must bear it; the heart's all.   *Exit*
SHALLOW Be merry, Master Bardolph; and, my little soldier
  there, be merry.
SILENCE (*sings*)
  Be merry, be merry, my wife has all,
  For women are shrews, both short and tall.
  'Tis merry in hall, when beards wag all,
  And welcome merry Shrovetide! Be merry, be merry.
FALSTAFF I did not think Master Silence had been a man
  of this mettle.
SILENCE Who, I? I have been merry twice and once ere
  now.

                      Enter Davy

DAVY (*to Bardolph*) There's a dish of russets for you.
SHALLOW Davy!
DAVY Your worship? I'll be with you straight. (*To Bardolph*)
  A cup of wine, sir?
SILENCE (*sings*)
          A cup of wine that's brisk and fine,
          And drink unto you, sweetheart mine,
          And a merry heart lives long-a.
FALSTAFF Well said, Master Silence.
SILENCE If we shall be merry, now comes in the sweet of
  the night.
FALSTAFF Health and long life to you, Master Silence.
SILENCE (*sings*)
          Fill the cup, and let it come,
          I'll pledge you a mile to the bottom.

SHALLOW Honest Bardolph, welcome! If you want anything
   and will not call, bless your heart. (*To the Page*) Welcome,
   my little tiny thief, and welcome indeed, too! I'll drink
   to Master Bardolph, and to all the gallants about London.
DAVY I hope to see London once ere I die.
BARDOLPH If I might see you there, Davy—
SHALLOW By the mass, you'll crack a quart together—ha!
   will you not, Master Bardolph?
BARDOLPH Yes, sir, in a two quart-pot.
SHALLOW By God's lights, I thank you. The knave will
   stick by you, I can assure you that; he will not out, he;
   'tis true bred!
BARDOLPH And I'll stick by him, sir.
SHALLOW Why, there spoke a king. Lack nothing! Be
   merry!

                    Knocking within

   Look who's at door there, ho! Who knocks?
                                        Exit Davy
FALSTAFF (*to Silence, seeing him drink*) Why, now you
   have done me right.
SILENCE (*sings*)
            Do me right,
            And dub me knight:
            Sir Mingo.
   Is it not so?
FALSTAFF It is so.
SILENCE Is it so? Why then, say an old man can do
   somewhat.

                    Enter Davy

DAVY If it please your worship, there's one Pistol come
   from the Court with news.
FALSTAFF From the Court? Let him come in.

Enter Pistol

How now, Pistol?

PISTOL Sir John, God save you!

FALSTAFF What wind blew you hither, Pistol?

PISTOL Not the ill wind which blows no man to good.
Sweet knight, you are now one of the greatest men in
this realm.

SILENCE By our lady, I think he is, but goodman Puff of
Barson.

PISTOL
Puff?
Puff in your teeth, most recreant coward base!
Sir John, I am your Pistol and your friend,
And helter-skelter have I ridden to you,
And tidings do I bring, and lucky joys,
And golden times, and happy news of price.

FALSTAFF I pray you now, deliver them like a man of this
world.

PISTOL
A farthing for the world and worldlings base!
I speak of Africa and golden joys.

FALSTAFF
O base Assyrian knight, what are your news?
Let King Cophetua know the truth thereof.

SILENCE (*sings*)
          And Robin Hood, Scarlet, and John.

PISTOL
Shall dunghill curs confront the Helicons?
And shall good news be baffled?
Then, Pistol, lay your head in Furies' lap.

SHALLOW Honest gentleman, I know not your breeding.

PISTOL Why then, lament therefor.

SHALLOW Give me pardon, sir. If, sir, you come with news
from the Court, I take it there's but two ways, either to

utter them or conceal them. I am, sir, under the King, in some authority.

PISTOL

Under which king, Besonian? Speak, or die.

SHALLOW

Under King Harry.

PISTOL   Harry the Fourth, or Fifth?

SHALLOW

Harry the Fourth.

PISTOL   A farthing for your office!

Sir John, your tender lambkin now is King;

Harry the Fifth's the man. I speak the truth—

When Pistol lies, do this, and fig me, like

The bragging Spaniard.

FALSTAFF   What, is the old King dead?

PISTOL

As nail in door! The things I speak are just.

FALSTAFF Away, Bardolph, saddle my horse! Master Robert Shallow, choose what office you will in the land, it is yours. Pistol, I will double-charge you with dignities.

BARDOLPH O joyful day! I would not take a knighthood for my fortune.

PISTOL What, I do bring good news?

FALSTAFF Carry Master Silence to bed. Master Shallow, my lord Shallow—be what you will—I am fortune's steward! Get on your boots; we'll ride all night. O sweet Pistol! Away, Bardolph!   *Exit Bardolph*

Come, Pistol, utter more to me, and devise something to do yourself good. Boot, boot, Master Shallow! I know the young King is sick for me. Let us take any man's horses—the laws of England are at my commandment. Blessed are they that have been my friends, and woe to my Lord Chief Justice!

PISTOL
  Let vultures vile seize on his lungs also!
  'Where is the life that late I led?' say they;
  Why, here it is. Welcome these pleasant days!

                                                    Exeunt

SCENE IV
London. A street.

*Enter Beadles dragging in Hostess Quickly
and Doll Tearsheet*

HOSTESS No, you arrant knave! I would to God that I
  might die, that I might have you hanged. You have
  drawn my shoulder out of joint.

FIRST BEADLE The constables have delivered her over to
  me, and she shall have whipping-cheer, I warrant her.
  There have been a man or two killed about her.

DOLL Nut-hook, nut-hook, you lie! Come on, I'll tell you
  what, you damned tripe-visaged rascal, if the child I go
  with does miscarry, you were better you had struck your
  mother, you paper-faced villain.

HOSTESS O the Lord, that Sir John were come! I would
  make this a bloody day to somebody. But I pray God the
  fruit of her womb miscarries.

FIRST BEADLE If it does, you shall have a dozen of cushions
  again—you have but eleven now. Come, I charge you
  both, go with me, for the man is dead that you and
  Pistol beat among you.

DOLL I'll tell you what you thin man in a censer, I will
  have you as soundly thrashed for this—you bluebottle
  rogue, you filthy famished correctioner, if you are not
  thrashed I'll forswear skirts.

FIRST BEADLE Come, come, you she knight-errant, come!

HOSTESS O god, that right should thus overcome might!
　　Well, of sufferance comes ease.
DOLL Come, you rogue, come, bring me to a justice.
HOSTESS Ay, come, you starved bloodhound.
DOLL Goodman death, goodman bones!
HOSTESS You anatomy, you!
DOLL Come, you thin thing, come, you rascal!
FIRST BEADLE Very well.   *Exeunt*

SCENE V
Before Westminster Abbey.

Enter three Grooms, strewers of rushes

FIRST GROOM More rushes, more rushes!
SECOND GROOM The trumpets have sounded twice.
THIRD GROOM 'Twill be two o'clock ere they come from
　　the coronation. Dispatch, dispatch!
                                                        Exeunt

*Trumpets sound, and the King and his train pass over the
stage. After them enter Falstaff, Shallow, Pistol, Bardolph,
　　　　　　　　and the Page*

FALSTAFF Stand here by me, Master Shallow; I will make
　　the King do you grace. I will leer upon him as he comes
　　by, and do but mark the countenance that he will give me.
PISTOL God bless your lungs, good knight!
FALSTAFF Come here, Pistol, stand behind me. (*To Shallow*)
　　O, if I had had time to have made new liveries, I would
　　have bestowed the thousand pound I borrowed of you.
　　But 'tis no matter; this poor show does better; this does
　　infer the zeal I had to see him.
SHALLOW It does so.
FALSTAFF It shows my earnestness of affection—

PISTOL It does so.

FALSTAFF My devotion—

PISTOL It does, it does, it does!

FALSTAFF As it were, to ride day and night, and not to
deliberate, not to remember, not to have patience to
change my clothes—

SHALLOW It is best, certain.

FALSTAFF But to stand stained with travel, and sweating
with desire to see him, thinking of nothing else, putting
all affairs else in oblivion, as if there were nothing else
to be done but to see him.

PISTOL 'Tis *semper idem*,[2] for *obsque hoc nihil est;* 'tis
all in every part.

SHALLOW 'Tis so, indeed.

PISTOL

My knight, I will inflame your noble liver,

And make you rage.

Your Doll, and Helen of your noble thoughts,

Is in base durance and contagious prison,

Haled thither

By most mechanical and dirty hand.

Rouse up Revenge from ebon den with fell Alecto's
    snake,

For Doll is in. Pistol speaks naught but truth.

FALSTAFF I will deliver her.

The trumpets sound

PISTOL

There roared the sea, and trumpet-clangour sounds.

Enter the King and his train, the Lord Chief Justice
among them

FALSTAFF God save your grace, King Hal, my royal Hal!

---

[2]*Semper eadem*, ever the same, was Elizabeth I's motto.

PISTOL The heavens you guard and keep, most royal imp
    of fame!

FALSTAFF God save you, my sweet boy!

KING HENRY V My Lord Chief Justice, speak to that vain
    man.

LORD CHIEF JUSTICE Have you your wits? Know you what
    'tis you speak?

FALSTAFF
    My King! My Jove! I speak to you, my heart!

KING HENRY V
    I know you not, old man. Fall to your prayers.
    How ill white hairs become a fool and jester.
    I have long dreamt of such a kind of man,
    So surfeit-swelled, so old, and so profane,
    But being awake I do despise my dream.
    Make less your body hence, and more your grace;
    Leave gormandizing; know the grave does gape
    For you thrice wider than for other men.
    Reply not to me with a fool-born jest.
    Presume not that I am the thing I was,
    For God does know, so shall the world perceive,
    That I have turned away my former self;
    So will I those that kept me company.
    When you do hear I am as I have been,
    Approach me, and you shall be as you were,
    The tutor and the feeder of my riots.
    Till then I banish you, on pain of death,
    As I have done the rest of my misleaders,
    Not to come near our person by ten miles.
    For competence of life I will allow you,
    That lack of means enforces you not to evils;
    And as we hear you do reform yourselves,
    We will, according to your strengths and qualities,
    Give you advancement. (*To the Lord Chief Justice*) Be it
      your charge, my lord,

To see performed the tenor of my word.

Set on.   *Exeunt King and his train*

FALSTAFF Master Shallow, I owe you a thousand pound.

SHALLOW Yes, indeed, Sir John, which I beseech you to let me have home with me.

FALSTAFF That can hardly be, Master Shallow. Do not you grieve at this. I shall be sent for in private to him. Look you, he must seem thus to the world. Fear not your advancement; I will be the man yet that shall make you great.

SHALLOW I cannot perceive how, unless you give me your doublet, and stuff me out with straw. I beseech you, good Sir John, let me have five hundred of my thousand.

FALSTAFF Sir, I will be as good as my word. This that you heard was but a colour.

SHALLOW A colour that I fear you will die in, Sir John.

FALSTAFF Fear no colours. Go with me to dinner. Come, Lieutenant Pistol; come, Bardolph. I shall be sent for soon at night.

Enter the Lord Chief Justice and Prince John, with officers

LORD CHIEF JUSTICE

Go, carry Sir John Falstaff to the Fleet.

Take all his company along with him.

FALSTAFF

My lord, my lord—

LORD CHIEF JUSTICE

I cannot now speak; I will hear you soon.

Take them away.

PISTOL

Si fortuna me tormenta, spero me contenta.

                                    Exeunt all but Prince John and
                                    the Lord Chief Justice

PRINCE JOHN
    I like this fair proceeding of the King's.
    He has intent his wonted followers
    Shall all be very well provided for;
    But all are banished till their conversations
    Appear more wise and modest to the world.
LORD CHIEF JUSTICE
    And so they are.
PRINCE JOHN
    The King has called his parliament, my lord.
LORD CHIEF JUSTICE
    He has.
PRINCE JOHN
    I will lay odds that, ere this year expires,
    We bear our civil swords and native fire
    As far as France. I heard a bird so sing,
    Whose music, to my thinking, pleased the King.
    Come, will you hence?   *Exeunt*

Epilogue

First, my fear; then, my curtsy; last, my speech.

My fear is your displeasure; my curtsy, my duty; and my speech, to beg your pardons. If you look for a good speech now, you undo me, for what I have to say is of my own making; and what indeed I should say will, I fear, prove my own marring. But to the purpose, and so to the venture. Be it known to you, as it is very well, I was lately here in the end of a displeasing play, to pray your patience for it, and to promise you a better. I meant indeed to pay you with this, which, if like an ill venture it comes unluckily home, I break, and you, my gentle creditors, lose. Here I promised you I would be, and here I commit my body to your mercies. Let me off some, and I will pay you some and, as most debtors do, promise you infinitely. And so I kneel down before you—but, indeed, to pray for the Queen.

If my tongue cannot entreat you to acquit me, will you command me to use my legs? And yet that were but light payment, to dance out of your debt. But a good conscience will make any possible satisfaction, and so would I. All the gentlewomen here have forgiven me. If the gentlemen will not, then the gentlemen do not agree with the gentlewomen, which was never seen in such an assembly.

One word more, I beseech you. If you are not too much cloyed with fat meat, our humble author will continue the story, with Sir John in it, and make you merry with fair Katherine of France—where, for anything I know, Falstaff shall die of a sweat, unless already he is killed with your hard opinions; for Oldcastle died a martyr, and this is not the man. My tongue is weary; when my legs are too, I will bid you good night.

Love's Labour's Lost

INTRODUCTION

L ove's *Labour's Lost*, a brilliant early play, bristling
with verbal virtuosity and linguistic difficulties,
stands most in need of judicious clarification for the
modern reader. It used to be thought an enigma, to which
the key and its numerous topical allusions had been lost.
Dr. Johnson, wisely as usual, was 'always inclined to believe
that Shakespeare has more allusions to particular facts
and persons than his readers commonly suppose'—and
than his critics realise, we may add. With regard to this
play he was not of the critics' opinion that 'the satire of
Shakespeare is so seldom personal'. 'Nor is there any play
that has more evident marks of the hand' of its author. All
this is borne out now by the vastly more detailed knowledge
that we have of his age and time than the 18th century
had at its disposal. Shakespeare did not write to create an
enigma, any more than he did with his Sonnets: his nature
was open, honest and candid, as Ben Jonson testified; he
wrote out of himself and his experience for his audience.

The original audience for which this play was written was
the private one of his patron Southampton's circle; it was
subsequently revised and 'augmented' for the public theatre.
That it had particular association with Southampton is
pointed up by his choosing it for special performance
to entertain James I—though by then an old play—at
Southampton House in 1605. But its ambiance is obvious

from the theme and characters, several of whom are immediately recognisable.

The theme relates to that with which the Sonnets had originated—the young patron's reluctance to embark on the love of women and rejection of family ties. The play is a skit on this theme by the patron's clever poet—the verbal cleverness is indescribable, and does create difficulties even for those familiar with Elizabethan language—the conceits, the puns, innuendoes, three-piled hyperboles and taffeta phrases, the nonsense he could invent! The names themselves are topical—the King of Navarre, Longaville, Dumaine (Mayenne), Berowne (Biron). The King binds himself and his circle by a vow to abstain from the company of women and devote themselves to study. Berowne thinks this is nonsense: one learns life only from love and women, they are the only 'academe', etc. The Princess from France —where Marguerite de Valois had something of such an academy—arrives with her ladies, to upset the plan and conquer the men's hearts. As a poet Shakespeare was chiefly known as the poet *par excellence* of Love, the English Ovid. This is what he thought.[1]

It has always been realised that Berowne speaks for Shakespeare; it has hardly been realised yet that Berowne *is* Shakespeare's skit on himself:

> but a merrier man
> Within the limit of becoming mirth—
> another joke, for the play is full of bawdiness—
> I never spent an hour's talk with yet.
> His eye begets occasion for his wit,
> For every object that the one does catch
> The other turns to a mirth-moving jest.

---

[1] cf. my *What Shakespeare Read and Thought.*

He describes himself succinctly as 'conceit's expositor', and the play fully bears him out in its numerous conceits and fancies, puns, quibbles and *double-entendres* which he could never resist. Other characteristics of his euphoric personality are touched on in his objections to taking the vow: he likes his food and plenty of sleep—he doesn't want to be seen to wink (!) all day,

> When I was wont to think no harm all night,
> And make a dark night too of half the day—

indeed! Or, as Elizabethans would say, forsooth!

We all know that Berowne-Shakespeare's mistress, Rosaline, is the Dark Lady of the Sonnets, for she is described in practically the same language as in the Sonnets, raven-black hair, etc.

> O, if in black my lady's brows be decked,
>   It mourns that painting and usurping hair
> Should ravish doters with a false aspèct;
>   And therefore is she born to make black fair . . .
> No face is fair that is not full so black.

There is a great deal more of this, and recognisable by-play between Berowne-Shakespeare and Rosaline-Emilia, born a Bassano with her more than half Italian characteristics. The Bassanos were from Venice, which comes in for a compliment: Venezia, Venezia! Che non te vede, non te pretia. Why all the unnecessary Italian bits and phrases in the play, when its term of reference is French? No doubt they were compliments to Emilia, though they also may come from John Florio, who was Southampton's Italian tutor: both he and Shakespeare were acquainted in the Earl's service, who also receives an appropriate compliment:

Yourself, held precious in the world's esteem . . .
                                        the sole inheritor
Of all perfections that a man may owe [own].

It is the very language of the Sonnets—with which there are a number of verbal parallels—and of the dedications of the Poems to the patron.

Years ago the historian of contemporary Spain, Martin Hume, was obviously right in identifying Antonio Pérez, caricatured as Don Adriano de Armado. Philip II's exiled Secretary of State was a familiar of the Essex-Southampton circle, a resident at Essex House.[2] They were all bored with him, his self-importance, his boasts, his inflated rhetoric—he prided himself as a rhetorician, his Latin style full of absurd and flattering phrases. All this is in the play:

Our Court, you know, is haunted
With a refinèd traveller of Spain:
A man in all the world's new fashion planted,
That has a mint of phrases in his brain;
One whom the music of his own vain tongue
Does ravish like enchanting harmony,
A man of compliments . . .
From tawny Spain, lost in the world's debate.

He was indeed: he had lost his way, outlived his usefulness like many exiles, and outstayed his welcome. He was a great bore. He is made to say, 'I must tell you, it will please his grace, by the world, sometimes to lean upon my poor shoulder, and with his royal finger thus dally with my excrement, with my mustachio—but, sweetheart, let that pass.' It is true that in the heyday of his favour with the

---

[2] cf. G. Ungerer, *A Spaniard in Elizabethan England*, and G. Marañon, *Antonio Pérez*.

King, Philip would take him familiarly with him in his coach. But, now, he was pathetic; *pour comble de tout,* he is made to fall in love with a country wench, for he was a known homosexual.

Other features of members of the circle are touched: something of Florio the tutor in Holofernes the school-master: his odd language too is made fun of, and there was an indication that Florio was touchy about it. Something of Nashe is caricatured in Moth, the 'tender Juvenal', and some phrases score off Nashe's controversy with Gabriel Harvey at the time. Another literary reference, about Ajax sitting on his close-stool, refers to Harington's amusing and scabrous work on the subject, *The Metamorphosis of Ajax* (a jakes). Fun is made of the contemporary cult of Melancholy among intellectuals, for Shakespeare was not overburdened with respect for them—such as Chapman— far cleverer and more successful than they.

The plague of 1593 is present in the background—the play belongs to that year:

Thus pour the stars down plagues for perjury . . .

And

                  Bear with me, I am sick.
Write 'Lord have mercy on us' on those three.
They are infected; in their hearts it lies;
They have the plague, and caught it of your eyes.
These lords are visited; you are not free,
For the Lord's tokens [plague spots] on you do I see.

The play was revised and added to for public performance later, in 1597, and no doubt equipped with the masque of Muscovites then. Relations between the English and Russian Courts were particularly close, for the Elizabethans were first to open up oceanic contacts for Russia via Archangel.

(Thus it is that the Kremlin has the largest collection of Elizabethan silver in existence.) The Gray's Inn Revels at Christmas 1594 put on a pageant of Russians. Evidences in other plays too show Shakespeare reading about the sea-voyages of the time in Hakluyt's famous book, of 1589, besides what he observed for himself along the Thames.

More personal touches are numerous. Naturally we have the theatre in the presentation of the masque of the Nine Worthies, in which Shakespeare makes fun of bucolic performances so familiar to him in the provinces. We even have the way people were rehearsed for their parts with the boy Moth, who is put out of countenance by the mockery of the grandees. Very funny, rather cruel. Then as usual a kind comment follows—

> That sport best pleases that does least know how,
> Where zeal strives to content, and the contents
> Die in the zeal of that which it presents.

We have too the countryman's familiarity with everything about deer-hunting. Years ago I explained a typical pun on the Latin *haud credo* (I don't think), which the country bumpkin takes for auld grey doe.

The actor turned dramatist makes a parade of Latin tags from his schoolmastership. Apart from his caricature of schoolmastering (again!) with Holofernes, he is showing off that he can do as well as the university wits—as with the defiant challenge of the epigraph from Ovid to *Venus and Adonis* this same year. 'Let the mob admire what is base: for me let Apollo minister cups of water from the pure Castalian spring.' Very superior—again as usual.

With so much throwing about of brains, with puns galore both English and Latin, this is the most difficult of the plays to make plain to the modern reader. No wonder people had lost the key to it as the centuries passed. But, with our far greater knowledge of Shakespeare's time and language today, the play does not present insuperable difficulties. I have clarified the more esoteric for the reader, either by translating the Latin words in brackets, or with a few footnotes—not to bury the text in superfluous commentary, as so often otherwise, but enough to explain what is necessary for the reader.

The play has a great deal of high-spirited nonsense and fooling in it, for the rest, let it speak for itself.

CHARACTERS

KING FERDINAND OF NAVARRE
BEROWNE ⎫
LONGAVILLE ⎬ lords attending the King
DUMAINE ⎭

DON ADRIANO DE ARMADO, a Spanish gentleman
MOTH, his page
HOLOFERNES, a schoolmaster
SIR NATHANIEL, a curate
DULL, a constable
COSTARD, a clown
JAQUENETTA, a country girl
A FORESTER

THE PRINCESS OF FRANCE
ROSALINE ⎫
MARIA ⎬ ladies attending the Princess
KATHARINE ⎭
BOYET, a French lord
MARCADE, a messenger

Lords and attendants

Act I

SCENE I
The King's park.

Enter King of Navarre, Berowne, Longaville, and Dumaine

KING

 Let fame, that all hunt after in their lives,
 Live registered upon our brazen tombs,
 And then grace us in the disgrace of death;
 When, spite of cormorant devouring Time,
 The endeavour of this present breath may buy
 That honour which shall blunt his scythe's keen edge,
 And make us heirs of all eternity.
 Therefore, brave conquerors—for so you are,
 That war against your own affections
 And the huge army of the world's desires—
 Our late edict shall strongly stand in force.
 Navarre shall be the wonder of the world;
 Our court shall be a little academe,
 Still and contemplative in living art.
 You three, Berowne, Dumaine, and Longaville,
 Have sworn for three years' term to live with me,
 My fellow-scholars, and to keep those statutes
 That are recorded in this schedule here.
 Your oaths are passed; and now subscribe your names,
 That his own hand may strike his honour down
 That violates the smallest branch herein.
 If you are armed to do as sworn to do,
 Subscribe to your deep oaths, and keep it too.

LONGAVILLE
    I am resolved. 'Tis but a three years' fast.
    The mind shall banquet though the body pines
    Fat paunches have lean pates, and dainty bits
    Make rich the ribs but bankrupt quite the wits.

DUMAINE
    My loving lord, Dumaine is mortified.
    The grosser manner of these world's delights
    He throws upon the gross world's baser slaves.
    To love, to wealth, to pomp, I pine and die,
    With all these living in philosophy.

BEROWNE
    I can but say their protestation over.
    So much, dear liege, I have already sworn,
    That is, to live and study here three years.
    But there are other strict observances:
    As not to see a woman in that term—
    Which I hope well is not enrollèd there.
    And one day in a week to touch no food,
    And but one meal on every day beside—
    Which too I hope is not enrollèd there:
    And then to sleep but three hours in the night,
    And not be seen to wink of all the day,
    When I was wont to think no harm all night,
    And make a dark night too of half the day—
    Which I hope well is not enrollèd there.
    O, these are barren tasks, too hard to keep,
    Not to see ladies, study, fast, not sleep.

KING
    Your oath is passed, to pass away from these.

BEROWNE
    Let me say no, my liege, then if you please.
    I only swore to study with your grace,
    And stay here in your court for three years' space.

LONGAVILLE
    You swore to that, Berowne, and to the rest.

BEROWNE
    By yea and nay, sir, then I swore in jest.
    What is the end of study, let me know?
KING
    Why, that to know which else we should not know.
BEROWNE
    Things hid and barred, you mean, from common sense?
KING
    Ay, that is study's god-like recompense.
BEROWNE
    Come on then, I will swear to study so,
    To know the thing I am forbidden to know:
    As thus—to study where I well may dine,
    When I to feast expressly am forbid,
    Or study where to meet some mistress fine,
    When mistresses from common sense are hid;
    Or, having sworn too hard-a-keeping oath,
    Study to break it and not break my troth.
    If study's gain is thus, and this is so,
    Study knows that which yet it does not know.
    Swear me to this, and I will never say no.
KING
    These are the stops that hinder study quite,
    And train our intellects to vain delight.
BEROWNE
    Why, all delights are vain, but that most vain
    Which, with pain purchased, does inherit pain:
    As painfully to pore upon a book
    To seek the light of truth, while truth the while
    Does falsely blind the eyesight of its look.
    Light seeking light does light of light beguile;
    So, ere you find where light in darkness lies,
    Your light grows dark by losing of your eyes.
    Study me how to please the eye indeed
    By fixing it upon a fairer eye,

Which dazzling so, that eye shall be his heed,
And give him light that it was blinded by.
Study is like the heaven's glorious sun,
That will not be deep-searched with saucy looks.
Small have continual plodders ever won,
Save base authority from others' books.
These earthly godfathers of heaven's lights,
That give a name to every fixèd star,
Have no more profit of their shining nights
Than those that walk and know not what they are.
Too much to know is to know naught but fame,
And every godfather can give a name.

KING
How well he's read, to reason against reading.

DUMAINE
Proceeded well, to stop all good proceeding.

LONGAVILLE
He weeds the corn, and still lets grow the weeding.

BEROWNE
The spring is near when green geese are a-breeding.

DUMAINE
How follows that?

BEROWNE   Fit in its place and time.

DUMAINE
In reason nothing.

BEROWNE   Something then in rhyme.

KING
Berowne is like an envious nipping frost
That bites the first-born infants of the spring.

BEROWNE
Well, say I am! Why should proud summer boast
Before the birds have any cause to sing?
Why should I joy in an abortive birth?
At Christmas I no more desire a rose
Than wish a snow in May's new-fangled shows,
But liking each thing that in season grows.

So you, to study now it is too late,
Climb over the house to unlock the little gate.

KING
Well, sit you out. Go home, Berowne. Adieu!

BEROWNE
No, my good lord, I have sworn to stay with you.
And though I have for barbarism said more
Than for that angel knowledge you can say,
Yet, confident, I'll keep what I have sworn,
And bide the penance of each three years' day.
Give me the paper, let me read the same,
And to the strictest decrees I'll write my name.

KING
How well this yielding rescues you from shame.

BEROWNE (*reading*) *Item: that no woman shall come within a mile of my court*—has this been proclaimed?

LONGAVILLE Four days ago.

BEROWNE Let's see the penalty—*on pain of losing her tongue*. Who devised this penalty?

LONGAVILLE Sure, that did I.

BEROWNE Sweet lord, and why?

LONGAVILLE
To fright them hence with that dread penalty.

BEROWNE
A dangerous law against gentility!
Item: if any man is seen to talk with a woman within the term of three years, he shall endure such public shame as the rest of the court can possibly devise.
This article, my liege, yourself must break;
For well you know here comes in embassy
The French King's daughter with yourself to speak—
A maid of grace and complete majesty—
About surrender up of Aquitaine
To her decrepit, sick, bedridden father.
Therefore this article is made in vain,
Or vainly comes the admirèd Princess hither.

KING
>What say you, lords? Why, this was quite forgot.

BEROWNE
>So study evermore is overshot.
>While it does study to have what it would,
>It does forget to do the thing it should;
>And when it has the thing it then hunts most,
>'Tis won as towns with fire—so won, so lost.

KING
>We must of force dispense with this decree.
>She must lie here on mere necessity.

BEROWNE
>Necessity will make us all forsworn
>Three thousand times within this three years' space;
>For every man with his affections born,
>Is not by might mastered, but by special grace.
>If I break faith, this word shall speak for me:
>I am forsworn on mere 'necessity'.
>So to the laws at large I write my name,
>And he that breaks them in the least degree
>Stands in attainder of eternal shame.
>Suggestions are to others as to me,
>But I believe, although I seem so loath,
>I am the last that will last, keep his oath.

He signs

>But is there no quick recreation granted?

KING
>Ay, that there is. Our court, you know, is haunted
>With a refinèd traveller of Spain;
>A man in all the world's new fashion planted,
>That has a mint of phrases in his brain,
>One whom the music of his own vain tongue
>Does ravish like enchanting harmony;

A man of compliments, whom right and wrong
Have chosen umpire of their mutiny.
This child of fancy, that Armado hight,
For interim to our studies shall relate
In high-born words the worth of many a knight
From tawny Spain, lost in the world's debate.
How you delight, my lords, I know not, I,
But I protest I love to hear him lie,
And I will use him for my minstrelsy.

BEROWNE
Armado is a most illustrious wight,
A man of fire-new words, fashion's own knight.

LONGAVILLE
Costard the swain and he shall be our sport,
And so to study three years is but short.

Enter Dull with a letter, and Costard

DULL Which is the Duke's own person?

BEROWNE This, fellow. What would you?

DULL I myself reprehend [represent] his own person, for
I am his grace's thirdborough.[1] But I would see his own
person in flesh and blood.

BEROWNE This is he.

DULL Signior Arm— Arm— commends you. There's
villainy abroad. This letter will tell you more.

COSTARD Sir, the contempts thereof are as touching me.

KING A letter from the magnificent Armado.

BEROWNE How low soever the matter, I hope in God for
high words.

LONGAVILLE A high hope for a low heaven. God grant us
patience!

BEROWNE To hear, or forbear hearing?

LONGAVILLE To hear meekly, sir, and to laugh moderately;
or to forbear both.

---

[1] A petty officer.

BEROWNE Well, sir, be it as the style shall give us cause to climb in the merriness.

COSTARD The matter is to me, sir, as concerning Jaquenetta. The manner of it is, I was taken with the manner.

BEROWNE In what manner?

COSTARD In manner and form following, sir—all those three: I was seen with her 'in' the 'manor'-house, sitting with her upon the 'form', and taken 'following' her into the park. Which, put together, is 'in manner and form following'. Now, sir, for the 'manner'—it is the manner of a man to speak to a woman. For the 'form'—in some form.

BEROWNE For the 'following', sir?

COSTARD As it shall follow in my correction—and God defend the right!

KING Will you hear this letter with attention?

BEROWNE As we would hear an oracle.

COSTARD Such is the simplicity of man to hearken after the flesh.

KING (reading) Great deputy, the welkin's vicegerent, and sole dominator of Navarre, my soul's earth's god, and body's fostering patron—

COSTARD Not a word of Costard yet.

KING So it is—

COSTARD It may be so; but if he says it is so, he is, in telling true—but so.

KING Peace!

COSTARD Be to me and every man that dares not fight.

KING No words!

COSTARD Of other men's secrets, I beseech you.

KING So it is, besieged with sable-coloured melancholy, I did commend the black oppressing humour to the most wholesome physic of your health-giving air; and, as I am a gentleman, betook myself to walk. The time when? About the sixth hour; when beasts most graze, birds best peck, and men sit down to that nourishment

which is called supper. So much for the time when.
Now for the ground which—which, I mean, I walked
upon. It is called your park. Then for the place where—
where, I mean, I did encounter that obscene and most
preposterous event that draws from my snow-white pen
the ebony-coloured ink which here you view, behold,
survey, or see. But to the place where. It stands north-
north-east and by east from the west corner of your
curious-knotted garden. There did I see that low-spirited
swain, that base minion of your mirth—

COSTARD Me?

KING That unlettered small-knowing soul—

COSTARD Me?

KING That shallow vassal—

COSTARD Still me?

KING Which, as I remember, hight Costard—

COSTARD O, me!

KING Sorted and consorted, contrary to your established
   proclaimed edict and continent canon, which with—
   O, with—but with this I passion to say wherewith—

COSTARD With a wench.

KING With a child of our grandmother Eve, a female or,
   for your more sweet understanding, a woman. Him I
   —as my ever-esteemed duty pricks me on—have sent to
   you, to receive the reward of punishment, by your sweet
   grace's officer, Anthony Dull, a man of good repute,
   carriage, bearing, and estimation.

DULL Me, if it shall please you. I am Anthony Dull.

KING For Jaquenetta—so is the weaker vessel called—which
   I apprehended with the aforesaid swain, I keep her as a
   vessel of your law's fury, and shall, at the least of your
   sweet notice, bring her to trial. Yours in all compliments
   of devoted and heart-burning heat of duty,

                    Don Adriano de Armado

BEROWNE This is not so well as I looked for, but the best
   that ever I heard.

KING Ay, the best for the worst. But, fellow, what say you to this?

COSTARD Sir, I confess the wench.

KING Did you hear the proclamation?

COSTARD I do confess much of the hearing it, but little of the marking of it.

KING It was proclaimed a year's imprisonment to be taken with a wench.

COSTARD I was taken with none, sir; I was taken with a damsel.

KING Well, it was proclaimed 'damsel'.

COSTARD This was no damsel either, sir; she was a virgin.

KING It is so varied too, for it was proclaimed 'virgin'.

COSTARD If it was, I deny her virginity. I was taken with a maid.

KING This 'maid' will not serve your turn, sir.

COSTARD This maid will serve my turn, sir.

KING Sir, I will pronounce your sentence: you shall fast a week with bran and water.

COSTARD I had rather pray a month with mutton and porridge.

KING

And Don Armado shall be your keeper.
My Lord Berowne, see him delivered over;
And go we, lords, to put in practice that
Which each to other has so strongly sworn.

Exeunt King, Longaville, and Dumaine

BEROWNE

I'll lay my head to any goodman's hat
These oaths and laws will prove an idle scorn.
Fellow, come on.

COSTARD I suffer for the truth, sir; for true it is I was taken with Jaquenetta, and Jaquenetta is a true girl. And therefore welcome the sour cup of prosperity! [adversity] Affliction may one day smile again, and till then sit you down, sorrow!   *Exeunt*

SCENE II
The same.

Enter Armado and Moth, his page

ARMADO Boy, what sign is it when a man of great spirit grows melancholy?

MOTH A great sign, sir, that he will look sad.

ARMADO Why, sadness is one and the self-same thing, dear imp.

MOTH No, no; O Lord, sir, no!

ARMADO How can you part sadness and melancholy, my tender juvenal?

MOTH By a familiar demonstration of the working, my tough signior.

ARMADO Why tough signior? Why tough signior?

MOTH Why tender juvenal? Why tender juvenal?

ARMADO I spoke it, tender juvenal, as a congruent epitheton appertaining to your young days, which we may nominate tender.

MOTH And I, tough signior, as an appertinent title to your old time, which we may name tough.

ARMADO Pretty and apt.

MOTH How mean you, sir? I pretty and my saying apt, or I apt and my saying pretty?

ARMADO You pretty, because little.

MOTH Little pretty, because little. Wherefore apt?

ARMADO And therefore apt, because quick.

MOTH Speak you this in my praise, master?

ARMADO In your condign praise.

MOTH I will praise an eel with the same praise.

ARMADO What, that an eel is ingenious?

MOTH That an eel is quick.

ARMADO I do say you art quick in answers. You heat my blood.

MOTH I am answered, sir.

ARMADO I love not to be crossed.

MOTH *(aside)* He speaks the mere contrary—crosses love not him.

ARMADO I have promised to study three years with the Duke.

MOTH You may do it in an hour, sir.

ARMADO Impossible.

MOTH How many is one thrice told?

ARMADO I am ill at reckoning. It fits the spirit of a tapster.

MOTH You are a gentleman and a gamester, sir.

ARMADO I confess both. They are both the varnish of a complete man.

MOTH Then I am sure you know how much the gross sum of deuce-ace amounts to.

ARMADO It does amount to one more than two.

MOTH Which the base vulgar do call three.

ARMADO True.

MOTH Why, sir, is this such a piece of study? Now here is three studied ere you'll thrice wink; and how easy it is to put 'years' to the word 'three', and study three years in two words, the dancing horse will tell you.

ARMADO A most fine figure!

MOTH *(aside)* To prove you a cipher.

ARMADO I will hereupon confess I am in love; and as it is base for a soldier to love, so am I in love with a base wench. If drawing my sword against the humour of affection would deliver me from the reprobate thought of it, I would take desire prisoner, and ransom him to any French courtier for a new-devised curtsy. I think scorn to sigh: I think I should outswear Cupid. Comfort me, boy. What great men have been in love?

MOTH Hercules, master.

ARMADO Most sweet Hercules! More authority, dear boy, name more; and, sweet my child, let them be men of good repute and carriage.

MOTH Samson, master: he was a man of good carriage—
   great carriage, for he carried the town-gates on his back
   like a porter—and he was in love.

ARMADO O well-knit Samson! Strong-jointed Samson!
   I do excel you in my rapier as much as you did me in
   carrying gates. I am in love too. Who was Samson's love,
   my dear Moth?

MOTH A woman, master.

ARMADO Of what complexion?

MOTH Of all the four, or the three, or the two, or one of
   the four.

ARMADO Tell me precisely of what complexion.

MOTH Of the sea-water green, sir.

ARMADO Is that one of the four complexions?

MOTH As I have read, sir; and the best of them too.

ARMADO Green indeed is the colour of lovers; but to have
   a love of that colour, it seems Samson had small reason
   for it. He surely affected her for her wit.

MOTH It was so, sir, for she had a green wit.

ARMADO My love is most immaculate white and red.

MOTH Most maculate thoughts, master, are masked under
   such colours.

ARMADO Define, define, well-educated infant.

MOTH My father's wit and my mother's tongue assist me!

ARMADO Sweet invocation of a child—most pretty and
   pathetical!

MOTH

    If she is made of white and red,
       Her faults will never be known,
    For blushing cheeks by faults are bred,
       And fears by pale white shown.
    Then if she fears or is to blame,
       By this you shall not know,
    For still her cheeks possess the same
       Which native she does owe [own].

A dangerous rhyme, master, against the reason of white
and red.

ARMADO Is there not a ballad, boy, of the King and the
Beggar?

MOTH The world was very guilty of such a ballad some
three ages since, but I think now it is not to be found; or,
if it is, it would neither serve for the writing nor the tune.

ARMADO I will have that subject newly written over, that
I may example my digression by some mighty precedent.
Boy, I do love that country girl that I took in the park
with the rational hind Costard. She deserves well.

MOTH (aside) To be whipped—and yet a better love than
my master.

ARMADO Sing, boy. My spirit grows heavy in love.

MOTH (aside) And that's great marvel, loving a light wench.

ARMADO I say, sing.

MOTH Forbear till this company has passed.

Enter Dull, Costard, and Jaquenetta

DULL Sir, the Duke's pleasure is that you keep Costard
safe; and you must suffer him to take no delight, and no
penance, but he must fast three days a week. For this
damsel, I must keep her at the park; she is allowed for
the dairy-woman. Fare you well.

ARMADO (aside) I do betray myself with blushing.—
Maid—

JAQUENETTA Man.

ARMADO I will visit you at the lodge.

JAQUENETTA That's hereby.

ARMADO I know where it is situate.

JAQUENETTA Lord, how wise you are!

ARMADO I will tell you wonders.

JAQUENETTA With that face?

ARMADO I love you.

JAQUENETTA So I heard you say.

ARMADO And so farewell.

JAQUENETTA Fair weather after you.

DULL Come, Jaquenetta, away!

Exeunt Dull and Jaquenetta

ARMADO Villain, you shall fast for your offences ere you be pardoned.

COSTARD Well, sir, I hope when I do it I shall do it on a full stomach.

ARMADO You shall be heavily punished.

COSTARD I am more bound to you than your fellows, for they are but lightly rewarded.

ARMADO Take away this villain. Shut him up.

MOTH Come, you transgressing slave, away!

COSTARD Let me not be pent up, sir. I will fast being loose.

MOTH No, sir, that were fast-and-loose.[2] You shall to prison.

COSTARD Well, if ever I do see the merry days of desolation that I have seen, some shall see—

MOTH What shall some see?

COSTARD Nay, nothing, Master Moth, but what they look upon. It is not for prisoners to be too silent in their words, and therefore I say nothing. I thank God I have as little patience as another man, and therefore I can be quiet.   *Exeunt Moth and Costard*

ARMADO I do affect the very ground, which is base, where her shoe, which is baser, guided by her foot, which is basest, does tread. I shall be forsworn, which is a great argument of falsehood, if I love. And how can that be true love which is falsely attempted? Love is a familiar; Love is a devil; there is no evil angel but Love. Yet was Samson so tempted, and he had an excellent strength; yet was Solomon so seduced, and he had a very good wit. Cupid's arrow is too hard for Hercules' club, and

---

[2]An Elizabethan game.

therefore too much odds for a Spaniard's rapier. The first and second cause will not serve my turn; the passado he respects not, the duello he regards not. His disgrace is to be called boy, but his glory is to subdue men. Adieu, valour; rust, rapier; be still, drum; for your manager is in love; yea, he loves. Assist me, some extemporal god of rhyme, for I am sure I shall turn sonnet. Devise, wit; write, pen; for I am for whole volumes in folio.   *Exit*

Act II

SCENE I
The same.

Enter the Princess of France, Rosaline, Maria,
and Katharine, with Boyet and Lords

BOYET

    Now, madam, summon up your dearest spirits.
    Consider whom the King your father sends,
    To whom he sends, and what's his embassy:
    Yourself, held precious in the world's esteem,
    To parley with the sole inheritor
    Of all perfections that a man may own,
    Matchless Navarre; the plea of no less weight
    Than Aquitaine, a dowry for a queen.
    Be now as prodigal of all dear grace
    As Nature was in making graces dear
    When she did starve the general world beside,
    And prodigally gave them all to you.

PRINCESS

    Good Lord Boyet, my beauty, though but mean,
    Needs not the painted flourish of your praise.
    Beauty is bought by judgement of the eye,
    Not uttered by base sale of chapmen's tongues.
    I am less proud to hear you tell my worth
    Than you much willing to be counted wise
    In spending your wit in the praise of mine.
    But now to task the tasker. Good Boyet,
    You are not ignorant all-telling fame
    Does noise abroad Navarre has made a vow,

Till careful study shall outwear three years,
No woman may approach his silent Court.
Therefore to us it seems a needful course,
Before we enter his forbidden gates,
To know his pleasure; and in that behalf,
Bold of your worthiness, we single you
As our best-moving fair solicitor.
Tell him the daughter of the King of France,
On serious business craving quick dispatch,
Importunes personal conference with his grace.
Haste, signify so much, while we attend,
Like humble-visaged suitors, his high will.

BOYET
Proud of employment, willingly I go.

PRINCESS
All pride is willing pride, and yours is so.

Exit Boyet

Who are the votaries, my loving lords,
That are vow-fellows with this virtuous Duke?

FIRST LORD
Lord Longaville is one.

PRINCESS   Know you the man?

MARIA
I know him, madam. At a marriage feast
Between Lord Perigort and the beauteous heir
Of Jacquès Falconbridge, solemnizèd
In Normandy, saw I this Longaville.
A man of sovereign parts he is esteemed;
Well fitted in arts, glorious in arms.
Nothing becomes him ill that he would well.
The only soil of his fair virtue's gloss—
If virtue's gloss will stain with any soil—
Is a sharp wit matched with too blunt a will,
Whose edge has power to cut, whose will still wills
It should none spare that come within his power.

PRINCESS
Some merry mocking lord, perhaps—it's so?
MARIA
They say so most that most his humours know.
PRINCESS
Such short-lived wits do wither as they grow.
Who are the rest?
KATHARINE
The young Dumaine, a well-accomplished youth,
Of all that virtue love for virtue loved;
Most power to do most harm, least knowing ill,
For he has wit to make an ill shape good,
And shape to win grace though he had no wit.
I saw him at the Duke Alençon's once;
And much too little of that good I saw
Is my report to his great worthiness.
ROSALINE
Another of these students at that time
Was there with him, if I have heard a truth.
Berowne they call him—but a merrier man,
Within the limit of becoming mirth,
I never spent an hoùr's talk with yet.
His eye begets occasion for his wit,
For every object that the one does catch
The other turns to a mirth-moving jest,
Which his fair tongue—conceit's expositor—
Delivers in such apt and gracious words
That agèd ears play truant at his tales
And younger hearings are quite ravishèd,
So sweet and voluble is his discourse.
PRINCESS
God bless my ladies! Are they all in love,
That every one her own has garnishèd
With such bedecking ornaments of praise?
FIRST LORD
Here comes Boyet.

Enter Boyet

PRINCESS   Now, what admittance, lord?

BOYET

Navarre had notice of your fair approach,
And he and his competitors in oath
Were all addressed to meet you, gentle lady,
Before I came. Indeed, thus much I have learned:
He rather means to lodge you in the field,
Like one that comes here to besiege his Court,
Than seek a dispensation from his oath,
To let you enter his unpeopled house.
Here comes Navarre.

Enter the King, Berowne, Longaville, and Dumaine

KING

Fair Princess, welcome to the Court of Navarre.

PRINCESS 'Fair' I give you back again, and 'welcome'
I have not yet. The roof of this Court is too high to be
yours, and welcome to the wide fields too base to be mine.

KING

You shall be welcome, madam, to my Court.

PRINCESS

I will be welcome, then. Conduct me thither.

KING

Hear me, dear lady. I have sworn an oath—

PRINCESS

Our Lady help my lord! He'll be forsworn.

KING

Not for the world, fair madam, by my will.

PRINCESS

Why, will shall break it; will, and nothing else.

KING

Your ladyship is ignorant what it is.

PRINCESS

    Were my lord so, his ignorance were wise,

    Where now his knowledge must prove ignorance.

    I hear your grace has sworn out house-keeping.

    'Tis deadly sin to keep that oath, my lord,

    And sin to break it.

    But pardon me, I am too sudden-bold;

    To teach a teacher ill beseems me then.

    Vouchsafe to read the purpose of my coming,

    And suddenly resolve me in my suit.

She gives the King a paper

KING

    Madam, I will, if suddenly I may.

PRINCESS

    You will the sooner that I am away,

    For you'll prove perjured if you make me stay.

BEROWNE Lady, I will commend you to my own heart.

ROSALINE Pray you, do my commendations; I would be
    glad to see it.

BEROWNE I would you heard it groan.

ROSALINE Is the fool sick?

BEROWNE Sick at the heart.

ROSALINE Alas, let it blood.

BEROWNE Would that do it good?

ROSALINE My physic says ay.

BEROWNE Will you prick it with your eye?

ROSALINE Not at all: with my knife.

BEROWNE Now God save your life.

ROSALINE And yours from long living.

BEROWNE I cannot stay thanksgiving.

KING

    Madam, your father here does intimate

    The payment of a hundred thousand crowns,

    Being but the one half of an entire sum

Disbursèd by my father in his wars.
But say that he, or we—as neither have—
Received that sum, yet there remains unpaid
A hundred thousand more, in surety of which
One part of Aquitaine is bound to us,
Although not valued to the money's worth.
If then the King your father will restore
But that one half which is unsatisfied,
We will give up our right in Aquitaine
And hold fair friendship with his majesty.
But that, it seems, he little purposes,
For here he does demand to have repaid
A hundred thousand crowns, and not demands,
On payment of a hundred thousand crowns,
To have his title live in Aquitaine.
Which we much rather had depart with now,
And have the money by our father lent,
Than Aquitaine, so gelded as it is.
Dear Princess, were not his requests so far
From reason's yielding, your fair self should make
A yielding against some reason in my breast,
And go well satisfied to France again.

PRINCESS
You do the King my father too much wrong,
And wrong the reputation of your name,
In so unseeming to confess receipt
Of that which has so faithfully been paid.

KING
I do protest I never heard of it;
And if you prove it, I'll repay it back
Or yield up Aquitaine.

PRINCESS   We arrest your word.
Boyet, you can produce acquittances
For such a sum from special officers
Of Charles his father.

KING   Satisfy me so.

BOYET
  So please your grace, the packet is not come
  Where that and other specialties are bound.
  Tomorrow you shall have a sight of them.
KING
  It shall suffice me; at which interview
  All liberal reason I will yield unto.
  Meantime, receive such welcome at my hand
  As honour, without breach of honour, may
  Make tender of to your true worthiness.
  You may not come, fair Princess, in my gates;
  But here without you shall be so received
  As you shall deem yourself lodged in my heart,
  Though so denied fair harbour in my house.
  Your own good thoughts excuse me, and farewell.
  Tomorrow shall we visit you again.
PRINCESS
  Sweet health and fair desires consort your grace.
KING
  Your own wish wish I you in every place.

                                        Exit King

DUMAINE
  Sir, I pray you, a word. What lady is that same?
BOYET
  The heir of Alençon, Katharine her name.
DUMAINE
  A gallant lady. Monsieur, fare you well.   *Exit*
LONGAVILLE
  I beseech you a word. What is she in the white?
BOYET
  A woman sometimes, if you saw her in the light.
LONGAVILLE
  Perchance light in the light. I desire her name.
BOYET
  She has but one for herself—to desire that were a shame.

LONGAVILLE
  Pray you, sir: whose daughter?
BOYET
  Her mother's, I have heard.
LONGAVILLE
  God's blessing on your beard!
BOYET
  Good sir, be not offended.
  She is an heir of Falconbridge.
LONGAVILLE
  Nay, my choler is ended.
  She is a most sweet lady.
BOYET
  Not unlikely, sir; that may be.

Exit Longaville

BEROWNE
  What's her name in the cap?
BOYET
  Rosaline, by good hap.
BEROWNE
  Is she wedded or no?
BOYET
  To her will, sir, or so.
BEROWNE
  You are welcome, sir! Adieu.
BOYET
  Farewell to me, sir, and welcome to you.

Exit Berowne

MARIA
  That last is Berowne, the merry madcap lord.
  Not a word with him but a jest.
BOYET   And every jest but a word.
PRINCESS
  It was well done of you to take him at his word.

BOYET

I was as willing to grapple as he was to board.

KATHARINE

Two hot sheeps, indeed!

BOYET   And wherefore not 'ships'?

No sheep, sweet lamb, unless we feed on your lips.

KATHARINE

You sheep, and I pasture. Shall that finish the jest?

BOYET

So you grant pasture for me.

He offers to kiss her

KATHARINE   Not so, gentle beast.

My lips are no common, though several they be.

BOYET

Belonging to whom?

KATHARINE   To my fortunes and me.

PRINCESS

Good wits will be jangling; but, gentles, agree.

This civil war of wits were much better used

On Navarre and his book-men, for here 'tis abused.

BOYET

If my observation, which very seldom lies,

By the heart's still rhetoric disclosèd with eyes

Deceive me not now, Navarre is infected.

PRINCESS

With what?

BOYET

With that which we lovers entitle 'affected'.

PRINCESS

Your reason?

BOYET

Why, all his behaviour did make their retire

To the court of his eye, peeping through desire.

His heart, like an agate with your print impressed.

Proud with his form, in his eye pride expressed.
His tongue, all impatient to speak and not see,
Did stumble with haste in his eyesight to be.
All senses to that sense did make their repair,
To feel only looking on fairest of fair.
I thought all his senses were locked in his eye,
As jewels in crystal for some prince to buy;
Who, tendering their own worth from where they were
    glassed,
Did point you to buy them along as you passed.
His face's own margin did quote such amazes
That all eyes saw his eyes enchanted with gazes.
I'll give you Aquitaine, and all that is his,
If you give him for my sake but one loving kiss.

PRINCESS
Come, to our pavilion. Boyet is disposed.

BOYET
But to speak that in words which his eye has disclosed.
I only have made a mouth of his eye
By adding a tongue which I know will not lie.

MARIA
You are an old love-monger, and speak skilfully.

KATHARINE
He is Cupid's grandfather, and learns news of him.

ROSALINE
Then was Venus like her mother, for her father is but
    grim.

BOYET
Do you hear, my mad wenches?

MARIA   No.

BOYET   What then, do you see?

MARIA
Ay, our way to be gone.

BOYET   You are too hard for me.

                                        Exeunt

Act III

SCENE I
The same.

Enter Armado and Moth

ARMADO Warble, child: make passionate my sense of hearing.

MOTH *(singing)* Concolinel.

ARMADO Sweet air! Go, tenderness of years, take this key, give enlargement to the swain, bring him festinately hither. I must employ him in a letter to my love.

MOTH Master, will you win your love with a French brawl?

ARMADO How mean you? Brawling in French?

MOTH No, my complete master; but to jig off a tune at the tongue's end, canary to it with your feet, humour it with turning up your eyelids, sigh a note and sing a note; sometimes through the throat as if you swallowed love with singing love, sometimes through the nose as if you snuffed up love by smelling love; with your hat penthouse-like over the shop of your eyes, with your arms crossed on your thin-belly doublet like a rabbit on a spit, or your hands in your pocket like a man after the old painting; and keep not long in one tune, but a snip and away. These are compliments, these are humours, these betray nice wenches, that would be betrayed without these; and make them men of note—do you note me?— that most are affected to these.

ARMADO How have you purchased this experience?

MOTH By my penny of observation.

ARMADO But O—but O—

MOTH 'The hobby-horse is forgot.'

ARMADO Call you my love 'hobby-horse'?

MOTH No, master. The hobby-horse is but a colt, (*aside*) and your love perhaps a hackney. (*To him*) But have you forgotten your love?

ARMADO Almost I had.

MOTH Negligent student! Learn her by heart.

ARMADO By heart and in heart, boy.

MOTH And out of heart, master. All those three I will prove.

ARMADO What will you prove?

MOTH A man, if I live; and this 'by', 'in', and 'without', upon the instant. 'By' heart you love her, because your heart cannot come by her; 'in' heart you love her, because your heart is in love with her; and 'out' of heart you love her, being out of heart that you cannot enjoy her.

ARMADO I am all these three.

MOTH And three times as much more, and yet nothing at all.

ARMADO Fetch hither the swain. He must carry for me a letter.

MOTH A message well matched—a horse to be ambassador for an ass.

ARMADO Ha, ha, what say you?

MOTH Sure, sir, you must send the ass upon the horse, for he is very slow-gaited. But I go.

ARMADO The way is but short. Away!

MOTH As swift as lead, sir.

ARMADO The meaning, pretty ingenious? Is not lead a metal heavy, dull, and slow?

MOTH

   Not so, honest master; or rather, master, no.

ARMADO

   I say lead is slow.

MOTH   You are too swift, sir, to say so.
    Is that lead slow which is fired from a gun?
ARMADO Sweet smoke of rhetoric!
    He reputes me a cannon; and the bullet, that's he.
    I shoot you at the swain.
MOTH   Thump then, and I flee.
                                 Exit

ARMADO
    A most acute juvenal, voluble and free of grace!
    By your favour, sweet heaven, I must sigh in your face.
    Most rude melancholy, valour gives you place.
    My herald is returned.

Enter Moth with Costard

MOTH
    A wonder, master! Here's a costard broken in a shin.
ARMADO
    Some enigma, some riddle. Come, your *envoi*[1]—begin.
COSTARD No egma, no riddle, no envoy, no salve in the
    bag, sir! O, sir, plantain, a plain plantain! No envoy, no
    envoy, no salve, sir, but a plantain!
ARMADO By virtue, you enforce laughter; your silly
    thought, my spleen; the heaving of my lungs provokes
    me to ridiculous smiling! O, pardon me, my stars! Does
    the inconsiderate take *salve*[2] for *envoi* and the word
    '*envoi*' for a *salve?*
MOTH Do the wise think them other? Is not envoi a *salve?*
ARMADO
    No, page; it is an epilogue or discourse to make plain
    Some obscure precedence that has tofore been sain. [said].
    I will example it:

---

[1]Message, on conclusion.
[2]i.e., take hail for farewell.

      The fox, the ape, and the humble-bee
      Were still at odds, being but three.
  There's the moral. Now the *envoi*—

MOTH I will add the *envoi*. Say the moral again.

ARMADO
      The fox, the ape, and the humble-bee
      Were still at odds, being but three.

MOTH
      Until the goose came out of door,
      And stayed the odds by adding four.
  Now will I begin your moral, and do you follow with
  my *envoi*.
      The fox, the ape, and the humble-bee
      Were still at odds, being but three.

ARMADO
      Until the goose came out of door,
      Staying the odds by adding four.

MOTH A good *envoi*, ending in the goose. Would you
  desire more?

COSTARD
  The boy has sold him a bargain, a goose, that's flat.
  Sir, your pennyworth is good, if your goose is fat.
  To sell a bargain well is as cunning as fast-and-loose.
  Let me see: a fat *envoi*—ay, that's a fat goose.

ARMADO
  Come hither, come hither. How did this argument begin?

MOTH
  By saying that a costard was broken in a shin.
  Then called you for the *envoi*.

COSTARD True, and I for a plantain—thus came your
  argument in; then the boy's fat *envoi*, the goose that you
  bought—and he ended the market.

ARMADO But tell me, how was there a costard broken in a
  shin?

MOTH I will tell you sensibly.

COSTARD You have no feeling of it, Moth. I will speak
  that envoy:
  I, Costard, running out, that was safely within,
  Fell over the threshold and broke my shin.
ARMADO We will talk no more of this matter.
COSTARD Till there be more matter in the shin.
ARMADO Sir Costard, I will enfranchise you.
COSTARD O, marry me to one Frances! I smell some envoy,
  some goose in this.
ARMADO By my sweet soul, I mean setting you at liberty,
  enfreedoming your person. You were immured, restrained,
  captivated, bound.
COSTARD True, true, and now you will be my purgation
  and let me loose.
ARMADO I give you your liberty, set you from durance,
  and in lieu thereof impose on you nothing but this:
  (*giving Costard a letter*) bear this significant to the
  country maid Jaquenetta. There is remuneration (*giving
  him a coin*), for the best ward of my honour is rewarding
  my dependants. Moth, follow.
MOTH
  Like the sequel, I. Signior Costard, adieu.
                              Exeunt Armado and Moth
COSTARD
  My sweet ounce of man's flesh, my fine jewel!—Now
  will I look to his remuneration. 'Remuneration'! O, that's
  the Latin word for three farthings. Three farthings—
  remuneration. 'What's the price of this tape?' 'One
  penny.' 'No, I'll give you a remuneration.' Why, it carries
  it! 'Remuneration'! Why, it is a fairer name than French
  crown.[3] I will never buy and sell out of this word.

                    Enter Berowne

---

[3]Implying bald head from venereal infection.

BEROWNE My good knave Costard, exceedingly well met.

COSTARD Pray you, sir, how much carnation ribbon may
a man buy for a remuneration?

BEROWNE What is a remuneration?

COSTARD Sure, sir, halfpenny farthing.

BEROWNE Why then, three-farthing worth of silk.

COSTARD I thank your worship. God be with you.

BEROWNE Stay, slave. I must employ you.
    As you will win my favour, good my knave,
    Do one thing for me that I shall entreat.

COSTARD When would you have it done, sir?

BEROWNE This afternoon.

COSTARD Well, I will do it, sir. Fare you well.

BEROWNE You know not what it is.

COSTARD I shall know, sir, when I have done it.

BEROWNE Why, villain, you must know first.

COSTARD I will come to your worship tomorrow morning.

BEROWNE It must be done this afternoon.
    Hark, slave, it is but this:
    The Princess comes to hunt here in the park,
    And in her train there is a gentle lady;
    When tongues speak sweetly, then they name her name,
    And Rosaline they call her. Ask for her,
    And to her white hand see you do commend
    This sealed-up counsel.

He gives Costard a letter

                    There's your guerdon [reward]—go.

He gives him money

COSTARD Guerdon, O sweet guerdon! Better than
remuneration—elevenpence farthing better. Most
sweet guerdon! I will do it, sir, in print. Guerdon!
Remuneration!   *Exit*

BEROWNE
   And I, in truth, in love!
   I, that have been love's whip,
   A very beadle to a humorous sigh,
   A critic, nay, a night-watch constable,
   A domineering pedant over the boy,
   Than whom no mortal so magnificent!
   This wimpled, whining, purblind, wayward boy,
   This Signior Junior, giant-dwarf, Dan Cupid,
   Regent of love-rhymes, lord of folded arms,
   The anointed sovereign of sighs and groans,
   Liege of all loiterers and malcontents,
   Dread prince of skirts, king of codpieces,
   Sole imperator and great general
   Of trotting censors—O my little heart!
   And I to be a corporal of his field,
   And wear his colours like a tumbler's hoop!
   What? I love? I sue? I seek a wife?
   A woman, that is like a German clock;
   Still a-repairing, ever out of frame,
   And never going aright, being a watch,
   But being watched that it may still go right!
   Nay, to be perjured, which is worst of all;
   And among three to love the worst of all—
   A whitely wanton with a velvet brow,
   With two pitch-balls stuck in her face for eyes;
   Ay, and, by heaven, one that will do the deed
   Though Argus were her eunuch and her guard!
   And I to sigh for her, to watch for her,
   To pray for her! Go to, it is a plague
   That Cupid will impose for my neglect
   Of his almighty dreadful little might.
   Well, I will love, write, sigh, pray, sue, and groan;
   Some men must love my lady, and some Joan.   *Exit*

Act IV

SCENE I
The same.

Enter the Princess, Rosaline, Maria, Katharine, Boyet, two
more Lords, and a Forester

PRINCESS
    Was that the King that spurred his horse so hard
    Against the steep-up rising of the hill?

FIRST LORD
    I know not, but I think it was not he.

PRINCESS
    Whoever he was, he showed a mounting mind.
    Well, lords, today we shall have our dispatch;
    On Saturday we will return to France.
    Then, forester, my friend, where is the bush
    That we must stand and play the murderer in?

FORESTER
    Hereby, upon the edge of yonder coppice;
    A stand where you may make the fairest shoot.

PRINCESS
    I thank my beauty, I am fair that shoot,
    And thereupon you speak 'the fairest shoot'.

FORESTER
    Pardon me, madam, for I meant not so.

PRINCESS
    What, what? First praise me, and again say no?
    O short-lived pride! Not fair? Alas for woe!

FORESTER
    Yes, madam, fair.

PRINCESS   Nay, never paint me now!
   Where fair is not, praise cannot mend the brow.
   Here, good my glass, take this for telling true;

                  (She gives him money)

   Fair payment for foul words is more than due.
FORESTER
   Nothing but fair is that which you inherit.
PRINCESS
   See, see, my beauty will be saved by merit!
   O heresy in fair, fit for these days!
   A giving hand, though foul, shall have fair praise.
   But come, the bow! Now mercy goes to kill,
   And shooting well is then accounted ill.
   Thus will I save my credit in the shoot:
   Not wounding, pity would not let me do't;
   If wounding, then it was to show my skill,
   That more for praise than purpose meant to kill.
   And out of question so it is sometimes;
   Glory grows guilty of detested crimes,
   When, for fame's sake, for praise, an outward part,
   We bend to that the working of the heart.
   As I for praise alone now seek to spill
   The poor deer's blood, that my heart means no ill.
BOYET
   Do not curst wives hold that self-sovereignty
   Only for praise' sake, when they strive to be
   Lords over their lords?
PRINCESS
   Only for praise, and praise we may afford
   To any lady that subdues a lord.

                Enter Costard

BOYET Here comes a member of the commonwealth.

COSTARD Good even all! Pray you, which is the head
    lady?

PRINCESS You shall know her, fellow, by the rest that have
    no heads.

COSTARD Which is the greatest lady, the highest?

PRINCESS The thickest and the tallest.

COSTARD The thickest and the tallest! It is so—truth is
    truth.

  If your waist, mistress, were as slender as my wit,
    One of these maids' girdles for your waist should be fit.
  Are not you the chief woman? You are the thickest here.

PRINCESS What's your will, sir? What's your will?

COSTARD I have a letter from Monsieur Berowne to one
    Lady Rosaline.

PRINCESS

  O, your letter, your letter! He's a good friend of mine.
  Stand aside, good bearer. Boyet, you can carve—
  Break up this capon.

BOYET   I am bound to serve.

He reads

  This letter is mistaken, it imports none here.
  It is written to Jaquenetta.

PRINCESS   We will read it, I swear.

  Break the neck of the wax, and everyone give ear.

BOYET (*reading*) *By heaven, that you are fair is most
    infallible; true that you are beauteous; truth itself that
    you are lovely. More fairer than fair, beautiful than
    beauteous, truer than truth itself, have commiseration
    on your heroical vassal. The magnanimous and most
    illustrate King Cophetua set eye upon the pernicious
    and most indubitate beggar Zenelophon, and he it was
    that might rightly say Veni, vidi, vici; which to anatomize
    in the vulgar—O base and obscure vulgar!—namely, he*

came, see, and overcame. He came, one; see, two;
overcame, three. Who came? The king. Why did he
come? To see. Why did he see? To overcome. To whom
came he? To the beggar. What saw he? The beggar. Who
overcame he? The beggar. The conclusion is victory. On
whose side? The king's. The captive is enriched. On
whose side? The beggar's. The catastrophe is a nuptial.
On whose side? The king's. No; on both in one, or one
in both. I am the king, for so stands the comparison,
you the beggar, for so witnesses your lowliness. Shall I
command your love? I may. Shall I enforce your love? I
could. Shall I entreat your love? I will. What shall you
exchange for rags? Robes. For tittles? Titles. For yourself?
Me. Thus, expecting your reply, I profane my lips on
your foot, my eyes on your picture, and my heart on
your every part.

Yours in the dearest design of industry,
Don Adriano de Armado

Thus do you hear the Nemean lion roar
Against you, lamb, that stand as his prey.
Submissive fall his princely feet before,
And he from forage will incline to play.
But if you strive, poor soul, what are you then?
Food for his rage, repasture for his den.

PRINCESS

What plume of feathers is he that indited this letter?
What vane? What weathercock? Did you ever hear better?

BOYET

I am much deceived but I remember the style.

PRINCESS

Else your memory is bad, going over it erewhile.

BOYET

This Armado is a Spaniard that keeps here in Court;
A phantasm, a Monarcho, and one that makes sport
To the prince and his book-mates.

PRINCESS   You, fellow, a word.
Who gave you this letter?

COSTARD   I told you; my lord.
   PRINCESS
To whom should you give it?
COSTARD   From my lord to my lady.
PRINCESS
From which lord to which lady?
COSTARD
From my Lord Berowne, a good master of mine,
To a lady of France that he called Rosaline.
PRINCESS
You have mistaken his letter. Come, lords, away.

(*To Rosaline*)

Here, sweet, put up this; 'twill be yours another day.
   Exeunt all except Boyet, Rosaline, Maria, and Costard
BOYET
Who is the suitor? Who is the suitor?
ROSALINE   Shall I teach you to know?
BOYET
Ay, my continent of beauty.
ROSALINE   Why, she that bears the bow.
   Finely put off!
BOYET
My lady goes to kill horns, but, if you marry,
Hang me by the neck if horns that year miscarry.
   Finely put on!
ROSALINE
Well then, I am the shooter.
BOYET   And who is your deer?
ROSALINE
If we choose by the horns, yourself. Come not near.
   Finely put on indeed!
MARIA
You still wrangle with her, Boyet, and she strikes at the
   brow.

BOYET

But she herself is hit lower. Have I hit her now?

ROSALINE Shall I come upon you with an old saying that
was a man when King Pepin of France was a little boy,
as touching the hit it?

BOYET If I may answer you with one as old, that was a
woman when Queen Guinevere of Britain was a little
wench, as touching the hit it.

ROSALINE

You can not hit it, hit it, hit it,
    You can not hit it, my good man.

BOYET

If I cannot, cannot, cannot,
    If I cannot, another can.

Exit Rosaline

COSTARD

By my word, most pleasant! How both did fit it!

MARIA

A mark marvellous well shot, for they both did hit it.

BOYET

A mark! O, mark but that mark! 'A mark', says my lady!
Let the mark have a prick in it, to aim at if it may be.

MARIA

Wide of the bow hand! In faith, your hand is out.

COSTARD

Indeed, he must shoot nearer, or he'll never hit the clout
    [Mark].

BOYET

If my hand is out, then perhaps your hand is in.

COSTARD

Then will she get the upshot by cleaving the pin.

MARIA

Come, come, you talk greasily; your lips grow foul.

COSTARD

She's too hard for you at pricks, sir. Challenge her to
bowl.

BOYET
  I fear too much rubbing. Good night, my good owl.
                            Exeunt Boyet and Maria
COSTARD
  By my soul, a swain, a most simple clown!
  Lord, Lord, how the ladies and I have put him down!
  On my word, most sweet jests, most fine vulgar wit;
  When it comes so smoothly off, so obscenely as it were,
    so fit.
  Armado to the one side—O, a most dainty man!
  To see him walk before a lady, and to bear her fan!
  To see him kiss his hand, and how most sweetly he will
    swear!
  And his page on the other side, that handful of wit!
  Ah, heavens, it is a most pathetical nit!

                Shout within

  Sola, sola!   *Exit*

SCENE II
The same.

Enter Holofernes, Sir Nathaniel, and Dull

SIR NATHANIEL Very reverend sport, truly, and done in
  the testimony of a good conscience.
HOLOFERNES The deer was, as you know, in *sanguis*, blood;
  ripe as the pearmain, which now hangs like a jewel in
  the ear of *caelum*, the sky, the welkin, the heaven, and
  anon falls like a crabapple on the face of *terra*, the soil,
  the land, the earth.
SIR NATHANIEL Truly, Master Holofernes, the epithets are
  sweetly varied, like a scholar at the least; but, sir, I
  assure you it was a buck of the first head.

HOLOFERNES Sir Nathaniel, *haud credo.* [I think not]

DULL 'Twas not an aud grey doe, 'twas a pricket.[1]

HOLOFERNES Most barbarous intimation! Yet a kind of
insinuation, as it were, *in via,* in way, of explication;
facere, as it were, replication, or, rather, *ostentare,* to
show, as it were, his inclination—after his undressed,
unpolished, uneducated, unpruned, untrained, or, rather,
unlettered, or, ratherest, unconfirmed fashion—to insert
again my *haud credo* for a deer.

DULL I said the deer was not an aud grey doe, 'twas a
pricket.

HOLOFERNES Twice-sodden simplicity! *Bis coctus!* [twice
cooked]

O you monster Ignorance, how deformed do you look!

SIR NATHANIEL

Sir, he has never fed of the dainties that are bred in a book.

He has not eaten paper, as it were; he has not drunk

ink. His intellect is not replenished. He is only an

animal, only sensible in the duller parts.

And such barren plants are set before us that we thankful
should be—

Which we of taste and feeling are—for those parts that
do fructify in us more than he.

For as it would ill become me to be vain, indiscreet, or a
fool,

If were there an ass set on learning, to see him in a
school.

But *omne bene,* [all's well] say I, being of an old father's
mind;

Many can brook the weather that love not the wind.

DULL

You two are book-men—can you tell me by your wit

What was a month old at Cain's birth that's not five
weeks old as yet?

---

[1]Buck of the second year.

HOLOFERNES Dictynna, goodman Dull. Dictynna, goodman Dull.

DULL What is Dictima?

SIR NATHANIEL A title to Phoebe, to Luna, to the moon.

HOLOFERNES

The moon was a month old when Adam was no more,
And reached not to five weeks when he came to five-score.
The allusion holds in the exchange.

DULL 'Tis true, indeed; the collusion holds in the exchange.

HOLOFERNES God comfort your capacity! I say the allusion holds in the exchange.

DULL And I say the pollution holds in the exchange, for the moon is never but a month old; and I say beside that 'twas a pricket that the Princess killed.

HOLOFERNES Sir Nathaniel, will you hear an extemporal epitaph on the death of the deer? And, to humour the ignorant, call I the deer the Princess killed a pricket.

SIR NATHANIEL *Perge* [proceed], good Master Holofernes, *perge*, so it shall please you to abrogate scurrility.

HOLOFERNES I will something affect the letter, for it argues facility.

The preyful Princess pierced and pricked a pretty pleasing pricket;
Some say a sore,[2] but not a sore till now made sore with shooting.
The dogs did yell; put 'L' to sore, then sorel[3] jumps from thicket;
Or pricket, sore, or else sorel; the people fall a-hooting.
If sore be sore, then 'L' to sore makes fifty sores o'sorel:
Of one sore I a hundred make, by adding but one more 'L'.

SIR NATHANIEL A rare talent!

---

[2]A buck of the fourth year.
[3]A buck of the third year.

DULL If a talent [talon] is a claw, look how he claws him with a talent.

HOLOFERNES This is a gift that I have; simple, simple; a foolish extravagant spirit, full of forms, figures, shapes, objects, ideas, apprehensions, motions, revolutions. These are begot in the ventricle of memory, nourished in the womb of *pia mater* [the brain], and delivered upon the mellowing of occasion. But the gift is good in those in whom it is acute, and I am thankful for it.

SIR NATHANIEL Sir, I praise the Lord for you, and so may my parishioners, for their sons are well tutored by you, and their daughters profit very greatly under you. You are a good member of the commonwealth.

HOLOFERNES *Mehercle!* [By Hercules] If their sons are ingenious, they shall want no instruction; if their daughters are capable, I will put it to them. But *vir sapit qui pauca loquitur.* [It's a wise man who says little.] A soul feminine salutes us.

Enter Jaquenetta and Costard

JAQUENETTA God give you good morrow, Master Parson.

HOLOFERNES Master Parson—*quasi* pierce-one? If one should be pierced, which is the one?

COSTARD Sure, Master Schoolmaster, he that is likest to a hogshead.

HOLOFERNES Piercing a hogshead! A good lustre of conceit in a turf of earth, fire enough for a flint, pearl enough for a swine. 'Tis pretty; it is well.

JAQUENETTA Good Master Parson, be so good as read me this letter. It was given me by Costard, and sent me from Don Armado. I beseech you, read it.

HOLOFERNES

> *Fauste precor gelida quando pecus omne sub umbra*
> *   Ruminat—*[4]

and so forth. Ah, good old Mantuan, I may speak of you
as the traveller does of Venice:

> *Venetia, Venetia,*
> *Che non te vede, non te pretia.*[5]

Old Mantuan, old Mantuan! Who understands you
not, loves you not. *(He sings)* Ut, re, sol, la, mi, fa.—Under
pardon, sir, what are the contents? Or, rather, as Horace
says in his—What, my soul, verses?

SIR NATHANIEL Ay, sir, and very learned.

HOLOFERNES Let me hear a stave, a stanza, a verse. *Lege,*
domine. [Read, master]

SIR NATHANIEL *(reading)*

> *If love makes me forsworn, how shall I swear to love?*
> *   Ah, never faith could hold if not to beauty vowed!*
> *Though to myself forsworn, to you I'll faithful prove;*
> *   Those thoughts to me were oaks, to you like osiers*
> *   bowed.*
> *Study his bias leaves and makes his book your eyes,*
> *   Where all those pleasures live that art would*
> *   comprehend.*
> *If knowledge is the mark, to know you shall suffice:*
> *   Well learnèd is that tongue that well can you*
> *   commend,*
> *All ignorant that soul that sees you without wonder;*
> *   Which is to me some praise, that I your parts admire.*
> *Your eye Jove's lightning bears, your voice his dreadful*
> *   thunder,*
> *   Which, not to anger bent, is music and sweet fire.*

---

[4]Faustus, I pray when all the herd chew the cud in the
shade . . .
[5]Who sees you not does not prize you.

Celestial as you are, O, pardon love this wrong,
That sings heaven's praise with such an earthly tongue!
HOLOFERNES You find not the apostrophe, and so miss
the accent. Let me supervise the canzonet.

He takes the letter

Here are only numbers ratified; but, for the elegancy,
facility, and golden cadence of poesy, *caret.* [It is wanting]
Ovidius Naso was the man; and why indeed 'Naso' but
for smelling out the odoriferous flowers of fancy, the
jerks of invention? *Imitari* [to imitate] is nothing. So
does the hound its master, the ape its keeper, the tired
horse its rider. But, damosella virgin, was this directed
to you?
JAQUENETTA Ay, sir, from one Monsieur Boyet, one of the
strange Queen's lords.
HOLOFERNES I will overglance the superscript: (*reading*)
To the snow-white hand of the most beauteous Lady
Rosaline. I will look again on the intellect of the letter,
for the nomination of the party writing to the person
written unto: *Your ladyship's, in all desired employment,*
Berowne. Sir Nathaniel, this Berowne is one of the
votaries with the King; and here he has framed a letter
to a sequent of the stranger Queen's, which accidentally,
or by the way of progression, has miscarried. Trip and
go, my sweet; deliver this paper into the royal hand of the
King; it may concern much. Stay not your compliment;
I forgive your duty. Adieu.
JAQUENETTA Good Costard, go with me. Sir, God save
your life.
COSTARD Have with you, my girl.
                              Exeunt Costard and Jaquenetta
SIR NATHANIEL Sir, you have done this in the fear of God,
very religiously; and as a certain father saith—

HOLOFERNES Sir, tell not me of the father, I do fear dubious excuses. But to return to the verses: did they please you, Sir Nathaniel?

SIR NATHANIEL Marvellous well for the pen.

HOLOFERNES I do dine today at the father's of a certain pupil of mine; where, if before repast it shall please you to gratify the table with a grace, I will, on my privilege I have with the parents of the foresaid child or pupil, undertake your *ben venuto* [welcome]; where I will prove those verses to be very unlearned, neither savouring of poetry, wit, nor invention. I beseech your society.

SIR NATHANIEL And thank you too, for society—says the text—is the happiness of life.

HOLOFERNES And, certain, the text most infallibly concludes it. (*To Dull*) Sir, I do invite you too; you shall not say me nay. *Pauca verba.* [in short] Away! The gentlefolk are at their game, and we will to our recreation.

Exeunt

SCENE III
The same.

Enter Berowne with a paper alone

BEROWNE (*reading*)
The King he is hunting the deer;
  I am coursing myself—
They have pitched a toil; I am toiling in a pitch—pitch that defiles. 'Defile'—a foul word! Well, set you down, sorrow, for so they say the fool said, and so say I—and I the fool. Well proved, wit! By the Lord, this love is as mad as Ajax: it kills sheep, it kills me—I a sheep. Well proved again on my side! I will not love; if I do, hang me! In faith, I will not. O, but her eye! By this light, but for her eye I would not love her—yes, for her two eyes.

Well, I do nothing in the world but lie, and lie in my throat. By heaven, I do love, and it has taught me to rhyme, and to be melancholy; and here is part of my rhyme, and here my melancholy. Well, she has one of my sonnets already. The clown bore it, the fool sent it, and the lady has it—sweet clown, sweeter fool, sweetest lady! By the world, I would not care a pin if the other three were in. Here comes one with a paper. God give him grace to groan!

He stands aside
Enter the King with a paper

KING Ay me!
BEROWNE Shot, by heaven! Proceed, sweet Cupid. You have thumped him with your arrow under the left pap. In faith, secrets!
KING (*reading*)
So sweet a kiss the golden sun gives not
  To those fresh morning drops upon the rose,
As your eye-beams when their fresh rays have smote
  The night of dew that on my cheeks down flows.
Nor shines the silver moon one half so bright
  Through the transparent bosom of the deep
As does your face, through tears of mine, give light.
  You shine in every tear that I do weep;
No drop but as a coach does carry thee.
  So ride you triumphing in my woe.
Do but behold the tears that swell in me,
  And they your glory through my grief will show.
But do not love yourself; then you will keep
My tears for glasses and still make me weep.
O queen of queens, how far do you excel,
No thought can think, nor tongue of mortal tell!
How shall she know my griefs? I'll drop the paper.
Sweet leaves, shade folly. Who is he comes here?

He stands aside
Enter Longaville

What, Longaville, and reading! Listen, ear!
BEROWNE
  Now, in your likeness, one more fool appear!
LONGAVILLE Ay me, I am forsworn!
BEROWNE Why, he comes in like a perjurer, wearing papers.
KING
  In love, I hope—sweet fellowship in shame!
BEROWNE
  One drunkard loves another of the name.
LONGAVILLE
  Am I the first that have been perjured so?
BEROWNE
  I could put you in comfort—not by two that I know.
  You make the triumvirate, the corner-cap of society,
  The shape of Love's Tyburn, that hangs up simplicity.
LONGAVILLE
  I fear these stubborn lines lack power to move.
  (*Reading*) O sweet Maria, empress of my love!—
  These numbers will I tear, and write in prose.
BEROWNE
  O, rhymes are guards on wanton Cupid's hose;
  Disfigure not his shop.
LONGAVILLE
                This same shall go:

(*Reading*)

Did not the heavenly rhetoric of your eye,
    Against whom the world cannot hold argument,
Persuade my heart to this false perjury?
    Vows for you broken deserve not punishment.
A woman I forswore, but I will prove—
    You being a goddess—I forswore not thee.

My vow was earthly, you a heavenly love;
*   Your grace, being gained, cures all disgrace in me.*
Vows are but breath, and breath a vapour is;
*   Then you, fair sun, which on my earth do shine,*
Exhale this vapour-vow; in you it is.
*   If broken, then, it is no fault of mine;*
If by me broken what fool is not so wise
To lose an oath to win a paradise?

BEROWNE
This is the liver vein, which makes flesh a deity,
A green goose a goddess. Pure, pure idolatry.
God amend us, God amend! We are much out of the way.

Enter Dumaine

LONGAVILLE
By whom shall I send this?—Company? Stay.

He stands aside

BEROWNE
All hid, all hid—an old infant play.
Like a demi-god here sit I in the sky,
And wretched fools' secrets heedfully over-eye.
More sacks to the mill! O heavens, I have my wish!
Dumaine transformed! Four woodcocks in a dish!
DUMAINE O most divine Kate!
BEROWNE O most profane coxcomb!
DUMAINE
By heaven, the wonder in a mortal eye!
BEROWNE
By earth, she is not, corporal. There you lie!
DUMAINE
Her amber hairs for foul has amber quoted.
BEROWNE
An amber-coloured raven was well noted.

DUMAINE
   As upright as the cedar.
BEROWNE   Stoop, I say!
   Her shoulder is with child.
DUMAINE   As fair as day.
BEROWNE
   Ay, as some days; but then no sun must shine.
DUMAINE
   O that I had my wish!
LONGAVILLE   And I had mine!
KING
   And I mine too, good Lord!
BEROWNE
   Amen, so I had mine! Is not that a good word?
DUMAINE
   I would forget her, but a fever she
   Reigns in my blood, and will remembered be.
BEROWNE
   A fever in your blood? Why, then incision
   Would let her out in saucers. Sweet misprision!
      [mistaking]
DUMAINE
   Once more I'll read the ode that I have writ.
BEROWNE
   Once more I'll mark how love can vary wit.
DUMAINE *(reading)*
   On a day—alas the day!—
   Love, whose month is ever May,
   Spied a blossom passing fair
   Playing in the wanton air.
   Through the velvet leaves the wind,
   All unseen, can passage find;
   That the lover, sick to death,
   Wished himself the heaven's breath.
   Air, said he, your cheeks may blow;

Air, would I might triumph so!
But, alas, my hand is sworn
Never to pluck you from your thorn.
Vow, alas, for youth unmeet,
Youth so apt to pluck a sweet!
Do not call it sin in me,
That I am forsworn for thee;
You for whom Jove would swear
Juno but an Ethiope were,
And deny himself for Jove,
Turning mortal for your love.
This will I send, and something else more plain,
That shall express my true love's fasting pain.
O, would the King, Berowne, and Longaville
Were lovers too! Ill, to example ill,
Would from my forehead wipe a perjured note,
For none offends where all alike do dote.

LONGAVILLE (*advancing*)
Dumaine, your love is far from charity,
That in love's grief desire society.
You may look pale, but I should blush, I know,
To be overheard and taken napping so.

KING
Come, sir, you blush! As his your case is such;
You chide at him, offending twice as much.
You do not love Maria! Longaville
Did never sonnet for her sake compile,
Nor ever lay his wreathèd arms athwart
His loving bosom to keep down his heart.
I have been closely shrouded in this bush
And marked you both, and for you both did blush.
I heard your guilty rhymes, observed your fashion,
Saw sighs reek from you, noted well your passion.
'Ay me!' says one; 'O Jove!' the other cries.
One, her hairs were gold; crystal the other's eyes.

(*To Longaville*)

You would for paradise break faith and troth;

(*To Dumaine*)

And Jove, for your love, would infringe an oath.
What will Berowne say when he shall hear
Faith infringèd, which such zeal did swear?
How will he scorn, how will he spend his wit!
How will he triumph, leap, and laugh at it!
For all the wealth that ever I did see,
I would not have him know so much by me.

BEROWNE
Now step I forth to whip hypocrisy.
Ah, good my liege, I pray you pardon me.
Good heart, what grace have you, thus to reprove
These worms for loving, that are most in love?
Your eyes do make no coaches; in your tears
There is no certain princess that appears;
You'll not be perjured, 'tis a hateful thing;
Tush, none but minstrels like of sonneting!
But are you not ashamed? Nay, are you not,
All three of you, to be thus much overshot?
You found his mote, the King your mote did see;
But I a beam do find in each of three.
O, what a scene of foolery have I seen,
Of sighs, of groans, of sorrow, and of teen! [woe]
O me, with what strict patience have I sat,
To see a king transformèd to a gnat!
To see great Hercules whipping a gig, [top]
And profound Solomon to tune a jig,
And Nestor play at push-pin with the boys,
And critic Timon laugh at idle toys!
Where lies your grief? O, tell me, good Dumaine.
And, gentle Longaville, where lies your pain?

And where my liege's? All about the breast.
A caudle,[6] ho!
KING   Too bitter is your jest.
Are we betrayed thus to your over-view?
BEROWNE
Not you to me, but I betrayed by you;
I that am honest, I that hold it sin
To break the vow I am engagèd in,
I am betrayed by keeping company
With men like you, men of inconstancy.
When shall you see me write a thing in rhyme?
Or groan for Joan? Or spend a minute's time
In pruning me? When shall you hear that I
Will praise a hand, a foot, a face, an eye,
A gait, a state, a brow, a breast, a waist,
A leg, a limb—
KING   Soft! Whither away so fast?
A true man or a thief that gallops so?
BEROWNE
I post from love. Good lover, let me go.

Enter Jaquenetta and Costard

JAQUENETTA
God bless the King!
KING   What present have you there?
COSTARD
Some certain treason.
KING   What makes treason here?
COSTARD
Nay, it makes nothing, sir.
KING   If it mars nothing either,
The treason and you go in peace away together.

---
[6]Warm gruel.

JAQUENETTA
I beseech your grace let this letter be read.
Our parson misdoubts it; 'twas treason, he said.
KING Berowne, read it over.

(To Jaquenetta)

Where had you it?
JAQUENETTA Of Costard.
KING Where had you it?
COSTARD Of Dun Adramadio, Dun Adramadio.

Berowne tears the letter

KING
How now, what is in you? Why do you tear it?
BEROWNE
A toy, my liege, a toy. Your grace needs not fear it.
LONGAVILLE
It did move him to passion, and therefore let's hear it.
DUMAINE (picks up the pieces)
It is Berowne's writing, and here is his name.
BEROWNE (to Costard)
Ah, you bloody blockhead, you were born to do me shame!
Guilty, my lord, guilty! I confess, I confess!
KING
What?
BEROWNE
That you three fools lacked me fool to make up the mess.
He, he, and you—and you, my liege!—and I,
Are pick-purses in love, and we deserve to die.
O, dismiss this audience, and I shall tell you more.
DUMAINE
Now the number is even.
BEROWNE   True, true, we are four.
Will these turtles be gone?

KING   Hence, sirs, away!
COSTARD
  Walk aside the true folk, and let the traitors stay.
                    Exeunt Costard and Jaquenetta
BEROWNE
  Sweet lords, sweet lovers, O, let us embrace!
    As true we are as flesh and blood can be.
  The sea will ebb and flow, heaven show his face;
    Young blood does not obey an old decree.
  We cannot cross the cause why we were born;
  Therefore of all hands must we be forsworn.
KING
  What, did these rent lines show some love of thine?
BEROWNE
  'Did they?' say you! Who sees the heavenly Rosaline
  That, like a rude and savage man of Inde
    At the first opening of the gorgeous east,
  Bows not his vassal head and, stricken blind,
    Kisses the base ground with obedient breast?
  What pèremptory eagle-sighted eye
    Dares look upon the heaven of her brow
  That is not blinded by her majesty?
KING
    What zeal, what fury has inspired you now?
  My love, her mistress, is a gracious moon;
    She, an attending star, scarce seen a light.
BEROWNE
  My eyes are then no eyes, nor I Berowne.
    O, but for my love, day would turn to night!
  Of all complexions the culled sovereignty
    Do meet as at a fair in her fair cheek,
  Where several worthies make one dignity,
    Where nothing wants that want itself does seek.
  Lend me the flourish of all gentle tongues—
    Fie, painted rhetoric! O, she needs it not!

To things of sale a seller's praise belongs:
    She passes praise; then praise too short does blot.
A withered hermit, five-score winters worn,
    Might shake off fifty, looking in her eye.
Beauty does varnish age, as if new-born,
    And gives the crutch the cradle's infancy.
O, 'tis the sun that makes all things shine!

KING

By heaven, your love is black as ebony!

BEROWNE

Is ebony like her? O wood divine!
    A wife of such wood were felicity.
O, who can give an oath? Where is a book?
    That I may swear beauty does beauty lack
If now she learns not of her eye to look.
    No face is fair that is not full so black.

KING

O paradox! Black is the badge of hell,
    The hue of dungeons, and the school of night;
And beauty's crest becomes the heavens well.

BEROWNE

    Devils soonest tempt, resembling spirits of light.
O, if in black my lady's brows be decked,
    It mourns that painting and usurping hair
Should ravish doters with a false aspèct;
    And therefore is she born to make black fair.
Her favour turns the fashion of the days,
    For native blood is counted painting now;
And therefore red, that would avoid dispraise,
    Paints itself black, to imitate her brow.

DUMAINE

To look like her are chimney-sweepers black.

LONGAVILLE

    And since her time are colliers counted bright.

KING

And Ethiopes of their sweet complexion crack.

DUMAINE
    Dark needs no candles now, for dark is light.
BEROWNE
  Your mistresses dare never come in rain,
    For fear their colours should be washed away.
KING
    'Twere good yours did; for, sir, to tell you plain,
    I'll find a fairer face not washed today.
BEROWNE
  I'll prove her fair, or talk till doomsday here.
KING
    No devil will fright you then so much as she.
DUMAINE
  I never knew man hold vile stuff so dear.
LONGAVILLE
    Look, here's your love; my foot and her face see.
BEROWNE
  O, if the streets were pavèd with your eyes,
    Her feet were much too dainty for such tread.
DUMAINE
  O, vile! Then, as she goes, what upward lies
    The street should see as she walked overhead.
KING
  But what of this? Are we not all in love?
BEROWNE
    O, nothing so sure, and thereby all forsworn.
KING
    Then leave this chat, and, good Berowne, now prove
    Our loving lawful and our faith not torn.
DUMAINE
  Ay, indeed, there; some flattery for this evil!
LONGAVILLE
    O, some authority how to proceed!
  Some tricks, some quillets, how to cheat the devil!
DUMAINE
    Some salve for perjury.

BEROWNE   'Tis more than need.
  Have at you then, affection's men-at-arms!
  Consider what you first did swear unto:
  To fast, to study, and to see no woman—
  Flat treason against the kingly state of youth.
  Say, can you fast? Your stomachs are too young,
  And abstinence engenders maladies.
  O, we have made a vow to study, lords,
  And in that vow we have forsworn our books;
  For when would you, my liege, or you, or you,
  In leaden contemplation have found out
  Such fiery numbers as the prompting eyes
  Of beauty's tutors have enriched you with?
  Other slow arts entirely keep the brain,
  And therefore, finding barren practisers,
  Scarce show a harvest of their heavy toil.
  But love, first learnèd in a lady's eyes,
  Lives not alone immurèd in the brain,
  But with the motion of all elements
  Courses as swift as thought in every power,
  And gives to every power a double power,
  Above their functions and their offices.
  It adds a precious seeing to the eye:
  A lover's eyes will gaze an eagle blind.
  A lover's ear will hear the lowest sound
  When the suspicious head of theft is stopped.
  Love's feeling is more soft and sensible
  Than are the tender horns of cockled snails.
  Love's tongue proves dainty Bacchus gross in taste.
  For valour, is not Love a Hercules,
  Still climbing trees in the Hesperides?
  Subtle as Sphinx; as sweet and musical
  As bright Apollo's lute, strung with his hair.
  And when Love speaks, the voice of all the gods
  Make heaven drowsy with the harmony.
  Never durst poet touch a pen to write

Until his ink was tempered with Love's sighs.
O, then his lines would ravish savage ears
And plant in tyrants mild humility.
From women's eyes this doctrine I derive:
They sparkle still the right Promethean fire;
They are the books, the arts, the academes,
That show, contain, and nourish all the world;
Else none at all in aught proves excellent.
Then fools you were these women to forswear,
Or, keeping what is sworn, you will prove fools.
For wisdom's sake, a word that all men love,
Or for love's sake, a word that loves all men,
Or for men's sake, the authors of these women,
Or women's sake, by whom we men are men—
Let us once lose our oaths to find ourselves,
Or else we lose ourselves to keep our oaths.
It is religion to be thus forsworn,
For charity itself fulfils the law,
And who can sever love from charity?

KING
Saint Cupid, then! And, soldiers, to the field!

BEROWNE
Advance your standards, and upon them, lords!
Pell-mell, down with them! But be first advised
In conflict that you get the sun of them.

LONGAVILLE
Now to plain-dealing. Lay these glosses by.
Shall we resolve to woo these girls of France?

KING
And win them too! Therefore let us devise
Some entertainment for them in their tents.

BEROWNE
First from the park let us conduct them thither;
Then homeward every man attach the hand
Of his fair mistress. In the afternoon
We will with some strange pastime solace them,

Such as the shortness of the time can shape;
For revels, dances, masques, and merry hours
Forerun fair Love, strewing her way with flowers.
KING
Away, away! No time shall be omitted
That will betime and may by us be fitted
BEROWNE
Allons! Allons! [*Let us go!*]
                    Exeunt King, Longaville, and Dumaine
          Sowed cockle reaped no corn,
And justice always whirls in equal measure.
Light wenches may prove plagues to men forsworn;
If so, our copper buys no better treasure.   *Exit*

Act V

SCENE I
The same.

Enter Holofernes, Sir Nathaniel, and Dull

HOLOFERNES *Satis quod sufficit.* [Enough is enough.]

SIR NATHANIEL I praise God for you, sir. Your reasons at dinner have been sharp and sententious, pleasant without scurrility, witty without affectation, audacious without impudency, learned without bias, and strange without heresy. I did converse this *quondam* [former] day with a companion of the King's, who is entitled, nominated, or called Don Adriano de Armado.

HOLOFERNES *Novi hominem tanquam te.*[1] His humour is lofty, his discourse peremptory, his tongue refined, his eye ambitious, his gait majestical, and his general behaviour vain, ridiculous, and boastful. He is too fine, too spruce, too affected, too odd, as it were, too peregrinate, as I may call it.

SIR NATHANIEL A most singular and choice epithet.

He draws out his table-book

HOLOFERNES He draws out the thread of his verbosity finer than the staple of his argument. I abhor such fanatical phantasms, such unsociable and precise companions, such rackers of orthography, as to speak 'dout' *sine* [without] 'b', when he should say 'doubt', 'det' when he should pronounce 'debt'—d, e, b, t, not d,

---

[1] I know the man as well as I know you.

e, t. He calls a calf 'cauf', half 'hauf'; neighbour *vocatur* [is called] 'nebour', neigh abbreviated 'ne'. This is abhominable, which he would call 'abominable'. It insinuates me of insanity. *Ne intelligis, domine?* [You understand, sir?] To make frantic, lunatic.

SIR NATHANIEL *Laus Deo, bone intelligo.* [Thank God, I understand good]

HOLOFERNES *Bone?* 'Bone' for *'bene'!* Priscian a little scratched; it will serve.

Enter Armado, Moth, and Costard

SIR NATHANIEL *Videsne quis venit?* [Do you see who comes?]

HOLOFERNES *Video et gaudeo.* [I see and am glad]

ARMADO Chirrah!

HOLOFERNES *Quare* [why] 'chirrah', not 'sirrah'?

ARMADO Men of peace, well encountered.

HOLOFERNES Most military sir, salutation.

MOTH *(to Costard)* They have been at a great feast of languages and stolen the scraps.

COSTARD *(to Moth)* O, they have lived long on the almsbasket of words! I marvel your master has not eaten you for a word, for you are not so long by the head as *honorificabilitudinitatibus.*[2] You are easier swallowed than a pip.

MOTH Peace! The peal begins.

ARMADO *(to Holofernes)* Monsieur, are you not lettered?

MOTH Yes, yes! He teaches boys the horn-book. What is a, b, spelt backward with the horn on its head?

HOLOFERNES Ba, *pueritia,* [childishness] with a horn added.

---

[2] A nonsense coinage meaning roughly by the capabilities of being honoured.

MOTH Ba, most silly sheep with a horn. You hear his learning.

HOLOFERNES *Quis,* [who] *quis,* you consonant?

MOTH The last of the five vowels, if you repeat them; or the fifth, if I.

HOLOFERNES I will repeat them: a, e, i—

MOTH The sheep. The other two concludes it—o, u.

ARMADO Now, by the salt wave of the Mediterranean, a sweet touch, a quick venue of wit! Snip, snap, quick and home! It rejoices my intellect. True wit!

MOTH Offered by a child to an old man—which is witold.

HOLOFERNES What is the figure? What is the figure?

MOTH Horns.

HOLOFERNES You dispute like an infant. Go whip your top.

MOTH Lend me your horn to make one, and I will whip about your infamy, a top of a cuckold's horn!

COSTARD If I had but one penny in the world, you should have it to buy gingerbread. Hold, there is the very remuneration I had of your master, you halfpenny purse of wit, you pigeon-egg of discretion. O, if the heavens were so pleased that you were but my bastard, what a joyful father would you make me! Come, you have it *ad dunghill,* at the fingers' ends, as they say.

HOLOFERNES O, I smell false Latin! 'Dunghill' for '*unguem*'. [to a nicety]

ARMADO Arts-man, preambulate. We will be singled from the barbarous. Do you not educate youth at the charge-house on the top of the mountain?

HOLOFERNES Or *mons,* the hill.

ARMADO At your sweet pleasure, for the mountain.

HOLOFERNES I do, no question.

ARMADO Sir, it is the King's most sweet pleasure and affection to congratulate the Princess at her pavilion in the posteriors of this day, which the rude multitude call the afternoon.

HOLOFERNES The posterior of the day, most generous sir, is liable, congruent, and measurable for the afternoon. The word is well culled, choice, sweet, and apt, I do assure you, sir, I do assure.

ARMADO Sir, the King is a noble gentleman, and my familiar, I do assure you, very good friend. For what is inward between us, let it pass—I do beseech you, remember your courtesy; I beseech you, apparel your head. And among other importunate and most serious designs, and of great import indeed, too—but let that pass; for I must tell you, it will please his grace, by the world, sometimes to lean upon my poor shoulder, and with his royal finger thus dally with my excrement, with my mustachio—but, sweet heart, let that pass. By the world, I recount no fable! Some certain special honours it pleases his greatness to impart to Armado, a soldier, a man of travel, that has seen the world—but let that pass. The very all of all is—but, sweet heart, I do implore secrecy—that the King would have me present the Princess—sweet chuck—with some delightful ostentation, or show, or pageant, or antic, or firework. Now, understanding that the curate and your sweet self are good at such eruptions and sudden breaking out of mirth, as it were, I have acquainted you with, to the end to crave your assistance.

HOLOFERNES Sir, you shall present before her the Nine Worthies. Sir Nathaniel, as concerning some entertainment of time, some show in the posterior of this day, to be rendered by our assistance, the King's command, and this most gallant, illustrate, and learned gentleman, before the Princess—I say, none so fit as to present the Nine Worthies.

SIR NATHANIEL Where will you find men worthy enough to present them?

HOLOFERNES Joshua, yourself; this gallant gentleman, Judas
    Maccabaeus; this swain, because of his great limb or
    joint, shall pass Pompey the Great; the page, Hercules—
ARMADO Pardon, sir—error! He is not quantity enough
    for that Worthy's thumb; he is not so big as the end of
    his club.
HOLOFERNES Shall I have audience? He shall present
    Hercules in minority. His enter and exit shall be
    strangling a snake; and I will have an apology for that
    purpose.
MOTH An excellent device! So if any of the audience hiss,
    you may cry 'Well done, Hercules! Now you crush the
    snake!' That is the way to make an offence gracious,
    though few have the grace to do it.
ARMADO For the rest of the Worthies?
HOLOFERNES I will play three myself.
MOTH Thrice-worthy gentleman!
ARMADO Shall I tell you a thing?
HOLOFERNES We attend.
ARMADO We will have, if this fits not, a farce. I beseech
    you, follow.
HOLOFERNES *Via,* [Come!] goodman Dull! You have spoken
    no word all this while.
DULL Nor understood one either, sir.
HOLOFERNES *Allons!* [Let's go] We will employ you.
DULL I'll make one in a dance, or so; or I will play on the
    drum to the Worthies, and let them dance the hay.
HOLOFERNES Most dull, honest Dull! To our sport, away!
                                              Exeunt

SCENE II
The same.

Enter the Princess, Rosaline, Maria, and Katharine

PRINCESS

Sweet hearts, we shall be rich ere we depart
If fairings come thus plentifully in.
A lady walled about with diamonds!
Look you what I have from the loving King.

ROSALINE

Madam, came nothing else along with that?

PRINCESS

Nothing but this? Yes, as much love in rhyme
As would be crammed up in a sheet of paper,
Written on both sides the leaf, margin and all,
That he was fain to seal on Cupid's name.

ROSALINE

That was the way to make his godhead wax,
For he has been five thousand year a boy.

KATHARINE

Ay, and a shrewd unhappy gallows bird.

ROSALINE

You'll never be friends with him; he killed your sister.

KATHARINE

He made her melancholy, sad, and heavy;
And so she died. Had she been light, like you,
Of such a merry, nimble, stirring spirit,
She might have been a grandam ere she died.
And so may you, for a light heart lives long.

ROSALINE

What's your dark meaning, mouse, of this light word?

KATHARINE

A light condition in a beauty dark.

ROSALINE

We need more light to find your meaning out.

ROSALINE
KATHARINE

    You'll mar the light by taking it in snuff;
    Therefore, I'll darkly end the argument.

ROSALINE

    Look what you do, you do it ever in the dark.

KATHARINE

    So do not you, for you are a light wench.
    Indeed I weigh not you, and therefore light.

KATHARINE

    You weigh me not? O, that's you care not for me!

ROSALINE

    Great reason, for past cure is still past care.

PRINCESS

    Well bandied both! A set of wit well played.
    But, Rosaline, you have a favour too—
    Who sent it? And what is it?

ROSALINE   I would you knew.

    For if my face were but as fair as yours,
    My favour were as great. Be witness this—
    Nay, I have verses too, I thank Berowne;
    The numbers true, and, were the numbering too,
    I were the fairest goddess on the ground.
    I am compared to twenty thousand fairs.
    O, he has drawn my picture in his letter!

PRINCESS

    Anything like?

ROSALINE

    Much in the letters, nothing in the praise.

PRINCESS

    Beauteous as ink—a good conclusion.

KATHARINE

    Fair as a text B in a copy-book.

ROSALINE

    Beware pencils, ho! Let me not die your debtor,

    My red dominical, my golden letter.[3]

    O that your face were not so full of O's![4]

PRINCESS

    A pox of that jest, and I beshrew [curse] all shrews.

    But, Katharine, what was sent to you from fair Dumaine?

KATHARINE

    Madam, this glove.

PRINCESS   Did he not send you twain?

KATHARINE

    Yes, madam; and, moreover,

    Some thousand verses of a faithful lover;

    A huge translation of hypocrisy,

    Vilely compiled, profound simplicity.

MARIA

    This, and these pearls, to me sent Longaville.

    The letter is too long by half a mile.

PRINCESS

    I think no less. Do you not wish in heart

    The chain were longer and the letter short?

MARIA

    Ay, or I would these hands might never part.

PRINCESS

    We are wise girls to mock our lovers so.

ROSALINE

    They are worse fools to purchase mocking so.

    That same Berowne I'll torture ere I go.

    O that I knew he were but in by the week!

    How I would make him fawn, and beg, and seek,

    And wait the season, and observe the times,

    And spend his prodigal wits in useless rhymes,

---

[3]Red and gold letters marked Sundays and saints' days in the almanac.

[4]Marks of small pox.

And shape his service wholly to my behests,
And make him proud to make me proud that jests!
So planet-like would I o'ersway his state
That he should be my fool, and I his fate.

PRINCESS
None are so surely caught, when they are catched,
As wit turned fool. Folly, in wisdom hatched,
Has wisdom's warrant and the help of school
And wit's own grace to grace a learnèd fool.

ROSALINE
The blood of youth burns not with such excess
As gravity's revolt to wantonness.

MARIA
Folly in fools bears not so strong a note
As foolery in the wise when wit does dote,
Since all the power thereof it does apply
To prove, by wit, worth in simplicity.

Enter Boyet

PRINCESS
Here comes Boyet, and mirth is in his face.

BOYET
O, I am stabbed with laughter! Where's her grace?

PRINCESS
Your news, Boyet?

BOYET   Prepare, madam, prepare!
Arm, wenches, arm! Encounters mounted are
Against your peace. Love does approach disguised,
Armèd in arguments. You'll be surprised.
Muster your wits, stand in your own defence,
Or hide your heads like cowards and fly hence.

PRINCESS
Saint Denis to Saint Cupid! What are they
That charge their breath against us? Say, scout, say.

BOYET
> Under the cool shade of a sycamore
> I thought to close my eyes some half an hour,
> When, lo, to interrupt my purposed rest,
> Toward that shade I might behold addressed
> The King and his companions! Warily
> I stole into a neighbour thicket by,
> And overheard what you shall overhear—
> That, by and by, disguised they will be here.
> Their herald is a pretty knavish page
> That well by heart has conned his embassage.
> Action and accent did they teach him there:
> 'Thus must you speak' and 'thus your body bear'.
> And ever and anon they made a doubt
> Presence majestical would put him out,
> 'For', said the King, 'an angel shall you see;
> Yet fear not you, but speak audaciously.'
> The boy replied 'An angel is not evil;
> I should have feared her had she been a devil.'
> With that all laughed and clapped him on the shoulder,
> Making the bold wag by their praises bolder.
> One rubbed his elbow thus, and grinned, and swore
> A better speech was never spoken before.
> Another, with his finger and his thumb,
> Cried 'Via, [Come] we will do't, come what will come!'
> The third he capered and cried 'All goes well!'
> The fourth turned on the toe, and down he fell.
> With that they all did tumble on the ground,
> With such a zealous laughter, so profound,
> That in this fit ridiculous appears,
> To check their folly, passion's solemn tears.

PRINCESS
> But what, but what? Come they to visit us?

BOYET
> They do, they do, and are apparelled thus,
> Like Muscovites or Russians, as I guess.

Their purpose is to parley, court, and dance,
And every one his love-suit will advance
Unto his several mistress, which they'll know
By favours several which they did bestow.

PRINCESS

And will they so? The gallants shall be tasked;
For, ladies, we will every one be masked,
And not a man of them shall have the grace,
Despite of suit, to see a lady's face.
Hold, Rosaline, this favour you shall wear,
And then the King will court you for his dear.
Hold, take you this, my sweet, and give me thine;
So shall Berowne take me for Rosaline.
And change you favours too; so shall your loves
Woo contrary, deceived by these removes.

ROSALINE

Come on, then, wear the favours most in sight.

KATHARINE

But in this changing what is your intent?

PRINCESS

The effect of my intent is to cross theirs.
They do it but in mockery merriment,
And mock for mock is only my intent.
Their several counsels they unbosom shall
To loves mistook, and so be mocked withal
Upon the next occasion that we meet,
With visages displayed, to talk and greet.

ROSALINE

But shall we dance if they desire us to't?

PRINCESS

No, to the death we will not move a foot;
Nor to their penned speech render we our grace,
But while 'tis spoken each turn away her face.

BOYET

Why, that contempt will kill the speaker's heart,
And quite divorce his memory from his part.

PRINCESS
    Therefore I do it, and I make no doubt
    The rest will never come in, if he is out.
    There's no such sport as sport by sport o'erthrown,
    To make theirs ours, and ours none but our own.
    So shall we stay, mocking intended game,
    And they, well mocked, depart away with shame.

A trumpet sounds

BOYET
    The trumpet sounds. Be masked—the masquers come.

Enter blackamoors with music, Moth with a speech, and the King and the rest of the lords disguised like Russians

MOTH
    All hail, the richest beauties on the earth!
BOYET
    Beauties no richer than rich taffeta.
MOTH
    A holy parcel of the fairest dames

(The ladies turn their backs to him)

    That ever turned their—backs—to mortal views!
BEROWNE
    'Their eyes', villain, 'their eyes'!
MOTH
    That ever turned their eyes to mortal views!
    Out—
BOYET
    True! 'Out' indeed!
MOTH
    Out of your favours, heavenly spirits, grant
    Not to behold—

BEROWNE
'Once to behold', rogue!
MOTH
Once to behold with your sun-beamèd eyes—
With your sun-beamèd eyes—
BOYET
They will not answer to that epithet.
You were best call it 'daughter-beamèd eyes'.
MOTH
They do not mark me, and that brings me out.
BEROWNE
Is this your perfectness? Be gone, you rogue!

Exit Moth

ROSALINE
What would these strangers? Know their minds, Boyet.
If they do speak our language, 'tis our will
That some plain man recount their purposes.
Know what they would.
BOYET   What would you with the Princess?
BEROWNE
Nothing but peace and gentle visitation.
ROSALINE
What would they, say they?
BOYET
Nothing but peace and gentle visitation.
ROSALINE
Why, that they have, and bid them so be gone.
BOYET
She says you have it and you may be gone.
KING
Say to her, we have measured many miles
To tread a measure with her on this grass.
BOYET
They say that they have measured many a mile
To tread a measure with you on this grass.

ROSALINE

It is not so. Ask them how many inches
Is in one mile. If they have measured many,
The measure then of one is easily told.

BOYET

If to come hither you have measured miles,
And many miles, the Princess bids you tell
How many inches do fill up one mile.

BEROWNE

Tell her we measure them by weary steps.

BOYET

She hears herself.

ROSALINE   How many weary steps,
Of many weary miles you have o'ergone,
Are numbered in the travel of one mile?

BEROWNE

We number nothing that we spend for you.
Our duty is so rich, so infinite,
That we may do it still without account.
But deign to show the sunshine of your face,
That we like savages may worship it.

ROSALINE

My face is but a moon, and clouded too.

KING

Blessèd are clouds, to do as such clouds do.
Deign, bright moon, and these your stars, to shine—
Those clouds removed—upon our watery eyne. [eyes]

ROSALINE

O vain petitioner, beg a greater matter!
You now request but moonshine in the water.

KING

Then in our measure grant us but one change.
You bid me beg; this begging is not strange.

ROSALINE

Play music then! Nay, you must do it soon.
Not yet? No dance! Thus change I like the moon.

KING
    Will you not dance? How come you thus estranged?
ROSALINE
    You took the moon at full, but now she's changed.
KING
    Yet still she is the moon, and I the man.
    The music plays; grant us some motion to it.
ROSALINE
    Our ears do grant it.
KING   But your legs should do it.
ROSALINE
    Since you are strangers and come here by chance,
    We'll not be nice. Take hands. We will not dance.
KING
    Why take we hands then?
ROSALINE   Only to part friends.
    Curtsy, sweet hearts. And so the measure ends.
KING
    More measure of this measure! Be not nice.
ROSALINE
    We can afford no more at such a price.
KING
    Price you yourselves. What buys your company?
ROSALINE
    Your absence only.
KING   That can never be.
ROSALINE
    Then cannot we be bought; and so adieu—
    Twice to your visor, [mask] and half once to you!
KING
    If you deny to dance, let's hold more chat.
ROSALINE
    In private then.
KING   I am best pleased with that.

                    They talk apart

BEROWNE
   White-handed mistress, one sweet word with thee.
PRINCESS
   Honey, and milk, and sugar—there are three.
BEROWNE
   Nay then, two triplets, if you grow so nice,
   Metheglin,[5] wort, and malmsey. Well run, dice!
   There's half a dozen sweets.
PRINCESS   Seventh sweet, adieu.
   Since you can cheat, I'll play no more with you.
BEROWNE
   One word in secret.
PRINCESS   Let it not be sweet.
BEROWNE
   You grieve my gall.
PRINCESS   Gall? Bitter.
BEROWNE   Therefore meet.

                    They talk apart

DUMAINE
   Will you deign with me to change a word?
MARIA
   Name it.
DUMAINE Fair lady—
MARIA   Say you so? Fair lord!
   Take that for your 'fair lady'.
DUMAINE   Please it you,
   As much in private, and I'll bid adieu.

                    They talk apart

---

[5]A Welsh drink made of honey and wort.

KATHARINE
    What, was your visor made without a tongue?
LONGAVILLE
    I know the reason, lady, why you ask.
KATHARINE
    O for your reason! Quickly, sir; I long.
LONGAVILLE
    You have a double tongue within your mask,
    And would afford my speechless visor half.
KATHARINE
    'Veal', said the Dutchman. Is not 'veal' a calf?[6]
LONGAVILLE
    A calf, fair lady!
KATHARINE   No, a fair lord calf.
LONGAVILLE
    Let's part the word.
KATHARINE   No, I'll not be your half.
    Take all and wean it; it may prove an ox.
LONGAVILLE
    Look how you butt yourself in these sharp mocks.
    Will you give horns, chaste lady? Do not so.
KATHARINE
    Then die a calf before your horns do grow.
LONGAVILLE
    One word in private with you ere I die.
KATHARINE
    Bleat softly then. The butcher hears you cry.

                    They talk apart

BOYET
    The tongues of mocking wenches are as keen
        As is the razor's edge invisible,

---

[6]Pun on well, veil and French *veau*, i.e. veal and calf.

Cutting a smaller hair than may be seen;
  Above the sense of sense, so sensible
Seems their conference. Their conceits have wings
Fleeter than arrows, bullets, wind, thought, swifter things.

ROSALINE
Not one word more, my maids; break off, break off!

BEROWNE
By heaven, all dry-beaten with pure scoff!

KING
Farewell, mad wenches. You have simple wits.

                    Exeunt the King, lords, and blackamoors

PRINCESS
Twenty adieus, my frozen Muscovits.
Are these the breed of wits so wondered at?

BOYET
Tapers they are, with your sweet breaths puffed out.

ROSALINE
Well-liking wits they have; gross, gross; fat, fat.

PRINCESS
  O poverty in wit, kingly-poor flout!
Will they not, think you, hang themselves tonight?
  Or ever but in visors show their faces?
This pert Berowne was out of countenance quite.

ROSALINE
  They were all in lamentable cases.
The King was weeping-ripe for a good word.

PRINCESS
Berowne did swear himself out of all suit.

MARIA
Dumaine was at my service, and his sword.
  'Non point',[7] said I; my servant straight was mute.

KATHARINE
Lord Longaville said I came over his heart;
  And know you what he called me?

---

[7]Certainly not.

PRINCESS   Qualm, perhaps.

KATHARINE
  Yes, in good faith.

PRINCESS   Go, sickness as you are!

ROSALINE
    Well, better wits have worn plain statute-caps.[8]
    But will you hear? The King is my love sworn.

PRINCESS
    And quick Berowne has plighted faith to me.

KATHARINE
And Longaville was for my service born.

MARIA
Dumaine is mine as sure as bark on tree.

BOYET
  Madam, and pretty mistresses, give ear:
  Immediately they will again be here
  In their own shapes, for it can never be
  They will digest this harsh indignity.

PRINCESS
  Will they return?

BOYET   They will, they will, God knows;
  And leap for joy though they are lame with blows.
  Therefore change favours, and, when they repair,
  Blow like sweet roses in this summer air.

PRINCESS
  How 'blow'? How 'blow'? Speak to be understood.

BOYET
  Fair ladies masked are roses in their bud;
  Dismasked, their damask sweet commixture shown,
  Are angels lowering clouds, or roses blown.

PRINCESS
  Away, perplexity! What shall we do
  If they return in their own shapes to woo?

---

[8]Elizabethan law laid down that lower class people should wear plain head-gear.

ROSALINE

    Good madam, if by me you'll be advised,
    Let's mock them still, as well known as disguised.
    Let us complain to them what fools were here,
    Disguised like Muscovites in shapeless gear;
    And wonder what they were, and to what end
    Their shallow shows and prologue vilely penned,
    And their rough carriage so ridiculous,
    Should be presented at our tent to us.

BOYET

    Ladies, withdraw. The gallants are at hand.

PRINCESS

    Whip to our tents, as roes runs o'er the land.

                    Exeunt the Princess and ladies

Enter the King, Berowne, Longaville, and Dumaine, in
their proper habits

KING

    Fair sir, God save you. Where's the Princess?

BOYET

    Gone to her tent. Please it your majesty
    Command me any service to her thither?

KING

    That she will grant me audience for one word.

BOYET

    I will; and so will she, I know, my lord.   *Exit*

BEROWNE

    This fellow pecks up wit, as pigeons peas,
    And utters it again when God does please.
    He is wit's pedlar, and retails his wares
    At wakes and wassails, meetings, markets, fairs;
    And we that sell by gross, the Lord does know,
    Have not the grace to grace it with such show.
    This gallant pins the wenches on his sleeve.
    Had he been Adam, he had tempted Eve.

He can carve too, and lisp. Why, this is he
That kissed his hand away in courtesy.
This is the ape of form, Monsieur the Nice,
That, when he plays at tables, chides the dice
In honourable terms. Nay, he can sing
A mean[9] most meanly; and in ushering
Mend him who can. The ladies call him sweet.
The stairs, as he treads on them, kiss his feet.
This is the flower that smiles on everyone,
To show his teeth as white as whale's bone;
And consciences that will not die in debt
Pay him the due of 'honey-tongued Boyet'.

KING

A blister on his sweet tongue, with my heart,
That put Armado's page out of his part!

Enter the Princess, Rosaline, Maria, and Katharine,

BEROWNE

See where it comes! Behaviour, what were you
Till this man showed you, and what are you now?

KING

All hail, sweet madam, and fair time of day.

PRINCESS

'Fair' in 'all hail' is foul, as I conceive.

KING

Construe my speeches better, if you may.

PRINCESS

Then wish me better; I will give you leave.

KING

We came to visit you, and purpose now
To lead you to our Court. Allow it then.

---

[9] A midde part, tenor or alto.

PRINCESS

This field shall hold me, and so hold your vow.

Nor God nor I delight in perjured men.

KING

Rebuke me not for that which you provoke.

The virtue of your eye must break my oath.

PRINCESS

You nickname virtue—'vice' you should have spoke;

For virtue's office never breaks men's troth.

Now, by my maiden honour, yet as pure

As the unsullied lily, I protest,

A world of torments though I should endure,

I would not yield to be your house's guest,

So much I hate a breaking cause to be

Of heavenly oaths, vowed with integrity.

KING

O, you have lived in desolation here,

Unseen, unvisited, much to our shame.

PRINCESS

Not so, my lord. It is not so, I swear.

We have had pastimes here and pleasant game:

A group of Russians left us but of late.

KING

How, madam? Russians?

PRINCESS   Ay, in truth, my lord;

Trim gallants, full of courtship and of state.

ROSALINE

Madam, speak true! It is not so, my lord.

My lady, to the manner of the days,

In courtesy gives undeserving praise.

We four indeed confronted were with four

In Russian habit. Here they stayed an hour

And talked apace; and in that hour, my lord,

They did not bless us with one happy word.

I dare not call them fools, but this I think,

When they are thirsty, fools would fain have drink.

BEROWNE
    This jest is dry to me. My gentle sweet,
    Your wit makes wise things foolish. When we greet,
    With eyes' best seeing, heaven's fiery eye,
    By light we lose light. Your capacity
    Is of that nature that to your huge store
    Wise things seem foolish and rich things but poor.
ROSALINE
    This proves you wise and rich, for in my eye—
BEROWNE
    I am a fool, and full of poverty.
ROSALINE
    But that you take what does to you belong,
    It were a fault to snatch words from my tongue.
BEROWNE
    O, I am yours, and all that I possess.
ROSALINE
    All the fool mine?
BEROWNE   I cannot give you less.
ROSALINE
    Which of the visors was it that you wore?
BEROWNE
    Where, when, what visor? Why demand you this?
ROSALINE
    There, then, that visor: that superfluous case
    That hid the worse and showed the better face.
KING
    We were descried. They'll mock us now downright.
DUMAINE
    Let us confess, and turn it to a jest.
PRINCESS
    Amazed, my lord? Why looks your highness sad?
ROSALINE
    Help! Hold his brows! He'll swoon. Why look you pale?
    Sea-sick, I think, coming from Muscovy!

BEROWNE
> Thus pour the stars down plagues for perjury.
>> Can any face of brass hold longer out?
> Here stand I, lady; dart your skill at me.
>> Bruise me with scorn, confound me with a flout,
> Thrust your sharp wit quite through my ignorance,
>> Cut me to pieces with your keen conceit,
> And I will wish you never more to dance,
>> Nor ever more in Russian habit wait.
> O, never will I trust to speeches penned,
>> Nor to the motion of a schoolboy's tongue,
> Nor ever come in visor to my friend,
>> Nor woo in rhyme, like a blind harper's song.
> Taffeta phrases, silken terms precise,
>> Three-piled hyperboles, spruce affection,
> Figures pedantical—these summer flies
>> Have blown me full of maggot ostentation.
> I do forswear them; and I here protest
>> By this white glove—how white the hand, God
>> knows!—
> Henceforth my wooing mind shall be expressed
>> In russet yeas and honest kersey noes.
> And, to begin: wench—so God help me, law!—
> My love to you is sound, *sans* [without] crack or flaw.

ROSALINE
> *Sans 'sans'*, I pray you.

BEROWNE   Yet I have a trick
> Of the old rage. Bear with me, I am sick;
> I'll leave it by degrees. Soft, let us see:
> Write 'Lord have mercy on us' on those three.
> They are infected; in their hearts it lies;
> They have the plague, and caught it of your eyes.
> These lords are visited; you are not free,
> For the Lord's tokens on you do I see.

PRINCESS
   No, they are free that gave these tokens to us.
BEROWNE
   Our states are forfeit. Seek not to undo us.
ROSALINE
   It is not so; for how can this be true,
   That you stand forfeit, being those that sue?
BEROWNE
   Peace! for I will not have to do with you.
ROSALINE
   Nor shall you if I do as I intend.
BEROWNE
   Speak for yourselves. My wit is at an end.
KING
   Teach us, sweet madam, for our rude transgression
   Some fair excuse.
PRINCESS   The fairest is confession.
   Were not you here but even now disguised?
KING
   Madam, I was.
PRINCESS   And were you well advised?
KING
   I was, fair madam.
PRINCESS   When you then were here,
   What did you whisper in your lady's ear?
KING
   That more than all the world I did respect her.
PRINCESS
   When she shall challenge this, you will reject her.
KING
   Upon my honour, no.
PRINCESS   Peace, peace, forbear!
   Your oath once broken, you force not to forswear.
KING
   Despise me when I break this oath of mine.

PRINCESS

    I will; and therefore keep it. Rosaline,

    What did the Russian whisper in your ear?

ROSALINE

    Madam, he swore that he did hold me dear

    As precious eyesight, and did value me

    Above this world; adding thereto, moreover,

    That he would wed me or else die my lover.

PRINCESS

    God give you joy of him. The noble lord

    Most honourably does uphold his word.

KING

    What mean you, madam? By my life, my troth,

    I never swore this lady such an oath.

ROSALINE

    By heaven you did! And, to confirm it plain,

    You gave me this; but take it, sir, again.

KING

    My faith and this the Princess I did give.

    I knew her by this jewel on her sleeve.

PRINCESS

    Pardon me, sir, this jewel did she wear,

    And Lord Berowne, I thank him, is my dear.

    What! Will you have me, or your pearl again?

BEROWNE

    Neither of either; I remit both twain.

    I see the trick of it. Here was a consent,

    Knowing beforehand of our merriment,

    To dash it like a Christmas comedy.

    Some carry-tale, some please-man, some slight zany,

    Some mumble-news, some trencher-knight, some Dick,

    That smiles his cheek in years, and knows the trick

    To make my lady laugh when she's disposed,

    Told our intents before. Which once disclosed,

    The ladies did change favours, and then we,

    Following the signs, wooed but the sign of She.

Now, to our perjury to add more terror,
We are again forsworn, in will and error.
Much upon this it is. *(To Boyet)* And might not you
Forestall our sport, to make us thus untrue?
Do not you know my lady's foot by the square,
    And laugh upon the apple of her eye?
And stand between her back, sir, and the fire,
    Holding a trencher, jesting merrily?
You put our page out—go, you are allowed;
Die when you will, a smock shall be your shroud.
You leer upon me, do you? There's an eye
Wounds like a leaden sword.

BOYET   Full merrily
Has this brave gallop, this career, been run.

BEROWNE
Lo, he is tilting straight. Peace! I have done.

Enter Costard

Welcome, pure wit! You part now a fair fray.

COSTARD
O Lord, sir, they would know
Whether the three Worthies shall come in or no.

BEROWNE
What, are there but three?

COSTARD   No, sir; but it is very fine,
For every one presents three.

BEROWNE   And three times thrice is nine.

COSTARD
Not so, sir—under correction, sir—I hope it is not so.
You cannot beg us, sir, I can assure you, sir; we know
    what we know.
I hope, sir, three times thrice, sir—

BEROWNE   Is not nine?

COSTARD Under correction, sir, we know whereunto it
    does amount.

BEROWNE
By Jove, I always took three threes for nine.

COSTARD O Lord, sir, it were pity you should get your living by reckoning, sir.

BEROWNE How much is it?

COSTARD O Lord, sir, the parties themselves, the actors, sir, will show whereunto it does amount. For my own part, I am, as they say, but to perfect one man in one poor man—Pompion the Great, sir.

BEROWNE Are you one of the Worthies?

COSTARD It pleased them to think me worthy of Pompey the Great. For my own part, I know not the degree of the Worthy, but I am to stand for him.

BEROWNE Go bid them prepare.

COSTARD We will turn it finely off, sir; we will take some care.   *Exit*

KING
Berowne, they will shame us. Let them not approach.

BEROWNE
We are shame-proof, my lord; and 'tis some policy
To have one show worse than the King's and his company.

KING
I say they shall not come.

PRINCESS
Nay, my good lord, let me o'errule you now.
That sport best pleases that does least know how—
Where zeal strives to content, and the contènts
Die in the zeal of that which it presents;
Their form confounded makes most form in mirth,
When great things labouring perish in their birth.

BEROWNE
A right description of our sport, my lord.

Enter Armado

ARMADO Anointed, I implore so much expense of your
   royal sweet breath as will utter a brace of words.

Armado gives the King a paper

PRINCESS Does this man serve God?
BEROWNE Why ask you?
PRINCESS He speaks not like a man of God's making.
ARMADO That is all one, my fair sweet honey monarch;
   for, I protest, the schoolmaster is exceeding fantastical;
   too, too vain; too, too vain; but we will put it, as they
   say, to *fortuna de la guerra* [the fortune of war]. I wish
   you the peace of mind, most royal couplement.
                                                      Exit
KING Here is like to be a good presence of Worthies. He
   presents Hector of Troy; the swain, Pompey the Great;
   the parish curate, Alexander; Armado's page, Hercules;
   the pedant, Judas Maccabaeus.

(Reading)

And if these four Worthies in their first show thrive,
These four will change habits and present the other
   five.
BEROWNE
There are five in the first show.
KING
You are deceivèd. 'Tis not so.
BEROWNE The pedant, the braggart, the hedge-priest, the
   fool, and the boy.
   Abate throw at novum,[10] and the whole world again
   Cannot pick out five such, take each one in his vein.

---

[10]An Elizabethan dice-game.

KING
  The ship is under sail, and here she comes amain.

Enter Costard as Pompey

COSTARD *as Pompey*
  I Pompey am—
BEROWNE   You lie! You are not he.
COSTARD *as Pompey*
  I Pompey am—
BOYET   With leopard's head on knee.
BEROWNE
  Well said, old mocker. I must needs be friends with
      thee.
COSTARD *as Pompey*
  I Pompey am, Pompey surnamed the Big—
DUMAINE
  The 'Great'.
COSTARD *as Pompey*
  It is 'Great', sir—Pompey surnamed the Great,
  That oft in field, with targe and shield, did make my
      foe to sweat;
  And travelling along this coast, I here am come by
      chance,
  And lay my arms before the legs of this sweet lass of
      France.
  If your ladyship would say 'Thanks, Pompey', I had
      done.
PRINCESS Great thanks, great Pompey.
COSTARD 'Tis not so much worth, but I hope I was perfect.
  I made a little fault in 'Great'.
BEROWNE My hat to a halfpenny, Pompey proves the best
  Worthy.

Enter Sir Nathaniel as Alexander

SIR NATHANIEL *as Alexander*
  When in the world I lived, I was the world's commander;
  By east, west, north, and south, I spread my conquering
    might;
  My scutcheon plain declares that I am Alisander.
BOYET
  Your nose says no, you are not; for it stands too right.
BEROWNE
  Your nose smells 'no' in this, most tender-smelling knight.
PRINCESS
  The conqueror is dismayed. Proceed, good Alexander.
SIR NATHANIEL *as Alexander*
  When in the world I lived, I was the world's commander—
BOYET
  Most true, 'tis right—you were so, Alisander.
BEROWNE Pompey the Great—
COSTARD Your servant, and Costard.
BEROWNE Take away the conqueror; take away Alisander.
COSTARD (*to Sir Nathaniel*) O, sir, you have overthrown
  Alisander the conqueror. You will be scraped out of the
  painted cloth for this. Your lion, that holds his pole-axe
  sitting on a close-stool, will be given to Ajax. He will be
  the ninth Worthy. A conqueror, and afraid to speak?
  Run away for shame, Alisander.

Sir Nathaniel retires

  There, if it shall please you, a foolish mild man;
  an honest man, look you, and soon dashed. He is a
  marvellous good neighbour, faith, and a very good
  bowler; but for Alisander, alas, you see how 'tis—a
  little overparted. But there are Worthies a-coming will
  speak their mind in some other sort.
PRINCESS Stand aside, good Pompey.

Enter Holofernes as Judas and Moth as Hercules

HOLOFERNES *as presenter*
   Great Hercules is presented by this imp,
      Whose club killed Cerberus, that three-headed *canus,*
      [dog]
   And when he was a babe, a child, a shrimp,
      Thus did he strangle serpents in his *manus.* [hand]
   Quoniam [since] he seems now in minority,
   Ergo [therefore] I come with this apology.
   Keep some state in your exit, and retire.

          Moth retires Holofernes speaks as Judas

   Judas I am—
DUMAINE A Judas!
HOLOFERNES Not Iscariot, sir.

                  (as Judas)

   Judas I am, yclept [called] Maccabaeus.
DUMAINE Judas Maccabaeus clipped is plain Judas.
BEROWNE A kissing traitor. How, are you proved Judas?
HOLOFERNES *as Judas*
   Judas I am—
DUMAINE The more shame for you, Judas.
HOLOFERNES What mean you, sir?
BOYET To make Judas hang himself.
HOLOFERNES Begin, sir; you are my elder.
BEROWNE Well followed: Judas was hanged on an elder.
HOLOFERNES I will not be put out of countenance.
BEROWNE Because you have no face.
HOLOFERNES What is this?
BOYET A guitar-head.
DUMAINE The head of a bodkin.
BEROWNE A death's face in a ring.
LONGAVILLE The face of an old Roman coin, scarce seen.
BOYET The pommel of Caesar's sword.

DUMAINE The carved bone face on a flask.

BEROWNE Saint George's half-cheek in a brooch.

DUMAINE Ay, in a brooch of lead.

BEROWNE Ay, and worn in the cap of a toothdrawer. And
now forward, for we have put you in countenance.

HOLOFERNES You have put me out of countenance.

BEROWNE False! We have given you faces.

HOLOFERNES But you have outfaced them all.

BEROWNE
If you were a lion, we would do so.

BOYET
Therefore, as he is an ass, let him go.
And so adieu, sweet Jude. Nay, why do you stay?

DUMAINE For the latter end of his name.

BEROWNE
For the ass to the Jude? Give it him. Jude-as, away!

HOLOFERNES
This is not generous, not gentle, not humble.

BOYET
A light for Monsieur Judas! It grows dark; he may
stumble.

Holofernes retires

PRINCESS Alas, poor Maccabaeus, how has he been baited!

Enter Armado as Hector

BEROWNE Hide your head, Achilles! Here comes Hector in
arms.

DUMAINE Though my mocks come home by me, I will
now be merry.

KING Hector was but a Trojan in respect of this.

BOYET But is this Hector?

KING I think Hector was not so clean-timbered.

LONGAVILLE His leg is too big for Hector's.

DUMAINE More calf, certain.

BOYET No; he is best equipped in the small.

BEROWNE This cannot be Hector.

DUMAINE He's a god or a painter; for he makes faces.

ARMADO *as Hector*

    The armipotent Mars, of lances the almighty,
        Gave Hector a gift—

DUMAINE A gilt nutmeg.

BEROWNE A lemon.

LONGAVILLE Stuck with cloves.

DUMAINE No, cloven.

ARMADO Peace!

               (as Hector)

    The armipotent Mars, of lances the almighty,
        Gave Hector a gift, the heir of Ilion;
    A man so breathed that certain he would fight, yea,
        From morn till night, out of his pavilion.
    I am that flower—

DUMAINE   That mint!

LONGAVILLE   That columbine!

ARMADO Sweet Lord Longaville, rein your tongue.

LONGAVILLE I must rather give it the rein, for it runs against Hector.

DUMAINE Ay, and Hector's a greyhound.

ARMADO The sweet war-man is dead and rotten. Sweet chucks, beat not the bones of the buried. When he breathed, he was a man. But I will forward with my device. Sweet royalty, bestow on me the sense of hearing.

        Berowne whispers to Costard

PRINCESS Speak, brave Hector; we are much delighted.

ARMADO I do adore your sweet grace's slipper.

BOYET Loves her by the foot.

DUMAINE He may not by the yard.[11]

ARMADO *as Hector*
  This Hector far surmounted Hannibal;
      The party is gone—

COSTARD Fellow Hector, she is gone! She is two months on her way.

ARMADO What mean you?

COSTARD Faith, unless you play the honest Trojan, the poor wench is cast away. She's quick; the child brags in her belly already. 'Tis yours.

ARMADO Do you infamonize me among potentates? You shall die!

COSTARD Then shall Hector be whipped for Jaquenetta that is quick by him, and hanged for Pompey that is dead by him.

DUMAINE Most rare Pompey!

BOYET Renowned Pompey!

BEROWNE Greater than 'Great'! Great, great, great Pompey! Pompey the Huge!

DUMAINE Hector trembles.

BEROWNE Pompey is moved. More Ates, more Ates![12] Stir them on, stir them on!

DUMAINE Hector will challenge him.

BEROWNE Ay, if he has no more man's blood in his belly than will sup a flea.

ARMADO By the north pole, I do challenge you.

COSTARD I will not fight with a pole like a northern man. I'll slash; I'll do it by the sword. I bepray you, let me borrow my arms again.

DUMAINE Room for the incensed Worthies.

COSTARD I'll do it in my shirt.

DUMAINE Most resolute Pompey!

MOTH Master, let me take you a buttonhole lower. Do you

---

[11]Bawdy innuendo.
[12]Goddess of discord.

not see, Pompey is undressing for the combat. What mean you? You will lose your reputation.

ARMADO Gentlemen and soldiers, pardon me. I will not combat in my shirt.

DUMAINE You may not deny it. Pompey has made the challenge.

ARMADO Sweet bloods, I both may and will.

BEROWNE What reason have you for it?

ARMADO The naked truth of it is, I have no shirt. I go woolward for penance.

MOTH True, and it was enjoined him in Rome for want of linen. Since when, I'll be sworn, he wore none but a dishclout of Jaquenetta's, and that he wears next his heart for a favour.

Enter Marcade

MARCADE
God save you, madam.

PRINCESS   Welcome, Marcade,
But that you interrupt our merriment.

MARCADE
I am sorry, madam, for the news I bring
Is heavy in my tongue. The King your father—

PRINCESS
Dead, for my life!

MARCADE   Even so; my tale is told.

BEROWNE
Worthies, away! The scene begins to cloud.

ARMADO For my own part, I breathe free breath. I have seen the day of wrong through the little hole of discretion, and I will right myself like a soldier.

Exeunt Worthies

KING How fares your majesty?

PRINCESS
  Boyet, prepare. I will away tonight.

KING
  Madam, not so. I do beseech you, stay.

PRINCESS
  Prepare, I say. I thank you, gracious lords,
  For all your fair endeavours, and entreat,
  Out of a new-sad soul, that you will grant
  In your rich wisdom to excuse or hide
  The liberal opposition of our spirits,
  If over-boldly we have borne ourselves
  In the converse of breath. Your gentleness
  Was guilty of it. Farewell, worthy lord!
  A heavy heart bears not a nimble tongue.
  Excuse me so, coming too short of thanks
  For my great suit so easily obtained.

KING
  The extreme parts of time extremely forms
  All causes to the purpose of its speed,
  And often at its very loose decides
  That which long process could not arbitrate.
  And though the mourning brow of progeny
  Forbids the smiling courtesy of love
  The holy suit which fain it would convince,
  Yet, since love's argument was first on foot,
  Let not the cloud of sorrow jostle it
  From what it purposed. Since to wail friends lost
  Is not by much so wholesome-profitable
  As to rejoice at friends but newly found.

PRINCESS
  I understand you not. My griefs are double.

BEROWNE
  Honest plain words best pierce the ear of grief;
  And by these badges understand the King.
  For your fair sakes have we neglected time,

Played foul play with our oaths. Your beauty, ladies,
Has much deformed us, fashioning our humours
Even to the opposèd end of our intents.
And what in us has seemed ridiculous—
As love is full of unbefitting strains,
All wanton as a child, skipping and vain,
Formed by the eye and therefore, like the eye,
Full of straying shapes, of habits, and of forms,
Varying in subjects as the eye does roll
To every varied object in its glance:
Which parti-coated presence of loose love
Put on by us, if, in your heavenly eyes,
Has misbecomed our oaths and gravities,
Those heavenly eyes, that look into these faults,
Suggested us to make. Therefore, ladies,
Our love being yours, the error that love makes
Is likewise yours. We to ourselves prove false
By being once false for ever to be true
To those that make us both—fair ladies, you.
And even that falsehood, in itself a sin,
Thus purifies itself and turns to grace.

PRINCESS
We have received your letters, full of love;
Your favours, the ambassadors of love;
And in our maiden counsel rated them
At courtship, pleasant jest, and courtesy,
As bombast and as lining to the time.
But more devout than this in our respects
Have we not been; and therefore met your loves
In their own fashion, like a merriment.

DUMAINE
Our letters, madam, showed much more than jest.

LONGAVILLE
So did our looks.

ROSALINE   We did not note them so.

KING

    Now, at the latest minute of the hour,
    Grant us your loves.

PRINCESS   A time, I think, too short
    To make a world-without-end bargain in.
    No, no, my lord, your grace is perjured much,
    Full of dear guiltiness; and therefore this:
    If for my love—as there is no such cause—
    You will do aught, this shall you do for me:
    Your oath I will not trust; but go with speed
    To some forlorn and naked hermitage,
    Remote from all the pleasures of the world;
    There stay until the twelve celestial signs
    Have brought about the annual reckoning.
    If this austere unsociable life
    Changes not your offer made in heat of blood;
    If frosts and fasts, hard lodging and thin clothes
    Nip not the gaudy blossoms of your love,
    But that it bears this trial, and last love—
    Then, at the expiration of the year,
    Come challenge me, challenge by these deserts,
    And, by this virgin palm now kissing yours,
    I will be yours. And, till that instance, shut
    My woeful self up in a mourning house,
    Raining the tears of lamentation
    For the remembrance of my father's death.
    If this you do deny, let our hands part,
    Neither entitled in the other's heart.

KING

    If this, or more than this, I would deny,
    To flatter up these powers of mine with rest,
    The sudden hand of death close up my eye!
    Hence hermit then—my heart is in your breast.

DUMAINE

    But what to me, my love? But what to me?
    A wife?

KATHARINE A beard, fair health, and honesty;
  With threefold love I wish you all these three.
DUMAINE
  O, shall I say 'I thank you, gentle wife'?
KATHARINE
  Not so, my lord. A twelvemonth and a day
  I'll mark no words that smooth-faced wooers say.
  Come when the King does to my lady come;
  Then, if I have much love, I'll give you some.
DUMAINE
  I'll serve you true and faithfully till then.
KATHARINE
  Yet swear not, lest you be forsworn again.
LONGAVILLE
  What says Maria?
MARIA   At the twelvemonth's end
  I'll change my black gown for a faithful friend.
LONGAVILLE
  I'll stay with patience, but the time is long.
MARIA
  The liker you; few taller are so young.
BEROWNE
  Studies my lady? Mistress, look on me.
  Behold the window of my heart, my eye,
  What humble suit attends your answer there.
  Impose some service on me for your love.
ROSALINE
  Oft have I heard of you, my Lord Berowne,
  Before I saw you, and the world's large tongue
  Proclaims you for a man replete with mocks,
  Full of comparisons and wounding flouts,
  Which you on all estates will execute
  That lie within the mercy of your wit.
  To weed this wormwood from your fruitful brain,
  And therewith then to win me, if you please,
  Without which yet I am not to be won,

You shall this twelvemonth term from day to day
Visit the speechless sick, and still converse
With groaning wretches. And your task shall be
With all the fierce endeavour of your wit
To enforce the painèd impotent to smile.

BEROWNE

To move wild laughter in the throat of death?
It cannot be; it is impossible;
Mirth cannot move a soul in agony.

ROSALINE

Why, that's the way to choke a gibing spirit,
Whose influence is begot of that loose grace
Which shallow laughing hearers give to fools.
A jest's prosperity lies in the ear
Of him that hears it, never in the tongue
Of him that makes it. Then, if sickly ears,
Deafened with the clamours of their own dear groans,
Will hear your idle scorns, continue then,
And I will have you and that fault with it.
But if they will not, throw away that spirit,
And I shall find you empty of that fault,
Right joyful of your reformatiòn.

BEROWNE

A twelvemonth? Well, befall what will befall,
I'll jest a twelvemonth in an hospital.

PRINCESS *(to the King)*

Ay, sweet my lord, and so I take my leave.

KING

No, madam, we will bring you on your way.

BEROWNE

Our wooing does not end like an old play;
Jack has not Jill. These ladies' courtesy
Might well have made our sport a comedy.

KING
   Come, sir, it wants a twelvemonth and a day,
   And then 'twill end.
BEROWNE   That's too long for a play.

Enter Armado

ARMADO Sweet majesty, permit me—
PRINCESS Was not that Hector?
DUMAINE The worthy knight of Troy.
ARMADO I will kiss your royal finger, and take leave. I
   am a votary; I have vowed to Jaquenetta to hold the
   plough for her sweet love three year. But, most esteemed
   greatness, will you hear the dialogue that the two learned
   men have compiled in praise of the owl and the cuckoo?
   It should have followed in the end of our show.
KING Call them forth quickly; we will do so.
ARMADO Holla! Approach!

Enter all

This side is Hiems, winter; this Ver, the spring; the one
maintained by the owl, the other by the cuckoo. Ver,
begin.

THE SONG

VER   When daisies pied and violets blue
        And lady-smocks all silver-white
     And cuckoo-buds of yellow hue
        Do paint the meadows with delight,
     The cuckoo then, on every tree,
     Mocks married men; for thus sings he:
           'Cuckoo!

Cuckoo, cuckoo!' O, word of fear,
Unpleasing to a married ear!

When shepherds pipe on oaten straws,
    And merry larks are ploughmen's clocks,
When turtles tread, and rooks, and daws,
    And maidens bleach their summer smocks,
The cuckoo then, on every tree,
Mocks married men; for thus sings he:
                'Cuckoo!
Cuckoo, cuckoo!' O, word of fear,
Unpleasing to a married ear!

HIEMS When icicles hang by the wall,
    And Dick the shepherd blows his nail,
And Tom bears logs into the hall,
    And milk comes frozen home in pail,
When blood is nipped, and ways be foul,
Then nightly sings the staring owl:
                'Tu-whit
Tu-who!'—a merry note,
While greasy Joan does cool the pot.

When all aloud the wind does blow,
    And coughing drowns the parson's saw,
And birds sit brooding in the snow,
    And Marian's nose looks red and raw,
When roasted crabs hiss in the bowl,
Then nightly sings the staring owl:
                'Tu-whit
'Tu-who!'—a merry note,
While greasy Joan does cool the pot.

ARMADO The words of Mercury are harsh after the songs
    of Apollo. You that way; we this way.   *Exeunt*

Othello

INTRODUCTION

Othello, within its own terms, is a perfect master-piece; its date 1604, the same year as *Measure for Measure*. Think of turning out two such master-pieces in one year! This play was performed at Court in the old banqueting house at Whitehall on All Saints day, 1 November 1604—other Court performances are recorded. Probably written at home in the country that summer, for we know from John Aubrey that Shakespeare was in the habit of returning to Stratford once a year from the winter's playing in London and (earlier) touring.

Dr. Johnson's judgment was that 'the beauties of this play impress themselves so strongly that they can draw no aid from critical illustration.' What the commonsense of this great writer means is that the play stands in no need of criticism—it speaks for itself. In one sense it is simple, stream-lined, no sub-plot, few characters—unlike the complexities and the large cast of *Hamlet*. Its impact is no less fine, its psychological truth no less searching and revealing, if less complex. Its appeal to other creative artists is far more eloquent than mere criticism, and this has appealed strongly alike to painters and composers. Verdi made a fine opera of it, and indeed the play—like *Macbeth*—moves like an opera.

Shakespeare's contemporary, even the critical Ben Jonson, allowed that 'he was not for an age, but for all time'—a true prophecy. And *Othello* points to a prime issue of our own day, that of race relations. Just as *The Merchant of Venice* highlights the Jewish question and anti-Semitism, so *Othello* underscores the relation between black and white. Actually Othello is not a negro, though he calls himself 'black'; he is a Moor, of North Africa.

Nevertheless, the tragedy between Othello and Desdemona is due to this. Deeply in love with this very masculine, soldierly man, years older than herself, she did wrong in marrying him; for this was against her father's will, and that was a serious offence to sixteenth century minds. It exposed her to the disapprobation of her friends, and left her alone, face to face with a very passionate and unreasonable man, himself exposed to the envy of others, and within himself to his own sense of inferiority on account of race and age: an easy victim because of the simplicity, devotion and magnanimity of his own nature. He murders out of excessive love, turned to jealousy by the machinations of an envious, evil man.

Iago is by far the most interesting character in the play, a fascinating psychological study for those interested in such things. He is often presented as a man of motiveless malignity, a monster of mere evil. This is inadequate: he has his motives—he has been downgraded by Othello—and his suspicions, for he suspects Othello with his wife. But *he* is not motivated by sexual jealousy; like Richard III, he is rather strait-laced—a type that did not commend itself to the very sexy Shakespeare. He belongs to that rare kind of person who hates the sight of other people's happiness—that is to say, he is not incredible, a monster: he is real, but rare.

He also hates human beings for their foolery—and this too is understandable, if rare: Swift understood it all right. One cannot but admire the sheer skill with which he takes in fool after fool—beginning with the silly gentleman Roderigo, who aspires to Desdemona's favours. Well, if people like to be such fools, they get what is coming to them —and they should certainly keep out of the way of a clever, scheming villain like Iago. 'Thus credulous fools are caught', he sums up: he had no compunction or mercy for their credulity—serve them out for it would be his attitude.

All the same, it *is* terrible to watch Othello falling into his snare. Terrible, and also fascinating, for Iago sails so brazenly, so truthfully, close to the wind. Like Hitler, Iago knows that to tell human fools the truth is often the most effective way of taking them in. He actually warns Othello of the danger of being jealous—Othello of course thinks him all the more honest for that. He speaks a good word to Othello on behalf of Cassio whom he means to destroy: Othello believes him all the more when it comes to sowing suspicion as to Cassio's relations with Othello's wife. 'Honest Iago' is his misnomer. And of course the simple, innocent girl that Desdemona is becomes a helpless victim in such hands. One is torn with compassion as one watches the bird fluttering into the net; one's heart turns over at the final act of the tragedy in her bed-chamber, her last talk with the faithful Emilia (that name!)—who has also been an innocent instrument in bringing it about—her total incomprehension of why such a fate has come upon her.

Shakespeare got the well-known story from an Italian *novella*, one of Cinthio's again; but, as Sisson reminds us, he transformed what was 'a brutal and vulgar story' in the original by 'the splendour of his art.' It reminds one of the transformation he wrought from Arthur Brooke's pedestrian poem into *Romeo and Juliet*, with which *Othello* may profitably be compared.

More of the age is reflected in the later play. Desdemona's father can account for her falling for the Moor only by witchcraft or charms, spells or drugs. Jacobean society was very conscious of this kind of thing, with the King himself such an authority on witches, and such people as 'Dr.' Forman so successful in London (Ben Jonson put him into *The*

Alchemist). In a few years Forman would be compounding love-philtres for the wicked young Countess of Essex to compel the love of the King's boy-friend, Robert Carr, fatally towards herself. The handkerchief given to Othello's mother by an Egyptian charmer—which Desdemona lost so suspiciously—had a magical potency:

> The worms were hallowed that did breed the silk,
> And it was dyed in mummy—

supposed to have been concocted from mummies (what credulity!), and Forman dealt also in that. He had had a good record for sticking to his post in plague-time, when orthodox doctors absconded from London. The year 1603 saw one of the severe decennial visitations, and we see it in the background in the image:

> As does the raven over the infected house
> Boding to all.

Other images bring the time clearly before us. Othello's marriage, for instance:

> Faith, tonight he has boarded a land carrack:
> If it proves lawful prize, he's made for ever.

We note the doubt upon the marriage from the first; but carracks were the contemporary Portuguese ships bringing the treasures of the East to Europe. The Elizabethans boarded and made prizes of several, notably the *Madre de Dios*, taken by Ralegh's ships.

> The Anthropophagi, and men whose heads
> Do grow beneath their shoulders—

this observation lodged in the mind of that reading man,[1] the dramatist, from Ralegh's *Discovery . . . of Guiana* of 1596. The description of the Hellespont and the Pontic Sea came straight from Philemon Holland's translation of Pliny.

From the beginning Shakespeare had always had a leaning to grand language—in itself an index to his character: the style is the man. With the plays of this late-middle period we see the addiction to rare words and idiosyncratic phrases growing upon him, until we come to the difficult, elliptical, eccentric language of the last plays. *Othello* already provides many examples of rare words— all the more necessary to give them modern equivalents, for few know what they mean. No one else seems ever to have used the word 'exsufflicate' for inflated, or 'antres' for caves. We are used to the grand words he liked to use, like 'conjunctive', 'sequent messengers', 'iterance' for repetition, 'indign' for unworthy, 'portance' for conduct. But why accept unnecessary difficulty with such forms as 'ingredience' for ingredients, 'arrivance' for arrivals, 're-stem' for retrace, 'injointed' for united, 'designment' for design, etc.? Who but Shakespeare would use the word 'fortitude' for the strength of a place; or 'my speculative and officed instruments', to mean my visual and (other) usual faculties? Or we may take a more simple example to illustrate the necessity of removing obscurities where possible: 'Be not acknown on't' is here rendered simply, 'Acknowledge it not.'

---

[1] cf. my *What Shakespeare Read and Thought*.

CHARACTERS

OTHELLO, a Moor in the service of Venice
DESDEMONA, his wife
CASSIO, his Lieutenant
IAGO, his Ancient, i.e. Ensign
EMILIA, wife of Iago
BIANCA, mistress of Cassio
RODERIGO, a Venetian gentleman
THE DUKE OF VENICE
BRABANTIO, a Venetian Senator, Desdemona's father
GRATIANO, his brother
LODOVICO, his kinsman
MONTANO, Governor of Cyprus

Senators, Gentlemen, Musicians, Officers, Attendants.

Act I

SCENE I
Venice. Before Brabantio's house.

Enter Roderigo and Iago

RODERIGO
Tush, never tell me! I take it much unkindly
That you, Iago, who have had my purse
As if the strings were yours, should know of this.

IAGO
God, but you will not hear me!
If ever I did dream of such a matter,
Abhor me.

RODERIGO
You told me you did hold him in your hate.

IAGO
Despise me, if I do not. Three great ones of the city,
In personal suit to make me his Lieutenant,
Off-capped to him: and by the faith of man,
I know my price, I am worth no worse a place.
But he, as loving his own pride and purposes,
Evades them with a bombast circumstance
Horribly stuffed with epithets of war,
And in conclusion
Non-suits my mediators. For 'Sure,' says he,
'I have already chosen my officer.'
And what was he?
Indeed, a great arithmeticiàn,
One Michael Cassio, a Florentine—
A fellow almost damned in a fair wife—

That never set a squadron in the field,
Nor the division of an army knows
More than a spinster—unless the bookish theory,
Wherein the togaed consuls can propose
As masterly as he. Mere prattle without practice
Is all his soldiership. But he, sir, had the election.
And I, of whom his eyes had seen the proof
At Rhodes, at Cyprus, and on other grounds
Christian and heathen, must be leed and calmed
By debitor and creditor. This counter-caster,
He in good time must his Lieutenant be,
And I—God bless the mark!—his Moorship's Ensign.

RODERIGO

By heaven, I rather would have been his hangman.

IAGO

Why, there's no remedy. It is the curse of service:
Preferment goes by letter and affection,
And not by old gradation, where each second
Stood heir to the first. Now sir, be judge yourself
Whether I in any just term am obliged
To love the Moor.

RODERIGO

I would not follow him then.

IAGO   O, sir, content you:
I follow him to serve my turn upon him.
We cannot all be masters, nor all masters
Cannot be truly followed. You shall mark
Many a duteous and knee-crooking knave
That, doting on his own obsequious bondage,
Wears out his time, much like his master's ass,
For naught but provender, and when he's old—cashiered!
Whip me such honest knaves. Others there are
Who, trimmed in forms and visages of duty,
Keep yet their hearts attending on themselves,
And, throwing but shows of service on their lords,

Do thrive by them; and when they have lined their
   coats,
Do themselves homage. These fellows have some soul,
And such a one do I profess myself.
For, sir,
It is as sure as you are Roderigo,
Were I the Moor, I would not be Iago:
In following him, I follow but myself.
Heaven is my judge, not I for love and duty,
But seeming so for my peculiar end:
For when my outward action demonstrates
The native act and figure of my heart
In compliment extern, 'tis not long after,
But I will wear my heart upon my sleeve
For daws to peck at. I am not what I am.

RODERIGO

What a full fortune does the thick-lips own
If he can carry it thus!

IAGO   Call up her father,
Rouse him, make after him, poison his delight,
Proclaim him in the streets; incense her kinsmen,
And, though he in a fertile climate dwells,
Plague him with flies; though now his joy is joy,
Yet throw such chances of vexation on it,
As it may lose some colour.

RODERIGO

Here is her father's house; I'll call aloud.

IAGO

Do, with like fearsome accent and dire yell,
As when, by night and negligence, the fire
Is spied in populous cities.

RODERIGO

What, ho, Brabantio! Signior Brabantio, ho!

IAGO

Awake! What, ho, Brabantio! Thieves, thieves!
Look to your house, your daughter, and your bags!
Thieves, thieves!

Enter Brabantio above at a window

BRABANTIO

What is the reason of this terrible summons?
What is the matter there?

RODERIGO

Signior, is all your family within?

IAGO

Are your doors locked?

BRABANTIO   Why, wherefore ask you this?

IAGO

Zounds, sir, you're robbed; for shame, put on your
    gown;
Your heart is burst, you have lost half your soul.
Even now, now, very now, an old black ram
Is tupping your white ewe. Arise, arise,
Awake the snorting citizens with the bell,
Or else the devil will make a grandsire of you.
Arise, I say!

BRABANTIO What, have you lost your wits?

RODERIGO

Most reverend signior, do you know my voice?

BRABANTIO

Not I: what are you?

RODERIGO   My name is Roderigo.

BRABANTIO

The worser welcome!
I have charged you not to haunt about my doors.
In honest plainness you have heard me say
My daughter is not for you. And now in madness,
Being full of supper and distempering draughts,

Upon malicious bravery do you come
To startle my quiet.

RODERIGO
Sir, sir, sir—

BRABANTIO   But you must needs be sure
My spirit and my place have in them power
To make this bitter to you.

RODERIGO   Patience, good sir.

BRABANTIO
What tell you me of robbing? This is Venice:
My house is not a grange.

RODERIGO   Most grave Brabantio,
In simple and pure soul I come to you ...

IAGO Zounds, sir, you are one of those that will not serve
God if the devil bids you. Because we come to do you
service, and you think we are ruffians, you'll have your
daughter covered with a Barbary horse; you'll have your
nephews neigh to you, you'll have coursers for cousins,
and jennets for kin.

BRABANTIO What profane wretch are you?

IAGO I am one, sir, that comes to tell you, your daughter
and the Moor are now making the beast with two backs.

BRABANTIO
You are a villain.

IAGO   You are a Senator.

BRABANTIO
This you shall answer. I know you, Roderigo.

RODERIGO
Sir, I will answer anything. But I beseech you
If it is your pleasure and most wise consent,
As partly I find it is, that your fair daughter,
At this odd-even and dull watch of the night,
Transported with no worse nor better guard
But with a knave of common hire, a gondolier,
To the gross clasps of a lascivious Moor—

If this is known to you, and your allowance,
We then have done you bold and saucy wrongs.
But if you know not this, my manners tell me
We have your wrong rebuke. Do not believe
That from the sense of all civility
I thus would play and trifle with your reverence.
Your daughter, if you have not given her leave,
I say again has made a gross revolt,
Tying her duty, beauty, wit, and fortunes
In an extravagant and wheeling stranger
Of here and everywhere. Straight satisfy yourself:
If she is in her chamber or your house,
Let loose on me the justice of the state
For thus deluding you.

BRABANTIO   Strike on the tinder, ho!
Give me a taper; call up all my people!
This accident is not unlike my dream:
Belief of it oppresses me already.
Light, I say, light!   *Exit above*

IAGO   Farewell, for I must leave you.
It seems not meet, nor wholesome to my place,
To be produced—as if I stay, I shall—
Against the Moor. For I do know the state,
However this may gall him with some check,
Cannot with safety sack him. For he's embarked
With such loud reason to the Cyprus wars,
Which even now stand in act, that for their souls
Another of his fathom they have none
To lead their business. In which regard,
Though I do hate him as I do hell pains,
Yet for necessity of present life
I must show out a flag and sign of love,
Which is indeed but sign. That you shall surely find
    him,
Lead to the Sagittary the raisèd search;
And there will I be with him. So farewell.   *Exit*

Enter Brabantio below with servants and torches

BRABANTIO
   It is too true an evil. Gone she is,
   And what's to come of my despisèd time
   Is naught but bitterness. Now, Roderigo,
   Where did you see her?—O unhappy girl!—
   With the Moor, say you?—Who would be a father?—
   How did you know it was she?—She deceives me
   Past thought!—What said she to you?—Get more tapers.
   Raise all my kindred.—Are they married, think you?
RODERIGO
   Truly I think they are.
BRABANTIO
   O heaven! How got she out? O treason of the blood!
   Fathers, from hence trust not your daughters' minds
   By what you see them act. Are there not charms
   By which the property of youth and maidenhood
   May be abused? Have you not read, Roderigo,
   Of some such thing?
RODERIGO   Yes, sir, I have indeed.
BRABANTIO
   Call up my brother—O would you had had her!
   Some one way, some another. Do you know
   Where we may apprehend her and the Moor?
RODERIGO
   I think I can discover him, if you please
   To get good guard and go along with me.
BRABANTIO
   Pray you, lead on. At every house I'll call—
   I may command at most. Get weapons, ho!
   And raise some special officers of night.
   On, good Roderigo, I'll reward your pains.   *Exeunt*

SCENE II
A street.

Enter Othello, Iago, attendants with torches

IAGO
  Though in the trade of war I have slain men,
  Yet do I hold it very stuff of the conscience
  To do no contrived murder: I lack iniquity
  Sometimes to do me service. Nine or ten times
  I had thought to yerk him here under the ribs.
OTHELLO
  It is better as it is.
IAGO   Nay, but he prated
  And spoke such scurvy and provoking terms
  Against your honour,
  That with the little godliness I have,
  I did full hard forbear him. But I pray, sir,
  Are you fast married? For be assured of this,
  That the Magnifico is much beloved,
  And has in his effect a voice potential
  As double as the Duke's. He will divorce you,
  Or put upon you what restraint and grievance
  That law, with all its might to enforce it on,
  Will give him cable.
OTHELLO   Let him do his spite:
  My services, which I have done the signiory,
  Shall out-tongue his complaints. It is not yet known—
  That, when I know that boasting is an honour,
  I shall promùlgate—I fetch my life and being
  From men of royal rank, and my demerits
  May speak, unbonneted, to as proud a fortune
  As this that I have reached. For know, Iago,
  But that I love the gentle Desdemona,
  I would not my unhousèd free condition

Put into circumscription and confine
For the seas' worth. But look, what lights come there!

IAGO

Those are the raisèd father and his friends:
You were best go in.

OTHELLO   Not I: I must be found.
My parts, my title, and my perfect soul
Shall manifest me rightly. Is it they?

IAGO

By Janus, I think no.

Enter Cassio, with men bearing torches

OTHELLO

The servants of the Duke and my Lieutenant!
The goodness of the night upon you, friends.
What is the news?

CASSIO   The Duke does greet you, General,
And he requires your haste-post-haste appearance
Even on the instant.

OTHELLO   What is the matter, think you?

CASSIO

Something from Cyprus, as I may divine:
It is a business of some heat. The galleys
Have sent a dozen sequent messengers
This very night at one another's heels;
And many of the consuls, raised and met,
Are at the Duke's already. You have been hotly called for,
When being not at your lodging to be found.
The senate has sent about three several quests
To search you out.

OTHELLO   'Tis well I am found by you:
I will but spend a word here in the house
And go with you.   *Exit*

CASSIO   Ensign, what makes he here?

IAGO
   Faith, he tonight has boarded a land carack:
   If it proves lawful prize, he's made for ever.

CASSIO
   I do not understand.

IAGO   He's married.

CASSIO   To whom?

IAGO
   Marry, to—Come, Captain, will you go?

Enter Othello

OTHELLO   Along with you.

CASSIO
   Here comes another troop to seek for you.

Enter Brabantio, Roderigo, with officers and torches

IAGO
   It is Brabantio: General, be advised,
   He comes to bad intent.

OTHELLO   Holla, stand there.

RODERIGO
   Signior, it is the Moor.

BRABANTIO   Down with him, thief!

IAGO
   You, Roderigo? Come, sir, I am for you.

OTHELLO
   Keep up your bright swords, for the dew will rust them.
   Good signior, you shall more command with years
   Than with your weapons.

BRABANTIO
   O you foul thief! Where have you stowed my daughter?
   Damned as you are, you have enchanted her.
   For I'll refer me to all things of sense,

If she in chains of magic is not bound,
Whether a maid, so tender, fair, and happy,
So opposite to marriage that she shunned
The wealthy curlèd darlings of our nation,
Would ever have—to incur a general mock—
Run from her wardship to the sooty bosom
Of such a thing as you. To fear, not to delight.
Judge me the world, if 'tis not gross in sense
That you have practised on her with foul charms,
Abused her delicate youth with drugs or minerals
That weaken willpower. I'll have it disputed on;
'Tis probable, and palpable to thinking.
I therefore apprehend, and do attach you
For an abuser of the world, a practiser
Of arts inhibited, and out of warrant.
Lay hold upon him: if he does resist,
Subdue him, at his peril.

OTHELLO   Hold your hands,
Both you of my inclining and the rest.
Were it my cue to fight, I should have known it
Without a prompter. Where will you that I go
To answer this your charge?

BRABANTIO   To prison, till fit time
Of law and course of direct sessiòn
Calls you to answer.

OTHELLO   What if I do obey?
How may the Duke be therewith satisfied,
Whose messengers are here about my side,
Upon some urgent business of the state
To bring me to him?

OFFICER   'Tis true, most worthy signior:
The Duke's in council, and your noble self
I am sure is sent for.

BRABANTIO   How? The Duke in council?
In this time of the night? Bring him away.
Mine's not an idle cause; the Duke himself,

Or any of my brothers of the state,
Cannot but feel this wrong as if their own:
For if such actions may have passage free,
Bondslaves and pagans shall our statesmen be. *Exeunt*

SCENE III
The Duke's palace.

*The Duke and Senators at table with lights
and attendants*

DUKE
There is no consistency in these news
That gives them credit.
FIRST SENATOR   Indeed they are inconsistent.
My letters say a hundred and seven galleys.
DUKE
And mine, a hundred and forty.
SECOND SENATOR   And mine two hundred;
But though they tally not on a just account—
As in these cases where the aim reports
'Tis oft with difference—yet do they all confirm
A Turkish fleet, and bearing up to Cyprus.
DUKE
Nay, it is possible enough to judgement:
I do not so secure me in the error,
But the main article I do approve
In fearful sense.
SAILOR (*without*) What, ho! What, ho! What, ho!
FIRST OFFICER
A messenger from the galleys.

Enter Sailor

DUKE   Now, what's the business?
SAILOR
  The Turkish preparation makes for Rhodes;
  So was I bid report here to the state
  By Signior Angelo.
DUKE
  How say you by this change?
FIRST SENATOR   This cannot be,
  By any test of reason. It is a pageant
  To keep us in false gaze. When we consider
  The importance of Cyprus to the Turk,
  And let ourselves again but understand
  That as it more concerns the Turk than Rhodes,
  So may he with more facile question bear it:
  Because it stands not in such warlike brace,
  But altogether lacks the abilities
  That Rhodes is dressed in. If we make thought of this,
  We must not think the Turk is so unskilful
  To leave that latest which concerns him first,
  Neglecting an attempt of ease and gain
  To wake and wage a danger profitless.
DUKE
  Nay, in all confidence he's not for Rhodes.
FIRST OFFICER
  Here is more news.

Enter a Messenger

MESSENGER
  The Ottomites, reverend and gracious,
  Steering with due course toward the isle of Rhodes,
  Have there united with an after-fleet.
FIRST SENATOR
  Ay, so I thought. How many, as you guess?

MESSENGER
    Of thirty sail; and now they do retrace
    Their backward course, bearing with frank appearance
    Their purposes toward Cyprus. Signior Montano,
    Your trusty and most valiant servitor,
    With his free duty recommends you thus,
    And prays you to believe him.

DUKE
    It is certain then for Cyprus.
    Marcus Luccicos, is not he in town?

FIRST SENATOR
    He is now in Florence.

DUKE   Write from us: wish him
    Post-post-haste dispatch.

FIRST SENATOR
    Here comes Brabantio and the valiant Moor.

Enter Brabantio, Othello, Iago, Roderigo, and officers

DUKE
    Valiant Othello, we must straight employ you
    Against the general enemy Ottoman.
    (*To Brabantio*) I did not see you: welcome, gentle signior;
    We lacked your counsel and your help tonight.

BRABANTIO
    So did I yours. Good your grace, pardon me:
    Neither my place, nor aught I heard of business,
    Has raised me from my bed; nor does the general care
    Take hold on me. For my particular grief
    Is of so flood-gate and overbearing nature
    That it engulfs and swallows other sorrows
    And yet is still itself.

DUKE   Why? What's the matter?

BRABANTIO
    My daughter! O, my daughter!

SENATORS   Dead?

BRABANTIO   Ay, to me.
   She is abused, stolen from me, and corrupted
   By spells and medicines bought of mountebanks;
   For nature so preposterously to err,
   Being not deficient, blind, or lame of sense,
   Without witchcraft could not.
DUKE
   Whoever he is that in this foul proceeding
   Has thus beguiled your daughter of herself
   And you of her, the bloody book of law
   You shall yourself read in the bitter letter
   After your own sense—yea, though our very son
   Stood in your action.
BRABANTIO   Humbly I thank your grace.
   Here is the man: this Moor, whom now it seems
   Your special mandate for the state affairs
   Has hither brought.
ALL   We are very sorry for it.
DUKE
   What in your own part can you say to this?
BRABANTIO
   Nothing, but this is so.
OTHELLO
   Most potent, grave and reverend signiors,
   My very noble and approved good masters,
   That I have taken away this old man's daughter,
   It is most true. True I have married her;
   The very head and front of my offending
   Has this extent, no more. Rude am I in my speech
   And little blessed with the soft phrase of peace;
   For since these arms of mine had seven years' pith
   Till now some nine moons wasted, they have used
   Their dearest action in the tented field.
   And little of this great world can I speak
   More than pertains to feats of broil and battle;
   And therefore little shall I grace my cause

In speaking for myself. Yet, by your gracious patience.
I will a round unvarnished tale deliver
Of my whole course of love: what drugs, what charms,
What conjuration and what mighty magic—
For such proceedings I am charged with too—
I won his daughter.

BRABANTIO   A maiden never bold;
Of spirit so still and quiet that her motion
Blushed at herself: and she, in spite of nature,
Of years, of country, credit, everything,
To fall in love with what she feared to look on!
It is a judgement maimed and most imperfect
That will confess perfection so could err
Against all rules of nature, and must be driven
To find out practices of cunning hell
Why this should be. I therefore vowed again
That with some mixtures powerful o'er the blood,
Or with some dram conjured to this effect,
He wrought upon her.

DUKE   To vouch this is no proof,
Without much wider and more overt test
Than these thin habits and poor likelihoods
Of common seeming do prefer against him.

FIRST SENATOR
But, Othello, speak:
Did you by indirect and forcèd courses
Subdue and poison this young maid's affections?
Or came it by request and such fair question
As soul to soul affords?

OTHELLO   I do beseech you,
Send for the lady to the Sagittary,
And let her speak of me before her father.
If you do find me foul in her report,
The trust, the office I do hold of you
Not only take away, but let your sentence
Even fall upon my life.

DUKE   Fetch Desdemona hither.
OTHELLO
   Ensign, conduct them: you best know the place.
                       Exit Iago with attendants
   And till she comes, as truly as to heaven
   I do confess the vices of my blood,
   So justly to your grave ears I'll present
   How I did thrive in this fair lady's love,
   And she in mine.
DUKE   Say it, Othello.
OTHELLO
   Her father loved me, oft invited me,
   Ever questioned me the story of my life
   From year to year—the battles, sieges, fortunes
   That I have passed.
   I ran it through, even from my boyish days
   To the very moment that he bade me tell it.
   Wherein I spoke of most disastrous chances,
   Of moving accidents by flood and field,
   Of hair-breadth escapes in the imminent deadly breach,
   Of being taken by the insolent foe,
   And sold to slavery; of my redemption thence,
   And conduct in my travels' history.
   Wherein of caverns vast and deserts idle,
   Rough quarries, rocks, and hills whose heads touch
      heaven,
   It was my hint to speak—such was the process.
   And of the cannibals that each other eat,
   The anthropophagi, and men whose heads
   Do grow beneath their shoulders. This to hear
   Would Desdemona seriously incline.
   But still the house affairs would draw her thence,
   Which ever as she could with haste dispatch
   She'd come again, and with a greedy ear
   Devour up my discourse. This I observing
   Took once a pliant hour, and found good means

To draw from her a prayer of earnest heart
That I would all my pilgrimage dilate,
Whereof by parcels she had something heard,
But not attentively. I did consent,
And often did beguile her of her tears
When I did speak of some distressful stroke
That my youth suffered. My story being done,
She gave me for my pains a world of sighs:
She swore, in faith 'twas strange, 'twas passing strange,
'Twas pitiful, 'twas wondrous pitiful;
She wished she had not heard it, yet she wished
That heaven had made her such a man. She thanked
    me,
And bade me, if I had a friend that loved her,
I should but teach him how to tell my story,
And that would woo her. Upon this hint I spoke:
She loved me for the dangers I had passed,
And I loved her, that she did pity them.
This only is the witchcraft I have used.
Here comes the lady: let her witness it.

           Enter Desdemona, Iago, and attendants

DUKE
    I think this tale would win my daughter too.
    Good Brabantio, take up this mangled matter at the
        best:
    Men do their broken weapons rather use
    Than their bare hands.
BRABANTIO   I pray you hear her speak.
    If she confesses that she was half the wooer,
    Destruction on my head, if my bad blame
    Light on the man! Come hither, gentle mistress;
    Do you perceive in all this company
    Where most you owe obedience?

DESDEMONA   My noble father,
   I do perceive here a divided duty:
   To you I am bound for life and education;
   My life and education both do teach me
   How to respect you. You are lord of all my duty,
   I am hitherto your daughter. But here's my husband;
   And so much duty as my mother showed
   To you, preferring you before her father,
   So much I challenge, that I may profess
   Due to the Moor, my lord.

BRABANTIO   Goodbye! I have done.
   Please it your grace, on to the state affairs.
   I had rather to adopt a child than get it.
   Come hither, Moor:
   I here do give you that with all my heart
   What, but you have already, with all my heart
   I would keep from you. For your sake, jewel,
   I am glad at soul I have no other child,
   For your escape would teach me tyranny
   To hang clogs on them. I have done, my lord.

DUKE
   Let me speak like yourself and lay a sentence
   Which as a ladder or step may help these lovers
   Into your favour.
   When remedies are past the griefs are ended
   By seeing the worst which late on hopes depended.
   To mourn a mischief that is past and gone
   Is the next way to draw new mischief on.
   What cannot be preserved when fortune takes,
   Patience her injury a mockery makes.
   The robbed that smiles steals something from the thief;
   He robs himself that spends a useless grief.

BRABANTIO
   So let the Turk of Cyprus us beguile,
   We lose it not so long as we can smile;
   He bears the sentence well that nothing bears

But the free comfort which from thence he hears;
But he bears both the sentence and the sorrow
That to pay grief must of poor patience borrow.
These sentences, to sugar or to gall
Being strong on both sides, are equivocal.
But words are words; I never yet did hear
That the bruised heart was mended through the ear.
I humbly beseech you proceed to the affairs of state.

DUKE The Turk with a most mighty preparation makes
for Cyprus. Othello, the strength of the place is best
known to you: and though we have there a substitute of
most allowed sufficiency, yet opinion, a more sovereign
mistress of effects, throws a safer voice on you. You
must therefore be content to darken the gloss of your
new fortunes with this more stubborn and boisterous
expedition.

OTHELLO
The tyrant, custom, most grave Senators,
Has made the flinty and steel couch of war
My thrice-driven bed of down. I do acknowledge
A natural and prompt alacrity
I find in hardness; and do undertake
This present war against the Ottomites.
Most humbly, therefore, bending to your state,
I crave fit disposition for my wife,
Due reference of place, provision too.
With such accommodation and attendance
As levels with her breeding.

DUKE   If you please,
Be it at her father's.

BRABANTIO   I will not have it so.

OTHELLO
Nor I.

DESDEMONA Nor I: I would not there reside
To put my father in impatient thoughts
By being in his eye. Most gracious Duke,

To my unfolding lend your prosperous ear,
And let me find a charter in your voice
To assist my simpleness.
DUKE   What would you? Speak.
DESDEMONA
That I did love the Moor to live with him,
My downright violence and storm of fortunes
May trumpet to the world. My heart is subdued
Even to the very quality of my lord.
I saw Othello's visage in his mind,
And to his honours and his valiant parts
Did I my soul and fortunes consecrate.
So that, dear lords, if I am left behind
A moth of peace, and he goes to the war,
The rites for which I love him are bereft me;
And I a heavy interim shall support
By his dear absence. Let me go with him.
OTHELLO
Let her have your voice.
Hear with me, heaven, I therefore beg it not
To please the palate of my appetite,
Nor to comply with heat—the young desires
In me defunct—and my own satisfaction;
But to be free and bounteous to her mind.
And heaven defend your good souls that you think
I will your serious and great business scant
Because she is with me. No, when light-winged toys
Of feathered Cupid blind with wanton dullness
My visual and other faculties,
That pleasure may corrupt and taint my business—
Let housewives make a skillet of my helm,
And all unworthy and base adversities
Make head against my reputatiòn!

DUKE

    Be it as you shall privately determine,

    Either for her stay, or going. The affair cries haste,

    And speed must answer it. You must hence tonight.

DESDEMONA

    Tonight, my lord?

DUKE   This night.

OTHELLO   With all my heart.

DUKE

    At nine in the morning, here we'll meet again.

    Othello, leave some officer behind,

    And he shall our commission bring to you,

    With such things else of quality and respect

    As do concern you.

OTHELLO   So please your grace, my Ensign.

    A man he is of honesty and trust:

    To his conveyance I assign my wife,

    With what else needful your good grace shall think

    To be sent after me.

DUKE   Let it be so.

    Good night to everyone. And, noble signior,

    If virtue no delighted beauty lack,

    Your son-in-law is far more fair than black.

FIRST SENATOR

    Adieu, brave Moor: use Desdemona well.

BRABANTIO

    Look to her, Moor, if you have eyes to see.

    She has deceived her father, and may thee.

OTHELLO

    My life upon her faith!

                  Exeunt Duke, Senators, and attendants

                  Honest Iago,

    My Desdemona must I leave to you.

    I pray you let your wife attend on her,

    And bring them after in the best advantage.

    Come, Desdemona, I have but an hour

Of love, of worldly matters and direction
To spend with you. We must obey the time.

Exeunt Othello and Desdemona

RODERIGO Iago.

IAGO What say you, noble heart?

RODERIGO What will I do, think you?

IAGO Why, go to bed and sleep.

RODERIGO I will incontinently drown myself.   *wimp*

IAGO If you do, I shall never love you after. Why, you silly
gentleman!

RODERIGO It is silliness to live, when to live is torment:
and then we have a prescription to die, when death is
our physician.

IAGO O villainous! I have looked upon the world for four
times seven years, and since I could distinguish between
a benefit and an injury, I never found a man that knew
how to love himself. Ere I would say I would drown
myself for the love of a guinea-hen, I would change my
humanity with a baboon.   *call himself*

RODERIGO What should I do? I confess it is my shame to *foolish*
be so foolish, but it is not in my virtue to amend it.

IAGO Virtue? A fig! 'Tis in ourselves that we are thus, or
thus. Our bodies are our gardens, to which our wills are
gardeners. So that if we will plant nettles or sow lettuce,
set hyssop and weed up thyme, supply it with one
gender of herbs or distract it with many, either to have
it sterile with idleness or manured with industry, why   *?*
the power and corrigible authority of this lies in our
wills. If the beam of our lives had not one scale of
reason to poise another of sensuality, the blood and
baseness of our natures would conduct us to most
preposterous conclusions. But we have reason to cool
our raging motions, our carnal stings, our unbitted
lusts: whereof I take this, that you call love, to be a sect
or scion.

RODERIGO It cannot be.

IAGO It is merely a lust of the blood and a permission of the will. Come, be a man. Drown yourself? Drown cats and blind puppies. I have professed me your friend, and I confess me knit to your deserving with cables of perdurable toughness. I could never better help you than now. Put money in your purse. Follow you these wars; disguise your face with an usurped beard. I say, put money in your purse. It cannot be that Desdemona should long continue her love to the Moor—put money in your purse—nor he his to her. It was a violent commencement, and you shall see an answerable sequestration—put but money in your purse. These Moors are changeable in their wills—fill your purse with money. The food that to him now is as luscious as locusts shall be to him shortly as bitter as quinine. She must change for youth: when she is sated with his body she will find the error of her choice. Therefore put money in your purse. If you will needs damn yourself, do it a more delicate way than drowning. Raise all the money you can. If sanctimony and a frail vow between an erring barbarian and a super-subtle Venetian are not too hard for my wits and all the tribe of hell, you shall enjoy her—therefore raise money. A pox of drowning yourself! It is clean out of the way. Seek you rather to be hanged in compassing your joy than to be drowned and go without her.

RODERIGO Will you be fast to my hopes, if I depend on the issue?

IAGO You are sure of me. Go raise money. I have told you often, and I re-tell you again and again, I hate the Moor. My cause is heart-felt: yours has no less reason. Let us be conjunctive in our revenge against him. If you can cuckold him, you do yourself a pleasure, me a sport. There are many events in the womb of time, which will be delivered. About turn! Go, provide your money. We will have more of this tomorrow. Adieu.

RODERIGO Where shall we meet in the morning?

IAGO At my lodging.

RODERIGO I'll be with you betimes.

IAGO Very well; farewell. Do you hear, Roderigo?

RODERIGO What say you?

IAGO No more of drowning, do you hear?

RODERIGO I am changed.

IAGO Good; farewell. Put money enough in your purse.

RODERIGO I'll sell all my land.   *Exit*

IAGO

   Thus do I ever make my fool my purse:
   For I my own gained knowledge should profane
   If I would time expend with such a snipe
   But for my sport and profit. I hate the Moor,
   And it is thought abroad that between my sheets
   He's done my office. I know not if it is true,
   But I, for mere suspicion in that kind,
   Will do as if for surety. He thinks well of me;
   The better shall my purpose work on him.
   Cassio's a goodly man: let me see now;
   To get his place and to plume up my will
   In double knavery. How? How? Let's see.
   After some time, to abuse Othello's ear
   That he is too familiar with his wife;
   He has a person and a smooth disposition
   To be suspected, framed to make women false.
   The Moor is of a free and open nature,
   That thinks men honest that but seem to be so,
   And will as tenderly be led by the nose
   As asses are.
   I have it. It is engendered. Hell and night
   Must bring this monstrous birth to the world's light.
                             Exit

Act II

SCENE I
Cyprus. The port.

Enter Montano and two Gentlemen

MONTANO
    What from the cape can you discern at sea?
FIRST GENTLEMAN
    Nothing at all; it is a high-wrought flood.
    I cannot between the heaven and the main
    Descry a sail.
MONTANO
    I think the wind does speak aloud at land;
    A fuller blast never shook our battlements.
    If it has ruffianed so upon the sea,
    What ribs of oak, when mountains melt on them,
    Can hold the mortise? What shall we hear of this?
SECOND GENTLEMAN
    It seems the dispersal of the Turkish fleet:
    For do but stand upon the cursing shore,
    The chidden billow seems to pelt the clouds;
    The wind-shaked surge, with high and monstrous mane,
    Seems to cast water on the burning Bear
    And quench the guards of the ever-fixèd Pole.
    I never did like molestation view
    On the angry flood.
MONTANO   If the Turkish fleet
    Is not sheltered and embayed, they are drowned:
    It is impossible they bear it out.

Enter a Gentleman

405

THIRD GENTLEMAN
    News, lads! Our wars are done:
    The desperate tempest has so banged the Turks
    That their design halts. A ship of Venice
    Has seen a grievous wreck and sufferance
    On most part of their fleet.
MONTANO
    How! Is this true?
THIRD GENTLEMAN The ship is here put in,
    A Veronesa; Michael Cassio,
    Lieutenant to the warlike Moor, Othello,
    Is come on shore; the Moor himself at sea,
    And is in full commission here for Cyprus.
MONTANO
    I am glad of it: a worthy governor.
THIRD GENTLEMAN
    But this same Cassio, though he speaks of comfort
    Touching the Turkish loss; yet he looks sadly
    And prays the Moor is safe; for they were parted
    With foul and violent tempest.
MONTANO   Pray heaven he is:
    For I have served him, and the man commands
    Like a full soldier. Let's to the sea-side, ho!
    As well to see the vessel that's come in,
    As to throw out our eyes for brave Othello,
    Even till we make the main and the aerial blue
    An indistinct regard.
THIRD GENTLEMAN Come, let's do so;
    For every minute is expectancy
    Of more arrivals.

                        Enter Cassio

CASSIO
    Thanks, you the valiant of this warlike isle
    That so approve the Moor! O, let the heavens

Give him defence against the elements,
For I have lost him on a dangerous sea.

MONTANO
Is he well shipped?

CASSIO
His bark is stoutly timbered, and his pilot
Of very expert and approved allowance;
Therefore my hopes, not surfeited to death,
Stand in bold shape.

(*Cry within* 'A sail, a sail, a sail!')

CASSIO
What noise?

FOURTH GENTLEMAN
The town is empty; on the brow of the sea
Stand ranks of people, and they cry 'A sail!'

CASSIO
My hopes do shape him for the Governor.

Salvo

SECOND GENTLEMAN
They do discharge their shot of courtesy:
Our friends at least.

CASSIO   I pray you, sir, go forth,
And give us truth who 'tis that is arrived.

SECOND GENTLEMAN
I shall.   *Exit*

MONTANO
But, good Lieutenant, is your General wived?

CASSIO
Most fortunately: he has achieved a maid
That paragons description and wild fame;
One that excels the quirks of blazoning pens,
And in the essential vesture of creation
Does tire the inventor.

Enter Second Gentleman

               How now? Who has put in?

SECOND GENTLEMAN
  'Tis one Iago, Ensign to the General.

CASSIO
  He's had most favourable and happy speed:
  Tempests themselves, high seas, and howling winds,
  The guttered rocks and congregated sands,
  Traitors enscarped to clog the guiltless keel,
  As having sense of beauty, do omit
  Their mortal natures, letting go safely by
  The divine Desdemona.

MONTANO   What is she?

CASSIO
  She that I spake of, our great Captain's Captain,
  Left in the conduct of the bold Iago,
  Whose footing here anticipates our thoughts
  A sevennight's speed. Great Jove, Othello guard,
  And swell his sail with your own powerful breath,
  That he may bless this bay with his tall ship,
  Make love's quick pants in Desdemona's arms,
  Give renewed fire to our extinguished spirits,
  And bring all Cyprus comfort.

Enter Desdemona, Emilia, Iago, Roderigo, and attendants

               O, behold,
  The riches of the ship are come on shore!
  You men of Cyprus, let her have your knees.
  Hail to you, lady! And the grace of heaven,
  Before, behind you, and on every hand,
  Enwheel you round.

DESDEMONA   I thank you, valiant Cassio.
  What tidings can you tell me of my lord?

CASSIO
 He has not yet arrived; nor know I aught
 But that he's well, and will be shortly here.
DESDEMONA
 O, but I fear! How lost you company?
CASSIO
 The great contention of the sea and skies
 Parted our fellowship.
    (*Cry within*) 'A sail, a sail!'
       But hark, a sail!

GENTLEMAN
 They give their greeting to the citadel:
 This likewise is a friend.
CASSIO   See for the news.
 Good Ensign, you are welcome. Welcome, mistress.
 Let it not gall your patience, good Iago,
 That I extend my manners. 'Tis my breeding
 That gives me this bold show of courtesy.

     He kisses Emilia

IAGO
 Sir, would she give you so much of her lips
 As of her tongue she oft bestows on me,
 You would have enough.
DESDEMONA
 Alas, she has no speech.
IAGO   In faith, too much.
 I find it ever when I have wish to sleep.
 However, before your ladyship, I grant
 She puts her tongue a little in her heart
 And chides with thinking.
EMILIA   You have little cause to say so.
IAGO Come on, come on: you are pictures out of doors,
 bells in your parlours, wild-cats in your kitchens, saints

in your injuries, devils being offended, players in your
housewifery, and housewives in your beds.
DESDEMONA

O, fie upon you, slanderer!
IAGO

Nay, it is true, or else I am a Turk:
You rise to play and go to bed to work.
EMILIA

You shall not write my praise.
IAGO   No, let me not.
DESDEMONA

What would you write of me, if you should praise me?
IAGO

O, gentle lady, do not put me to it,
For I am nothing if not critical.
DESDEMONA

Come on, try. There's one gone to the harbour?
IAGO

Ay, madam.
DESDEMONA

(*aside*) I am not merry, but I do beguile
The thing I am by seeming otherwise.
Come, how would you praise me?
IAGO

I am about it, but indeed my invention
Comes from my pate as birdlime does from frieze—
It plucks out brains and all. But my muse labours,
And thus she is delivered.
If she is fair and wise, fairness and wit,
The one is for use, the other uses it.
DESDEMONA

Well praised! How if she is black and witty?
IAGO

If she is black, and thereto has a wit,
She'll find a white that shall her blackness fit.

DESDEMONA
  Worse and worse.
EMILIA   How if fair and foolish?
IAGO
  She never yet was foolish that was fair,
  For even her folly helped her to an heir.
DESDEMONA These are old fond paradoxes to make fools
  laugh in the alehouse. What miserable praise have you
  for her that's foul and foolish?
IAGO
  There's none so foul and foolish thereunto,
  But does foul pranks which fair and wise ones do.
DESDEMONA O heavy ignorance! You praise the worst
  best. But what praise could you bestow on a deserving
  woman indeed? One that in the authority of her merit
  did justly put on the proof of very malice itself?
IAGO
  She that was ever fair and never proud,
  Had tongue at will, and yet was never loud;
  Never lacked gold, and yet went never gay;
  Fled from her wish, and yet said 'Now I may';
  She that being angered, her revenge being nigh,
  Bade her wrong wait, and her displeasure fly;
  She that in wisdom never was so frail
  To change the cod's head for the salmon's tail;
  She that could think and never disclose her mind:
  See suitors following and not look behind:
  She was a one, if ever such one were—
DESDEMONA
  To do what?
IAGO
  To suckle fools and chronicle small beer.
DESDEMONA
  O, most lame and impotent conclusion!
  Do not learn of him, Emilia, though he is your husband.

How say you, Cassio, is he not a most profane and
liberal counsellor?

CASSIO He speaks home, madam; you may relish him
more in the soldier than in the scholar.

IAGO (aside) He takes her by the palm. Ay, well said,
whisper. With as little a web as this will I ensnare as
great a fly as Cassio. Ay, smile upon her, do. I will fetter
you in your own courtship. You say true, it is so indeed.
If such tricks as these strip you out of your lieutenantry,
it had been better you had not kissed your three fingers
so oft, which now again you are most apt to play the sir
in. Very good: well kissed, an excellent courtesy! It is so
indeed. Yet again your fingers to your lips? Would they
were screw-pipes for your sake!

Trumpet

(aloud) The Moor! I know his trumpet.

CASSIO   'Tis truly so.

DESDEMONA

Let's meet him and receive him.

CASSIO   Lo, where he comes!

Enter Othello and attendants

OTHELLO

O, my fair warrior!

DESDEMONA   My dear Othello!

OTHELLO

It gives me wonder great as my content
To see you here before me. O, my soul's joy!
If after every tempest come such calms,
May the winds blow till they have wakened death;
And let the labouring bark climb hills of seas,
Olympus-high, and duck again as low
As hell's from heaven. If it were now to die,

It were now to be most happy; for I fear
My soul has her content so absolute
That not another comfort like to this
Succeeds in unknown fate.

DESDEMONA   The heavens forbid
But that our loves and comforts should increase,
Even as our days do grow.

OTHELLO   Amen to that, sweet Powers!
I cannot speak enough of this content;
It stops me here; it is too much of joy.

They kiss

And this, and this the greatest discords be
That ever our hearts shall make.

IAGO *(aside)*   O, you are well tuned now!
But I'll lower the pegs that make this music,
As honest as I am.

OTHELLO   Come, let's to the castle.
News, friends; our wars are done; the Turks are drowned.
How do my old acquaintance of this isle?
Honey, you shall be well desired in Cyprus:
I have found great love among them. O my sweet,
I prattle out of fashion and I dote
In my own comforts. I pray you, good Iago,
Go to the bay and disembark my coffers;
Bring you the Master to the citadel;
He is a good one, and his worthiness
Does challenge much respect. Come, Desdemona,
Once more well met at Cyprus!

                    Exeunt all except Iago and Roderigo
IAGO *(to soldiers, who go off)* Do you meet me presently at
the harbour. *(To Roderigo)* Come hither. If you are
valiant—as they say base men being in love have then a
nobility in their natures more than is native to them—
listen to me. The Lieutenant tonight watches on the

court of guard. First, I must tell you this: Desdemona is
directly in love with him.

RODERIGO With him? Why, 'tis not possible!

IAGO Lay your finger thus, and let your soul be instructed.
Mark me with what violence she first loved the Moor,
but for bragging and telling her fantastical lies. And
will she love him still for prating? Let not your discreet
heart think it. Her eye must be fed. And what delight
shall she have to look on the devil? When the blood is
made dull with the act of sport, there should be, again
to inflame it and give satiety a fresh appetite, loveliness
in favour, sympathy in years, manners and beauties:
all which the Moor is defective in. Now for want of
these required conveniences, her delicate tenderness will
find itself abused, begin to heave the gorge, disrelish
and abhor the Moor. Very nature will instruct her in it
and compel her to some second choice. Now, sir, this
granted—as it is a most obvious and unforced position—
who stands so eminently in the degree of this fortune
as Cassio does?—A knave very voluble; no further
conscionable than in putting on the mere form of civil
and humane seeming for the better compassing of his
lustful and most hidden loose affection. Why, none;
why, none—a slippery and subtle knave, a finder out of
occasions; that has an eye that can stamp and counterfeit
advantages, though true advantage never presents itself;
a devilish knave! Besides, the knave is handsome, young,
and has all those requisites in him that folly and green
minds look after. A pestilent complete knave; and the
woman has found him already.

RODERIGO I cannot believe that in her: she's full of most
blessed condition.

IAGO Blessed fig's end! The wine she drinks is made of
grapes. If she had been blessed, she would never have
loved the Moor. Blessed pudding! Did you not see her
fiddle with the palm of his hand? Did you not mark that?

RODERIGO Yes, that I did: but that was but courtesy.

IAGO Lechery, by this hand: an index and obscure prologue
  to the history of lust and foul thoughts. They met so
  near with their lips that their breaths embraced together.
  Villainous thoughts, Roderigo! When these mutualities
  so marshal the way, hard at hand comes the master and
  main exercise, the incorporate conclusion. Pish! But,
  sir, be you ruled by me. I have brought you from Venice.
  Watch you tonight: for the command, I'll lay it upon
  you. Cassio knows you not; I'll not be far from you. Do
  you find some occasion to anger Cassio, either by speaking
  too loud, or crabbing his discipline, or from what other
  course you please, which the time shall more favourably
  minister.

RODERIGO Well.

IAGO Sir, he's rash and very sudden in anger, and haply
  with his truncheon may strike at you: provoke him that
  he may, for even out of that will I cause these of Cyprus
  to mutiny, whose appeasement shall come into no true
  taste again but by the displanting of Cassio. So shall
  you have a shorter journey to your desires by the means
  I shall then have to prefer them, and the impediment
  most profitably removed, without which there is no
  expectation of our prosperity.

RODERIGO I will do this, if you can bring it to any
  opportunity.

IAGO I warrant you. Meet me by and by at the citadel. I
  must fetch his necessaries ashore. Farewell.

RODERIGO Adieu.   *Exit*

IAGO
  That Cassio loves her, I do well believe it:
  That she loves him, 'tis apt and of great credit.
  The Moor—howbeit that I endure him not—
  Is of a constant, loving, noble nature,
  And, I dare think, he'll prove to Desdemona
  A most dear husband. Now, I do love her too;

Not out of absolute lust—though peradventure
I stand accountable for as great a sin—
But partly led to diet my revenge
For that I do suspect the lusty Moor
Has leaped into my seat: the thought whereof
Does, like a poisonous mineral, gnaw my inwards,
And nothing can, or shall, content my soul
Till I am evened with him, wife for wife.
Or failing so, yet that I put the Moor
At least into a jealousy so strong
That judgement cannot cure. Which thing to do
If this poor trash of Venice, whom I track
For his quick hunting, responds to incitement,
I'll have our Michael Cassio on the hip,
Abuse him to the Moor in the rank garb—
For I fear Cassio with my night-cap too—
Make the Moor thank me, love me, and reward me
For making him egregiously an ass,
And practising upon his peace and quiet,
Even to madness. 'Tis here, but yet confused:
Knavery's plain face is never seen till used.   *Exit*

SCENE II
Cyprus. A street.

Enter Herald, with a proclamation

HERALD It is Othello's pleasure, our noble and valiant
General, that upon certain tidings now arrived importing
the mere perdition of the Turkish fleet, every man puts
himself into triumph: some to dance, some to make
bonfires, each man to what sport and revels his addiction
leads him. For, besides these beneficial news, it is the
celebration of his nuptials. So much was his pleasure
should be proclaimed. All stores are open, and there is

full liberty of feasting from this present hour of five till
the bell has told eleven. Heaven bless the isle of Cyprus
and our noble General Othello!   *Exit*

SCENE III
The citadel.

Enter Othello, Desdemona, Cassio, and attendants

OTHELLO
  Good Michael, look you to the guard tonight.
  Let's teach ourselves that honourable stop,
  Not to outsport discretion.
CASSIO
  Iago has direction what to do;
  But, notwithstanding, with my personal eye
  Will I look to it.
OTHELLO   Iago is most honest.
  Michael, good night. Tomorrow with your earliest
  Let me have speech with you. *(To Desdemona)* Come,
      my dear love,
  The purchase made, the fruits are to ensue:
  That profit's yet to come between me and you.
  Good night.
              Exeunt Othello, Desdemona, and attendants

              Enter Iago

CASSIO Welcome, Iago; we must to the watch.
IAGO Not this hour, Lieutenant; 'tis not yet ten o'clock.
  Our General cast us thus early for the love of his
  Desdemona; whom let us not therefore blame. He has
  not yet made wanton the night with her; and she is
  sport for Jove.
CASSIO She is a most exquisite lady.

IAGO And, I'll warrant her, full of game.

CASSIO Indeed, she is a most fresh and delicate creature.

IAGO What an eye she has! I think it sounds a parley to
provocation.

CASSIO An inviting eye, and yet I think right modest.

IAGO And when she speaks, is it not an alarum to love?

CASSIO She is indeed perfection.

IAGO Well, happiness to their sheets! Come, Lieutenant,
I have a stoup of wine; and here without are a brace of
Cyprus gallants that would gladly have a measure to
the health of black Othello.

CASSIO Not tonight, good Iago. I have very poor and
unhappy brains for drinking. I could well wish courtesy
would invent some other custom of entertainment.

IAGO O, they are our friends! But one cup; I'll drink for
you.

CASSIO I have drunk but one cup tonight, and that was
well watered too; and behold what innovation it makes
here. I am unfortunate in the infirmity and dare not tax
my weakness with any more.

IAGO What, man! 'Tis a night of revels; the gallants desire
it.

CASSIO Where are they?

IAGO Here, at the door: I pray you call them in.

CASSIO I'll do it, but it dislikes me.   *Exit*

IAGO

If I can fasten but one cup upon him,
With that which he has drunk tonight already,
He'll be as full of quarrel and offence
As my young mistress' dog. Now my sick fool Roderigo,
Whom love has turned almost the wrong side out,
To Desdemona has tonight caroused
Potations bottle-deep; and he's to watch.
Three else of Cyprus, noble swelling spirits—
That hold their honours in a wary distance,
The very elements of this warlike isle—

Have I tonight flustered with flowing cups,
And they watch too. Among this flock of drunkards,
Am I to put our Cassio in some action
That may offend the isle. But here they come;
If consequence does but approve my dream,
My boat sails freely both with wind and stream.

*Enter Cassio with Montano and Gentlemen,
and servants with wine*

CASSIO Before God, they have given me a rouse already.
MONTANO Good faith, a little one; not past a pint, as I am
a soldier.
IAGO Some wine, ho!
(*sings*) And let me the canakin clink, clink;
     And let me the canakin clink;
         A soldier's a man
         O, man's life's but a span;
     Why, then, let a soldier drink.
Some wine, boys.
CASSIO Before God, an excellent song.
IAGO I learned it in England, where indeed they are most
potent in potting. Your Dane, your German, and your
swag-bellied Hollander—drink, ho!—are nothing to your
English.
CASSIO Is your Englishman so expert in his drinking?
IAGO Why, he drinks with facility your Dane dead drunk;
he sweats not to overthrow your German; he gives your
Hollander a vomit, ere the next bottle can be filled.
CASSIO To the health of our General!
MONTANO I am for it, Lieutenant; and I'll do you justice.

IAGO O, sweet England!

    (*sings*) King Stephen was and-a worthy peer,

        His breeches cost him but a crown;

        He held them sixpence all too dear;

           With that he called the tailor lown.

        He was a wight of high renown,

           And you are but of low degree;

        'Tis pride that pulls the country down;

           Then take your auld cloak about thee.

    Some wine, ho!

CASSIO Before God, this is a more exquisite song than the other.

IAGO Will you hear it again?

CASSIO No, for I hold him to be unworthy of his place that does those things. Well, God's above all; and there are souls must be saved, and there are souls must not be saved.

IAGO It's true, good Lieutenant.

CASSIO For my own part—no offence to the General, nor any man of quality—I hope to be saved.

IAGO And so do I too, Lieutenant.

CASSIO Ay, but, by your leave, not before me. The Lieutenant is to be saved before the Ensign. Let's have no more of this; let's to our affairs. God forgive us our sins. Gentlemen, let's look to our business. Do not think, gentlemen, I am drunk: this is my Ensign, this is my right hand, and this is my left. I am not drunk now: I can stand well enough and I speak well enough.

GENTLEMEN Excellent well.

CASSIO Why, very well; you must not think then that I am drunk.   *Exit*

MONTANO To the platform, masters; come, let's set the watch.

IAGO

    You see this fellow that is gone before:

    He is a soldier, fit to stand by Caesar

And give direction; and do but see his vice:
It is to his virtue a just equinox,
The one as long as the other. 'Tis pity of him.
I fear the trust Othello puts in him,
On some odd time of his infirmity,
Will shake this island.

MONTANO   But is he often thus?

IAGO
It is evermore the prologue to his sleep:
He'll watch the horologe a double set,
If drink rocks not his cradle.

MONTANO   It were well
The General were put in mind of it:
Perhaps he sees it not, or his good nature
Prizes the virtue that appears in Cassio
And looks not on his evils. Is not this true?

Enter Roderigo

IAGO
(*aside*) How now, Roderigo!
I pray you after the Lieutenant go!   *Exit Roderigo*

MONTANO
It is great pity that the noble Moor
Should hazard such a place as his own second
With one of an ingrafted infirmity.
It were an honest action to say
So to the Moor.

IAGO   Not I, for this fair island!
I do love Cassio well and would do much
To cure him of this evil.
    (*Cry within*) 'Help! Help!'
                        But hark, what noise?
    Enter Cassio, pursuing Roderigo

CASSIO Zounds, you rogue, you rascal!

MONTANO What's the matter, Lieutenant?

CASSIO A knave teach me my duty? I'll beat the knave
  into a wicker-bottle.
RODERIGO Beat me?
CASSIO Do you prate, rogue?

He strikes Roderigo

MONTANO Nay, good Lieutenant; I pray you, sir, hold
  your hand.
CASSIO Let me go, sir, or I'll knock you over the nut.
MONTANO Come, come, you're drunk.
CASSIO Drunk!
IAGO *(to Roderigo)* Away, I say; go out and cry a mutiny.
                                                          Exit Roderigo
  Nay, good Lieutenant. God's will, gentleman!
  Help, ho! Lieutenant! Sir! Montano! Sir!
  Help, masters. Here's a goodly watch indeed.

Bell rings

  Who's that who rings the bell? Diablo, ho!
  The town will rise. God's will, Lieutenant, hold!
  You will be shamed for ever!

Enter Othello and attendants

OTHELLO
  What is the matter here?
MONTANO   Zounds, I bleed still.
  I am hurt to the death.
OTHELLO   Hold for your lives!
IAGO
  Hold, ho, Lieutenant, sir, Montano, gentlemen!
  Have you forgotten all sense of place and duty?
  Hold! The General speaks to you: hold, for shame!

OTHELLO

Why, how now, ho! From whence arises this?
Are we turned Turks and to ourselves do that
Which heaven has forbidden the Ottomites?
For Christian shame, put by this barbarous brawl.
He that stirs next to carve for his own rage
Holds his soul light: he dies upon his motion.
Silence that dreadful bell: it frightens the isle
From its propriety. What is the matter, masters?
Honest Iago, that looks dead with grieving,
Speak, who began this? On your love I charge you.

IAGO

I do not know. Friends all but now, even now,
In quarter and in terms like bride and groom
Divesting them for bed. And then but now—
As if some planet had unwitted men—
Swords out, and tilting one at others' breasts
In opposition bloody. I cannot speak
Any beginning to this peevish odds;
And would in action glorious I had lost
Those legs that brought me to a part of it.

OTHELLO

How comes it, Michael, you are thus forgotten?

CASSIO

I pray you pardon me: I cannot speak.

OTHELLO

Worthy Montano, you were wont to be civil:
The gravity and stillness of your youth
The world has noted; and your name is great
In mouths of wisest judgement. What's the matter
That you unlace your reputation thus
And spend your good standing for the name
Of a night-brawler? Give me answer to it.

MONTANO

Worthy Othello, I am hurt to danger.
Your officer, Iago, can inform you,

While I spare speech, which somewhat now offends me,
Of all that I do know; nor know I aught
By me that's said or done amiss this night,
Unless self-charity be sometimes a vice,
And to defend ourselves it is a sin
When violence assails us.

OTHELLO   Now, by heaven,
My blood begins my safer guides to rule,
And passion, having my best judgement darkened,
Attempts to lead the way. Zounds, if I stir,
Or do but lift this arm, the best of you
Shall sink in my rebuke. Give me to know
How this foul rout began, who set it on;
And he that is proved guilty in this offence,
Though he had twinned with me, both at a birth,
Shall lose me. What! In a town of war
Yet wild, the people's hearts brimful of fear,
To manage private and domestic quarrel
At night, and on the court and guard of safety,
It is monstrous. Iago, who began it?

MONTANO
If partially allied or leagued in office,
You do deliver more or less than truth,
You are no soldier.

IAGO   Touch me not so near.
I had rather have this tongue cut from my mouth
Than it should do offence to Michael Cassio.
Yet, I persuade myself, to speak the truth
Shall nothing wrong him. This it is, General.
Montano and myself being in speech,
There comes a fellow, crying out for help,
And Cassio following with determined sword
To execute upon him. Sir, this gentleman
Steps in to Cassio and entreats his pause:
Myself the crying fellow did pursue
Lest by his clamour—as it so fell out—

The town might fall in fright. He, swift of foot,
Outran my purpose and I returned the rather
For that I heard the clink and fall of swords
And Cassio high in oath, which till tonight
I never might say before. When I came back—
For this was brief—I found them close together
At blow and thrust, even as again they were
When you yourself did part them.
More of this matter can I not report:
But men are men; the best sometimes forget.
Though Cassio did some little wrong to him,
As men in rage strike those that wish them best,
Yet surely Cassio, I believe, received
From him that fled some strange indignity
Which patience could not pass.

OTHELLO   I know, Iago,
Your honesty and love do mince this matter,
Making it light to Cassio. Cassio, I love you
But nevermore be officer of mine.

Enter Desdemona, attended

Look, if my gentle love be not raised up.
I'll make you an example.

DESDEMONA   What is the matter, dear?

OTHELLO
All's well now, sweeting: come away to bed.
Sir, for your hurts myself will be your surgeon.

Montano is led off

Iago, look with care about the town
And silence those whom this vile brawl distracted.
Come, Desdemona, it is the soldiers' life
To have their balmy slumbers waked with strife.

Exeunt all but Iago and Cassio

IAGO What, are you hurt, Lieutenant?

CASSIO Ay, past all surgery.

IAGO God forbid!

CASSIO Reputation, reputation, reputation! O, I have lost
my reputation! I have lost the immortal part of myself,
and what remains is bestial. My reputation, Iago, my
reputation!

IAGO As I am an honest man I thought you had received
some bodily wound: there is more of sense in that than
in reputation. Reputation is an idle and most false
imposition; often got without merit and lost without
deserving. You have lost no reputation at all, unless you
repute yourself such a loser. What, man! There are ways
to recover the General again. You are but now sack in
his mood—a punishment more in policy than in malice
—even so as one would beat his offenceless dog to affright
an imperious lion. Sue to him again, and he's yours.

CASSIO I will rather sue to be despised than to deceive so
good a commander with so slight, so drunken, and so
indiscreet an officer. Drunk! And speak parrot! And
squabble! Swagger! Swear! And discourse fustian with
one's own shadow! O, you invisible spirit of wine, if
you have no name to be known by, let us call you devil.

IAGO What was he that you followed with your sword?
What had he done to you?

CASSIO I know not.

IAGO Is it possible?

CASSIO I remember a mass of things, but nothing distinctly:
a quarrel, but nothing wherefore. O God, that men
should put an enemy in their mouths to steal away their
brains! That we should with joy, pleasure, revel and
applause transform ourselves into beasts!

IAGO Why, but you are now well enough! How came you
thus recovered?

CASSIO It has pleased the devil drunkenness to give place
to the devil wrath: one unperfectness shows me another,
to make me frankly despise myself.

IAGO Come, you are too severe a moralist. As the time, the
place and the condition of this country stand, I could

heartily wish this had not so befallen: but since it is as it is, mend it for your own good.

CASSIO I will ask him for my place again; he shall tell me I am a drunkard. Had I as many mouths as Hydra, such an answer would stop them all. To be now a sensible man, by and by a fool, and presently a beast! O, strange! Every inordinate cup is unblessed and the ingredients a devil.

IAGO Come, come; good wine is a good familiar creature if it is well used: exclaim no more against it. And, good Lieutenant, I think you think I love you.

CASSIO I have well proved it, sir. I drunk!

IAGO You or any man living may be drunk at a time, man. I'll tell you what you shall do. Our General's wife is now the General. I may say so in this respect, for he has devoted and given up himself to the contemplation, mark, and denotement of her parts and graces. Confess yourself freely to her; importune her help to put you in your place again. She is of so free, so kind, so apt, so blessed a disposition, that she holds it a vice in her goodness not to do more than she is requested. This broken joint between you and her husband, entreat her to put in a splint; and my fortunes against any lay worth naming, this crack of your love shall grow stronger than it was before.

CASSIO You advise me well.

IAGO I protest in the sincerity of love and honest kindness.

CASSIO I think it freely; and betimes in the morning I will beseech the virtuous Desdemona to undertake for me. I am desperate of my fortunes if they check me here.

IAGO You are in the right. Good night, Lieutenant, I must to the watch.

CASSIO Good night, honest Iago. *Exit*

IAGO
And what's he then that says I play the villain,
When this advice is free I give, and honest,

Proven to thinking, and indeed the course
To win the Moor again? For it is most easy
The inclining Desdemona to subdue
In any honest suit. She's framed as fruitful
As the free elements; and then for her
To win the Moor, were it to renounce his baptism,
All seals and symbols of redeemèd sin,
His soul is so enfettered to her love,
That she may make, unmake, do what she likes,
Even as her appetite shall play the god
With his weak function. How am I then a villain
To counsel Cassio to this parallel course
Directly to his good? Divinity of hell!
When devils will the blackest sins put on,
They do suggest at first with heavenly shows
As I do now. For while this honest fool
Plies Desdemona to repair his fortunes,
And she for him pleads strongly to the Moor,
I'll pour this pestilence into his ear:
That she affects him for her body's lust,
And by how much she strives to do him good,
She shall undo her credit with the Moor.
So will I turn her virtue into pitch,
And out of her own goodness make the net
That shall enmesh them all.

Enter Roderigo

How now, Roderigo?

RODERIGO I do follow here in the chase, not like a hound
that hunts, but one that fills up the cry. My money is
almost spent; I have been tonight exceedingly well
cudgelled; and I think the issue will be, I shall have so
much experience for my pains; and so, with no money
at all, and a little more wit, return again to Venice.

IAGO
    How poor are they that have not patiènce!
    What wound did ever heal but by degrees?
    You know we work by wit, and not by witchcraft,
    And wit depends on dilatory time.
    Does it not go well? Cassio has beaten you,
    And you by that small hurt have cashiered Cassio.
    Though other things grow fair against the sun,
    Yet fruits that blossom first will first be ripe.
    Content yourself awhile. By the mass, 'tis morning:
    Pleasure and action make the hours seem short.
    Retire you; go where you are billeted.
    Away, I say, you shall know more hereafter:
    Nay, get you gone.   *Exit Roderigo*
              Two things are to be done.
    My wife must move for Cassio to her mistress:
    I'll set her on.
    Myself the while to draw the Moor apart,
    And bring him just when he may Cassio find
    Soliciting his wife. Ay, that's the way.
    Dull not device by coldness and delay.   *Exit*

Act III

SCENE I
Before the citadel.

Enter Cassio and Musicians

CASSIO
    Masters, play here—I will content your pains—
    Something that's brief; and bid 'Good morrow, General'.

              They play
              Enter Clown

CLOWN Why, masters, have your instruments been in Naples, that they speak in the nose thus?
FIRST MUSICIAN How, sir, how?
CLOWN Are these, I pray you, wind instruments?
FIRST MUSICIAN Ay, indeed are they, sir.
CLOWN O, thereby hangs a tail.
FIRST MUSICIAN Whereby hangs a tale, sir?
CLOWN Sure, sir, by many a wind instrument that I know. But, masters, here's money for you: and the General so likes your music that he desires you, for love's sake, to make no more noise with it.
FIRST MUSICIAN Well, sir, we will not.
CLOWN If you have any music that may not be heard, to it again. But, as they say, to hear music the General does not greatly care.
FIRST MUSICIAN We have none such, sir.
CLOWN Then put up your pipes in your bag, for I'll away. Go, vanish into air, away. *Exeunt Musicians*

CASSIO Do you hear, my honest friend?

CLOWN No, I hear not your honest friend: I hear you.

CASSIO Pray keep up your quibbles—there's a poor piece
of gold for you. If the gentlewoman that attends the
General's wife is stirring, tell her there's one Cassio
entreats her a little favour of speech. Will you do this?

CLOWN She is stirring, sir. If she will stir hither, I shall
seem to notify unto her.

CASSIO Do, good my friend.   *Exit Clown*

Enter Iago

In happy time, Iago.

IAGO   You have not been abed then?

CASSIO
Why, no: the day had broken before we parted.
I have made bold, Iago,
To send in to your wife. My suit to her
Is that she will to virtuous Desdemona
Procure me some access.

IAGO   I'll send her to you at once;
And I'll devise a means to draw the Moor
Out of the way, that your converse and business
May be more free.

CASSIO   I humbly thank you for it.

Exit Iago

I never knew a Florentine more kind and honest.

Enter Emilia

EMILIA
Good morrow, good Lieutenant; I am sorry
For your displeasure: but all will sure be well.
The General and his wife are talking of it,
And she speaks for you stoutly. The Moor replies
That he you hurt is of great fame in Cyprus,

And great affinity; and that in wholesome wisdom
He might not but refuse you. But he protests he loves
   you
And needs no other suitor but his likings
To take the safest occasion by the front
To bring you in again.

CASSIO   Yet I beseech you,
If you think fit, or that it may be done,
Give me advantage of some brief discourse
With Desdemona alone.

EMILIA   Pray you, come in:
I will bestow you where you shall have time
To speak your bosom freely.

CASSIO   I am much bound to you.

Exeunt

SCENE II
The citadel.

Enter Othello, Iago, and Gentlemen

OTHELLO
These letters give, Iago, to the pilot,
And by him do my duties to the senate.
That done, I will be walking on the works:
Repair there to me.

IAGO   Well, my good lord, I'll do it.   *Exit*

OTHELLO
This fortification, gentlemen, shall we see it?

GENTLEMEN
We'll wait upon your lordship.   *Exeunt*

SCENE III
The same.

Enter Desdemona, Cassio, and Emilia

DESDEMONA
  Be you assured, good Cassio, I will do
  All my abilities in your behalf.

EMILIA
  Good madam, do: I warrant it grieves my husband
  As if the case were his.

DESDEMONA
  O, that's an honest fellow! Do not doubt, Cassio,
  But I will have my lord and you again
  As friendly as you were.

CASSIO   Bounteous madam,
  Whatever shall become of Michael Cassio,
  He's never anything but your true servant.

DESDEMONA
  I know it: I thank you. You do love my lord;
  You have known him long, and be you well assured
  He shall in strangeness stand no farther off
  Than in a politic distance.

CASSIO   Ay, but, lady,
  That policy may either last so long,
  Or feed upon such nice and waterish diet,
  Or breed itself so out of circumstance,
  That I being absent and my place supplied,
  My General will forget my love and service.

DESDEMONA
  Do not doubt that. Before Emilia here,
  I give you warrant of your place. Assure you,
  If I do vow a friendship, I will perform it
  To the last article. My lord shall never rest.
  I'll watch him tame and talk him out of patience;
  His bed shall seem a school, his board a shrift;

I'll intermingle everything he does
With Cassio's suit. Therefore be merry, Cassio,
For your solicitor shall rather die
Than give your cause away.

Enter Othello and Iago

EMILIA
Madam, here comes my lord.
CASSIO
Madam, I'll take my leave.
DESDEMONA
Why, stay and hear me speak.
CASSIO
Madam, not now: I am very ill at ease,
Unfit for my own purposes.
DESDEMONA
Well, do your discretion.   *Exit Cassio*
IAGO
Ha! I like not that.
OTHELLO   What do you say?
IAGO
Nothing, my lord; or if—I know not what.
OTHELLO
Was not that Cassio parted from my wife?
IAGO
Cassio, my lord? No, sure, I cannot think it
That he would sneak away so guilty-like,
Seeing you coming.
OTHELLO   I do believe it was he.
DESDEMONA
How now, my lord?
I have been talking with a suitor here,
A man that languishes in your displeasure.
OTHELLO
Who is it you mean?

DESDEMONA

    Why, your Lieutenant, Cassio. Good my lord,
    If I have any grace or power to move you,
    His present reconciliation take.
    For if he is not one that truly loves you,
    That errs in ignorance, and not in cunning,
    I have no judgement in an honest face.
    I pray you call him back.

OTHELLO   Went he hence now?

DESDEMONA

    Yes, faith; so humbled
    That he has left part of his grief with me
    To suffer with him. Good love, call him back.

OTHELLO

    Not now, sweet Desdemon; some other time.

DESDEMONA

    But shall it be shortly?

OTHELLO   The sooner, sweet, for you.

DESDEMONA

    Shall it be tonight, at supper?

OTHELLO   No, not tonight.

DESDEMONA

    Tomorrow dinner then?

OTHELLO   I shall not dine at home.
    I meet the captains at the citadel.

DESDEMONA

    Why, then, tomorrow night, or Tuesday morn,
    On Tuesday noon, or night; on Wednesday morn.
    Pray you name the time, but let it not
    Exceed three days. In faith, he is penitent:
    And yet his trespass in our common reason—
    Save that, they say, the wars must make example
    Out of their best—is not almost a fault
    To incur a private check. When shall he come?
    Tell me, Othello. I wonder in my soul
    What you would ask me that I should deny,

Or stand so stammering on? What! Michael Cassio,
That came a-wooing with you? And so many a time—
When I have spoken of you dispraisingly—
Has taken your part, to have so much to do
To bring him in? By our Lady, I could do much.

OTHELLO
Pray you, no more: let him come when he will;
I will deny you nothing.

DESDEMONA   Why, this is not a boon:
'Tis as I should entreat you wear your gloves
Or feed on nourishing dishes, or keep you warm;
Or sue to you to do a peculiar profit
To your own person. Nay, when I have a suit
Wherein I mean to touch your love indeed
It shall be full of poise and difficult weight,
And fearful to be granted.

OTHELLO   I will deny you nothing.
Whereon, I do beseech you, grant me this:
To leave me but a little to my self.

DESDEMONA
Shall I deny you? No; farewell, my lord.

OTHELLO
Farewell, my Desdemona, I'll come to you straight.

DESDEMONA
Emilia, come. Be as your fancies teach you.
Whatever you are, I am obedient.

                         Exeunt Desdemona and Emilia

OTHELLO
Excellent wench! Perdition catch my soul
But I do love you! And when I love you not,
Chaos is come again.

IAGO   My noble lord—

OTHELLO
What do you say, Iago?

IAGO   Did Michael Cassio,
When you wooed my lady, know of your love?

OTHELLO
He did, from first to last. Why do you ask?
IAGO
But for a satisfaction of my thought—
No further harm.
OTHELLO   Why of your thought, Iago?
IAGO
I did not think he had been acquainted with her.
OTHELLO
O yes, and went between us very often.
IAGO
Indeed!
OTHELLO
Indeed? Ay, indeed. Discern you aught in that?
Is he not honest?
IAGO   Honest, my lord?
OTHELLO   Honest? Ay, honest.
IAGO
My lord, for aught I know.
OTHELLO   What do you think?
IAGO
Think, my lord?
OTHELLO
Think, my lord! By heaven, he echoes me,
As if there were some monster in his thought
Too hideous to be shown. You do mean something.
I heard you say even now, you like not that,
When Cassio left my wife. What did you not like?
And when I told you he was of my counsel
In my whole course of wooing, you cried 'Indeed!'
And did contract and purse your brow together,
As if you then had shut up in your brain
Some horrible idea. If you do love me,
Show me your thought.
IAGO
My lord, you know I love you.

OTHELLO   I think you do:
  Because I know you are full of love and honesty,
  And weigh your words before you give them breath,
  Therefore these stops of yours affright me more.
  For such things in a false disloyal knave
  Are tricks of custom; but in a man that's just,
  They're close dilations, working from the heart,
  That passion cannot rule.

IAGO   For Michael Cassio,
  I dare be sworn I think that he is honest.

OTHELLO
  I think so too.

IAGO   Men should be what they seem;
  Or those that are not, would they might seem none!

OTHELLO
  Certain, men should be what they seem.

IAGO
  Why, then, I think Cassio's an honest man.

OTHELLO
  Nay, yet there's more in this.
  I pray speak to me as to your thinkings,
  As you do ruminate, and give your worst of thoughts
  The worst of words.

IAGO   Good my lord, pardon me;
  Though I am bound to every act of duty,
  I am not bound to that all slaves are free to:
  Utter my thoughts. Why, say they are vile and false?
  As where's that palace whereinto foul things
  Sometimes intrude not? Who has a breast so pure,
  But some uncleanly apprehensions
  Keep courts and law-days, and in session sit
  With meditations lawful?

OTHELLO
  You do conspire against your friend, Iago,
  If you but think him wronged, and make his ear
  A stranger to your thoughts.

IAGO   I do beseech you,
    Though I perhaps am vicious in my guess—
    As I confess it is my nature's plague
    To spy into abuses, and of suspicion
    Shape faults that are not—that your wisdom then,
    From one that so imperfectly conjectures,
    Would take no notice, nor build yourself a trouble
    Out of his scattering and unsure observance.
    It were not for your quiet nor your good,
    Nor for my manhood, honesty, and wisdom,
    To let you know my thoughts.
OTHELLO   What do you mean?
IAGO
    Good name in man and woman, dear my lord,
    Is the immediate jewel of their souls.
    Who steals my purse, steals trash; 'tis something, nothing;
    'Twas mine, 'tis his, and has been slave to thousands.
    But he that filches from me my good name
    Robs me of that which not enriches him
    And makes me poor indeed.
OTHELLO   By heaven, I'll know your thoughts.
IAGO
    You cannot, if my heart were in your hand,
    And shall not, while 'tis in my custody.
OTHELLO
    Ha!
IAGO O, beware, my lord, of jealousy!
    It is the green-eyed monster, which does mock
    The meat it feeds on. That cuckold lives in bliss
    Who certain of his fate loves not his wronger;
    But O, what damnèd minutes tells he over,
    Who dotes yet doubts, suspects yet fondly loves!
OTHELLO
    O misery!

IAGO

    Poor and content is rich, and rich enough;
    But riches boundless are as poor as winter,
    To him that ever fears he shall be poor.
    Good God, the souls of all my tribe defend
    From jealousy!

OTHELLO   Why, why is this?

    Think you I'd make a life of jealousy,
    To follow still the changes of the moon
    With fresh suspicions? No, to be once in doubt
    Is once to be resolved. Exchange me for a goat,
    When I shall turn the business of my soul
    To such inflated and blown-up surmises,
    Matching your inference. 'Tis not to make me jealous
    To say my wife is fair, loves company,
    Is free of speech, sings, plays, and dances well:
    Where virtue is, these are more virtuous.
    Nor from my own weak merits will I draw
    The smallest fear or suspicion of her change,
    For she had eyes and chose me. No, Iago,
    I'll see before I doubt; when I doubt, prove;
    And on the proof, there is no more but this:
    Away at once with love or jealousy!

IAGO

    I am glad of this: for now I shall have reason
    To show the love and duty that I bear you
    With franker spirit. Therefore, as I am bound,
    Receive it from me. I speak not yet of proof.
    Look to your wife; observe her well with Cassio.
    Wear your eye thus: not jealous, nor secure.
    I would not have your free and noble nature,
    Out of self-bounty, be abused. Look to it.
    I know our country disposition well:
    In Venice they do let God see the pranks
    They dare not show their husbands; their best conscience
    Is not to leave it undone, but keep it unknown.

OTHELLO
  Do you say so?
IAGO
  She did deceive her father, marrying you,
  And when she seemed to shake, and fear your looks,
  She loved them most.
OTHELLO   And so she did.
IAGO   Why, very well then!
  She that so young could give out such a seeming,
  To sew her father's eyes up close as oak—
  He thought it was witchcraft.—But I am much to blame,
  I humbly do beseech you of your pardon
  For too much loving you.
OTHELLO   I am bound to you for ever.
IAGO
  I see this has a little dashed your spirits.
OTHELLO
  Not a jot, not a jot.
IAGO   In faith, I fear it has.
  I hope you will consider that what is spoken
  Comes from my love. But I do see you are moved.
  I am to pray you, not to strain my speech
  To grosser issues, nor to larger reach
  Than to suspicion.
OTHELLO
  I will not.
IAGO   Should you do so, my lord,
  My speech should fall into such vile result
  Which my thoughts aimed not at. Cassio's my worthy
      friend.
  My lord, I see you are moved.
OTHELLO   No, not much moved.
  I do not think but Desdemona's honest.
IAGO
  Long live she so! And long live you to think so!

OTHELLO
  I have a pain upon my forehead here.
DESDEMONA
  Faith, that's with watching: 'twill away again.
  Let me but bind it hard, within this hour
  It will be well.
OTHELLO   Your napkin is too little.

  He puts the handkerchief from him, and she drops it

  Let it alone. Come, I'll go in with you.
DESDEMONA
  I am very sorry that you are not well.
                    Exeunt Othello and Desdemona
EMILIA
  I am glad I have found this napkin:
  This was her first remembrance from the Moor.
  My wayward husband has a hundred times
  Wooed me to steal it. But she so loves the token—
  For he conjùred her she should ever keep it—
  That she reserves it evermore about her
  To kiss and talk to. I'll have the work taken out,
  And give it Iago.
  What he will do with it, heaven knows, not I:
  I nothing, but to please his fantasy.

                    Enter Iago

IAGO
  How now? What do you here alone?
EMILIA
  Do not you chide: I have a thing for you.
IAGO
  A thing for me? It is a common thing.
EMILIA
  Ha!

IAGO

To have a foolish wife.

EMILIA

O, is that all? What will you give me now
For that same handkerchief?

IAGO   What handkerchief?

EMILIA

What handkerchief!
Why that the Moor first gave to Desdemona;
That which so often you did bid me steal.

IAGO

Have you stolen it from her?

EMILIA

No, faith, she let it drop by negligence,
And to the advantage, I, being here, took it up.
Look, here it is.

IAGO   A good wench! Give it me.

EMILIA

What will you do with it, that you have been so earnest
To have me filch it?

IAGO *(snatching it)*   Why, what is that to you?

EMILIA

If it is not for some purpose of import,
Give it me again. Poor lady, she'll run mad
When she shall lack it.

IAGO

Acknowledge it not: I have use for it.
Go, leave me.   *Exit Emilia*
I will in Cassio's lodging lose this napkin,
And let him find it. Trifles light as air
Are to the jealous confirmations strong
As proofs of holy writ. This may do something.
The Moor already changes with my poison.
Dangerous conceits are in their natures poisons,
Which at the first are scarce found to distaste,

But, with a little act upon the blood,
Burn like the mines of sulphur.

Enter Othello

                    I did say so.
Look where he comes! Not poppy, nor mandragora,
Nor all the drowsy syrups of the world,
Shall ever medicine you to that sweet sleep
Which you owned yesterday.

OTHELLO   Ha, ha, false to me!

IAGO

Why, how now, General! No more of that.

OTHELLO

Away! Be gone! You have set me on the rack.
I swear it is better to be much abused,
Than but to know it a little.

IAGO   How now, my lord!

OTHELLO

What sense had I of her stolen hours of lust?
I saw it not, thought it not, it harmed not me.
I slept the next night well, was free and merry;
I found not Cassio's kisses on her lips.
He that is robbed, not wanting what is stolen,
Let him not know it, and he's not robbed at all.

IAGO

I am sorry to hear this.

OTHELLO

I had been happy if the general camp,
Sappers and all, had tasted her sweet body,
So I had nothing known. O, now, for ever
Farewell the tranquil mind! Farewell content!
Farewell the plumèd troops and the big wars
That make ambition virtue—O, farewell!
Farewell the neighing steed, and the shrill trump,
The spirit-stirring drum, the ear-piercing fife,

The royal banner and all quality,
Pride, pomp and circumstance of glorious war!
And, O you mortal engines, whose rude throats
The immortal Jove's dread clamours counterfeit,
Farewell! Othello's occupation's gone.

IAGO

Is it possible, my lord?

OTHELLO

Villain, be sure you prove my love a whore.
Be sure of it: give me the ocular proof,
Or by the worth of my eternal soul,
You had been better have been born a dog
Than answer my waked wrath!

IAGO   Is it come to this?

OTHELLO

Make me to see it: or, at the least, so prove it
That the probation bears no hinge or loop
To hang a doubt on—or woe upon your life!

IAGO

My noble lord—

OTHELLO

If you do slander her and torture me,
Never pray more; abandon all remorse;
On horror's head horrors accumulate,
Do deeds to make heaven weep, all earth amazed:
For nothing can you to damnation add
Greater than that.

IAGO   O grace! O heaven defend me!
Are you a man? Have you a soul? Or sense?
Goodbye to you: take my office. O wretched fool,
That loves to make your honesty a vice!
O monstrous world! Take note, take note, O world!
To be direct and honest is not safe.
I thank you for this profit, and from hence
I'll love no friend, since love breeds such offence.

OTHELLO
  Nay, stay: you should be honest.
IAGO
  I should be wise; for honesty's a fool
  And loses what it works for.
OTHELLO   By the world,
  I think my wife is chaste, and think she is not;
  I think that you are just, and think you are not.
  I'll have some proof. Her name that was as fresh
  As Dian's visage is now begrimed and black
  As my own face. If there are cords or knives,
  Poison or fire or suffocating streams,
  I'll not endure it. Would I were satisfied!
IAGO
  I see, sir, you are eaten up with passion.
  I do repent me that I put it to you.
  You would be satisfied?
OTHELLO   Would! Nay, I will.
IAGO
  And may. But how? How satisfied, my lord?
  Would you, the supervisor, grossly gape on?
  Behold her topped?
OTHELLO   Death and damnation! O!
IAGO
  It were a tedious difficulty, I think,
  To bring them to that prospect. Damn them then
  If ever mortal eyes do see them bolster
  More than their own! What then? How then?
  What shall I say? Where's satisfactiòn?
  It is impossible you should see this,
  Were they as prime as goats, as hot as monkeys,
  As salt as wolves in pride, and fools as gross
  As ignorance made drunk. But yet, I say,
  If imputation and strong circumstance,
  Which lead directly to the door of truth,
  Will give you satisfaction, you might have it.

OTHELLO
  Give me a living reason she is disloyal.
IAGO
  I do not like the office.
  But since I am entered in this cause so far—
  Pricked to it by foolish honesty and love—
  I will go on. I lay with Cassio lately,
  And being troubled with a raging tooth
  I could not sleep.
  There are a kind of men so loose of soul
  That in their sleep will mutter their affairs:
  One of this kind is Cassio.
  In sleep I heard him say: 'Sweet Desdemona,
  Let us be wary, let us hide our loves';
  And then, sir, would he grip and wring my hand,
  Cry 'O sweet creature!' and then kiss me hard,
  As if he plucked up kisses by the roots,
  That grew upon my lips. Then laid his leg
  Over my thigh, and sighed and kissed, and then
  Cried 'Cursèd fate that gave you to the Moor!'
OTHELLO
  O monstrous! Monstrous!
IAGO   Nay, this was but his dream.
OTHELLO
  But this denoted a foregone conclusiòn.
IAGO
  It is suspicious, though it is but a dream:
  And this may help to thicken other proofs
  That do demonstrate thinly.
OTHELLO   I'll tear her all to pieces!
IAGO
  Nay, but be wise: yet we see nothing done,
  She may be honest yet. Tell me but this:
  Have you not sometimes seen a handkerchief,
  Spotted with strawberries, in your wife's hand?

OTHELLO
  I gave her such a one: it was my first gift.
IAGO
  I know not that: but such a handkerchief—
  I am sure it was your wife's—did I today
  See Cassio wipe his beard with.
OTHELLO   If it is that—
IAGO
  If it is that, or any that was hers,
  It speaks against her with the other proofs.
OTHELLO
  O, that the slave had forty thousand lives!
  One is too poor, too weak for my revenge.
  Now do I see it is true. Look here, Iago—
  All my fond love thus do I blow to heaven:
  It is gone.
  Arise, black vengeance, from your hollow cell!
  Yield up, O love, your crown and hearted throne
  To tyrannous hate! Swell, bosom, with your freight,
  For 'tis of serpents' tongues!
IAGO   Yet be content.
OTHELLO
  O, blood, blood, blood!
IAGO
  Patience, I say: your mind perhaps may change.
OTHELLO
  Never, Iago. Like to the Pontic sea,
  Whose icy current and compulsive course
  Never feels retiring ebb, but keeps due on
  To the Propontic and the Hellespont.
  Even so my bloody thoughts with violent pace
  Shall never look back, never ebb to humble love,
  Till that a capable and wide revenge
  Swallow them up. Now, by yon marble heaven,
  In the due reverence of a sacred vow
  I here engage my words.

He kneels

IAGO   Do not rise yet.

He kneels

Witness you ever-burning lights above,
You elements, that embrace us round about,
Witness that here Iago does give up
The execution of his wit, hands, heart,
To wronged Othello's service. Let him command,
And to obey shall be in me compassion,
What bloody business ever.

They rise

OTHELLO   I greet your love,
   Not with vain thanks, but with acceptance bounteous;
   And will upon the instant put you to it.
   Within these three days let me hear you say
   That Cassio's not alive.
IAGO   My friend is dead;
   It is done at your request. But let her live.
OTHELLO
   Damn her, lewd minx! O, damn her, damn her!
   Come go with me apart. I will withdraw
   To furnish me with some swift means of death
   For the fair devil. Now are you my Lieutenant.
IAGO
   I am your own for ever.   *Exeunt*

SCENE IV
The same.

Enter Desdemona, Emilia, and Clown

DESDEMONA Do you know, fellow, where Lieutenant Cassio lies?

CLOWN I dare not say he lies anywhere.

DESDEMONA Why, man?

CLOWN He's a soldier, and for one to say a soldier lies is stabbing.

DESDEMONA Very well, where lodges he?

CLOWN To tell you where he lodges is to tell you where I lie.

DESDEMONA Can anything be made of this?

CLOWN I know not where he lodges, and for me to devise a lodging, and say he lies here, or he lies there, were to lie in my own throat.

DESDEMONA Can you inquire him out? And be edified by report?

CLOWN I will catechize the world for him, that is, make questions, and by them answer.

DESDEMONA Seek him; bid him come hither; tell him I have moved my lord on his behalf, and hope all will be well.

CLOWN To do this is within the compass of man's wit, and therefore I will attempt the doing of it.   *Exit*

DESDEMONA
Where should I lose that handkerchief, Emilia?

EMILIA
I know not, madam.

DESDEMONA
Believe me, I had rather have lost my purse
Full of florins; and, but that my noble Moor
Is true of mind, and made of no such baseness
As jealous creatures are, it were enough
To put him to ill-thinking.

EMILIA   Is he not jealous?

DESDEMONA
   Who? He? I think the sun where he was born
   Drew all such humours from him.
EMILIA   Look where he comes.

Enter Othello

DESDEMONA
   I will not leave him now till Cassio
   Is called to him. How is it with you, my lord?
OTHELLO
   Well, my good lady. (*Aside*) O, hardness to dissemble!
   How do you, Desdemona?
DESDEMONA   Well, my good lord.
OTHELLO
   Give me your hand. This hand is moist, my lady.
DESDEMONA
   It yet has felt no age, and known no sorrow.
OTHELLO
   This argues fruitfulness and liberal heart.
   Hot, hot and moist. This hand of yours requires
   A sequester from liberty, fasting and prayer,
   Much castigation, exercise devout;
   For there's a young and sweating devil here
   That commonly rebels. It is a good hand,
   A frank one.
DESDEMONA You may, indeed, say so:
   For it was that hand that gave away my heart.
OTHELLO
   A liberal hand! The hearts of old gave hands;
   But our new heraldry is hands, not hearts.
DESDEMONA
   I cannot speak of this. Come now, your promise.
OTHELLO
   What promise, chuck?
DESDEMONA
   I have sent to bid Cassio come speak with you.

OTHELLO
 I have a salt and sorry cold offends me:
 Lend me your handkerchief.
DESDEMONA   Here, my lord.
OTHELLO
 That which I gave you.
DESDEMONA   I have it not about me.
OTHELLO
 Not?
DESDEMONA No, faith, my lord.
OTHELLO   That is a fault.
 That handkerchief
 Did an Egyptian to my mother give:
 She was a charmer and could almost read
 The thoughts of people. She told her, while she kept it,
 It would make her amiable and subdue my father
 Entirely to her love. But, if she lost it
 Or made a gift of it, my father's eye
 Should hold her loathèd, and his spirits should hunt
 After new fancies. She, dying, gave it me,
 And bid me, when my fate would have me wive,
 To give it her. I did so; and take heed of it:
 Make it a darling, like your precious eye.
 To lose or give it away were such perdition
 As nothing else could match.
DESDEMONA   Is it possible?
OTHELLO
 It is true: there's magic in the web of it.
 A sibyl, that had numbered in the world
 The sun to course two hundred compasses,
 In her prophetic fury sewed the work:
 The worms were hallowed that did breed the silk,
 And it was dyed in mummy,[1] which the skilful
 Conserved of maidens' hearts.

---

[1]A compound made from mummies or dead bodies.

DESDEMONA   Indeed! Is it true?
OTHELLO
  Most veritable; therefore look to it well.
DESDEMONA
  Then would to God that I had never seen it!
OTHELLO
  Ha! Wherefore?
DESDEMONA
  Why do you speak so startingly and rash?
OTHELLO
  Is it lost? Is it gone? Speak: is it out of the way?
DESDEMONA
  Heaven bless us!
OTHELLO   Say you?
DESDEMONA   It is not lost.
  But what if it were?
OTHELLO   How!
DESDEMONA
  I say it is not lost.
OTHELLO   Fetch it: let me see it.
DESDEMONA
  Why, so I can, sir; but I will not now.
  This is a trick to put me from my suit.
  Pray you let Cassio be received again.
OTHELLO
  Fetch me the handkerchief: my mind misgives.
DESDEMONA
  Come, come:
  You'll never meet a more sufficient man.
OTHELLO
  The handkerchief!
DESDEMONA   I pray, talk to me of Cassio.
OTHELLO
  The handkerchief!

DESDEMONA   A man that all his time
  Has founded his good fortunes on your love;
  Shared dangers with you—
OTHELLO
  The handkerchief!
DESDEMONA   In faith you are to blame.
OTHELLO
  Zounds!   *Exit*
EMILIA
  Is not this man jealous?
DESDEMONA   I never saw this before.
  Sure, there's some wonder in this handkerchief:
  I am most unhappy in the loss of it.
EMILIA
  'Tis not a year or two shows us a man.
  They are all but stomachs, and we all but food;
  They eat us hungerly, and when they are full,
  They belch us. Look you, Cassio and my husband.

Enter Iago and Cassio

IAGO
  There is no other way: it is she must do it.
  And lo, the happiness! Go, and importune her.
DESDEMONA
  How now, good Cassio! What's the news with you?
CASSIO
  Madam, my former suit. I do beseech you
  That by your virtuous means I may again
  Exist and be a member of his love;
  Whom I, with all the office of my heart,
  Entirely honour. I would not be delayed.
  If my offence is of such mortal kind
  That neither service past, nor present sorrow,
  Nor purposed merit in futurity,
  Can ransom me into his love again,

But to know so must be my benefit.
So shall I clothe me in a forced content,
And shut myself up in some other course
To Fortune's alms.

DESDEMONA   Alas, thrice-gentle Cassio!
My advocation is not now in tune:
My lord is not my lord; nor should I know him,
Were he in feature as in humour altered.
So help me every spirit sanctified
As I have spoken for you all my best,
And stood within the blank of his displeasure
For my free speech! You must awhile be patient.
What I can do, I will; and more I will,
Than for myself I dare. Let that suffice you.

IAGO
Is my lord angry?

EMILIA   He went hence but now
And certainly in strange unquietness.

IAGO
Can he be angry? I have seen the cannon
When it has blown his ranks into the air,
And like the devil from his very arm
Puffed his own brother—and can he be angry?
Something of moment then. I will go meet him.
There's matter in it indeed if he is angry.

DESDEMONA
I pray you do so.   *Exit Iago*
          Something, sure, of state,
Either from Venice, or some unhatched plot
Made demonstrable here in Cyprus to him,
Has puddled his clear spirit. And in such cases
Men's natures wrangle with inferior things,
Though great ones are their object. 'Tis even so.
For let our finger ache, and it endues
Our healthful members even to that sense
Of pain. Nay, we must think men are not gods,

Nor of them look for such observant care
As fits the bridal. Bless me indeed, Emilia,
I was—unhandsome warrior as I am—
Arraigning his unkindness with my soul;
But now I find I had suborned the witness
And he is indicted falsely.

EMILIA

Pray heaven it is state matters, as you think,
And no conception nor any jealous fancy
Concerning you.

DESDEMONA

Alas the day, I never gave him cause.

EMILIA

But jealous souls will not be answered so;
They are not ever jealous for the cause,
But jealous because they're jealous. It is a monster
Begotten upon itself, born on itself.

DESDEMONA

Heaven keep that monster from Othello's mind.

EMILIA

Lady, amen!

DESDEMONA

I will go seek him. Cassio, walk here about.
If I do find him fit, I'll move your suit,
And seek to effect it to my uttermost.

CASSIO

I humbly thank your ladyship.

> *Exeunt Desdemona and Emilia*

> *Enter Bianca*

BIANCA

God save you, friend Cassio.

CASSIO   What make you from home?
How is it with you, my most fair Bianca?
In faith, sweet love, I was coming to your house.

BIANCA
    And I was going to your lodging, Cassio.
    What! Keep a week away? Seven days and nights?
    Eight score eight hours? And lovers' absent hours
    More tedious than the dial eight score times!
    O weary reckoning!
CASSIO   Pardon me, Bianca.
    I have this while with leaden thoughts been pressed:
    But I shall in a more continuate time
    Strike off this score of absence. Sweet Bianca,
    Take me this work out.
BIANCA   O Cassio, whence came this?
    This is some token from a newer friend.
    To the felt absence now I feel a cause.
    Is it come to this? Well, well.
CASSIO   Go to, woman!
    Throw your vile guesses in the devil's teeth
    From whence you have them. You are jealous now
    That this is from some mistress, some remembrance:
    No, by my faith, Bianca.
BIANCA   Why, whose is it?
CASSIO
    I know not, sweet. I found it in my chamber.
    I like the work well. Ere it be demanded—
    As like enough it will—I'd have it copied.
    Take it and do it, and leave me for this time.
BIANCA
    Leave you? Wherefore?
CASSIO
    I do attend here on the General,
    And think it no addition, nor my wish,
    To have him see me womaned.
BIANCA   Why, I pray you?
CASSIO
    Not that I love you not.

BIANCA   But that you do not love me.
  I pray you, bring me on the way a little,
  And say if I shall see you soon at night.
CASSIO
  It is but a little way that I can bring you,
  For I attend here: but I'll see you soon.
BIANCA
  'Tis very good: I must await the chance.   *Exeunt*

Act IV

SCENE I
Before the citadel.

Enter Othello and Iago

IAGO
  Will you think so?

OTHELLO   Think so, Iago?

IAGO   What!
  To kiss in private?

OTHELLO   An unauthorized kiss.

IAGO
  Or to be naked with her friend in bed
  An hour or more, not meaning any harm?

OTHELLO
  Naked in bed, Iago, and not mean harm?
  It is hypocrisy against the devil.
  They that mean virtuously and yet do so,
  The devil their virtue tempts, and they tempt heaven.

IAGO
  So they do nothing, it is a venial slip.
  But if I give my wife a handkerchief—

OTHELLO
  What then?

IAGO
  Why, then, 'tis hers, my lord, and being hers,
  She may, I think, bestow it on any man.

OTHELLO
  She is protectress of her honour too.
  May she give that?

IAGO

  Her honour is an essence that is not seen:
  They have it very oft that have it not.
  But for the handkerchief—

OTHELLO

  By heaven, I would most gladly have forgot it!
  You said—O, it comes over my memory
  As does the raven over the infected house,
  Boding to all!—he had my handkerchief.

IAGO

  Ay, what of that?

OTHELLO   That's not so good now.

IAGO   What

  If I had said, I had seen him do you wrong,
  Or heard him say—as knaves are such abroad,
  Who having by their own importunate suit
  Or voluntary dotage of some mistress
  Convincèd or supplied them, cannot choose
  But they must blab—

OTHELLO   Has he said anything?

IAGO

  He has, my lord; but be you well assured,
  No more than he'll unswear.

OTHELLO   What has he said?

IAGO

  Faith, that he did—I know not what he did.

OTHELLO

  What? What?

IAGO

  Lie—

OTHELLO With her?

IAGO   With her, on her, what you will.

OTHELLO Lie with her? Lie on her? We say lie on her
  when they belie her. Lie with her! Zounds, that's fulsome!
  Handkerchief—confession—handkerchief! To confess and
  be hanged for his labour. First to be hanged and then to

confess! I tremble at it. Nature would not invest herself
in such shadowing passion without some instruction. It
is not words that shake me thus! Pish! Noses, ears, and
lips! Is it possible?—Confess? Handkerchief! O devil!

He falls

IAGO
Work on,
My medicine, work! Thus credulous fools are caught,
And many worthy and chaste dames even thus,
All guiltless, meet reproach. What ho, my lord!
My lord, I say! Othello!

Enter Cassio

How now, Cassio!
CASSIO
What's the matter?
IAGO
My lord is fallen into an epilepsy.
This is his second fit: he had one yesterday.
CASSIO
Rub him about the temples.
IAGO No, forbear.
Unconsciousness must have its quiet course.
If not, he foams at mouth; and by and by
Breaks out to savage madness. Look, he stirs.
Do you withdraw yourself a little while:
He will recover straight. When he is gone,
I would on great occasion speak with you.
                                    Exit Cassio
How is it, General? Have you not hurt your head?
OTHELLO
Do you mock me?

IAGO   I mock you? No, by heaven!
  Would you would bear your fortune like a man!
OTHELLO
  A hornèd man's a monster and a beast.
IAGO
  There's many a beast then in a populous city,
  And many a civil monster.
OTHELLO
  Did he confess it?
IAGO   Good sir, be a man.
  Think every bearded fellow that's but yoked
  May draw with you. There's millions now alive
  That nightly lie in those improper beds
  Which they dare swear peculiar. Your case is better.
  O, it is the spite of hell, the fiend's arch-mock,
  To lip a wanton in a secure couch,
  And to suppose her chaste! No, let me know;
  And knowing what I am, I know what shall be.
OTHELLO
  O, you are wise, 'tis certain.
IAGO   Stand you awhile apart;
  Confine yourself but in a patient mood.
  While you were here, overwhelmèd with your grief—
  A passion most unsuiting such a man—
  Cassio came hither. I shifted him away
  And laid a good excuse upon your fit;
  Bade him later return and here speak with me,
  And this he promised. Do but enclose yourself,
  And mark the sneers, the gibes, and notable scorns
  That dwell in every region of his face.
  For I will make him tell the tale anew,
  Where, how, how oft, how long ago, and when
  He has, and is again, to meet your wife.
  I say, but mark his gestures. For sure, patience!
  Or I shall say you're all in all in passion
  And nothing of a man.

OTHELLO Do you hear, Iago?
I will be found most cunning in my patience,
But—do you hear?—most bloody.
IAGO That's not amiss,
But yet keep time in all. Will you withdraw?

Othello retires

Now will I question Cassio of Bianca,
A housewife, that by selling her desires
Buys herself bread and clothes. It is a creature
That dotes on Cassio—as 'tis the strumpet's plague
To beguile many and be beguiled by one.
He, when he hears of her, cannot refrain
From the excess of laughter. Here he comes.

Enter Cassio

As he shall smile, Othello shall go mad;
And his unbookish jealousy must construe
Poor Cassio's smiles, gestures, and light behavior
Quite in the wrong. How do you now, Lieutenant?
CASSIO
The worse in that you give me the addition
Whose want even kills me.
IAGO
Ply Desdemona well and you are sure of it.
Now if this suit lay in Bianca's power,
How quickly should you speed!
CASSIO Alas, poor wretch!
OTHELLO
(*aside*) Look, how he laughs already!
IAGO
I never knew a woman love man so.
CASSIO
Alas, poor rogue! I think in faith she loves me.
OTHELLO
(*aside*) Now he denies it faintly, and laughs it out.

IAGO

  Do you hear, Cassio?

OTHELLO

  (*aside*) Now he importunes him to tell it over.

  Go to, well said, well said!

IAGO

  She gives it out that you shall marry her.

  Do you intend it?

CASSIO

  Ha, ha, ha!

OTHELLO

  (*aside*) Do you triumph, Roman? Do you triumph?

CASSIO I marry her! What! A customer! Pray bear some
  charity to my wit: do not think it so unwholesome. Ha,
  ha, ha!

OTHELLO (*aside*) So, so, so, so: they laugh that win.

IAGO Faith, the cry goes that you shall marry her.

CASSIO Pray, say true.

IAGO I am a very villain else.

OTHELLO (*aside*) Have you scarred me? Well.

CASSIO This is the monkey's own giving out. She is
  persuaded I will marry her out of her own love and
  flattery, not out of my promise.

OTHELLO (*aside*) Iago beckons me. Now he begins the
  story.

CASSIO She was here even now. She haunts me in every
  place. I was the other day talking on the sea-bank with
  certain Venetians, and thither comes the bauble and, by
  this hand, falls thus about my neck.

OTHELLO (*aside*) Crying 'O dear Cassio!' as it were. His
  gesture imports it.

CASSIO So hangs and lolls and weeps upon me, so hales
  and pulls me. Ha, ha, ha!

OTHELLO (*aside*) Now he tells how she plucked him to my
  chamber. O, I see that nose of yours, but not that dog I
  shall throw it to!

CASSIO Well, I must leave her company.

IAGO Before me! Look where she comes.

CASSIO 'Tis such another strumpet! Sure, a perfumed one!

Enter Bianca

What do you mean by this haunting of me?

BIANCA Let the devil and his dam haunt you! What did you mean by that same handkerchief you gave me even now? I was a fine fool to take it. I must take out the work! A likely piece of work, that you should find it in your chamber, and not know who left it there! This is some minx's token, and I must take out the work? There, give it your hobby-horse, wheresoever you had it. I'll take out no work on it.

CASSIO How now, my sweet Bianca! How now, how now!

OTHELLO *(aside)* By heaven, that should be my handkerchief!

BIANCA If you'll come to supper tonight, you may. If you will not, come when you are next prepared for.   *Exit*

IAGO After her, after her!

CASSIO Faith I must: she'll rail in the street else.

IAGO Will you sup there?

CASSIO Faith, I intend to.

IAGO Well, I may chance to see you: for I would very gladly speak with you.

CASSIO Pray come, will you?

IAGO Go to! Say no more.   *Exit Cassio*

OTHELLO *(coming forward)* How shall I murder him, Iago?

IAGO Did you perceive how he laughed at his vice?

OTHELLO O, Iago!

IAGO And did you see the handkerchief?

OTHELLO Was that mine?

IAGO Yours, by this hand! And to see how he prizes the foolish woman your wife: she gave it him, and he has given it his whore.

OTHELLO I would have him nine years a-killing!—A fine woman, a fair woman, a sweet woman!

IAGO Nay, you must forget that.

OTHELLO Ay, let her rot and perish, and be damned tonight, for she shall not live! No, my heart is turned to stone: I strike it, and it hurts my hand.—O, the world has not a sweeter creature! She might lie by an emperor's side and command him tasks.

IAGO Nay, that's not your way.

OTHELLO Hang her! I do but say what she is: so delicate with her needle, an admirable musician! O, she will sing the savageness out of a bear! Of so high and plenteous wit and invention!

IAGO She is the worse for all this.

OTHELLO O, a thousand, thousand times!—And then of so gentle a condition.

IAGO Ay, too gentle.

OTHELLO Nay, that's certain—but yet the pity of it, Iago! O, Iago, the pity of it, Iago!

IAGO If you are so silly over her iniquity, give her patent to offend, for if it touches not you, it comes near nobody.

OTHELLO I will chop her into bits of meat! Cuckold me!

IAGO O, it is foul in her!

OTHELLO With my officer!

IAGO That is fouler.

OTHELLO Get me some poison, Iago, this night. I'll not expostulate with her, lest her body and beauty unprovide my mind again—this night, Iago.

IAGO Do it not with poison; strangle her in her bed, even the bed she has contaminated.

OTHELLO Good, good! The justice of it pleases; very good!

IAGO And for Cassio, let me be his undertaker. You shall hear more by midnight.

OTHELLO
    Excellent good!

Trumpet sounds

What trumpet is that same?

IAGO
I warrant, something from Venice.

Enter Lodovico, Desdemona, and attendants

It is Lodovico,
Come from the Duke; and see your wife is with him.

LODOVICO
God save you, worthy General!

OTHELLO   With all my heart, sir.

LODOVICO
The Duke and Senators of Venice greet you.

He gives him a letter

OTHELLO
I kiss the instrument of their pleasures.

He reads the letter

DESDEMONA
And what's the news, good cousin Lodovico?

IAGO
I am very glad to see you, signior:
Welcome to Cyprus.

LODOVICO
I thank you. How does Lieutenant Cassio?

IAGO
Lives, sir.

DESDEMONA
Cousin, there's fallen between him and my lord
An unkind breach; but you shall make all well.

OTHELLO
  Are you sure of that?
DESDEMONA
  My lord?
OTHELLO
  'This fail you not to do, as you will'—
LODOVICO
  He did not call: he's busy in the paper.
  Is there division between my lord and Cassio?
DESDEMONA
  A most unhappy one; I would do much
  To atone them, for the love I bear to Cassio.
OTHELLO
  Fire and brimstone!
DESDEMONA
  My lord?
OTHELLO
  Are you wise?
DESDEMONA
  What, is he angry?
LODOVICO   Maybe the letter moved him.
  For, as I think, they do command him home,
  Deputing Cassio in his government.
DESDEMONA
  By my faith, I am glad of it.
OTHELLO   Indeed!
DESDEMONA   My lord?
OTHELLO
  I am glad to see you mad.
DESDEMONA   Why, sweet Othello!
OTHELLO
  Devil!

                    He strikes her

DESDEMONA
  I have not deserved this.
LODOVICO
  My lord, this would not be believed in Venice,
  Though I should swear I saw it. 'Tis very much.
  Make her amends; she weeps.
OTHELLO   O devil, devil!
  If the earth could conceive with woman's tears,
  Each drop she falls would prove a crocodile.
  Out of my sight!
DESDEMONA   I will not stay to offend you.
LODOVICO
  Truly an obedient lady.
  I do beseech your lordship call her back.
OTHELLO
  Mistress!
DESDEMONA
  My lord?
OTHELLO
  What would you with her, sir?
LODOVICO
  Who? I, my lord?
OTHELLO
  Ay, you did wish that I would make her turn.
  Sir, she can turn, and turn, and yet go on,
  And turn again. And she can weep, sir, weep.
  And she's obedient; as you say, obedient,
  Very obedient—proceed you in your tears—
  Concerning this, sir—O, well-painted passion!—
  I am commanded home—get you away!
  I'll send for you anon.—Sir, I obey the mandate,
  And will return to Venice.—Hence, be gone!
                                        Exit Desdemona

Cassio shall have my place. And sir, tonight
I do entreat that we may sup together.
You are welcome, sir, to Cyprus. Goats and monkeys!

Exit

LODOVICO
Is this the noble Moor, whom our full senate
Call all-in-all sufficient? Is this the nature
Whom passion could not shake? Whose solid virtue
The shot of accident nor dart of chance
Could neither graze nor pierce?
IAGO   He is much changed.
LODOVICO
Are his wits safe? Is he not light of brain?
IAGO
He is that he is: I may not breathe my thought
What he might be. If what he might he is not,
I would to heaven he were.
LODOVICO   What! Strike his wife!
IAGO
Faith, that was not so well: yet would I knew
That stroke would prove the worst!
LODOVICO   Is it his use?
Or did the letters work upon his blood
And new-create this fault?
IAGO   Alas, alas!
It is not honesty in me to speak
What I have seen and known. You shall observe him,
And his own courses will denote him so,
That I may save my speech. Do but go after,
And mark how he continues.
LODOVICO
I am sorry that I am deceived in him.

SCENE II
The citadel.

Enter Othello and Emilia

OTHELLO
  You have seen nothing then?
EMILIA
  Nor ever heard, nor ever did suspect.
OTHELLO
  Yes, you have seen Cassio and her together.
EMILIA
  But then I saw no harm; and then I heard
  Each syllable that breath made up between them.
OTHELLO
  What! Did they never whisper?
EMILIA   Never, my lord.
OTHELLO
  Nor send you out of the way?
EMILIA   Never.
OTHELLO
  To fetch her fan, her gloves, her mask, nor anything?
EMILIA
  Never, my lord.
OTHELLO
  That is strange.
EMILIA
  I durst, my lord, to wager she is chaste,
  Lay down my soul at stake. If you think otherwise
  Remove your thought: it does abuse your bosom.
  If any wretch has put this in your head,
  Let heaven requite it with the serpent's curse!
  For if she is not honest, chaste, and true,
  There's no man happy. The purest of their wives
  Is foul as slander.

OTHELLO   Bid her come hither: go!

Exit Emilia

She says enough; yet she's a simple bawd
That cannot say as much. This is a subtle whore,
A closet lock and key of villainous secrets;
And yet she'll kneel and pray—I have seen her do it.

Enter Desdemona and Emilia

DESDEMONA
My lord, what is your will?
OTHELLO   Pray, chuck, come hither.
DESDEMONA
What is your pleasure?
OTHELLO   Let me see your eyes.
Look in my face.
DESDEMONA   What horrible fancy is this?
OTHELLO *(to Emilia)*
Some of your function, mistress.
Leave procreants alone and shut the door.
Cough or cry 'hem' if anybody comes.
Your mystery, your mystery! Nay, dispatch! *Exit Emilia*
DESDEMONA
Upon my knees, what does your speech import?
I understand a fury in your words,
But not the words.
OTHELLO   Why, what are you?
DESDEMONA
Your wife, my lord; your true and loyal wife.
OTHELLO
Come, swear it; damn yourself;
Lest being like one of heaven, the devils themselves
Should fear to seize you. Therefore be double-damned:
Swear you are chaste.
DESDEMONA   Heaven does truly know it.

OTHELLO
  Heaven truly knows that you are false as hell.
DESDEMONA
  To whom, my lord? With whom? How am I false?
OTHELLO
  Ah, Desdèmon! Away, away, away!
DESDEMONA
  Alas, the heavy day! Why do you weep?
  Am I the motive of these tears my lord?
  If haply you my father do suspect
  An instrument of this your calling back,
  Lay not your blame on me. If you have lost him,
  I have lost him too.
OTHELLO   Had it pleased heaven
  To try me with affliction, had they rained
  All kind of sores and shames on my bare head,
  Steeped me in poverty to the very lips,
  Given to captivity me and my utmost hopes,
  I should have found in some place of my soul
  A drop of patience. But alas, to make me
  A fixèd figure for the time of scorn
  To point its slow unmoving finger at!
  Yet could I bear that too, well, very well:
  But there where I have garnered up my heart,
  Where either I must live, or bear no life,
  The fountain now from which my current runs,
  Or else dries up—to be discarded thence
  Or keep it as a cistern for foul toads
  To knot and gender in! Turn your complexion there,
  Patience, you young and rose-lipped cherubin,
  Ay, there look grim as hell!
DESDEMONA
  I hope my noble lord esteems me chaste.
OTHELLO
  O, ay! As summer flies are in the shambles,
  That quicken even with blowing, O, you weed,

Who are so lovely fair, and smell so sweet
That the sense aches at you, would you had never been
   born!

DESDEMONA

Alas, what ignorant sin have I committed?

OTHELLO

Was this fair paper, this most goodly book,
Made to write 'whore' upon? What committed!
Committed? O, you public commoner!
I should make very forges of my cheeks,
That would to cinders burn up modesty,
Did I but speak your deeds. What committed?
Heaven stops the nose at it, and the moon winks;
The bawdy wind, that kisses all it meets,
Is hushed within the hollow mine of earth
And will not hear it. What committed?
Impudent strumpet!

DESDEMONA   By heaven, you do me wrong.

OTHELLO

Are you not a strumpet?

DESDEMONA   No, as I am a Christian.

If to preserve this vessel for my lord
From any other foul unlawful touch,
Be not to be a strumpet, I am none.

OTHELLO

What! Not a whore?

DESDEMONA   No, as I shall be saved.

OTHELLO

Is it possible?

DESDEMONA

O, heaven forgive us!

OTHELLO   I cry you mercy then:
I took you for that cunning whore of Venice
That married with Othello. (*Calling*) You, mistress,
That have the office opposite to Saint Peter
And keep the gate of hell!

Enter Emilia

You, you, ay, you!
We have done our course: there's money for your pains.
I pray you turn the key, and keep our counsel.   *Exit*

EMILIA
Alas, what does this gentleman conceive?
How do you, madam? How do you, my good lady?

DESDEMONA
Faith, half asleep.

EMILIA
Good madam, what's the matter with my lord?

DESDEMONA
With whom?

EMILIA
Why, with my lord, madam.

DESDEMONA
Who is your lord?

EMILIA   He that is yours, sweet lady.

DESDEMONA
I have none. Do not talk to me, Emilia:
I cannot weep; and answers have I none,
But what should go by water. Pray you tonight
Lay on my bed my wedding sheets, remember,
And call your husband hither

EMILIA   Here's a change indeed!
                                                Exit

DESDEMONA
It is meet I should be used so, very meet.
How have I behaved, that he might stick
The smallest opinion on my least misuse?

Enter Emilia and Iago

IAGO
What is your pleasure, madam? How is it with you?

DESDEMONA

    I cannot tell: those that do teach young babes
    Do it with gentle means and easy tasks:
    He might have chidden me so, for, in good faith,
    I am a child to chiding.

IAGO   What is the matter, lady?

EMILIA

    Alas, Iago, my lord has so bewhored her,
    Thrown such despite and heavy terms upon her
    As true heart cannot bear.

DESDEMONA

    Am I that name, Iago?

IAGO   What name, fair lady?

DESDEMONA

    Such as she said my lord did say I was.

EMILIA

    He called her whore: a beggar in his drink
    Could not have laid such terms upon his strumpet.

IAGO

    Why did he so?

DESDEMONA

    I do not know: I am sure I am none such.

IAGO

    Do not weep, do not weep. Alas the day!

EMILIA

    Did she forsake so many noble matches,
    Her father, and her country, all her friends,
    To be called whore? Would it not make one weep?

DESDEMONA

    It is my wretched fortune.

IAGO   Curse him for it!
    How comes this whim upon him?

DESDEMONA   Nay, heaven does know.

EMILIA

    I will be hanged if some eternal villain,
    Some busy and insinuating rogue,

Some lying, cozening slave, to get some office,
Has not devised this slander; I'll be hanged else.

IAGO

Fie, there is no such man! It is impossible.

DESDEMONA

If any such there is, heaven pardon him.

EMILIA

A halter pardon him and hell gnaw his bones!
Why should he call her whore? Who keeps her company?
What place, what time, what form, what likelihood?
The Moor's abused by some most villainous knave,
Some base notorious knave, some scurvy fellow.
O heaven, that such companions you'd unfold,
And put in every honest hand a whip
To lash the rascals naked through the world,
Even from the east to the west!

IAGO   Speak within door.

EMILIA

O fie upon them! Some such squire he was
That turned your wit the seamy side without
And made you to suspect me with the Moor.

IAGO

You are a fool, go to.

DESDEMONA   O good Iago,
What shall I do to win my lord again?
Good friend, go to him; for, by this light of heaven,
I know not how I lost him. Here I kneel:
If ever my will did trespass against his love,
Either in discourse of thought or actual deed;
Or that my eyes, my ears, or any sense
Delighted them in any other form;
Or that I do not yet, and ever did,
And ever will—though he does shake me off
To beggarly divorcement—love him dearly,
Comfort forswear me! Unkindness may do much,
And his unkindness may defeat my life,

But never taint my love. I cannot say 'whore':
It does abhor me now I speak the word;
To do the act that might the addition earn
Not the world's mass of vanity could make me.

IAGO

I pray you, be content: 'tis but his humour;
The business of the state does him offence,
And he does chide with you.

DESDEMONA

If it were no other—

IAGO   It is so, I warrant.
Hark how these instruments summon to supper!
The messengers of Venice stay the meat.
Go in, and weep not; all things shall be well.

Exeunt Desdemona and Emilia

Enter Roderigo

How now, Roderigo?

RODERIGO I do not find that you deal justly with me.

IAGO What in the contrary?

RODERIGO Every day you put me off with some device, Iago, and rather, as it seems to me now, keep from me all conveniency, than supply me with the least advantage of hope. I will indeed no longer endure it. Nor am I yet persuaded to put up in peace what already I have foolishly suffered.

IAGO Will you hear me, Roderigo?

RODERIGO Faith, I have heard too much; for your words and performances are no kin together.

IAGO You charge me most unjustly.

RODERIGO With naught but truth. I have wasted myself out of my means. The jewels you have had from me to deliver to Desdemona would half have corrupted a votarist. You have told me she has received them, and

returned me expectations and comforts of sudden respect
and acquaintance, but I find none.

IAGO Well, go to; very well.

RODERIGO Very well, go to! I cannot go to, man, and it is
not very well. Nay, I think it is scurvy and begin to find
myself cheated in it.

IAGO Very well.

RODERIGO I tell you, it is not very well. I will make
myself known to Desdemona. If she will return me my
jewels, I will give over my suit and repent my unlawful
solicitation. If not, assure yourself I will seek satisfaction
of you.

IAGO You have said now.

RODERIGO Ay, and said nothing but what I protest
intention of doing.

IAGO Why, now I see there's mettle in you; and even from
this instant do build on you a better opinion than ever
before. Give me your hand, Roderigo. You have taken
against me a most just exception; but yet I protest I have
dealt most directly in your affair.

RODERIGO It has not appeared.

IAGO I grant indeed it has not appeared; and your suspicion
is not without wit and judgement. But, Roderigo, if you
have that in you indeed, which I have greater reason to
believe now than ever—I mean purpose, courage, and
valour—this night show it. If you the next night
following enjoy not Desdemona, take me from this
world with treachery, and devise engines for my life.

RODERIGO Well, what is it? Is it within reason and
compass?

IAGO Sir, there is especial commission come from Venice
to depute Cassio in Othello's place.

RODERIGO Is that true? Why, then Othello and Desdemona
return again to Venice.

IAGO O, no: he goes into Mauritania and takes away
with him the fair Desdemona, unless his abode be

lingered here by some accident: wherein none can be so
determinate as the removing of Cassio.

RODERIGO How do you mean 'removing' of him?

IAGO Why, by making him incapable of Othello's place—
knocking out his brains.

RODERIGO And that you would have me to do?

IAGO Ay, if you dare do yourself a profit and a right. He
sups tonight with a harlot; and thither will I go to him.
He knows not yet of his honourable fortune. If you will
watch his going thence—which I will fashion to fall out
between twelve and one—you may take him at your
pleasure. I will be near to second your attempt, and he
shall fall between us. Come, stand not amazed at it, but
go along with me. I will show you such a necessity in
his death that you shall think yourself bound to put it
on him. It is now high supper-time and the night grows
to waste. About it!

RODERIGO I will hear further reason for this.

IAGO And you shall be satisfied.   *Exeunt*

SCENE III
The same.

*Enter Othello, Lodovico, Desdemona, Emilia, and
attendants*

LODOVICO

I do beseech you, sir, trouble yourself no further.

OTHELLO

O, pardon me: it will do me good to walk.

LODOVICO

Madam, good night. I humbly thank your ladyship.

DESDEMONA

Your honour is most welcome.

OTHELLO   Will you walk, sir?
  O, Desdemona!
DESDEMONA
  My lord?
OTHELLO Get you to bed on the instant. I will return
  forthwith. Dismiss your attendant there. Look it be
  done.
DESDEMONA I will, my lord.
                    Exeunt Othello, Lodovico, and attendants
EMILIA
  How goes it now? He looks gentler than he did.
DESDEMONA
  He says he will return incontinent.
  He has commanded me to go to bed,
  And bade me to dismiss you.
EMILIA   Dismiss me?
DESDEMONA
  It was his bidding: therefore, good Emilia,
  Give me my nightly wearing, and adieu.
  We must not now displease him.
EMILIA
  I would you had never seen him.
DESDEMONA
  So would not I: my love does so approve him
  That even his stubbornness, his checks, his frowns—
  Pray, unpin me—have grace and favour in them.
EMILIA
  I have laid those sheets, you bade me, on the bed.
DESDEMONA
  All's one. Good faith, how foolish are our minds!
  If I do die before you, pray shroud me
  In one of those same sheets.
EMILIA   Come, come, you talk.
DESDEMONA
  My mother had a maid called Barbary:
  She was in love: and him she loved proved mad

And did forsake her. She had a song of willow;
An old thing it was; but it expressed her fortune,
And she died singing it. That song tonight
Will not go from my mind: I have much to do
But to go hang my head all at one side,
And sing it like poor Barbary—pray, be quick.

EMILIA
Shall I go fetch your night-gown?

DESDEMONA   No, unpin me here.
This Lodovico is a proper man.

EMILIA
A very handsome man.

DESDEMONA   He speaks well.

EMILIA I know a lady in Venice would have walked barefoot
to Palestine for a touch of his nether lip.

DESDEMONA (*sings*)
    The poor soul sat sighing by a sycamore tree,
        Sing all a green willow;
    Her hand on her bosom, her head on her knee,
        Sing willow, willow, willow;
    The fresh streams ran by her and murmured her
    moans;
        Sing willow, willow, willow;
    Her salt tears fell from her and softened the stones—
Lay by these.
        Sing willow, willow, willow—
Pray make haste; he'll come anon.
    Sing all a green willow must be my garland.
    Let nobody blame him; his scorn I approve—
Nay, that's not next. Hark, who is it that knocks?

EMILIA It's the wind.

DESDEMONA
    I called my love false love, but what said he then?
        Sing willow, willow, willow:
    If I court more women, you'll couch with more men.

So get you gone; good night. My eyes do itch:
Does that bode weeping?

EMILIA   'Tis neither here nor there.

DESDEMONA

I have heard it said so. O, these men, these men!
Do you in conscience think—tell me, Emilia—
That there are women who abuse their husbands
In such gross kind?

EMILIA   There are some such, no question.

DESDEMONA

Would you do such a deed for all the world?

EMILIA

Why, would not you?

DESDEMONA   No, by this heavenly light.

EMILIA Nor I neither by this heavenly light: I might do it
    as well in the dark.

DESDEMONA Would you do such a deed for all the world?

EMILIA The world's a huge thing: it is a great price for a
    small vice.

DESDEMONA In truth, I think you would not.

EMILIA In truth I think I should, and undo it when I had
    done it. Sure, I would not do such a thing for a joint
    ring, nor for measures of lawn, nor for gowns, petticoats,
    nor caps, nor any petty exhibition. But for all the whole
    world! God's pity, who would not make her husband a
    cuckold, to make him a monarch? I should venture
    purgatory for it.

DESDEMONA Bless me, if I would do such a wrong for the
    whole world!

EMILIA Why, the wrong is but a wrong in the world; and
    having the world for your labour, 'tis a wrong in your
    own world, and you might quickly make it right.

DESDEMONA I do not think there is any such woman.

EMILIA Yes, a dozen: and as many in addition as would
    store the world they played for.
    But I do think it is their husbands' faults

If wives do fall. Say that they slack their duties,
And pour our treasures into foreign laps;
Or else break out in peevish jealousies,
Throwing restraint upon us; or say they strike us,
Or scant our former living out of spite—
Why, we have galls, and though we have some grace,
Yet have we some revenge. Let husbands know
Their wives have sense like them: they see and smell,
And have their palates both for sweet and sour
As husbands have. What is it that they do,
When they change us for others? Is it sport?
I think it is. And does affection breed it?
I think it does. Is it frailty that thus errs?
It is so too. And have not we affections,
Desires for sport, and frailty, as men have?
Then let them use us well: else let them know
The ills we do, their ills instruct us so.

DESDEMONA
Good night, good night. God me such uses send,
Not to pick bad from bad, but by bad mend!   *Exeunt*

Act V

SCENE I
A street.

Enter Iago and Roderigo

IAGO

Here, stand behind this bulk: straight will he come.
Wear your good rapier bare, and put it home.
Quick, quick; fear nothing: I'll be at your elbow.
It makes us, or it mars us; think on that,
And fix most firm your resolution.

RODERIGO

Be near at hand; I may miscarry in it.

IAGO

Here, at your hand: be bold, and take your stand.

He retires

RODERIGO

I have no great devotion to the deed,
And yet he has given me satisfying reasons.
'Tis but a man gone. Forth my sword! He dies!

IAGO

I have rubbed this young scab almost to the quick,
And he grows angry. Now, whether he kills Cassio,
Or Cassio him, or each does kill the other,
Every way makes my gain. Live Roderigo,
He calls me to a restitution large
Of gold and jewels, that I swindled from him
As gifts to Desdemona.
It must not be. If Cassio does remain
He has a daily beauty in his life

That makes me ugly: and besides, the Moor
May reveal me to him—there stand I in much peril.
No, he must die. But soft, I hear him coming.

Enter Cassio

RODERIGO
I know his gait; 'tis he. Villain, you die!
CASSIO
That thrust had been my enemy indeed,
But that my coat is better than you think.
I will make proof of yours.

He wounds Roderigo

RODERIGO   O, I am slain!
                   Iago wounds Cassio in the leg, and exit
CASSIO
I am maimed for ever. Help, ho! Murder, murder!

Enter Othello, above

OTHELLO
The voice of Cassio: Iago keeps his word.
RODERIGO
O, villain that I am!
OTHELLO   It is even so.
CASSIO
O, help, ho! Light! A surgeon!
OTHELLO
'Tis he! O brave Iago, honest and just,
That have such noble sense of your friend's wrong,
You teach me! Minion, your dear lies dead,
And your unblest fate hastes. Strumpet, I come!
Forth of my heart those charms, your eyes, are blotted;
Your bed, lust-stained, shall with lust's blood be spotted.

Exit Othello

Enter Lodovico and Gratiano

CASSIO
What, ho! No watch? No passage? Murder, murder!
GRATIANO
'Tis some mischance: the cry is very direful.
CASSIO
O, help!
LODOVICO
Hark!
RODERIGO
O wretched villain!
LODOVICO
Two or three groan. It is a heavy night.
These may be counterfeits. Let's think it unsafe
To come in to the cry without more help.
RODERIGO
Nobody come? Then shall I bleed to death.
LODOVICO
Hark!

Enter Iago, with a light

GRATIANO
Here's one comes in his shirt, with light and weapons.
IAGO
Who's there? Whose noise is this that cries on murder?
LODOVICO
We do not know.
IAGO   Did you not hear a cry?
CASSIO
Here, here: for heaven's sake help me!
IAGO   What's the matter?

GRATIANO
  This is Othello's Ensign, as I take it.
LODOVICO
  The same indeed, a very valiant fellow.
IAGO
  What are you here, that cry so grievously?
CASSIO
  Iago? O, I am spoiled, undone by villains!
  Give me some help.
IAGO
  O me, Lieutenant! What villains have done this?
CASSIO
  I think that one of them is hereabout
  And cannot make away.
IAGO   O treacherous villains!
  What are you there? Come in, and give some help.
RODERIGO
  O, help me here!
CASSIO
  That's one of them.
IAGO   O murderous slave! O villain!

He stabs Roderigo

RODERIGO
  O damned Iago! O inhuman dog!
IAGO
  Kill men in the dark? Where are these bloody thieves?
  How silent is this town! Ho, murder, murder!

Lodovico and Gratiano come forward

  What may you be? Are you of good or evil?
LODOVICO
  As you shall prove us, praise us.

IAGO
  Signior Lodovico?
LODOVICO
  He, sir.
IAGO
  I cry you mercy. Here's Cassio hurt by villains.
GRATIANO
  Cassio?
IAGO
  How is it, brother?
CASSIO
  My leg is cut in two.
IAGO   God, heaven forbid!
  Light, gentlemen. I'll bind it with my shirt.

Enter Bianca

BIANCA
  What is the matter, ho? Who is it that cried?
IAGO
  Who is it that cried?
BIANCA
  O, my dear Cassio, my sweet Cassio,
  O Cassio, Cassio, Cassio!
IAGO
  O notable strumpet! Cassio, may you suspect
  Who they should be that have thus mangled you?
CASSIO
  No.
GRATIANO
  I am sorry to find you thus: I have been to seek you.
IAGO
  Lend me a garter: so. O, for a chair
  To bear him easily hence!
BIANCA   Alas, he faints!
  O Cassio, Cassio, Cassio!

IAGO

    Gentlemen all, I do suspect this trash
    To be a party in this injury.
    Patience awhile, good Cassio. Come, come,
    Lend me a light. Know we this face or no?
    Alas, my friend, and my dear countryman
    Roderigo? No—yes, sure—O heaven, Roderigo!

GRATIANO

    What! Of Venice?

IAGO

    Even he, sir. Did you know him?

GRATIANO   Know him? Ay.

IAGO

    Signor Gratiano? I cry you gentle pardon.
    These bloody accidents must excuse my manners
    That so neglected you.

GRATIANO   I am glad to see you.

IAGO

    How do you, Cassio? O, a chair, a chair!

GRATIANO

    Roderigo!

IAGO

    He, he, 'tis he.

Enter attendants with chair

          O, that's well said, the chair!
    Some good man bear him carefully from hence.
    I'll fetch the General's surgeon. For you, mistress,
    Save you your labour. He that lies slain here, Cassio,
    Was my dear friend. What malice was between you?

CASSIO

    None in the world, nor do I know the man.

IAGO

    (*to Bianca*) What, look you pale? O, bear him out of the
        air.

                              Cassio and Roderigo are borne off

    Stay you, good gentlemen. Look you pale, mistress?
    Do you perceive the wildness of her eye?
    Nay, if you stare, we shall hear more anon.
    Behold her well; I pray you look upon her.
    Do you see, gentlemen? Nay, guiltiness will speak
    Though tongues were out of use.

Enter Emilia

EMILIA

    Alas, what's the matter? What's the matter, husband?

IAGO

    Cassio has here been set on in the dark
    By Roderigo and fellows that are escaped:
    He's almost slain and Roderigo quite.

EMILIA

    Alas, good gentleman! Alas, good Cassio!

IAGO

    This is the fruit of whoring. Pray, Emilia,
    Go know of Cassio where he supped tonight.
    What, do you shake at that?

BIANCA

    He supped at my house, but I therefore shake not.

IAGO

    O, did he so? I charge you go with me.

EMILIA

    O, fie upon you, strumpet!

BIANCA

    I am no strumpet, but of life as honest
    As you that thus abuse me.

EMILIA   As I? Foh! Fie upon you!

IAGO
    Kind gentlemen, let's see poor Cassio dressed.
    Come, mistress, you must tell us another tale.
    Emilia, run you to the citadel,
    And tell my lord and lady what has happened.
    Will you go on before? (*Aside*) This is the night
    That either makes me, or undoes me quite.   *Exeunt*

SCENE II
The citadel. A bedchamber.

Enter Othello, with a light, Desdemona in her bed

OTHELLO
    It is the cause, it is the cause, my soul:
    Let me not name it to you, you chaste stars!
    It is the cause. Yet I'll not shed her blood,
    Nor scar that whiter skin of hers than snow,
    And smooth as monumental alabaster.
    Yet she must die, else she'll betray more men.
    Put out the light, and then put out the light:
    If I quench you, you flaming minister,
    I can again your former light restore,
    Should I repent me. But once put out your light,
    You cunningest pattern of excelling nature,
    I know not where is that Promethean heat
    That can your light relume. When I have plucked your
        rose,
    I cannot give it vital growth again,
    It needs must wither. I'll smell it on the tree.

He kisses her

    O balmy breath, that do almost persuade
    Justice to break its sword! One more, one more.

Be thus when you are dead and I will kill you,
And love you after. One more, and this the last.
So sweet was never so fatal. I must weep.
But they are cruel tears: this sorrow's heavenly—
It strikes where it does love. She wakes.

DESDEMONA

Who's there? Othello?

OTHELLO

Ay, Desdemona.

DESDEMONA   Will you come to bed, my lord?

OTHELLO

Have you prayed tonight, Desdemon?

DESDEMONA   Ay, my lord.

OTHELLO

If you bethink yourself of any crime
Unreconciled as yet to heaven and grace,
Solicit for it straight.

DESDEMONA

Alas, my lord, what may you mean by that?

OTHELLO

Well, do it, and be brief; I will walk by:
I would not kill your unprepared spirit;
No—heaven forfend!—I would not kill your soul.

DESDEMONA

Talk you of killing?

OTHELLO   Ay, I do.

DESDEMONA   Then heaven

Have mercy on me!

OTHELLO   Amen, with all my heart!

DESDEMONA

If you say so, I hope you will not kill me.

OTHELLO

Hum!

DESDEMONA

   And yet I fear you: for you are fatal then

   When your eyes roll so. Why I should fear I know not,

   Since guiltiness I know not; but yet I feel I fear.

OTHELLO

   Think on your sins.

DESDEMONA   They are loves I bear to you.

OTHELLO

   Ay, and for that you die.

DESDEMONA

   That death's unnatural that kills for loving.

   Alas, why gnaw you so your nether lip?

   Some bloody passion shakes your very frame:

   These are portents; but yet I hope, I hope

   They do not point on me.

OTHELLO   Peace, and be still!

DESDEMONA

   I will—so. What is the matter?

OTHELLO

   That handkerchief which I so loved and gave you,

   You gave to Cassio.

DESDEMONA   No, by my life and soul!

   Send for the man and ask him.

OTHELLO   Sweet soul, take heed,

   Take heed of perjury: you are on your death-bed.

DESDEMONA

   Ay, but not yet to die.

OTHELLO   Yes, now at once.

   Therefore confess you freely of your sin;

   For to deny each article with oath

   Cannot remove nor choke the strong conception

   That I do groan with. For you are to die.

DESDEMONA

   Then Lord have mercy on me!

OTHELLO   I say, amen.

DESDEMONA

    And have you mercy too! I never did

    Offend you in my life; never loved Cassio

    But with such general warranty of heaven

    As I might love. I never gave him token.

OTHELLO

    By heaven, I saw my handkerchief in his hand!

    O perjured woman! You do stone my heart,

    And make me call what I intend to do

    A murder, which I thought a sacrifice.

    I saw the handkerchief.

DESDEMONA   He found it then.

    I never gave it him. Send for him hither.

    Let him confess a truth.

OTHELLO   He has confessed.

DESDEMONA

    What, my lord?

OTHELLO

    That he has used you.

DESDEMONA   How? Unlawfully?

OTHELLO

    Ay.

DESDEMONA

    He will not say so.

OTHELLO   No, his mouth is stopped:

    Honest Iago has taken order for it.

DESDEMONA

    O, my fear interprets! What, is he dead?

OTHELLO

    Had all his hairs been lives, my great revenge

    Had stomach for them all.

DESDEMONA

    Alas, he is betrayed, and I undone.

OTHELLO

    Out, strumpet! Weep you for him to my face?

DESDEMONA

O banish me, my lord, but kill me not!

OTHELLO

Down, strumpet!

DESDEMONA

Kill me tomorrow: let me live tonight!

OTHELLO

Nay, if you strive—

DESDEMONA

But half an hour!

OTHELLO   Being done, there is no pause.

DESDEMONA

But while I say one prayer!

OTHELLO   It is too late.

DESDEMONA

O Lord, Lord, Lord!

He smothers her

EMILIA

(*without*) My lord, my lord! What, ho! My lord, my
    lord!

OTHELLO

What noise is this? Not dead? Not yet quite dead?
I, that am cruel, am yet merciful:
I would not have you linger in your pain.
So, so.

EMILIA (*without*) What, ho! My lord, my lord!

OTHELLO   Who's there?

EMILIA

(*without*) O, good my lord, I'd speak a word with you.

OTHELLO

Yes, 'tis Emilia.—By and by.—She's dead.
'Tis like she comes to speak of Cassio's death:
The noise was high. Ha! No more moving?
Still as the grave. Shall she come in? Were it good?

I think she stirs again. No. What's best to do?
If she comes in, she'll sure speak to my wife—
My wife! My wife! What wife? I have no wife.
O, insupportable! O heavy hour!
I think it should be now a huge eclipse
Of sun and moon, and that the affrighted globe
Should yawn at alteration.

EMILIA   I do beseech you
That I may speak with you. O, good my lord!

OTHELLO

I had forgotten you. O, come in, Emilia.
Soft; by and by. Let me the curtains draw.
Where are you? (*He unlocks door.*) What's the matter
   with you now?

Enter Emilia

EMILIA

O, my good lord, yonder's foul murder done.

OTHELLO

What! Now?

EMILIA

But now, my lord.

OTHELLO

It is the very error of the moon;
She comes more near to earth than she was wont,
And makes men mad.

EMILIA

Cassio, my lord, has killed a young Venetian
Called Roderigo

OTHELLO   Roderigo killed?
And Cassio killed?

EMILIA   No, Cassio is not killed.

OTHELLO

Not Cassio killed! Then murder is out of tune,
And sweet revenge grows harsh.

DESDEMONA
  O, falsely, falsely murdered!
EMILIA   O Lord! What cry is that?
OTHELLO
  That? What?
EMILIA
  Out and alas, that was my lady's voice!

She draws back the curtains

  Help, help, ho, help! O, lady, speak again!
  Sweet Desdemona, O sweet mistress, speak!
DESDEMONA
  A guiltless death I die.
EMILIA
  O, who has done this deed?
DESDEMONA
  Nobody—I myself—farewell.
  Commend me to my kind lord—O, farewell!   *She dies*
OTHELLO
  Why, how should she be murdered?
EMILIA   Alas, who knows?
OTHELLO
  You heard her say herself it was not I.
EMILIA
  She said so: I must needs report the truth.
OTHELLO
  She's like a liar gone to burning hell:
  'Twas I that killed her.
EMILIA   O, the more angel she,
  And you the blacker devil!
OTHELLO
  She turned to folly; and she was a whore.
EMILIA
  You do belie her, and you are a devil.

OTHELLO

  She was false as water.

EMILIA   You are rash as fire to say

  That she was false. O, she was heavenly true!

OTHELLO

  Cassio did top her: ask your husband else.

  O, I were damned beneath all depth in hell

  But that I did proceed upon just grounds

  To this extremity. Your husband knew it all.

EMILIA

  My husband!

OTHELLO   Your husband.

EMILIA   That she was false to wedlock?

OTHELLO

  Ay, with Cassio. Nay, had she been true,

  If heaven would make me such another world

  Of one entire and perfect chrysolite,

  I'd not have sold her for it.

EMILIA   My husband!

OTHELLO

  Ay, 'twas he that told me on her first:

  An honest man he is, and hates the slime

  That sticks on filthy deeds.

EMILIA   My husband!

OTHELLO

  What needs this iterance, woman? I say your husband.

EMILIA

  O mistress, villainy has made mocks with love!

  My husband say that she was false?

OTHELLO   He, woman;

  I say your husband; do you understand the word?

  My friend, your husband, honest, honest Iago.

EMILIA

  If he says so, may his pernicious soul

  Rot half a grain a day! He lies to the heart.

  She was too fond of her most filthy bargain.

OTHELLO
  Ha!
EMILIA
  Do your worst:
  This deed of yours is no more worthy heaven
  Than you were worthy her.
OTHELLO   Peace, you were best.
EMILIA
  You have not half that power to do me harm
  As I have to be hurt. O gull! O dolt!
  As ignorant as dirt! You have done a deed—
  I care not for your sword—I'll make you known,
  Though I lost twenty lives. Help! Help, ho! Help!
  The Moor has killed my mistress! Murder! Murder!

            Enter Montano, Gratiano, and Iago

MONTANO
  What is the matter? How now, General?
EMILIA
  O, are you come, Iago? You have done well,
  That men must lay their murders on your neck.
GRATIANO
  What is the matter?
EMILIA
  Disprove this villain, if you are a man:
  He says you told him that his wife was false.
  I know you did not: you're not such a villain.
  Speak, for my heart is full.
IAGO
  I told him what I thought, and told no more
  Than what he found himself was apt and true.
EMILIA
  But did you ever tell him she was false?
IAGO
  I did.

EMILIA
You told a lie, an odious damnèd lie:
Upon my soul, a lie, a wicked lie!
She false with Cassio! Did you say with Cassio?

IAGO
With Cassio, mistress! Shut up, charm your tongue.

EMILIA
I will not charm my tongue; I am bound to speak:
My mistress here lies murdered in her bed.

ALL
O heavens forfend!

EMILIA
And your reports have set the murder on.

OTHELLO
Nay, stare not masters: it is true indeed.

GRATIANO
It is a strange truth.

MONTANO
O monstrous act!

EMILIA   Villainy, villainy, villainy!
I think upon it, I think—I smell it—O villainy!
I thought so then; I'll kill myself for grief.
O villainy, villainy!

IAGO
What, are you mad? I charge you get you home.

EMILIA
Good gentlemen, let me have leave to speak.
'Tis proper I obey him, but not now.
Perhaps, Iago, I will never go home.

OTHELLO
(falling on bed) O! O! O!

EMILIA   Nay, lay you down and roar,
For you have killed the sweetest innocent
That ever did lift up eye.

OTHELLO (rising)   O, she was foul!
I scarce did know you, uncle; there lies your niece,

Whose breath indeed these hands have newly stopped.
I know this act shows horrible and grim.

GRATIANO

Poor Desdemon, I am glad your father's dead:
Your match was mortal to him, and pure grief
Cut his old thread in twain. Did he live now,
This sight would make him do a desperate deed,
Yea, curse his better angel from his side,
And fall to damnation.

OTHELLO

'Tis pitiful: but yet Iago knows
That she with Cassio has the act of shame
A thousand times committed. Cassio confessed it,
And she did gratify his amorous works
With that recognizance and pledge of love
Which I first gave her. I saw it in his hand:
It was a handkerchief, an antique token
My father gave my mother.

EMILIA   O God! O heavenly Powers!

IAGO

Zounds, hold your peace!

EMILIA   'Twill out, 'twill out. I peace?
No, I will speak as liberal as the north;
Let heaven, and men, and devils, let them all,
All, all cry shame against me, yet I'll speak.

IAGO

Be wise, and get you home.

EMILIA   I will not.

Iago draws his sword

GRATIANO   Fie!
Your sword upon a woman!

EMILIA

O you dull Moor, that handkerchief you speak of
I found by fortune and did give my husband,

For often, with a solemn earnestness—
More than indeed belonged to such a trifle—
He begged of me to steal it.

IAGO   Villainous whore!

EMILIA
She give it Cassio? No, alas, I found it
And I did give it my husband.

IAGO   Filth, you lie!

EMILIA
By heaven I do not, I do not, gentlemen.
O murderous coxcomb, what should such a fool
Do with so good a wife?

OTHELLO   Are there no stones in heaven
But what serve for the thunder? Precious villain!

He runs at Iago; Montano disarms him; Iago stabs Emilia
from behind and exit

GRATIANO
The woman falls: sure he has killed his wife.

EMILIA
Ay, ay: O, lay me by my mistress' side.

GRATIANO
He's gone, but his wife is killed.

MONTANO
'Tis a notorious villain. Take you this weapon,
Which I have here recovered from the Moor.
Come guard the door without: let him not pass,
But kill him rather. I'll after that same villain,
For 'tis a damnèd slave.

                    Exeunt Montano and Gratiano

OTHELLO   I am not valiant either,
But every puny swordsman gets my sword.
But why should honour outlive honesty?
Let it go all.

EMILIA   What did your song bode, lady?
  Hark, can you hear me? I will play the swan
  And die in music. (*Singing*) Willow, willow, willow.
  Moor, she was chaste; she loved you, cruel Moor,
  So come my soul to bliss, as I speak true;
  So speaking as I think, I die, I die.   *She dies*
OTHELLO
  I have another weapon in this chamber:
  It was a sword of Spain, the ice-brook's temper.
  O, here it is. Uncle, I must come forth.
GRATIANO
  (*within*) If you attempt it, it will cost you dear;
  You have no weapon, and perforce must suffer.
OTHELLO
  Look in upon me then, and speak with me,
  Or naked as I am I will assault you.

Enter Gratiano

GRATIANO
  What is the matter?
OTHELLO   Behold, I have a weapon:
  A better never did itself sustain
  Upon a soldier's thigh. I have seen the day
  That with this little arm and this good sword,
  I have made my way through more impediments
  Than twenty times your stop. But, O vain boast!—
  Who can control his fate?—It is not so now.
  Be not afraid, though you do see me weaponed:
  Here is my journey's end, here is my butt
  And very sea-mark of my utmost sail.
  Do you go back dismayed? It is a lost fear:
  Man but a rush against Othello's breast,
  And he retires. Where should Othello go?

He goes to the bed

Now, how do you look now? O ill-starred wench!
Pale as your smock! When we shall meet at Doom
This look of yours will hurl my soul from heaven
And fiends will snatch at it. Cold, cold, my girl,
Even like your chastity.
O cursèd, cursèd slave! Whip me, ye devils,
From the possession of this heavenly sight!
Blow me about in winds! Roast me in sulphur!
Wash me in steep-down gulfs of liquid fire!
O Desdemòn! Dead Desdemòn! Dead! O! O!

Enter Lodovico, Cassio in a chair,
Montano and Iago with officers

LODOVICO
Where is this rash and most unfortunate man?
OTHELLO
That's he that was Othello: here I am.
LODOVICO
Where is that viper? Bring the villain forth.
OTHELLO
I look down towards his feet; but that's a fable.
If you are a devil, I cannot kill you.

He wounds Iago

LODOVICO
Wrench his sword from him.
IAGO   I bleed, sir, but not killed.
OTHELLO
I am not sorry either; I'd have you live,
For in my mind it is happiness to die.
LODOVICO
O, you Othello, that were once so good,
Fallen in the plots of a damnèd slave,
What shall be said to you?

OTHELLO   Why, anything:
  An honourable murderer, if you will:
  For naught did I in hate, but all in honour.
LODOVICO
  This wretch has part confessed his villainy.
  Did you and he consent in Cassio's death?
OTHELLO
  Ay.
CASSIO
  Dear General, I never gave you cause.
OTHELLO
  I do believe it, and I ask your pardon.
  Will you, I pray, demand that demi-devil
  Why he has thus ensnared my soul and body?
IAGO
  Demand me nothing; what you know, you know:
  From this time forth I never will speak word.
LODOVICO
  What! Not to pray?
GRATIANO
  Torture will open your lips.
OTHELLO   Well, you do best.
LODOVICO
  Sir, you shall understand what has befallen,
  Which, as I think, you know not. Here is a letter
  Found in the pocket of the slain Roderigo,
  And here another: the one of them imports
  The death of Cassio, to be undertaken
  By Roderigo.
OTHELLO   O villain!
CASSIO   Most heathenish and most gross!
LODOVICO
  Now here's another discontented paper
  Found in his pocket too; and this, it seems
  Roderigo meant to have sent this damnèd villain,

But that, belike, Iago, in the nick,
Came in and satisfied him.
OTHELLO   O the pernicious scoundrel!
How came you, Cassio, by that handkerchief
That was my wife's?
CASSIO   I found it in my chamber;
And he himself confessed but even now
That there he dropped it for a special purpose
Which wrought to his desire.
OTHELLO   O fool, fool, fool!
CASSIO
There is besides, in Roderigo's letter,
How he upbraids Iago, that he made him
Brave me upon the watch, whereon it came
That I was sacked; and even but now he spoke
After long seeming dead—Iago hurt him,
Iago set him on.
LODOVICO
You must forsake this room and go with us.
Your power and your command are taken off
And Cassio rules in Cyprus. For this slave,
If there is any cunning cruelty
That can torment him much, and hold him long,
It shall be his. You shall close prisoner rest,
Till the nature of your fault is known
To the Venetian state. Come, bring him away.
OTHELLO
Soft you; a word or two before you go.
I have done the state some service and they know it:
No more of that. I pray you in your letters
When you shall these unlucky deeds relate
Speak of me as I am: nothing extenuate,
Nor set down aught in malice. Then must you speak
Of one that loved not wisely, but too well;
Of one, not easily jealous but, being wrought,

Perplexed in the extreme; of one whose hand
Like the base Indian threw a pearl away
Richer than all his tribe; whose sùbdued eyes,
Albeit unusèd to the melting mood,
Drop tears as fast as the Arabian trees
Their medicinable gum. Set you down this:
And say, besides, that in Aleppo once
Where a malignant and a turbaned Turk
Beat a Venetian and traduced the state,
I took by the throat the circumcisèd dog
And smote him thus.

He stabs himself

LODOVICO
O bloody period!
GRATIANO   All that's spoken is marred!
OTHELLO
I kissed you, ere I killed you: no way but this,
Killing myself, to die upon a kiss.

He falls on the bed and dies

CASSIO
This did I fear, but thought he had no weapon,
For he was great of heart.
LODOVICO   O, Spartan dog,
More deadly than anguish, hunger, or the sea,
Look on the tragic loading of this bed:
This is your work. The object poisons sight:
Let it be hidden.

The curtains are drawn

Gratiano, keep the house
And seize upon the fortunes of the Moor,

For they succeed on you. To you, Lord Governor,
Remains the censure of this hellish villain:
The time, the place, the torture, O, enforce it!
Myself will straight aboard, and to the state
This heavy act with heavy heart relate.   *Exeunt*

The Winter's Tale

INTRODUCTION

This lovely play, which hovers for a good deal on the edge of the sorrowful (like the music of Mozart)—is classed as a comedy, for all ends happily. It is usual, and convenient, to class these last plays from *Pericles* onwards as romances, full as they are of improbable romantic happenings. These appealed greatly to the sophisticated audience of the Blackfriars theatre—much smaller than the Globe, covered over for indoor performances, more stage scenery and music—as also to the Jacobean Court, which hardly cared for brutal realism.

A great deal in it is calculated for a Court audience, with laughs that would specially appeal to it. Autolycus, the thieving pedlar—hence his name from the classical robber on the mountain-side, who escaped detection by changing the look of things—says in one of his disguises: 'Whether it likes me or no, I am a courtier. See you not the air of the Court in these enfoldings? [garments]. Has not my gait in it the measure of the Court? [A lofty strut]. Receives not your nose Court odour from me? [i.e. highly scented]. Reflect I not on your baseness, Court contempt?' etc.

The taking over of Blackfriars, hitherto a private theatre, by Shakespeare's Company, now the King's men, provided a new challenge to which he responded with two master-pieces, *The Winter's Tale* and *The Tempest*. The experienced master was capable of a flexible dramaturgy for all tastes—as we know, and has been proved throughout the centuries since—and Simon Forman saw the play at the Globe in May 1611.[1] He gives a fairly full account of it, but was mainly interested—as he would be—in the doings of Autolycus and drew the moral, as he usually did: 'Beware of trusting feigned beggars or fawning fellows.'

It was performed at Court on Gunpowder day, 5 November, that year; and was chosen along with five others of the master's plays—far more than anyone else's—for the grand entertainments to celebrate Princess Elizabeth's marriage to the Elector Palatine in 1613 (from which the present royal line in Britain descends). An appropriate choice, with the romantic marriage of the young princess of Sicilia to the young prince of Bohemia. (But Bohemia! in only a few years the foolish Elector would accept the Bohemian throne and thus start the Thirty Years' War, incurring a lifetime of exile for him and his Winter Queen. A winter's tale indeed!—we see nature imitating art once more.)

Shakespeare got the outline of his story from Robert Greene's early novel, *Pandosto*, the republication of which in 1607 drew his attention to it, in the way usual with him. But he changed a great deal. He made much more of the psychotic jealousy King Leontes suffers from over his wife, Hermione's, friendliness for his former friend, Polixenes. In the course of it he creates a marvellous character in the vein of King Lear, who learns truth and repentance from the sufferings he endures—and inflicts. In fact, Leontes is a completely modern study in psychosis; the way it operates is borne out by the findings of contemporary psychiatry. We might say that only shock-treatment— the death of his son, the presumed death of his wife,

---

[1] v. my *Simon Forman: Sex and Society in Shakespeare's Age*, 306–07.

corroborating the sentence of the Delphic Oracle—brings
him to his senses, faces him with the truth, brings healing
with repentance. But already in the 18th century Dr.
Johnson saw how psychologically veracious this was, however improbable the romantic circumstances of the tale for a
winter's hearthside.

As usual it is Shakespeare's own creations that are best.
He entirely re-creates Leontes and fills out his relations
with his Queen, spirited to begin with, then struck down
by the madness, and jealousy of her husband; entirely
innocent and forgiving, she has much in common with
Queen Catherine in *Henry VIII*. Paulina, her lady in
waiting, is a fine character fully portrayed: utterly loyal
to the injured Queen, fearless and outspoken, she is not
afraid to stand up to the King and tell him what she thinks.
A suggestion of comedy, for she is rather loquacious,
relieves the tension with her. Still more with Autolycus,
one of Shakespeare's most appealing creations; there is a
charm upon him, as he charms his victims with his patter
and his songs, his quick transformations of character and
disguises. An enchanting virtuoso of the roads—there is a
suggestion that he had known employment about the
Court, until dismissed for some misdemeanour, we do not
know what. And O, the beauty of his songs!

When daffodils begin to peer,
    With heigh! the doxy over the dale,
Why then comes in the sweet of the year,
    For the red blood reigns in the winter's pale.

(We can imagine William Shakespeare at home at Stratford
writing that.) No wonder all the country folk were taken
in by Autolycus—I am with Simon Forman in finding
my attention fixed by him and the delicious country life
surrounding him, the shepherds' shearing feast, the three-
men songs, the country folk bearing their part and think-

ing that what is in print must be true. All so true to the life of the age.

Professor Sisson notices that the story of Leontes and Hermione portrays the romance of middle age. No one notices that it is William Shakespeare getting older, looking back:

> Looking on the lines
> Of my boy's face, I thought I did recoil
> Twenty-three years, and saw myself unbreeched
> In my green velvet coat, my dagger muzzled
> Lest it should bite its master and so prove,
> As ornaments oft do, too dangerous.

Polixenes has a boy too:

> He's all my exercise, my mirth, my matter . . .
> He makes a July's day short as December.

Each has an only son. Leontes' boy dies — and Shakespeare knew that grief: his only son, who was to have carried on the name, had died as a boy of eleven. There was no boy to gladden the household at Stratford, which saw more of the master now, his strenuous hard-working days over.

The theme of gentility is there, and much is made of it. William Shakespeare had taken out his coat-of-arms, *Non sans droict* (indeed!), in his father's name, so as to have been born a gentleman:

> As you are certainly a gentleman, thereto
> Clerk-like experienced — which no less adorns
> Our gentry than our parents' noble names.

Sir Thomas Smith tells us at the time that university men were *ipso facto* gentlemen from their clerk-like experience.[2] Then, with his inveterate sense of humour, the dramatist makes a lot of fun of the theme later. The Clown: 'You denied to fight with me this other day, because I was no gentleman born. See you these clothes? Say you see them not and think me still no gentleman born! You were best say these robes are not gentleman born.' And so it goes on.

William Shakespeare did not qualify as a gentleman through being an actor: the theatre was his livelihood, his way of making his money. He was much more proud of being a poet. Dr. Johnson saw that: 'it is impossible for any man to rid his mind of his profession.' The authorship of Shakespeare has supplied him with a metaphor:

> How would he look, to see his work, so noble,
> Vilely bound up!

All the same, the theatre is ever-present. Autolycus had, or invented, an acquaintance who had put on a show of the Prodigal Son. Perdita, as mistress of the shepherds' feast:

> It seems I play as I have seen them do
> In Whitsun pastorals.

Camillo will have Prince Florizel (this romantic name had actually appeared earlier in Warwickshire)—who had come to the feast disguised as a country swain—'royally appointed as if the scene you play were mine.' Paulina, completely justified, and meeting her Queen's lost daughter: 'the dignity of this act was worth the audience of kings and princes, for by such was it acted.'—And such

---

[2]q. in G. W. Prothero, *Select Statutes and Documents . . . of Elizabeth and James I*, 177.

was Shakespeare's audience. The King sums up towards the end:

> and on this stage
> —Where we offenders now—appear soul-vexed.

Do we detect a personal note in the reflection?—

> Prosperity is the very bond of love,
> Whose fresh complexion and whose heart together
> Affliction alters.

We certainly have his regular wooing of the audience in Time, the Chorus:

> Of this allow
> If ever you have spent time worse than now;
> If never, yet that Time himself does say
> He wishes earnestly you never may.

Contemporary social actualities are there with the endearing marketings for the feast: 'Three pound of sugar, five pound of currants; rice—what will this sister of mine do with rice? . . . I must have saffron to colour the warden pies; mace; dates?—nutmegs seven; a root or two of ginger; four pounds of prunes, and as many of raisins of the sun.' The shearers are all good singers—'but one Puritan among them, and he sings psalms to hornpipes.'

One notices a certain casualness in the late verse of the master, for all its occasional beauties (especially in the description of flowers)—with so many lines ending in and, but, for, that, as. Never mind: the text offers few difficulties, and I have modernised the punctuation to help the reader. No sacrosanctity attaches to Elizabethan punctuation: it was often that of a compositor. And I have supplied accents, as throughout this edition, to help both reader and speaker of the verse with its scansion.

CHARACTERS

LEONTES, King of Sicilia
MAMILLIUS, his son, the young Prince
CAMILLO
ANTIGONUS
CLEOMENES } four lords of Sicilia
DION
POLIXENES, King of Bohemia
FLORIZEL, Prince of Bohemia
ARCHIDAMUS, a lord of Bohemia
OLD SHEPHERD, *supposed* father of Perdita
CLOWN, his son
AUTOLYCUS, a rogue
A MARINER
A GAOLER
HERMIONE, Queen to Leontes
PERDITA, daughter to Leontes and Hermione
PAULINA, wife to Antigonus
EMILIA, a lady attending on Hermione
MOPSA
DORCAS } shepherdesses
OTHER LORDS AND GENTLEMEN, LADIES, OFFICERS, AND
SERVANTS, SHEPHERDS, AND SHEPHERDESSES
TIME, as Chorus

Scene: Sicilia and Bohemia

Act I

SCENE I
Sicilia. Leontes' palace.

Enter Camillo and Archidamus.

ARCHIDAMUS If you shall chance, Camillo, to visit Bohemia on the like occasion whereon my services are now on foot, you shall see, as I have said, great difference betwixt our Bohemia and your Sicilia.

CAMILLO I think this coming summer the King of Sicilia means to pay Bohemia the visitation which he justly owes him.

ARCHIDAMUS Wherein our entertainment shall shame us, we will be justified in our loves; for indeed—

CAMILLO Beseech you—

ARCHIDAMUS Verily, I speak it in the freedom of my knowledge. We cannot with such magnificence—in so rare —I know not what to say. We will give you sleepy drinks, that your senses—unintelligent of our insufficiency— may, though they cannot praise us, as little accuse us.

CAMILLO You pay a great deal too dear for what is given freely.

ARCHIDAMUS Believe me, I speak as my understanding instructs me and as my honesty puts it to utterance.

CAMILLO Sicilia cannot show himself over-kind to Bohemia. They were trained together in their childhoods, and there rooted between them then such an affection which cannot choose but branch now. Since their more mature dignities and royal necessities made separation of their society, their encounters, though not personal, have been royally

525

attorneyed with interchange of gifts, letters, loving
embassies; that they have seemed to be together, though
absent; shook hands, as over a waste; and embraced, as
it were, from the ends of opposed winds. The heavens
continue their loves!

ARCHIDAMUS I think there is not in the world either
malice or matter to alter it. You have an unspeakable
comfort of your young prince Mamillius. It is a gentleman
of the greatest promise that ever came into my note.

CAMILLO I very well agree with you in the hopes of him.
It is a gallant child—one that indeed physics the subject,
makes old hearts fresh. They that went on crutches ere
he was born desire yet their life to see him a man.

ARCHIDAMUS Would they else be content to die?

CAMILLO Yes—if there were no other excuse why they
should desire to live.

ARCHIDAMUS If the king had no son, they would desire to
live on crutches till he had one.   *Exeunt.*

Scene II
The same.

Enter Leontes, Hermione, Mamillius, Polixenes,
Camillo, Lords.

POLIXENES
Nine changes of the watery star have been
The shepherd's note since we have left our throne
Without a burden. Time as long again
Would be filled up, my brother, with our thanks,
And yet we should, for perpetuity,
Go hence in debt. And therefore, like a cipher,
Yet standing in rich place, I multiply
With one 'We thank you' many thousands more
That go before it.

LEONTES   Stay your thanks a while
  And pay them when you part.
POLIXENES   Sir, that's to-morrow.
  I am questioned by my fears of what may chance
  Or breed upon our absence, that may blow
  No nipping winds at home to make us say,
  'This is put forth too truly.' Besides, I have stayed
  To tire your royalty.
LEONTES   We are tougher, brother,
  Than you can put us to it.
POLIXENES   No longer stay.
LEONTES
  One seven-night longer.
POLIXENES   Very true, to-morrow.
LEONTES
  We'll part the time between us then, and in that
  I'll no gainsaying.
POLIXENES   Press me not, beseech you, so.
  There is no tongue that moves, none in the world,
  So soon as yours could win me. So it should now
  Were there necessity in your request, although
  It were needful I denied it. My affairs
  Do even drag me homeward, which to hinder
  Were in your love a whip to me, my stay
  To you a charge and trouble. To save both,
  Farewell, our brother.
LEONTES   Tongue-tied our queen? Speak you.
HERMIONE
  I had thought, sir, to have held my peace until
  You had drawn oaths from him not to stay. You, sir,
  Charge him too coldly. Tell him you are sure
  All in Bohemia's well; this satisfaction
  The by-gone day proclaimed. Say this to him,
  He's beat from his best ward.
LEONTES   Well said, Hermione.

HERMIONE
> To tell he longs to see his son were strong.
> But let him say so then, and let him go;
> But let him swear so, and he shall not stay,
> We'll thwack him hence with distaffs.
> Yet of your royal presence I'll adventure
> The borrow of a week. When at Bohemia
> You take my lord, I'll give him my commission
> To leave him there a month behind the time
> Prefixed for his parting. Yet, good deed, Leontes,
> I love you not a tick of the clock behind
> Any lady she her lord. You'll stay?

POLIXENES   No, madam.

HERMIONE
> Nay, but you will?

POLIXENES   I may not, verily.

HERMIONE
> Verily?
> You put me off with feeble vows, but I,
> Though you would seek to unsphere the stars with
>   oaths,
> Should yet say, 'Sir, no going.' Verily,
> You shall not go. A lady's 'Verily' is
> As potent as a lord's. Will you go yet?
> Force me to keep you as a prisoner,
> Not like a guest, so you shall pay your fees
> When you depart and save your thanks. How say you?
> My prisoner or my guest? By your dread 'Verily,'
> One of them you shall be.

POLIXENES   Your guest, then, madam.
> To be your prisoner should import offending,
> Which is for me less easy to commit
> Than you to punish.

HERMIONE   Not your gaoler, then,
> But your kind hostess. Come, I'll question you

Of my lord's tricks and yours when you were boys.
You were pretty lordings then?
POLIXENES   We were, fair queen,
Two lads that thought there was no more behind
But such a day to-morrow as to-day,
And to be boy eternal.
HERMIONE   Was not my lord
The verier wag of the two?
POLIXENES
We were as twinned lambs that did frisk in the sun,
And bleat the one at the other. What we changed
Was innocence for innocence; we knew not
The doctrine of ill-doing, nor dreamed
That any did. Had we pursued that life,
And our weak spirits never been higher reared
With stronger blood, we should have answered heaven
Boldly 'Not guilty,' the imposition cleared
Hereditary ours.
HERMIONE   By this we gather
You have tripped since.
POLIXENES   O my most sacred lady,
Temptations have since then been born to us, for
In those unfledged days was my wife a girl.
Your precious self had then not crossed the eyes
Of my young playfellow.
HERMIONE   Grace to goodness!
Of this make no conclusion, lest you say
Your queen and I are devils. Yet go on.
The offenses we have made you do we'll answer:
If you first sinned with us, and that with us
You did continue fault, and that you slipped not
With any but with us.
LEONTES   Is he won yet?
HERMIONE
He will stay, my lord.

LEONTES   At my request he would not.
  Hermione, my dearest, you never spoke
  To better purpose.
HERMIONE   Never?
LEONTES   Never but once.
HERMIONE
  What? Have I twice said well? When was it before?
  I pray tell me. Cram us with praise, and make us
  As fat as tame things. One good deed dying tongueless
  Slaughters a thousand waiting upon that.
  Our praises are our wages. You may ride us
  With one soft kiss a thousand furlongs ere
  With spur we heat an acre. But to the goal.
  My last good deed was to entreat his stay.
  What was my first? It has an elder sister,
  Or I mistake you. O, would her name were Grace!
  But once before I spoke to the purpose. When?
  Nay, let me have it; I long.
LEONTES   Why, that was when
  Three crabbèd months had soured themselves to death
  Ere I could make you open your white hand
  And clap yourself my love. Then did you utter
  'I am yours for ever.'
HERMIONE   It is grace indeed.
  Why, lo you now, I have spoken to the purpose twice;
  The one for ever earned a royal husband,
  The other for some while a friend.

          Gives her hand to Polixenes, and they walk apart.

LEONTES [*aside*]   Too hot, too hot!
  To mingle friendship far is mingling bloods.
  I have tremor cordis[1] on me. My heart dances,
  But not for joy, not joy. This entertainment

---
[1]Palpitation of heart.

May a free face put on, derive a liberty
From heartiness, from bounty, fertile bosom,
And well become the agent. It may, I grant.
But to be paddling palms and pinching fingers,
As now they are, and making practiced smiles
As in a looking-glass, and then to sigh, as at
The death of the deer—O, that is entertainment
My bosom likes not, nor my brows. Mamillius,
Are you my boy?

MAMILLIUS   Ay, my good lord.

LEONTES In faith!
Why, that's my brave boy. What, smudged your nose?
They say it is a copy out of mine. Come, captain,
We must be neat—not neat but cleanly, captain.
And yet the steer, the heifer, and the calf
Are all called neat.—Still virginalling
Upon his palm?—How now, you wanton calf?
Are you my calf?

MAMILLIUS   Yes, if you will, my lord.

LEONTES
You want a rough head and the horns I have,
To be full like me; yet they say we are
Almost as like as eggs. Women say so,
That will say anything. But were they false
As over-dyed blacks, as wind, as waters, false
As dice are to be wished by one that fixes
No bourn between his and mine, yet were it true
To say this boy were like me. Come, sir page,
Look on me with your sky-blue eye. Sweet villain!
Most dearest! my treasure! Can your dam?—may it be?—
Affection, your intention stabs the center!
You do make possible things not so held,
Communicate with dreams—how can this be?
With what is unreal you coactive art,
And fellow nothing. Then it is very credent
You may co-join with something; and you do,

And that beyond commission, and I find it,
And that to the infection of my brains
And hardening of my brows.

POLIXENES   What means Sicilia?

HERMIONE
He something seems unsettled.

POLIXENES   How, my lord?
What cheer? How is it with you, best brother?

HERMIONE   You look
As if you held a brow of much distraction.
Are you moved, my lord?

LEONTES   No, in good earnest.
How sometimes nature will betray its folly,
Its tenderness, and make itself a pastime
To harder bosoms! Looking on the lines
Of my boy's face, I thought I did recoil
Twenty-three years, and saw myself unbreeched,
In my green velvet coat, my dagger muzzled
Lest it should bite its master and so prove,
As ornaments oft do, too dangerous.
How like, I thought, I then was to this kernel,
This squash, this gentleman. My honest friend,
Will you take eggs for money?

MAMILLIUS   No, my lord, I'll fight.

LEONTES
You will? Why, happy man be his lot! My brother,
Are you so fond of your young prince as we
Do seem to be of ours?

POLIXENES   If at home, sir,
He's all my exercise, my mirth, my matter,
Now my sworn friend and then my enemy,
My parasite, my soldier, statesman, all.
He makes a July's day short as December,
And with his varying childness cures in me
Thoughts that would thick my blood.

LEONTES   So stands this squire
   Officed with me. We two will walk, my lord,
   And leave you to your graver steps. Hermione,
   How you love us, show in our brother's welcome.
   Let what is dear in Sicily be cheap.
   Next to yourself and my young rover, he is
   Heir apparent to my heart.
HERMIONE   If you would seek us,
   We are yours in the garden. Shall we attend you there?
LEONTES
   To your own bents dispose you. You'll be found,
   Be you beneath the sky. [*aside*] I am angling now,
   Though you perceive me not how I give line.
   Go to, go to!
   How she holds up the beak, the bill to him,
   And arms her with the boldness of a wife
   To her allowing husband!
          Exeunt Polixenes, Hermione, and Attendants.
              Gone already!
   Inch-thick, knee-deep, o'er head and ears a forked one!
   Go play, boy, play. Your mother plays, and I
   Play too, but so disgraced a part, whose issue
   Will hiss me to my grave. Contempt and clamor
   Will be my knell. Go play, boy, play. There have been,
   Or I am much deceived, cuckolds ere now;
   And many a man there is, even at this present,
   Now while I speak this, holds his wife by the arm,
   That little thinks she has been sluiced in his absence
   And his pond fished by his next neighbor, by
   Sir Smile, his neighbor. Nay, there's comfort in it
   While other men have gates and those gates opened,
   As mine, against their will. Should all despair
   That have revolted wives, the tenth of mankind
   Would hang themselves. Physic for it there's none.
   It is a bawdy planet, that will strike
   Where 'tis predominant; it is powerful, think it,

From east, west, north, and south. Be it concluded,
No barricado for a belly. Know it,
It will let in and out the enemy
With bag and baggage. Many thousand of us
Have the disease and feel it not. How now, boy?
MAMILLIUS
I am like you, they say.
LEONTES   Why, that's some comfort.
What, Camillo there?
CAMILLO
Ay, my good lord.
LEONTES
Go play, Mamillius. You are an honest man.
                                        Exit Mamillius.
Camillo, this great sir will yet stay longer.
CAMILLO
You had much ado to make his anchor hold;
When you cast out, it still came home.
LEONTES   Did you note it?
CAMILLO
He would not stay at your petitions, made
His business more material
LEONTES   Did you perceive it?

                        [*Aside.*]

They're here with me already, whispering, rounding
'Sicilia is a so-forth.' It is far gone,
When I shall taste it last. How came it, Camillo,
That he did stay?
CAMILLO   At the good queen's entreaty.
LEONTES
At the queen's be it. 'Good' should be pertinent;
But so it is, it is not. Was this taken
By any understanding pate but yours?
For your conceit is soaking, will draw in

More than the common blocks. Not noted, is it,
But of the finer natures, by several
Of head-piece extraordinary? Lower messes
Perchance are to this business purblind? Say.

CAMILLO
Business, my lord? I think most understand
Bohemia stays here longer.

LEONTES   Ha?

CAMILLO   Stays here longer.

LEONTES
Ay, but why?

CAMILLO
To satisfy your highness and the entreaties
Of our most gracious mistress.

LEONTES   Satisfy
The entreaties of your mistress? Satisfy;
Let that suffice. I have trusted you, Camillo,
With all the nearest things to my heart, as well
My chamber-councils, wherein, priest-like, you
Have cleansed my bosom, I from you departed
Your penitent reformed. But we have been
Deceived in your integrity, deceived
In that which seems so.

CAMILLO   Be it forbidden, my lord!

LEONTES
To bide upon it, you are not honest; or,
If you incline that way, you are a coward,
Which hamstrings honesty behind, restraining
From course required. Or else you must be counted
A servant grafted in my serious trust
And therein negligent. Or else a fool
That see a game played home, the rich stake drawn,
And take it all for jest.

CAMILLO   My gracious lord,
I may be negligent, foolish, and fearful.
In every one of these no man is free,

But that his negligence, his folly, fear,
Among the infinite doings of the world,
Sometimes puts forth. In your affairs, my lord,
If ever I were willful-negligent,
It was my folly; if industriously
I played the fool, it was my negligence,
Not weighing well the end. If ever fearful
To do a thing where I the issue doubted,
Whereof the execution did cry out
Against the non-performance, it was a fear
Which oft infects the wisest. These, my lord,
Are such allowed infirmities that honesty
Is never free of. But, beseech your grace,
Be plainer with me; let me know my trespass
By its own visage. If I deny it,
It is none of mine.

LEONTES   Have not you seen, Camillo—
But that's past doubt, you have, or your eye-glass
Is thicker than a cuckold's horn—or heard—
For to a vision so apparent rumor
Cannot be mute—or thought—for cogitation
Resides not in that man that does not think—
My wife is slippery? If you will confess,
Or else be impudently negative,
To have nor eyes nor ears nor thought, then say
My wife is a hobby-horse, deserves a name
As rank as any flax-wench that gives way
Before her troth-plight. Say it and justify it.

CAMILLO
I would not be a stander-by to hear
My sovereign mistress clouded so, without
My present vengeance taken. Bless my heart,
You never spoke what did become you less
Than this, which to reiterate were sin
As deep as that, though true.

LEONTES   Is whispering nothing?
  Is leaning cheek to cheek? Is meeting noses?
  Kissing with inside lip? stopping the career
  Of laughter with a sigh?—a note infallible
  Of breaking honesty!—horsing foot on foot?
  Skulking in corners? wishing clocks more swift?
  Hours, minutes? noon, midnight? and all eyes
  Blind with cataract but theirs, theirs only,
  That would unseen be wicked? Is this nothing?
  Why, then the world and all that's in it is nothing,
  The covering sky is nothing, Bohemia nothing,
  My wife is nothing, and nothing have these nothings,
  If this is nothing.
CAMILLO   Good my lord, be cured
  Of this diseased opinion, and betimes,
  For it is most dangerous.
LEONTES   Say it be, it is true.
CAMILLO
  No, no, my lord.
LEONTES   It is. You lie, you lie.
  I say you lie, Camillo, and I hate you,
  Pronounce you a gross lout, a mindless slave,
  Or else a hovering temporizer, that
  Can with your eyes at once see good and evil,
  Inclining to them both. Were my wife's liver
  Infected as her life, she would not live
  The running of one glass.
CAMILLO   Who does infect her?
LEONTES
  Why, he that wears her like her medal, hanging
  About his neck—Bohemia. Who, if I
  Had servants true about me that bore eyes
  To see alike my honor as their profits,
  Their own particular thrifts, they would do that
  Which should undo more doing. Ay, and you,
  His cupbearer—whom I from meaner form

Have benched and reared to worship, who may see
Plainly as heaven sees earth and earth sees heaven,
How I am gallèd—might bespice a cup
To give my enemy a lasting wink,
Which draught to me were cordial.
CAMILLO   Sir, my lord,
I could do this and that with no rash potion,
But with a lingering dram that should not work
Maliciously like poison. But I cannot
Believe this crack to be in my dread mistress,
So sovereignly being honorable.
I have loved you—
LEONTES   Make that your question, and go rot!
Do you think I am so muddy, so unsettled,
To appoint myself in this vexation, sully
The purity and whiteness of my sheets—
Which to preserve is sleep, which being spotted
Is goads, thorns, nettles, tails of wasps—
Give scandal to the blood of the prince my son,
Who I do think is mine and love as mine,
Without ripe moving to it? Would I do this?
Could man so flinch?
CAMILLO   I must believe you, sir.
I do, and will fetch off Bohemia for it.
Provided that, when he's removed, your highness
Will take again your queen as yours at first—
Even for your son's sake, and thereby for sealing
The injury of tongues in Courts and kingdoms
Known and allied to yours.
LEONTES   You do advise me
Even so as I my own course have set down.
I'll give no blemish to her honor, none.
CAMILLO   My lord,
Go then, and with a countenance as clear
As friendship wears at feasts, keep with Bohemia
And with your queen. I am his cupbearer.

If from me he has wholesome beverage,
Account me not your servant.
LEONTES   This is all.
Do it, and you have the one half of my heart;
Do it not, you split your own.
CAMILLO   I'll do it, my lord.
LEONTES
I will seem friendly, as you have advised me.   *Exit.*
CAMILLO
O miserable lady! But for me,
What case stand I in? I must be the poisoner
Of good Polixenes; and my ground to do it
Is the obedience to a master, one
Who in rebellion with himself will have
All that are his so too. To do this deed,
Promotion follows. If I could find example
Of thousands that had struck anointed kings
And flourished after, I'd not do it; but since
Nor brass nor stone nor parchment bears not one,
Let villainy itself forswear it. I must
Forsake the court. To do it, or no, is certain
To me a break-neck. Happy star reign now!
Here comes Bohemia.

Enter Polixenes.

POLIXENES   This is strange. I think
My favor here begins to warp. Not speak?
Good day, Camillo.
CAMILLO   Hail, most royal sir!
POLIXENES
What is the news in the Court?
CAMILLO   None rare, my lord.
POLIXENES
The king has on him such a countenance
As he had lost some province and a region

Loved as he loves himself. Even now I met him
With customary compliment; when he,
Wafting his eyes to the contrary, letting fall
A lip of much contempt, speeds from me, and
So leaves me to consider what is breeding
That changes thus his manners.

CAMILLO
I dare not know, my lord.

POLIXENES
How dare not? do not? Do you know and dare not
Be intelligent to me? It is thereabouts,
For, to yourself, what you do know, you must,
And cannot say you dare not. Good Camillo,
Your changed complexions are to me a mirror
Which shows me mine changed too; for I must be
A party in this alteration, finding
Myself thus altered with it.

CAMILLO   There is a sickness
Which puts some of us in distemper, but
I cannot name the disease, and it is caught
Of you that yet are well.

POLIXENES   How caught of me?
Make me not sighted like the basilisk.[2]
I have looked on thousands who have sped the better
By my regard, but killed none so. Camillo,
As you are certainly a gentleman, thereto
Clerk-like experienced—which no less adorns
Our gentry than our parents' noble names,
In whose succession we are gentle—I beseech you,
If you know aught which does behove my knowledge
Thereof to be informed, imprison it not
In ignorant concealment.

CAMILLO   I may not answer.

---

[2]Fabled creature whose look killed.

POLIXENES
    A sickness caught of me, and yet I well?
    I must be answered. Do you hear, Camillo?
    I conjure you by all the parts of man
    Which honor does acknowledge, whereof the least
    Is not this suit of mine, that you declare
    What incidence you do guess of harm
    Is creeping toward me; how far off, how near;
    Which way to be prevented, if to be;
    If not, how best to bear it.

CAMILLO   Sir, I will tell you,
    Since I am charged in honor and by him
    That I think honorable. Therefore mark my counsel,
    Which must be even as swiftly followed as
    I mean to utter it, or both yourself and I
    Cry 'Lost,' and so good night!

POLIXENES   On, good Camillo.

CAMILLO
    I am appointed him to murder you.

POLIXENES
    By whom, Camillo?

CAMILLO   By the king.

POLIXENES   For what?

CAMILLO
    He thinks, nay, with all confidence he swears,
    As he had seen it or been an instrument
    To vice you to it, that you have touched his queen
    Forbiddenly.

POLIXENES O, then my best blood turn
    To an infected jelly and my name
    Be yoked with his that did betray the Best!
    Turn then my freshest reputation to
    A savor that may strike the dullest nostril
    Where I arrive, and my approach be shunned,
    Nay, hated too, worse than the worst infection
    That ever was heard or read!

CAMILLO   Swear his thought over
By each particular star in heaven and
By all their influences, you may as well
Forbid the sea then to obey the moon
As either by oath remove or counsel shake
The fabric of his folly, whose foundation
Is piled upon his faith and will continue
The standing of his body.
POLIXENES   How should this grow?
CAMILLO
I know not. But I am sure it is safer to
Avoid what's grown than question how 'tis born.
If therefore you dare trust my honesty,
That lies enclosèd in this trunk which you
Shall bear along impawned, away to-night!
Your followers I will whisper to the business,
And will by twos and threes at several posterns
Clear them of the city. For myself, I'll put
My fortunes to your service, which are here
By this discovery lost. Be not uncertain,
For, by the honor of my parents, I
Have uttered truth, which if you seek to prove,
I dare not stand by; nor shall you be safer
Than one condemnèd by the king's own mouth,
Thereon his execution sworn.
POLIXENES   I do believe you;
I saw his heart in his face. Give me your hand.
Be pilot to me and your places shall
Still neighbor mine. My ships are ready and
My people did expect my hence departure
Two days ago. This jealousy
Is for a precious creature. As she's rare,
Must it be great; as his person is mighty,
Must it be violent; and as he does conceive
He is dishonored by a man who ever
Professed love to him, his revenges must

In that be made more bitter. Fear overshades me.
Good expedition be my friend, and comfort
The gracious queen, part of his theme but nothing
Of his ill-taken suspicion! Come, Camillo.
I will respect you as a father if
You bear my life off hence. Let us away.

CAMILLO
It is in my authority to command
The keys of all the posterns. Please your highness
To take the urgent hour. Come, sir, away.   *Exeunt.*

Act II

SCENE I
The same.

Enter Hermione, Mamillius, and Ladies.

HERMIONE
 Take the boy to you. He so troubles me,
 It is past enduring.
LADY   Come, my gracious lord,
 Shall I be your playfellow?
MAMILLIUS   No, I'll none of you.
LADY
 Why, my sweet lord?
MAMILLIUS
 You'll kiss me hard and speak to me as if
 I were a baby still. I love you better.
SECOND LADY
 And why so, my lord?
MAMILLIUS   Not quite because
 Your brows are blacker. Yet black brows, they say,
 Become some women best, if there is not
 Too much hair there, but in a semicircle,
 Or a half-moon made with a pen.
SECOND LADY   Who taught you this?
MAMILLIUS
 I learned it out of women's faces. Pray now,
 What color are your eyebrows?
LADY   Blue, my lord.

MAMILLIUS

   Nay, that's a mock. I have seen a lady's nose

   That has been blue, but not her eyebrows.

LADY   Hark you.

   The queen your mother rounds apace. We shall

   Present our services to a fine new prince

   One of these days, and then you'd wanton with us,

   If we would have you.

SECOND LADY   She is spread of late

   Into a goodly bulk. Good time encounter her!

HERMIONE

   What wisdom stirs among you? Come, sir, now

   I am for you again. Pray you sit by us

   And tell us a tale.

MAMILLIUS   Merry or sad shall it be?

HERMIONE

   As merry as you will.

MAMILLIUS

   A sad tale is best for winter. I have one

   Of sprites and goblins.

HERMIONE   Let's have that, good sir.

   Come on, sit down. Come on, and do your best

   To fright me with your sprites; you're powerful at it.

MAMILLIUS

   There was a man—

HERMIONE   Nay, come sit down; then on.

MAMILLIUS

   Dwelt by a churchyard. I will tell it softly;

   Yon crickets shall not hear it.

HERMIONE   Come on, then,

   And give it me in my ear.

Enter Leontes, Antigonus, Lords and guards.

LEONTES
  Was he met there? his train? Camillo with him?
LORD
  Behind the tuft of pines I met them. Never
  Saw I men scour so on their way. I eyed them
  Even to their ships.
LEONTES   How blest am I
  In my just judgment, in my true opinion!
  Alas, for lesser knowledge! how accursed
  In being so blest! There may be in the cup
  A spider steeped, and one may drink, depart,
  And yet partake no venom, for his knowledge
  Is not infected. But if one present
  The abhorred ingredient to his eye, makes known
  How he has drunk, he cracks his gorge, his sides,
  With violent vomits. I have drunk, and seen the spider.
  Camillo was his help in this, his pander.
  There is a plot against my life, my crown.
  All's true that is mistrusted. That false villain
  Whom I employed was pre-employed by him.
  He has discovered my design, and I
  Remain a racked thing—yea, a very trick
  For them to play at will. How came the posterns
  So easily open?
LORD   By his great authority,
  Which often has no less prevailed than so
  On your command.
LEONTES   I know it too well.
  Give me the boy. I am glad you did not nurse him.
  Though he does bear some signs of me, yet you
  Have too much blood in him.
HERMIONE   What is this? sport?
LEONTES
  Bear the boy hence. He shall not come about her.
  Away with him! and let her sport herself

With that she's big with, for 'tis Polixenes
Has made you swell thus.

HERMIONE   But I'd say he had not,
And I'll be sworn you would believe my saying,
However you lean to the nayward.

LEONTES   You, my lords,
Look on her, mark her well. Be but about
To say 'She is a goodly lady,' and
The justice of your hearts will thereto add
''Tis pity she's not honest, honorable.'
Praise her but for this her without-door form—
Which on my faith deserves high speech—and straight
The shrug, the hum or ha, these petty brands
That calumny does use—O, I am out,
That mercy does, for calumny will sear
Virtue itself—these shrugs, these hums and ha's,
When you have said she's goodly, come between
Ere you can say she's honest. But be it known,
From him that has most cause to grieve it should be,
She's an adulteress.

HERMIONE   Should a villain say so,
The most replenished villain in the world,
He were as much more villain. You, my lord,
Do but mistake.

LEONTES   You have mistaken, my lady,
Polixenes for Leontes. O you thing!
Which I'll not call a creature of your place,
Lest barbarism, making me the precedent,
Should a like language use to all degrees
And mannerly distinguishment leave out
Between the prince and beggar. I have said
She's an adulteress; I have said with whom.
More, she's a traitor and Camillo is
A confederate with her, and one that knows
What she should shame to know herself
But with her most vile principal, that she's

A bed-swerver, even as bad as those
That vulgars give boldest titles—ay, and privy
To this their late escape.

HERMIONE   No, by my life,
Privy to none of this. How will this grieve you,
When you shall come to clearer knowledge, that
You thus have published me! Gentle my lord,
You scarce can right me thoroughly then to say
You did mistake.

LEONTES   No. If I mistake
In those foundations which I build upon,
The center is not big enough to bear
A schoolboy's top. Away with her to prison!
He who shall speak for her is afar off guilty
But that he speaks.

HERMIONE   There's some ill planet reigns.
I must be patient till the heavens look
With an aspect more favorable. Good my lords,
I am not prone to weeping, as our sex
Commonly are; the want of which vain dew
Perchance shall dry your pities. But I have
That honorable grief lodged here which burns
Worse than tears drown. Beseech you all, my lords,
With thoughts so qualified as your charities
Shall best instruct you, measure me; and so
The king's will be performed.

LEONTES   Shall I be heard?

HERMIONE
Who is it that goes with me? Beseech your highness,
My women may be with me, for you see
My plight requires it. Do not weep, good fools;
There is no cause. When you shall know your mistress
Has deserved prison, then abound in tears
As I come out. This action I now go on
Is for my better grace. Adieu, my lord.

I never wished to see you sorry; now
I trust I shall. My women, come; you have leave.

LEONTES

Go, do our bidding. Hence!

Exit Queen, guarded, with Ladies.

LORD

Beseech your highness, call the queen again.

ANTIGONUS

Be certain what you do, sir, lest your justice
Prove violence, in which three great ones suffer,
Yourself, your queen, your son.

LORD   For her, my lord,
I dare my life lay down and will do it, sir,
Please you to accept it, that the queen is spotless
In the eyes of heaven and to you—I mean,
In this which you accuse her.

ANTIGONUS   If it proves
She's otherwise, I'll keep my stables where
I lodge my wife. I'll go in couples with her,
Than when I feel and see her no farther trust her;
For every inch of woman in the world,
Ay, every dram of woman's flesh is false,
If she is.

LEONTES Hold your peaces.

LORD   Good my lord—

ANTIGONUS

It is for you we speak, not for ourselves.
You are abused and by some putter-on
That will be damned for it. Would I knew the villain,
I would make hell for him. Be she honor-flawed,
I have three daughters—the eldest is eleven,
The second and the third, nine and some five—
If this proves true, they'll pay for it. By my honor,
I'll geld them all; fourteen they shall not see
To bring false generations. They are co-heirs,

And I had rather geld myself than they
Should not produce fair issue.

LEONTES   Cease; no more.
You smell this business with a sense as cold
As is a dead man's nose. But I do see it and feel it,
As you feel doing thus [*pinches Antigonus*], and see
  with it
The instruments that feel.

ANTIGONUS   If it is so,
We need no grave to bury honesty.
There's not a grain of it the face to sweeten
Of the whole dungy earth.

LEONTES   What? Lack I credit?

LORD
I had rather you did lack than I, my lord,
Upon this ground; and more it would content me
To have her honor true than your suspicion,
Be blamed for it how you might.

LEONTES   Why, what need we
Commune with you of this, but rather follow
Our forceful instigation? Our prerogative
Calls not your counsels, but our natural goodness
Imparts this, which if you—or stupified
Or seeming so in skill—cannot or will not
Relish a truth like us, inform yourselves
We need no more of your advice. The matter,
The loss, the gain, the ordering of it, is all
Properly ours.

ANTIGONUS And I wish, my liege,
You had only in your silent judgment tried it,
Without more overture.

LEONTES   How could that be?
Either you are most ignorant by age
Or you were born a fool. Camillo's flight,
Added to their familiarity—
Which was as gross as ever touched conjecture,

That lacked sight only, nought for approbation
But only seeing, all other circumstances
Made up to the deed—does push on this proceeding.
Yet, for a greater confirmation—
For in an act of this importance it were
Most piteous to be wild—I have dispatched in post
To sacred Delphos, to Apollo's temple,
Cleomenes and Dion, whom you know
Of stuffed sufficiency. Now from the oracle
They will bring all, whose spiritual counsel had,
Shall stop or spur me. Have I done well?

LORD
Well done, my lord.

LEONTES
Though I am satisfied and need no more
Than what I know, yet shall the oracle
Give rest to the minds of others, such as he
Whose ignorant credulity will not
Come up to the truth. So have we thought it good
From our free person she should be confined,
Lest the treachery of the two fled hence
Be left her to perform. Come, follow us.
We are to speak in public, for this business
Will raise us all.

ANTIGONUS [aside] To laughter, as I take it,
If the good truth were known.   Exeunt.

SCENE II
A prison.

Enter Paulina, a Gentleman and Attendants.

PAULINA
The keeper of the prison, call to him;
Let him have knowledge who I am.   *Exit Gentleman.*

                                        Good lady,
No Court in Europe is too good for you.
What do you then in prison?

                    Enter Gentleman with the Gaoler.

                                        Now, good sir,
You know me, do you not?
GAOLER   For a worthy lady
And one whom much I honor.
PAULINA   Pray you then,
Conduct me to the queen.
GAOLER   I may not, madam.
To the contrary I have express commandment.
PAULINA
Here's ado,
To lock up honesty and honor from
The access of gentle visitors. Is it lawful, pray you,
To see her women? any of them? Emilia?
GAOLER
So please you, madam,
To put apart these your attendants, I
Shall bring Emilia forth.
PAULINA   I pray now, call her.
Withdraw yourselves.
                         Exeunt Gentleman and Attendants.
GAOLER   And, madam,
I must be present at your conference.
PAULINA
Well, be it so, pray.   *Exit Gaoler.*
Here's such ado to make no stain a stain
As passes coloring.

                    Enter Gaoler with Emilia.

Dear gentlewoman,
How fares our gracious lady?

EMILIA
As well as one so great and so forlorn
May hold together. On her frights and griefs,
Which never tender lady has borne greater,
She is something before her time delivered.

PAULINA
A boy?

EMILIA A daughter, and a goodly babe,
Lusty and like to live. The queen receives
Much comfort in it, says, 'My poor prisoner,
I am innocent as you.'

PAULINA   I dare be sworn.
These fits of lunacy in the king, curse them!
He must be told of it, and he shall. The office
Becomes a woman best; I'll take it upon me.
If I prove honey-mouthed, let my tongue blister
And never to my red-looked anger be
The trumpet any more. Pray you, Emilia,
Commend my best obedience to the queen.
If she dares trust me with her little babe,
I'll show it the king and undertake to be
Her advocate to the loudest. We do not know
How he may soften at the sight of the child.
The silence often of pure innocence
Persuades when speaking fails.

EMILIA   Most worthy madam,
Your honor and your goodness are so evident
That your free undertaking cannot miss
A thriving issue. There is no lady living
So meet for this great errand. Please your ladyship
To visit the next room, I'll presently
Acquaint the queen of your most noble offer,
Who but to-day hammered of this design;

But durst not tempt a minister of honor
Lest she should be denied.
PAULINA   Tell her, Emilia,
I'll use that tongue I have. If wit flows from it
As boldness from my bosom, let it not be doubted
I shall do good.
EMILIA   Now be you blest for it!
I'll to the queen. Please you, come something nearer.
GAOLER
Madam, if it pleases the queen to send the babe,
I know not what I shall incur to pass it,
Having no warrant.
PAULINA   You need not fear it, sir.
This child was prisoner to the womb and is
By law and process of great nature thence
Freed and enfranchised; not a party to
The anger of the king nor guilty of,
If any is, the trespass of the queen.
GAOLER
I do believe it.
PAULINA
Do not you fear. Upon my honor, I
Will stand between you and danger.   *Exeunt.*

SCENE III
Leontes' palace.

Enter Leontes, Antigonus, Lords and Attendants.

LEONTES
Nor night nor day no rest. It is but weakness
To bear the matter thus—mere weakness. If
The cause were not in being—part of the cause,
She, the adulteress; for the harlot king
Is quite beyond my arm, out of the blank

And level of my brain, plot-proof. But she
I can hook to me. Say that she were gone,
Given to the fire, a moiety of my rest
Might come to me again. Who's there?
SERVANT   My lord.
LEONTES
How does the boy?
SERVANT   He took good rest to-night.
'Tis hoped his sickness is discharged.
LEONTES
To see his nobleness!
Conceiving the dishonor of his mother,
He straight declined, drooped, took it deeply,
Fastened and fixed the shame of it in himself,
Threw off his spirit, his appetite, his sleep,
And downright languished. Leave me solely. Go
See how he fares.   *Exit Servant.*
                Fie, fie! no thought of him!
The very thought of my revenges that way
Recoil upon me—in himself too mighty,
And in his parties, his alliance. Let him be
Until a time may serve. For present vengeance,
Take it on her. Camillo and Polixenes
Laugh at me, make their pastime at my sorrow.
They should not laugh if I could reach them, nor
Shall she within my power.

                Enter Paulina with a Babe.

LORD   You must not enter.
PAULINA
Nay, rather, good my lords, be second to me.
Fear you his tyrannous passion more, alas,
Than the queen's life? a gracious innocent soul,
More free than he is jealous.
ANTIGONUS   That's enough.

SERVANT
   Madam, he has not slept to-night, commanded
   None should come at him.
PAULINA   Not so hot, good sir.
   I come to bring him sleep. It is such as you,
   That creep like shadows by him and do sigh
   At each his needless heavings, such as you
   Nourish the cause of his awaking. I
   Do come with words as medicinal as true,
   Honest as either, to purge him of that humor
   That presses him from sleep.
LEONTES   What noise there, ho?
PAULINA
   No noise, my lord, but needful conference
   About some godparents for your highness.
LEONTES   How?
   Away with that audacious lady! Antigonus,
   I charged you that she should not come about me.
   I knew she would.
ANTIGONUS   I told her so, my lord,
   On your displeasure's peril and on mine,
   She should not visit you.
LEONTES   What, can you not rule her?
PAULINA
   From all dishonesty he can. In this,
   Unless he takes the course that you have done,
   Commit me for committing honor, trust it,
   He shall not rule me.
ANTIGONUS   La you now, you hear!
   When she will take the rein I let her run,
   But she'll not stumble.
PAULINA   Good my liege, I come—
   And I beseech you hear me, who profess
   Myself your loyal servant, your physician,
   Your most obedient counsellor, yet that dare
   Less appear so in comforting your evils

Than such as most seem yours—I say I come
From your good queen.

LEONTES   Good queen?

PAULINA   Good queen, my lord,
Good queen. I say good queen,
And would by combat make her good, so were I
A man, the worst about you.

LEONTES   Force her hence.

PAULINA
Let him that makes but trifles of his eyes
First hand me. On my own accord I'll off,
But first I'll do my errand. The good queen,
For she is good, has brought you forth a daughter—
Here it is—commends it to your blessing.

Lays down the child.

LEONTES   Out!
A mankind witch! Hence with her, out of door!
A most intelligencing bawd.

PAULINA   Not so.
I am as ignorant in that as you
In so entitling me—and no less honest
Than you are mad; which is enough, I'll warrant,
As this world goes, to pass for honest.

LEONTES   Traitors!
Will you not push her out? Give her the bastard.
You dotard, you are woman-tired, unroosted
By your dame Partlet here. Take up the bastard.
Take it up, I say. Give it to your crone.

PAULINA   Forever
Unvenerable be your hands, if you
Take up the princess by that forcèd baseness
Which he has put upon it!

LEONTES   He dreads his wife.

PAULINA
   So I would you did. Then it were past all doubt
   You'd call your children yours.
LEONTES   A nest of traitors!
ANTIGONUS
   I am none, by this good light.
PAULINA   Nor I, nor any
   But one that's here, and that's himself; for he
   The sacred honor of himself, his queen's,
   His hopeful son's, his babe's, betrays to slander,
   Whose sting is sharper than the sword's. And will not—
   For, as the case now stands, it is a curse
   He cannot be compelled to it—once remove
   The root of his opinion, which is rotten
   As ever oak or stone was sound.
LEONTES   A strumpet
   Of boundless tongue, who late did beat her husband
   And now baits me! This brat is none of mine;
   It is the issue of Polixenes.
   Hence with it, and together with the dam
   Commit them to the fire!
PAULINA   It is yours,
   And, might we lay the old proverb to your charge,
   So like you 'tis the worse. Behold, my lords.
   Although the print is little, the whole matter
   And copy of the father—eye, nose, lip,
   The trick of his frown, his forehead, nay, the valley,
   The pretty dimples of its chin and cheek, its smiles,
   The very mould and frame of hand, nail, finger.
   And you, good goddess Nature, which have made it
   So like to him that got it, if you have
   The ordering of the mind too, among all colors
   No yellow in it, lest she suspects, as he does,
   Her children not her husband's!

LEONTES   A gross hag!
  And, scoundrel, you are worthy to be hanged
  That will not stay her tongue.
ANTIGONUS   Hang all the husbands
  That cannot do that feat, you'll leave yourself
  Hardly one subject.
LEONTES   Once more, take her hence!
PAULINA
  A most unworthy and unnatural lord
  Can do no more.
LEONTES   I'll have you burnt.
PAULINA   I care not.
  It is a heretic that makes the fire,
  Not she who burns in it. I'll not call you tyrant;
  But this most cruel usage of your queen,
  Not able to produce more accusation
  Than your own weak-hinged fancy, something savors
  Of tyranny and will ignoble make you,
  Yes, scandalous to the world.
LEONTES   On your allegiance,
  Out of the chamber with her! Were I a tyrant,
  Where were her life? She durst not call me so
  If she did know me one. Away with her!
PAULINA
  I pray you do not push me; I'll be gone.
  Look to your babe, my lord; 'tis yours. Jove send her
  A better guiding spirit. What need these hands?
  You that are thus so tender over his follies
  Will never do him good, not one of you.
  So, so. Farewell; we are gone.   *Exit.*
LEONTES
  You, traitor, have set on your wife to this.
  My child? away with it! Even you, that have
  A heart so tender over it, take it hence
  And see it instantly consumed with fire—
  Even you and none but you. Take it up straight.

Within this hour bring me word it is done,
And by good testimony, or I'll seize your life,
With what you else call yours. If you refuse
And will encounter with my wrath, say so.
The bastard brains with these my very hands
Shall I dash out. Go, take it to the fire,
For you set on your wife.

ANTIGONUS   I did not, sir.
These lords, my noble fellows, if they please,
Can clear me in it.

LORDS   We can. My royal liege,
He is not guilty of her coming hither.

LEONTES
You are liars all.

LORD
Beseech your highness, give us better credit.
We have always truly served you, and beseech you
So to esteem of us; and on our knees we beg,
As recompense of our dear services
Past and to come, that you do change this purpose,
Which being so horrible, so bloody, must
Lead on to some foul issue. We all kneel.

LEONTES
I am a feather for each wind that blows.
Shall I live on to see this bastard kneel
And call me father? Better burn it now
Than curse it then. But be it; let it live.
It shall not either. You, sir, come you hither,
You that have been so tenderly officious
With Lady Margery, your midwife there,
To save this bastard's life—for 'tis a bastard,
So sure as this beard's grey. What will you adventure
To save this brat's life?

ANTIGONUS   Anything, my lord,
That my ability may undergo
And nobleness impose. At least thus much.

I'll pawn the little blood which I have left
To save the innocent. Anything possible.

LEONTES
It shall be possible. Swear by this sword
You will perform my bidding.

ANTIGONUS   I will, my lord.

LEONTES
Mark and perform it, see you; for the fail
Of any point in it shall not only be
Death to yourself but to your lewd-tongued wife,
Whom for this time we pardon. We enjoin you,
As you are liege-man to us, that you carry
This female bastard hence, and that you bear it
To some remote and desert place quite out
Of our dominions, and that there you leave it,
Without more mercy, to its own protection
And favor of the climate. As by strange fortune
It came to us, I do in justice charge you,
On your soul's peril and your body's torture,
That you commend it strangely to some place
Where chance may nurse or end it. Take it up.

ANTIGONUS
I swear to do this, though a present death
Had been more merciful. Come on, poor babe.
Some powerful spirit instruct the kites and ravens
To be your nurses. Wolves and bears, they say,
Casting their savageness aside, have done
Like offices of pity. Sir, be prosperous
In more than this deed does require. And blessing
Against this cruelty fight on your side,
Poor thing, condemned to loss.   *Exit with the Babe.*

LEONTES   No, I'll not rear
Another's issue.

Enter a Servant.

SERVANT   Please your highness, posts
   From those you sent to the oracle are come
   An hour since. Cleomenes and Dion,
   Being well arrived from Delphos, are both landed,
   Hasting to the Court.
LORD   So please you, sir, their speed
   Has been beyond account.
LEONTES   Twenty-three days
   They have been absent. 'Tis good speed, foretells
   The great Apollo suddenly will have
   The truth of this appear. Prepare you, lords;
   Summon a session, that we may arraign
   Our most disloyal lady, for, as she has
   Been publicly accused, so shall she have
   A just and open trial. While she lives
   My heart will be a burden to me. Leave me,
   And think upon my bidding.   *Exeunt.*

Act III

SCENE I
Sicilia—A road.

Enter Cleomenes and Dion.

CLEOMENES
    The climate's delicate, the air most sweet,
    Fertile the isle, the temple much surpassing
    The common praise it bears.
DION   I shall report,
    For most it caught me, the celestial habits—
    It seems I so should term them—and the reverence
    Of the grave wearers. O, the sacrifice,
    How ceremonious, solemn, and unearthly
    It was in the offering!
CLEOMENES   But of all, the burst
    And the ear-deafening voice of the oracle,
    Kin to Jove's thunder, so surprised my sense
    That I was nothing.
DION   If the event of the journey
    Proves as successful to the queen—O be it so!—
    As it has been to us rare, pleasant, speedy,
    The time is worth the use of it.
CLEOMENES   Great Apollo
    Turn all to the best! These proclamatiòns,
    So forcing faults upon Hermione,
    I little like.
DION   The violent carriage of it
    Will clear or end the business. When the oracle,
    Thus by Apollo's great divine sealed up,

Shall the contents discover, something rare
Even then will rush to knowledge. Go. Fresh horses!
And gracious be the issue!   *Exeunt.*

SCENE II
A court of justice.

Enter Leontes, Lords and Officers.

LEONTES
This sessions, to our great grief we pronounce,
Even pushes against our heart—the party tried
The daughter of a king, our wife, and one
Of us too much beloved. Let us be cleared
Of being tyrannous, since we so openly
Proceed in justice, which shall have due course,
Even to the guilt or the purgatiòn.
Produce the prisoner.

OFFICER
It is his highness' pleasure that the queen
Appear in person here in court. Silence!

Enter Hermione, guarded, Paulina, and Ladies.

LEONTES
Read the indictment.

OFFICER [*reads*] Hermione, queen to the worthy Leontes,
king of Sicilia, you are here accused and arraigned of
high treason, in committing adultery with Polixenes,
king of Bohemia, and conspiring with Camillo to take
away the life of our sovereign lord the king, your royal
husband; the pretense whereof being by circumstances
partly laid open, you, Hermione, contrary to the faith
and allegiance of a true subject, did counsel and aid
them, for their better safety, to fly away by night.

HERMIONE
Since what I am to say must be but that
Which contradicts my accusation, and
The testimony on my part no other
But what comes from myself, it shall scarce help me
To say, 'Not guilty.' My integrity,
Being counted falsehood, shall, as I express it,
Be so received. But thus: if powers divine
Behold our human actions, as they do,
I doubt not then but innocence shall make
False accusation blush and tyranny
Tremble at patience. You, my lord, best know,
Who least will seem to do so, my past life
Has been as continent, as chaste, as true,
As I am now unhappy; which is more
Than history can pattern, though devised
And played to take spectators. For behold me—
A fellow of the royal bed, who own
A moiety of the throne, a great king's daughter,
The mother to a hopeful prince—here standing
To prate and talk for life and honor before
Who please to come and hear. For life, I prize it
As I weigh grief, which I would spare. For honor,
It is a derivative from me to mine,
And only that I stand for. I appeal
To your own conscience, sir, before Polixenes
Came to your Court, how I was in your grace,
How merited to be so. Since he came,
With what encounter so uncurrent I
Have strained to appear thus; if one jot beyond
The bound of honor, or in act or will
That way inclining, hardened be the hearts
Of all that hear me, and my nearest of kin
Cry fie upon my grave!

LEONTES   I never heard yet
    That any of these bolder vices wanted
    Less impudence to gainsay what they did
    Than to perform it first.
HERMIONE   That's true enough,
    Though it is a saying, sir, not due to me.
LEONTES
    You will not own it.
HERMIONE   More than mistress of
    Which comes to me in name of fault, I must not
    At all acknowledge. For Polixenes,
    With whom I am accused, I do confess
    I loved him as in honor he required—
    With such a kind of love as might become
    A lady like me, with a love even such,
    So and no other, as yourself commanded.
    Which not to have done I think had been in me
    Both disobedience and ingratitude
    To you and toward your friend, whose love had spoken,
    Even since it could speak, from an infant, freely
    That it was yours. Now, for conspiracy,
    I know not how it tastes, though it is dished
    For me to try how. All I know of it
    Is that Camillo was an honest man;
    And why he left your Court, the gods themselves,
    Knowing no more than I, are ignorant.
LEONTES
    You knew of his departure, as you know
    What you have undertaken to do in his absence.
HERMIONE
    Sir,
    You speak a language that I understand not,
    My life stands in the level of your dreams,
    Which I will lay down.

LEONTES   Your actions are my dreams.
   You had a bastard by Polixenes,
   And I but dreamed it. As you were past all shame—
   Those of your fact are so—so past all truth,
   Which to deny concerns more than avails; for as
   Your brat has been cast out, like to itself,
   No father owning it—which is, indeed,
   More criminal in you than it—so you
   Shall feel our justice, in whose easiest passage
   Look for no less than death.
HERMIONE   Sir, spare your threats.
   The threat which you would fright me with I seek.
   To me can life be no commodity.
   The crown and comfort of my life, your favor,
   I do give lost, for I do feel it gone,
   But know not how it went. My second joy
   And first-fruits of my body, from his presence
   I am barred, like one infectious. My third comfort,
   Starred most unluckily, is from my breast,
   The innocent milk in its most innocent mouth,
   Haled out to murder. Myself on every post
   Proclaimed a strumpet: with immodest hatred
   The child-bed privilege denied, which belongs
   To women of all fashion. Lastly, hurried
   Here to this place, in the open air, before
   I have got strength of limit. Now, my liege,
   Tell me what blessings I have here alive,
   That I should fear to die? Therefore proceed.
   But yet hear this—mistake me not, no life
   (I prize it not a straw) but for my honor,
   Which I would free. If I shall be condemned
   Upon surmises, all proofs sleeping else
   But what your jealousies awake, I tell you
   It is rigor and not law. Your honors all,
   I do refer me to the oracle.
   Apollo be my judge!

LORD   This your request
   Is altogether just. Therefore bring forth,
   And in Apollo's name, his oracle.
                                 Exeunt certain Officers.
HERMIONE
   The emperor of Russia was my father.
   O that he were alive, and here beholding
   His daughter's trial; that he did but see
   The flatness of my misery—yet with eyes
   Of pity, not revenge.

        Enter Officers with Cleomenes, and Dion.

OFFICER
   You here shall swear upon this sword of justice,
   That you, Cleomenes and Dion, have
   Been both at Delphos, and from thence have brought
   This sealed-up oracle, by the hand delivered
   Of great Apollo's priest; and that since then
   You have not dared to break the holy seal
   Nor read the secrets in it.
CLEOMENES, DION   All this we swear.
LEONTES
   Break up the seals and read.
OFFICER [*reads*] Hermione is chaste, Polixenes blameless,
   Camillo a true subject, Leontes a jealous tyrant, his
   innocent babe truly begotten; and the king shall live
   without an heir if that which is lost be not found.
LORDS
   Now blessèd be the great Apollo!
HERMIONE   Praisèd!
LEONTES
   Have you read truth?
OFFICER   Ay, my lord, even so
   As it is here set down.

LEONTES
>There is no truth at all in the oracle.
>The sessions shall proceed. This is mere falsehood.

Enter Servant.

SERVANT
>My lord the king, the king!

LEONTES   What is the business?

SERVANT
>O sir, I shall be hated to report it.
>The prince your son, with mere worry and fear
>Of the queen's fate, is gone.

LEONTES   How? gone?

SERVANT   Is dead.

LEONTES
>Apollo's angry, and the heavens themselves
>Do strike at my injustice.

Hermione swoons.

>How now there?

PAULINA
>This news is mortal to the queen. Look down
>And see what death is doing.

LEONTES   Take her hence.
>Her heart is but overcharged; she will recover.
>I have too much believed my own suspicion.
>Beseech you, tenderly apply to her
>Some remedies for life.
>   *Exeunt Paulina and Ladies with Hermione.*
>   Apollo, pardon
>My great profaneness against your oracle!
>I will reconcile me to Polixenes,
>New woo my queen, recall the good Camillo,
>Whom I proclaim a man of truth, of mercy.

For, being transported by my jealousies
To bloody thoughts and to revenge, I chose
Camillo for the minister to poison
My friend Polixenes. Which had been done,
But that the good mind of Camillo tardied
My swift command; though I with death and with
Reward did threaten and encourage him,
Not doing it and being done. He, most humane
And filled with honor, to my kingly guest
Unclasped my design, quit his fortunes here,
Which you knew great; and to the hazard
Of all uncertainties himself commended,
No richer than his honor. How he glisters
Through my rust! and how his piety
Does my deeds make the blacker!

Enter Paulina.

PAULINA   Woe the while!
  O, cut my lace, lest my heart, cracking it,
  Breaks too!
LORD   What fit is this, good lady?
PAULINA
  What studied torments, tyrant, have you for me?
  What wheels? racks? fires? what flaying? boiling
  In leads or oils? what old or newer torture
  Must I receive, whose every word deserves
  To taste of your most worst? Your tyranny,
  Together working with your jealousies,
  Fancies too weak for boys, too green and idle
  For girls of nine, O, think what they have done,
  And then run mad indeed, stark mad, for all
  Your bygone fooleries were but spices of it.
  That you betrayed Polixenes, was nothing;
  That did but show you, for a fool, inconstant
  And damnably ungrateful. Nor was it much

You would have poisoned good Camillo's honor,
To have him kill a king—poor trespasses,
More monstrous standing by. Whereof I reckon
The casting forth to crows your baby daughter
To be or none or little, though a devil
Would have shed water out of fire ere done it.
Nor is it directly laid to you, the death
Of the young prince, whose honorable thoughts,
Thoughts high for one so tender, cleft the heart
That could conceive a gross and foolish sire
Blemished his gracious dam. This is not, no,
Laid to your answer. But the last—O lords,
When I have said, cry 'Woe!'—the queen, the queen,
The sweetest dear creature's dead, and vengeance for it
Not dropped down yet.
LORD   The higher powers forbid!
PAULINA
I say she's dead; I'll swear it. If word nor oath
Prevails not, go and see. If you can bring
Tincture or lustre in her lip, her eye,
Heat outwardly or breath within, I'll serve you
As I would do the gods. But, O you tyrant,
Do not repent these things, for they are heavier
Than all your woes can stir. Therefore betake you
To nothing but despair. A thousand knees
Ten thousand years together, naked, fasting,
Upon a barren mountain, and ever winter
In storm perpetual, could not move the gods
To look that way you were.
LEONTES   Go on, go on.
You can not speak too much. I have deserved
All tongues to talk their bitterest.
LORD   Say no more.
However the business goes, you have made fault
In the boldness of your speech.

PAULINA   I am sorry for it.
All faults I make, when I shall come to know them,
I do repent. Alas, I have shown too much
The rashness of a woman. He is touched
To the noble heart. What's gone and what's past help
Should be past grief. Do not receive affliction
At my petition. I beseech you, rather
Let me be punished, that reminded you
Of what you should forget. Now, good my liege,
Sir, royal sir, forgive a foolish woman.
The love I bore your queen—lo, fool again!—
I'll speak of her no more, nor of your children;
I'll not remember you of my own lord,
Who is lost too. Take your patience to you,
And I will say nothing.
LEONTES   You did speak but well
When most the truth, which I receive much better
Than to be pitied of you. Pray you, bring me
To the dead bodies of my queen and son.
One grave shall be for both. Upon them shall
The causes of their death appear, unto
Our shame perpetual. Once a day I'll visit
The chapel where they lie, and tears shed there
Shall be my recreation. So long as nature
Will bear up with this exercise, so long
I daily vow to use it. Come, and lead me
To these sorrows.   *Exeunt.*

SCENE III
Bohemia. A sea-coast.

Enter Antigonus, and a Mariner, with a Babe.

ANTIGONUS
You are perfect then our ship has touched upon
The deserts of Bohemia?
MARINER   Ay, my lord, and fear
We have landed in ill time. The skies look grimly
And threaten present blusters. In my conscience,
The heavens with that we have in hand are angry
And frown upon us.
ANTIGONUS
Their sacred wills be done! Go, get aboard;
Look to your bark. I'll not be long before
I call upon you.
MARINER   Make your best haste, and go not
Too far in the land. 'Tis like to be loud weather.
Besides, this place is famous for the creatures
Of prey that keep upon it.
ANTIGONUS   Go you away;
I'll follow instantly.
MARINER   I am glad at heart
To be so rid of the business.   *Exit.*
ANTIGONUS   Come, poor babe.
I have heard, but not believed, the spirits of the dead
May walk again. If such thing be, your mother
Appeared to me last night, for never was dream
So like a waking. To me comes a creature,
Sometimes her head on one side, some another.
I never saw a vessel of like sorrow,
So filled and so becoming. In pure white robes,
Like very sanctity, she did approach
My cabin where I lay; thrice bowed before me,
And, gasping to begin some speech, her eyes

Became two spouts. The fury spent, anon
Did this break her from: 'Good Antigonus,
Since fate, against your better disposition,
Has made your person for the thrower-out
Of my poor babe, according to your oath,
Places remote enough are in Bohemia;
There weep and leave it crying. And, since the babe
Is counted lost for ever, Perdita,
I pray you, call it. For this ungentle business,
Put on you by my lord, you never shall see
Your wife Paulina more.' And so, with shrieks,
She melted into air. Affrighted much,
I did in time collect myself, and thought
This was so and no slumber. Dreams are toys;
Yet for this once, yes, superstitiously,
I will be squared by this. I do believe
Hermione has suffered death, and that
Apollo would, this being indeed the issue
Of King Polixenes, it should here be laid,
Either for life or death, upon the earth
Of its right father. Blossom, speed you well.
There lie, and there your inscription; there these,
Which may, if fortune please, both breed you, pretty,
And still rest yours. The storm begins. Poor wretch,
That for your mother's fault are thus exposed
To loss and what may follow. Weep I cannot,
But my heart bleeds; and most accursed am I
To be by oath enjoined to this. Farewell!
The day frowns more and more. You're likely to have
A lullaby too rough. I never saw
The heavens so dim by day. A savage clamor!
Well may I get aboard! This is the chase.
I am gone for ever.   *Exit, pursued by a bear.*

Enter Shepherd.

SHEPHERD I would there were no age between ten and three-and-twenty, or that youth would sleep out the rest; for there is nothing in between but getting wenches with child, wronging the ancientry, stealing, fighting. Hark you now. Would any but these boiled brains of nineteen and two-and-twenty hunt this weather? They have scared away two of my best sheep, which I fear the wolf will sooner find than the master. If anywhere I have them, 'tis by the seaside, browsing of ivy. Good luck, if it be your will! What have we here? Mercy on us, a bairn, a very pretty bairn! A boy or a girl, I wonder? A pretty one, a very pretty one. Sure, some scape. Though I am not bookish, yet I can read waiting-gentlewoman in the scape. This has been some stair-work, some trunk-work, some behind-door-work. They were warmer that got this than the poor thing is here. I'll take it up for pity. Yet I'll tarry till my son comes. He hallooed but even now. Whoa, ho, hoa!

Enter Clown.

CLOWN Hilloa, loa!
SHEPHERD What, are you so near? If you'd see a thing to talk on when you are dead and rotten, come hither. What ails you, man?
CLOWN I have seen two such sights, by sea and by land—but I am not to say it is a sea, for it is now the sky; betwixt the firmament and it you cannot thrust a bodkin's point.
SHEPHERD Why, boy, how is it?
CLOWN I would you did but see how it chafes, how it rages, how it takes up the shore. But that's not to the point. O, the most piteous cry of the poor souls! Sometimes to see them, and not to see them. Now the ship boring the moon with her main-mast, and anon swallowed with foam and froth, as you'd thrust a cork

into a hogshead. And then for the land-service—to see how the bear tore out his shoulder-bone, how he cried to me for help and said his name was Antigonus, a nobleman. But to make an end of the ship—to see how the sea swallowed up all. But, first, how the poor souls roared, and the sea mocked them, and how the poor gentleman roared and the bear mocked him, both roaring louder than the sea or weather.

SHEPHERD Name of mercy, when was this, boy?

CLOWN Now, now; I have not winked since I saw these sights. The men are not yet cold under water, nor the bear half dined on the gentleman. He's at it now.

SHEPHERD Would I had been by, to have helped the old man.

CLOWN I would you had been by the ship side, to have helped her. There your charity would have lacked footing.

SHEPHERD Heavy matters, heavy matters! But look you here, boy. Now bless yourself! You met with things dying, I with things new-born. Here's a sight for you. Look you, a christening-cloth for a squire's child. Look you here. Take up, take up, boy; open it. So, let's see. It was told me I should be rich by the fairies. This is some changeling. Open it. What's within, boy?

CLOWN You're a made old man. If the sins of your youth are forgiven you, you're well to live. Gold! all gold!

SHEPHERD This is fairy gold, boy, and it will prove so. Up with it, keep it close. Home, home, the next way. We are lucky, boy, and to be so always requires nothing but secrecy. Let my sheep go. Come, good boy, the next way home.

CLOWN Go you the next way with your findings. I'll go see if the bear is gone from the gentleman and how much he has eaten. They are never angry but when they are hungry. If there is any of him left, I'll bury it.

SHEPHERD That's a good deed. If you may discern by that
    which is left of him what he is, fetch me to the sight of
    him.
CLOWN Sure, will I; and you shall help to put him in the
    ground.
SHEPHERD 'Tis a lucky day, boy, and we'll do good deeds
    of it.   *Exeunt.*

Act IV

SCENE I

Enter Time, the Chorus.

TIME
   I, that please some, try all, both joy and terror
   Of good and bad, that makes and unfolds error,
   Now take upon me, in the name of Time,
   To use my wings. Impute it not a crime
   To me or my swift passage that I slide
   Over sixteen years and leave the growth untried
   Of that wide gap, since it is in my power
   To overthrow law and in one self-born hour
   To plant and o'erwhelm custom. Let me pass
   The same I am, ere ancientest order was
   Or what is now received. I witness to
   The times that brought them in. So shall I do
   To the freshest things now reigning, and make stale
   The glistering of this present, as my tale
   Now seems to it. Your patience this allowing,
   I turn my glass and give my scene such growing
   As you had slept between. Leontes leaving,
   The effects of his mad jealousies so grieving
   That he shuts up himself, imagine me,
   Gentle spectators, that I now may be
   In fair Bohemia. And remember well,
   I mentioned a son of the king's, which Florizel
   I now name to you, and with speed so pace
   To speak of Perdita, now grown in grace
   Equal with wondering. What of her ensues

I may not prophesy; but let Time's news
Be known when 'tis brought forth. A shepherd's daughter
And what to her adheres, which follows after,
Is the argument of Time. Of this allow
If ever you have spent time worse ere now;
If never, yet that Time himself does say
He wishes earnestly you never may.   *Exit.*

SCENE II
Bohemia. Polixenes' palace.

Enter Polixenes and Camillo.

POLIXENES I pray you, good Camillo, be no more importunate. It is a sickness denying you anything, a death to grant this.

CAMILLO It is fifteen years since I saw my country. Though I have for the most part been aired abroad, I desire to lay my bones there. Besides, the penitent king, my master, has sent for me, to whose feeling sorrows I might be some allay—or I overween to think so—which is another spur to my departure.

POLIXENES As you love me, Camillo, wipe not out the rest of your services by leaving me now. The need I have of you your own goodness has made. Better not to have had you than thus to want you. You, having made me businesses which none without you can sufficiently manage, must either stay to execute them yourself or take away with you the very services you have done. Which if I have not enough considered—as too much I cannot—to be more thankful to you shall be my study, and my profit therein the heaping friendships. Of that fatal country, Sicilia, pray speak no more, whose very naming punishes me with the remembrance of that penitent, as you call him, and reconciled king, my brother; whose loss of his most precious queen and children are even now to be afresh lamented. Say to me, when saw you the Prince Florizel, my son? Kings are no less unhappy, their issue not being gracious, than they are in losing them when they have approved their virtues.

CAMILLO Sir, it is three days since I saw the prince. What his happier affairs may be are to me unknown, but I have missingly noted he is of late much retired from Court and is less frequent to his princely exercises than formerly he has appeared.

POLIXENES I have considered so much, Camillo, and with some care—so far that I have eyes under my service which look upon his removedness. From whom I have this intelligence, that he is seldom from the house of a most homely shepherd; a man, they say, that from very nothing, and beyond the imagination of his neighbors, is grown into an unspeakable estate.

CAMILLO I have heard, sir, of such a man, who has a daughter of most rare note. The report of her is extended more than can be thought to begin from such a cottage.

POLIXENES That is likewise part of my intelligence; but, I fear, the angle that plucks our son thither. You shall accompany us to the place, where we will, not appearing what we are, have some question with the shepherd. From whose simplicity I think it not uneasy to get the cause of my son's resort thither. Pray be my present partner in this business, and lay aside the thoughts of Sicilia.

CAMILLO I willingly obey your command.

POLIXENES My best Camillo! We must disguise ourselves.

Exeunt.

SCENE III
Near the Shepherd's house.

Enter Autolycus, singing.

When daffodils begin to peer,
   With heigh! the doxy over the dale,
Why, then comes in the sweet of the year,
   For the red blood reigns in the winter's pale.

The white sheet bleaching on the hedge,
   With heigh! the sweet birds, O how they sing!
Does set my thieving tooth on edge,
   For a quart of ale is a dish for a king.

The lark, that tirra-lyra chants,
   With heigh! with heigh! the thrush and the jay,
Are summer songs for me and my aunts, [girls]
   While we lie tumbling in the hay.

I have served Prince Florizel and in my time worn
velvet, but now I am out of service.

But shall I go mourn for that, my dear?
   The pale moon shines by night.
And when I wander here and there,
   I then do most go right.

If tinkers may have leave to live,
   And bear the sow-skin budget,
Then my account I well may give,
   And in the stocks avouch it.

My traffic is sheets; when the kite builds, look to lesser
linen. My father named me Autolycus, who being, as I
am, littered under Mercury, was likewise a snapper-up
of unconsidered trifles. With dice and drab I purchased
this caparison, and my revenue is the silly cheat. Gallows
and knock are too powerful on the highway; beating

and hanging are terrors to me. For the life to come, I sleep out the thought of it. A prize! a prize!

Enter Clown.

CLOWN Let me see; every eleven wether tods;[1] every tod yields pound and odd shilling; fifteen hundred shorn, what comes the wool to?

AUTOLYCUS [*aside*]. If the springe holds, the cock's mine.

CLOWN I cannot do it without counters. Let me see; what am I to buy for our sheep-shearing feast? Three pound of sugar, five pound of currants, rice—what will this sister of mine do with rice? But my father has made her mistress of the feast, and she lays it on. She has made me four and twenty nosegays for the shearers—three-man songmen all, and very good ones. But they are most of them tenors and bases, but one puritan among them, and he sings psalms to hornpipes. I must have saffron to color the warden pies; mace; dates?—none, that's out of my note; nutmegs, seven; a root or two of ginger, but that I may beg; four pound of prunes, and as many of raisins of the sun.

AUTOLYCUS O that ever I was born!

[*Grovels on the ground.*]

CLOWN In the name of me—

AUTOLYCUS O, help me, help me! pluck but off these rags, and then death, death!

CLOWN Alas, poor soul, you have need of more rags to lay on you, rather than have these off.

AUTOLYCUS O, sir, the loathsomeness of them offends me more than the stripes I have received, which are mighty ones and millions.

---

[1] An old weight for wool.

CLOWN Alas, poor man! A million of beating may come to a great matter.

AUTOLYCUS I am robbed, sir, and beaten, my money and apparel taken from me, and these detestable things put upon me.

CLOWN What, by a horseman, or a footman?

AUTOLYCUS A footman, sweet sir, a footman.

CLOWN Indeed, he should be a footman by the garments he has left with you. If this is a horseman's coat, it has seen very hot service. Lend me your hand, I'll help you. Come, lend me your hand.

[*Helps him up.*]

AUTOLYCUS O, good sir, tenderly. O!

CLOWN Alas, poor soul!

AUTOLYCUS O, good sir, softly, good sir. I fear, sir, my shoulder-blade is out.

CLOWN How now? can you stand?

AUTOLYCUS [*picking his pocket*] Softly, dear sir; good sir, softly. You have done me a charitable office.

CLOWN Do you lack any money? I have a little money for you.

AUTOLYCUS No, good sweet sir; no, I beseech you, sir. I have a kinsman not past three quarters of a mile hence, unto whom I was going. I shall there have money, or anything I want. Offer me no money, I pray you; that kills my heart.

CLOWN What manner of fellow was he that robbed you?

AUTOLYCUS A fellow, sir, that I have known to go about with bagatelles. I knew him once a servant of the prince. I cannot tell, good sir, for which of his virtues it was, but he was certainly whipped out of the Court.

CLOWN His vices, you would say. There's no virtue whipped out of the Court. They cherish it to make it stay there, and yet it will no more but abide.

AUTOLYCUS Vices, I would say, sir. I know this man well.
He has been since an ape-bearer, then a process-server, a
bailiff. Then he compassed a show of the Prodigal Son,
and married a tinker's wife within a mile where my
land and living lie. And, having flown over many
knavish professions, he settled only in rogue. Some call
him Autolycus.

CLOWN Out upon him! Thief, for my life, thief! He haunts
wakes, fairs, and bear-baitings.

AUTOLYCUS Very true, sir; he, sir, he. That's the rogue
that put me into this apparel.

CLOWN Not a more cowardly rogue in all Bohemia. If you
had but looked big and spat at him, he'd have run.

AUTOLYCUS I must confess to you, sir, I am no fighter. I am
false of heart that way, and that he knew, I warrant him.

CLOWN How do you now?

AUTOLYCUS Sweet sir, much better than I was. I can stand
and walk. I will even take my leave of you and pace
softly towards my kinsman's.

CLOWN Shall I bring you on the way?

AUTOLYCUS No, good-faced sir; no, sweet sir.

CLOWN Then fare you well. I must go buy spices for our
sheep-shearing.

AUTOLYCUS Prosper you, sweet sir.   *Exit Clown.*
Your purse is not hot enough to purchase your spice. I'll be
with you at your sheep-shearing too. If I make not this
cheat bring out another and the shearers prove sheep, let
me be unrolled and my name put in the book of virtue.

Song.

Jog on, jog on, the foot-path way,
    And merrily take the stile-a.
A merry heart goes all the day,
    Your sad tires in a mile-a.   *Exit.*

SCENE IV
Before the Shepherd's house.

Enter Florizel and Perdita.

FLORIZEL
  These your unusual clothes to each part of you
  Do give a life—no shepherdess, but Flora
  Peering in April's front. This your sheep-shearing
  Is as a meeting of the petty gods,
  And you the queen of it.
PERDITA   Sir, my gracious lord,
  To chide at your extremes it not becomes me—
  O, pardon, that I name them. Your high self,
  The gracious mark of the land, you have obscured
  With a swain's wearing, and me, poor lowly maid,
  Most goddess-like dressed up. But that our feasts
  In every mess have folly, and the feeders
  Digest it with a custom, I should blush
  To see you so attired; swoon, I think,
  To show myself a glass.
FLORIZEL   I bless the time
  When my good falcon made her flight across
  Your father's ground.
PERDITA   Now Jove afford you cause!
  To me the difference forges dread; your greatness
  Has not been used to fear. Even now I tremble
  To think your father, by some accident,
  Should pass this way as you did. O, the Fates!
  How would he look, to see his work, so noble,
  Vilely bound up? What would he say? Or how
  Should I, in these my borrowed flaunts, behold
  The sternness of his presence?
FLORIZEL   Apprehend
  Nothing but jollity. The gods themselves,
  Humbling their deities to love, have taken

The shapes of beasts upon them. Jupiter
Became a bull, and bellowed; the green Neptune
A ram, and bleated; and the fire-robed god,
Golden Apollo, a poor humble swain,
As I seem now. Their transformatiòns
Were never for a piece of beauty rarer,
Nor in a way so chaste, since my desires
Run not before my honor, nor my lusts
Burn hotter than my faith.

PERDITA   O, but, sir,
Your resolution cannot hold when it is
Opposed, as it must be, by the power of the king.
One of these two must be necessities,
Which then will speak, that you must change this
    purpose,
Or I my life.

FLORIZEL   You dearest Perdita,
With these forced thoughts, I pray you, darken not
The mirth of the feast. Either I'll be yours, my fair,
Or not my father's. For I cannot be
My own, nor anything to any, if
I am not yours. To this I am most constant,
Though destiny says no. Be merry, gentle;
Strangle such thoughts as these with anything
That you behold the while. Your guests are coming.
Lift up your countenance, as it were the day
Of celebration of that nuptial which
We two have sworn shall come.

PERDITA   O lady Fortune,
Stand you auspicious!

FLORIZEL   See, your guests approach.
Address yourself to entertain them sprightly,
And let's be red with mirth.

Enter Shepherd, Clown, with Polixenes,
and Camillo disguised, Mopsa, Dorcas, Servants.

SHEPHERD

Fie, daughter! When my old wife lived, upon
This day she was both pantler,[2] butler, cook,
Both dame and servant; welcomed all, served all;
Would sing her song and dance her turn; now here
At upper end of the table, now in the middle;
On his shoulder, and his; her face on fire
With labor, and the thing she took to quench it
She would to each one sip. You are retirèd,
As if you were a feasted one and not
The hostess of the meeting. Pray you bid
These unknown friends to us welcome, for it is
A way to make us better friends, more known.
Come, quench your blushes and present yourself
That which you are, mistress of the feast. Come on,
And bid us welcome to your sheep-shearing,
As your good flock shall prosper.

PERDITA *to Polixenes*   Sir, welcome.

It is my father's will I should take on me
The hostess-ship of the day.

[*To Camillo.*]

                    You are welcome, sir.

Give me those flowers there, Dorcas. Reverend sirs,
For you there's rosemary and rue; these keep
Seeming and savor all the winter long.
Grace and remembrance be to you both,
And welcome to our shearing!

POLIXENES   Shepherdess—

A fair one are you—well you fit our ages
With flowers of winter.

---

[2]Pantryman.

PERDITA   Sir, the year growing ancient,
   Not yet on summer's death nor on the birth
   Of trembling winter, the fairest flowers of the season
   Are our carnations and streaked gillyflowers,
   Which some call nature's bastards. Of that kind
   Our rustic garden is barren, and I care not
   To get slips of them.
POLIXENES   Wherefore, gentle maiden,
   Do you neglect them?
PERDITA   For I have heard it said
   There is an art which in their colouring shares
   With great creating nature.
POLIXENES   Say there is;
   Yet nature is made better by no means
   But nature makes that means. So, over that art,
   Which you say adds to nature, is an art
   That nature makes. You see, sweet maid, we marry
   A gentler scion to the wildest stock,
   And make conceive a bark of baser kind
   By bud of nobler race. This is an art
   Which does mend nature—change it rather—but
   The art itself is nature.
PERDITA   So it is.
POLIXENES
   Then make your garden rich in gillyflowers,
   And do not call them bastards.
PERDITA   I'll not put
   The dibble in earth to set one slip of them,
   No more than, were I painted, I would wish
   This youth should say 'twere well, and only therefore
   Desire to breed by me. Here's flowers for you,
   Hot lavender, mints, savory, marjoram,
   The marigold, that goes to bed with the sun
   And with him rises weeping. These are flowers
   Of middle summer, and I think they are given
   To men of middle age. You are very welcome.

CAMILLO
  I should leave grazing, were I of your flock,
  And only live by gazing.
PERDITA   Out, alas!
  You'd be so lean that blasts of January
  Would blow you through and through. Now, my fair
    friend,
  I would I had some flowers of the spring that might
  Become your time of day, and yours, and yours,
  That wear upon your virgin branches yet
  Your maidenheads growing. O Proserpina,
  For the flowers now that, frighted, you let fall
  From Dis's wagon; daffodils,
  That come before the swallow dares, and take
  The winds of March with beauty; violets dim,
  But sweeter than the lids of Juno's eyes
  Or Cytherea's breath; pale primroses,
  That die unmarried, ere they can behold
  Bright Phoebus in his strength—a malady
  Most incident to maids; bold oxlips and
  The crown imperial; lilies of all kinds,
  The flower-de-luce being one. O, these I lack
  To make you garlands of, and my sweet friend,
  To strew him over and over!
FLORIZEL   What, like a corpse?
PERDITA
  No, like a bank for love to lie and play on.
  Not like a corpse; or if, not to be buried,
  But alive and in my arms. Come, take your flowers.
  It seems I play as I have seen them do
  In Whitsun pastorals. Sure this robe of mine
  Does change my disposition.
FLORIZEL   What you do
  Still betters what is done. When you speak, sweet,
  I'd have you do it ever. When you sing,
  I'd have you buy and sell so, so give alms,

Pray so, and for the ordering your affairs,
To sing them too. When you do dance, I wish you
A wave of the sea, that you might ever do
Nothing but that, move still, still so,
And own no other function. Each your doing,
So singular in each particular,
Crowns what you are doing in the present deeds,
That all your acts are queens.

PERDITA   O Doricles,
Your praises are too large. But that your youth,
And the true blood which peeps fairly through it,
Do plainly give you out an unstained shepherd,
With wisdom I might fear, my Doricles,
You wooed me the false way.

FLORIZEL   I think you have
As little skill to fear as I have purpose
To put you to it. But come; our dance, I pray.
Your hand, my Perdita. So turtledoves pair
That never mean to part.

PERDITA   I'll swear for them.

POLIXENES
This is the prettiest low-born lass that ever
Ran on the greensward. Nothing she does or seems
But smacks of something greater than herself,
Too noble for this place.

CAMILLO   He tells her something
That makes her blood blush at it. Truth, she is
The queen of curds and cream.

CLOWN   Come on, strike up!

DORCAS
Mopsa must be your mistress. Surely, garlic,
To mend her kissing with!

MOPSA   Now, in good time!

CLOWN
Not a word, a word! We stand upon our manners.
Come, strike up!

Music. Here a dance of Shepherds and Shepherdesses.

POLIXENES
Pray, good shepherd, what fair swain is this
Who dances with your daughter?

SHEPHERD
They call him Doricles, and boasts himself
To have a worthy feeding. But I have it
Upon his own report and I believe it;
He looks honest. He says he loves my daughter.
I think so too, for never gazed the moon
Upon the water as he'll stand and read
As it were my daughter's eyes; and, to be plain,
I think there is not half a kiss to choose
Who loves another best.

POLIXENES   She dances well.

SHEPHERD
So she does anything, though I report it
That should be silent. If young Doricles
Does light upon her, she shall bring him that
Which he not dreams of.

Enter Servant.

SERVANT O master, if you did but hear the pedlar at the
door, you would never dance again after a drum and
pipe—no, the bagpipe could not move you. He sings
several tunes faster than you'll tell money. He utters
them as he had eaten ballads and all men's ears grew to
his tunes.

CLOWN He could never come better. He shall come in. I
love a ballad but even too well if it is doleful matter
merrily set down, or a very pleasant thing indeed and
sung lamentably.

SERVANT He has songs for man or woman, of all sizes. No
milliner can so fit his customers with gloves. He has the

prettiest love-songs for maids, so without bawdry, which
is strange, with such delicate burdens of dildos and
fadings, 'Jump her and thump her.' And where some
broad-mouthed rascal would, as it were, mean mischief
and break a foul gap into the matter, he makes the maid
to answer, 'Whoop, do me no harm, good man'; puts
him off, slights him, with 'Whoop, do me no harm,
good man.'

POLIXENES This is a brave fellow.

CLOWN Believe me, you talk of an admirable witty fellow.
Has he any unfaded wares?

SERVANT He has ribbons of all the colors in the rainbow,
points more than all the lawyers in Bohemia can
learnedly handle, though they come to him by the gross
—linens, worsteds, cambrics, lawns. Why, he sings them
over as they were gods or goddesses. You would think a
smock were a she-angel, he so chants to the sleeve-hand
and the work about the square of it.

CLOWN Pray bring him in, and let him approach singing.

PERDITA Forewarn him that he uses no scurrilous words
in his tunes.   *Exit Servant.*

CLOWN You have of these pedlars that have more in them
than you'd think, sister.

PERDITA Ay, good brother, or go about to think.

Enter Autolycus, singing.

Lawn as white as driven snow,
Cyprus black as ever was crow;
Gloves as sweet as damask roses,
Masks for faces and for noses;
Beaded bracelet, necklace amber,
Perfume for a lady's chamber;
Golden quoifs and stomachers
For my lads to give their dears;
Pins and poking-sticks of steel,

What maids lack from head to heel.
Come buy of me, come; come buy, come buy.
Buy, lads, or else your lasses cry.
Come buy.

CLOWN If I were not in love with Mopsa, you should take
no money of me; but being enthralled as I am, it will
also be the bondage of certain ribbons and gloves.

MOPSA I was promised them against the feast, but they
come not too late now.

DORCAS He has promised you more than that, or there are
liars.

MOPSA He has paid you all he promised you. May be he has
paid you more, which will shame you to give him again.

CLOWN Are there no manners left among maids? Will
they wear their aprons where they should bear their
faces? Is there not milking-time, when you are going to
bed, or kiln-hole, to whistle off these secrets, but you
must be tittle-tattling before all our guests? 'Tis well
they are whispering. Run down your tongues, and not a
word more.

MOPSA I have done. Come, you promised me a coloured
kerchief and a pair of sweet gloves.

CLOWN Have I not told you how I was cozened by the way
and lost all my money?

AUTOLYCUS And indeed, sir, there are cozeners abroad;
therefore it behoves men to be wary.

CLOWN Fear not you, man; you shall lose nothing here.

AUTOLYCUS I hope so, sir, for I have about me many
parcels of value.

CLOWN What have you here? Ballads?

MOPSA Pray now, buy some. I love a ballad in print, on
my life, for then we are sure they are true.

AUTOLYCUS Here's one to a very doleful tune, how a
usurer's wife was brought to bed of twenty money-bags
at a burden, and how she longed to eat adders' heads
and toads grilled.

MOPSA Is it true, think you?

AUTOLYCUS Very true, and but a month old.

DORCAS Bless me from marrying a usurer!

AUTOLYCUS Here's the midwife's name to it, one Mistress
Tale-porter, and five or six honest wives that were present.
Why should I carry lies abroad?

MOPSA Pray you now, buy it.

CLOWN Come on, lay it by. And let's first see more ballads;
we'll buy the other things anon.

AUTOLYCUS Here's another ballad of a fish that appeared
upon the coast on Wednesday the fourscore of April,
forty thousand fathom above water, and sung this ballad
against the hard hearts of maids. It was thought she was
a woman and was turned into a cold fish, for she would
not exchange flesh with one that loved her. The ballad
is very pitiful and as true.

DORCAS Is it true too, think you?

AUTOLYCUS Five justices' hands at it, and witnesses more
than my pack will hold.

CLOWN Lay it by too. Another.

AUTOLYCUS This is a merry ballad, but a very pretty one.

MOPSA Let's have some merry ones.

AUTOLYCUS Why, this is a passing merry one and goes to
the tune of 'Two maids wooing a man.' There's scarce a
maid westward but she sings it. 'Tis in request, I can
tell you.

MOPSA We can both sing it; if you'll bear a part, you shall
hear. 'Tis in three parts.

DORCAS We had the tune of it a month ago.

AUTOLYCUS I can bear my part; you must know it is my
occupation. Have at it with you.

Song.

AUTOLYCUS Get you hence, for I must go
              Where it fits not you to know.
DORCAS   Whither?
MOPSA   O, whither?
DORCAS   Whither?
MOPSA   It becomes your oath full well,
              You to me your secrets tell.
DORCAS   Me too; let me go thither.
MOPSA   Either you go to the grange or mill.
DORCAS   If to either, you do ill.
AUTOLYCUS Neither.
DORCAS   What, neither?
AUTOLYCUS   Neither.
DORCAS   You have sworn my love to be.
MOPSA   You have sworn it more to me.
              Then whither go? say, whither?

CLOWN We'll have this song out anon by ourselves. My father and the gentlemen are in serious talk, and we'll not trouble them. Come, bring away your pack after me. Wenches, I'll buy for you both. Pedlar, let's have the first choice. Follow me, girls.

                  Exit with Dorcas and Mopsa.

AUTOLYCUS And you shall pay well for them.

            Follows singing.

              Song.

            Will you buy any tape,
     Or lace for your cape,
    My dainty duck, my dear-a?
       Any silk, any thread,
       Any toys for your head
    Of the newest and finest, wear-a?

Come to the pedlar.
Money's a meddler
That does sell all men's ware-a.   *Exit.*

Enter Servant.

SERVANT Master, there are three carters, three shepherds,
   three cowherds, three swineherds, that have made
   themselves all men of hair. They call themselves Satyrs,
   and they have a dance which the wenches say is a hodge-
   podge of gambols, because they are not in it. But they
   themselves are of the mind, if it is not too rough for some
   that know little but bowling, it will please plentifully.
SHEPHERD Away! we'll none of it. Here has been too much
   homely foolery already. I know, sir, we weary you.
POLIXENES You weary those that refresh us. Pray, let's see
   these four threes of herdsmen.
SERVANT One three of them, by their own report, sir, has
   danced before the king; and not the worst of the three
   but jumps twelve foot and a half by the square.
SHEPHERD Leave your prating. Since these good men are
   pleased, let them come in; but quickly now.
SERVANT Why, they stay at door, sir.   *Exit.*

Here a dance of twelve Satyrs, and exeunt.

POLIXENES
O, father, you'll know more of that hereafter.

[To Camillo.]

Is it not too far gone? 'Tis time to part them.
He's simple and tells much.—How now, fair shepherd,
Your heart is full of something that does take
Your mind from feasting. True, when I was young
And handed love as you do, I was wont

To load my she with knacks. I would have ransacked
The pedlar's silken treasury and have poured it
To her acceptance. You have let him go
And nothing traded with him. If your lass
Interpretation should abuse and call this
Your lack of love or bounty, you were straited
For a reply—at least if you make a care
Of happy holding her.

FLORIZEL   Old sir, I know
She prizes not such trifles as these are.
The gifts she looks from me are packed and locked
Up in my heart, which I have given already,
But not delivered. O, hear me breathe my life
Before this ancient sir, who, it should seem,
Has sometime loved. I take your hand, this hand
As soft as dove's down and as white as it,
Or Ethiopian's tooth, or the fanned snow that's sifted
By the northern blasts twice over.

POLIXENES   What follows this?
How prettily the young swain seems to wash
The hand that was fair before! I have put you out.
But to your protestation; let me hear
What you profess.

FLORIZEL   Do, and be witness to it.

POLIXENES
And this my neighbor too?

FLORIZEL   And he, and more
Than he, and men, the earth, the heavens, and all—
That, were I crowned the most imperial monarch,
Thereof most worthy, were I the fairest youth
That ever made eye swerve, had force and knowledge
More than was ever man's, I would not prize them
Without her love. For her employ them all;
Commend them and condemn them to her service
Or to their own perdition.

POLIXENES   Fairly offered.

CAMILLO
  This shows a sound affection.
SHEPHERD   But, my daughter,
  Say you the like to him?
PERDITA   I cannot speak
  So well, nothing so well; no, nor mean better.
  By the pattern of my own thoughts I cut out
  The purity of his.
SHEPHERD   Take hands, a bargain!
  And, friends unknown, you shall bear witness to it.
  I give my daughter to him and will make
  Her portion equal his.
FLORIZEL   O, that must be
  In the virtue of your daughter. One being dead,
  I shall have more than you can dream of yet,
  Enough then for your wonder. But, come on,
  Contract us before these witnesses.
SHEPHERD   Come, your hand;
  And, daughter, yours.
POLIXENES   Soft, swain, awhile, beseech you.
  Have you a father?
FLORIZEL   I have, but what of him?
POLIXENES
  Knows he of this?
FLORIZEL   He neither does nor shall.
POLIXENES
  I think a father
  Is at the nuptials of his son a guest
  That best becomes the table. Pray you once more,
  Is not your father grown incapable
  Of reasonable affairs? Is he not stupid
  With age and altering ills? Can he speak? hear?
  Know man from man? dispute his own estate?
  Lies he not bed-ridden? and again does nothing
  But what he did being childish?

FLORIZEL   No, good sir,
  He has his health and ampler strength indeed
  Than most have of his age.
POLIXENES   By my white beard,
  You offer him, if this is so, a wrong
  Something unfilial. Reason my son
  Should choose himself a wife; but as good reason
  The father, all whose joy is nothing else
  But fair posterity, should hold some counsel
  In such a business.
FLORIZEL   I yield all this;
  But for some other reasons, my grave sir,
  Which it is not fit you know, I not acquaint
  My father of this business.
POLIXENES   Let him know it.
FLORIZEL
  He shall not.
POLIXENES Pray you, let him.
FLORIZEL   No, he must not.
SHEPHERD
  Let him, my son. He shall not need to grieve
  At knowing of your choice.
FLORIZEL   Come, come, he must not.
  Mark our contract.
POLIXENES   Mark your divorce, young sir,

Discovers himself.

  Whom son I dare not call. You art too base
  To be acknowledged. You a sceptre's heir,
  That thus affects a sheep-hook!—You old traitor,
  I am sorry that by hanging you I can
  But shorten your life one week.—And you, fresh piece
  Of excellent witchcraft, who of force must know
  The royal fool you cope with—
SHEPHERD   O, my heart!

POLIXENES
  I'll have your beauty scratched with briers, and made
  More homely than your state.—For you, foolish boy,
  If I may ever know you do but sigh
  That you no more shall see this toy—as never
  I mean you shall—we'll bar you from succession,
  Not hold you of our blood, no, not our kin,
  Far than Deucalion off. Mark you my words.
  Follow us to the Court.—You churl, for this time,
  Though full of our displeasure, yet we free you
  From the dead blow of it.—And you, enchantment,
  Worthy enough a herdsman—yes, him too,
  That makes himself, but for our honor therein,
  Unworthy you—if ever henceforth you
  These rural latches to his entrance open,
  Or hoop his body more with your embraces,
  I will devise a death as cruel for you
  As you are tender to it.   *Exit.*
PERDITA   Even here undone!
  I was not much afraid; for once or twice
  I was about to speak and tell him plainly
  The selfsame sun that shines upon his Court
  Hides not his visage from our cottage, but
  Looks on alike. Will it please you, sir, be gone?
  I told you what would come of this. Beseech you,
  Of your own state take care. This dream of mine—
  Being now awake, I'll queen it no inch farther,
  But milk my ewes and weep.
CAMILLO   Why, how now, father?
  Speak ere you die.
SHEPHERD   I cannot speak, nor think,
  Nor dare to know that which I know. O sir,
  You have undone a man of fourscore three,
  That thought to fill his grave in quiet, yes,
  To die upon the bed my father died,
  To lie close by his honest bones. But now

Some hangman must put on my shroud and lay me
Where no priest shovels in dust. O cursèd wretch,
That knew this was the prince, and would adventure
To mingle faith with him. Undone! undone!
If I might die within this hour, I have lived
To die when I desire.   *Exit.*
FLORIZEL   Why look you so upon me?
I am but sorry, not afraid; delayed,
But nothing altered. What I was, I am,
More straining on for plucking back, not following
My leash unwillingly.
CAMILLO   Gracious my lord,
You know your father's temper. At this time
He will allow no speech, which I do guess
You do not purpose to him; and as hardly
Will he endure your sight as yet, I fear.
Then, till the fury of his highness settles,
Come not before him.
FLORIZEL   I do not purpose it.
I think—Camillo?
CAMILLO   Even he, my lord.
PERDITA
How often have I told you it would be thus?
How often said my dignity would last
But till it were known!
FLORIZEL   It cannot fail but by
The violation of my faith; and then
Let nature crush the sides of the earth together
And mar the seeds within. Lift up your looks.
From my succession wipe me, father. I
Am heir to my affection.
CAMILLO   Be advised.
FLORIZEL
I am, and by my fancy. If my reason
Will thereto be obedient, I have reason;

If not, my senses, better pleased with madness,
Do bid it welcome.
CAMILLO   This is desperate, sir.
FLORIZEL
So call it, but it does fulfil my vow.
I needs must think it honesty. Camillo,
Not for Bohemia nor the pomp that may
Be thereat gleaned, for all the sun sees or
The close earth wombs or the profound seas hide
In unknown fathoms, will I break my oath
To this my fair beloved. Therefore, I pray you,
As you have ever been my father's honored friend,
When he shall miss me—as, in faith, I mean not
To see him any more—cast your good counsels
Upon his passion. Let myself and fortune
Tug for the time to come. This you may know
And so deliver: I am put to sea
With her whom here I cannot hold on shore.
And most opportune to our need I have
A vessel rides fast by, but not prepared
For this design. What course I mean to hold
Shall nothing benefit your knowledge, nor
Concern me the reporting.
CAMILLO   O my lord,
I would your spirit were easier for advice
Or stronger for your need.
FLORIZEL   Hark, Perdita.

Draws her aside.

I'll hear you by and by.
CAMILLO   He's irremovable,
Resolved for flight. Now were I happy if
His going I could frame to serve my turn;
Save him from danger, do him love and honor;
Purchase the sight again of dear Sicilia

And that unhappy king, my master, whom
I so much thirst to see.

FLORIZEL   Now, good Camillo.
I am so fraught with weighty business that
I leave out ceremony.

CAMILLO   Sir, I think
You have heard of my poor services in the love
That I have borne your father?

FLORIZEL   Very nobly
Have you deserved. It is my father's music
To speak your deeds, not little of his care
To have them recompensed as thought on.

CAMILLO   Well, my lord,
If you may please to think I love the king
And, through him, what's nearest to him, which is
Your gracious self, embrace but my direction.
If your more ponderous and settled project
May suffer alteration, on my honor,
I'll point you where you shall have such receiving
As shall become your highness. Where you may
Enjoy your mistress, from whom, I see indeed,
There's no disjunction to be made but by—
As heavens forfend!—your ruin; marry her,
And, with my best endeavors in your absence,
Your discontenting father strive to qualify
And bring him up to liking.

FLORIZEL   How, Camillo,
May this, almost a miracle, be done?
That I may call you something more than man,
And after that trust to you.

CAMILLO   Have you thought on
A place whereto you will go?

FLORIZEL   Not any yet.
But as the unthought-on accident is guilty
To what we wildly do, so we profess

Ourselves to be the slaves of chance, and flies
Of every wind that blows.
CAMILLO   Then listen to me.
This follows: if you will not change your purpose
But undergo this flight, make for Sicilia,
And there present yourself and your fair princess,
For so I see she must be, before Leontes.
She shall be habited as it becomes
The partner of your bed. I think I see
Leontes opening his free arms and weeping
His welcome forth; asks you the son forgiveness,
As 'twere in the father's person; kisses the hands
Of your fresh princess; over and over divides him
Between his unkindness and his kindness. The one
He chides to hell and bids the other grow
Faster than thought or time.
FLORIZEL   Worthy Camillo,
What color for my visitation shall I
Hold up before him?
CAMILLO   Sent by the king your father
To greet him and to give him comfort. Sir,
The manner of your bearing towards him, with
What you, as from your father, shall deliver,
Things known betwixt us three, I'll write you down.
That shall point you forth at every sitting
What you must say, that he shall not perceive
But that you have your father's bosom there
And speak his very heart.
FLORIZEL   I am bound to you.
There is some sap in this.
CAMILLO   A course more promising
Than a wild dedication of yourselves
To unpathed waters, undreamed shores, most certain
To miseries enough. No hope to help you,
But as you shake off one to take another;
Nothing so certain as your anchors, which

Do their best office if they can but stay you
Where you'll be loath to be. Besides, you know
Prosperity is the very bond of love,
Whose fresh complexion and whose heart together
Affliction alters.

PERDITA   One of these is true.
I think affliction may subdue the cheek
But not take in the mind.

CAMILLO   Yea, say you so?
There shall not at your father's house these seven years
Be born another such.

FLORIZEL   My good Camillo,
She is as forward of her breeding as
She is in the rear of your birth.

CAMILLO   I cannot say
She lacks instruction, for she seems a mistress
To most that teach.

PERDITA   Your pardon, sir. For this
I'll blush you thanks.

FLORIZEL   My prettiest Perdita!
But O, the thorns we stand upon! Camillo,
Preserver of my father, now of me,
The medicine of our house, how shall we do?
We are not furnished like Bohemia's son,
Nor shall appear in Sicilia.

CAMILLO   My lord,
Fear none of this. I think you know my fortunes
Do all lie there. It shall be so my care
To have you royally appointed as if
The scene you play were mine. For instance, sir,
That you may know you shall not want, one word.

They talk aside. Enter Autolycus.

AUTOLYCUS Ha, ha, what a fool Honesty is! and Trust, his
sworn brother, a very simple gentleman! I have sold all

my trumpery. Not a counterfeit stone, not a ribbon,
glass, pomander, brooch, table-book, ballad, knife, tape,
glove, shoe-tie, bracelet, horn-ring, to keep my pack
from fasting. They throng who should buy first, as if
my trinkets had been hallowed and brought a benediction
to the buyer; by which means I saw whose purse was
best in picture, and what I saw, to my good use I
remembered. My clown, who wants but something to
be a reasonable man, grew so in love with the wenches'
song that he would not stir his toes till he had both tune
and words, which so drew the rest of the herd to me that
all their other senses stuck in ears. You might have
pinched a petticoat, it was senseless; 'twas nothing to
geld a codpiece of a purse; I would have filed keys off
that hung in chains. No hearing, no feeling, but my
sir's song and admiring the nothing of it. So that in this
time of lethargy I picked and cut most of their festival
purses; and had not the old man come in with a hub-
bub against his daughter and the king's son and scared
my choughs from the chaff, I had not left a purse alive
in the whole army.

Camillo, Florizel, and Perdita come forward.

CAMILLO
Nay, but my letters, by this means being there
So soon as you arrive, shall clear that doubt.
FLORIZÉL
And those that you shall procure from King Leontes—
CAMILLO
Shall satisfy your father.
PERDITA   Happy be you!
All that you speak shows fair.
CAMILLO [*seeing Autolycus*] Whom have we here?
We'll make an instrument of this, omit
Nothing may give us aid.

AUTOLYCUS If they have overheard me now, why, hanging.

CAMILLO
How now, good fellow? Why shake you so?
Fear not, man; here's no harm intended to you.

AUTOLYCUS I am a poor fellow, sir.

CAMILLO Why, be so ever; here's nobody will steal that
from you. Yet for the outside of your poverty we must
make an exchange. Therefore undress instantly—you
must think there's a necessity in it—and change garments
with this gentleman. Though the pennyworth on his
side is the worse, yet hold you, there's some help.

AUTOLYCUS I am a poor fellow, sir. [aside] I know you well
enough.

CAMILLO Nay, pray, dispatch. The gentleman is half flayed
already.

AUTOLYCUS Are you in earnest, sir? [aside] I smell the
trick of it.

FLORIZEL Dispatch, I pray.

AUTOLYCUS Indeed, I have had earnest, but I cannot with
conscience take it.

CAMILLO Unbuckle, unbuckle.

[Florizel and Autolycus exchange garments.]

Fortunate mistress—let my prophecy
Come home to you!—you must retire yourself
Into some covert. Take your sweetheart's hat
And pluck it over your brows, muffle your face,
Dismantle you and, as you can, disliken
The truth of your own seeming, that you may—
For I do fear eyes over—to shipboard
Get undescried.

PERDITA   I see the play so lies
That I must bear a part.

CAMILLO   No remedy.
Have you done there?

FLORIZEL   Should I now meet my father,
  He would not call me son.
CAMILLO   Nay, you shall have no hat.
                          Gives it to Perdita.
  Come, lady, come. Farewell, my friend.
AUTOLYCUS   Adieu, sir.
FLORIZEL
  O Perdita, what have we twain forgotten?
  Pray you, a word.
CAMILLO [*aside*]
  What I do next, shall be to tell the king
  Of this escape and whither they are bound.
  Wherein my hope is I shall so prevail
  To force him after; in whose company
  I shall review Sicilia, for whose sight
  I have a woman's longing.
FLORIZEL   Fortune speed us!
  Thus we set on, Camillo, to the seaside.
CAMILLO
  The swifter speed the better.
                  Exeunt Florizel, Perdita, and Camillo.
AUTOLYCUS I understand the business, I hear it. To have
  an open ear, a quick eye, and a nimble hand is necessary
  for a cutpurse. A good nose is requisite also, to smell out
  work for the other senses. I see this is the time that the
  unjust man does thrive. What an exchange had this
  been without profit! What profit is here with this
  exchange! Sure the gods do this year connive at us, and
  we may do any thing extempore. The prince himself is
  about a piece of iniquity, stealing away from his father
  with his clog at his heels. If I thought it were a piece of
  honesty to acquaint the king with it, I would not do it. I
  hold it the more knavery to conceal it, and therein am I
  constant to my profession.

                  Enter Clown and Shepherd.

Aside, aside! Here is more matter for a hot brain. Every lane's end, every shop, church, session, hanging, yield a careful man work.

CLOWN See, see! What a man you are now! There is no other way but to tell the king she's a changeling and none of your flesh and blood.

SHEPHERD Nay, but hear me.

CLOWN Nay, but hear me.

SHEPHERD Go to, then.

CLOWN She being none of your flesh and blood, your flesh and blood has not offended the king, and so your flesh and blood is not to be punished by him. Show those things you found about her, those secret things, all but what she has with her. This being done, let the law go whistle, I warrant you.

SHEPHERD I will tell the king all, every word—yes, and his son's pranks too, who, I may say, is no honest man, neither to his father nor to me, to go about to make me the king's brother-in-law.

CLOWN Indeed, brother-in-law was the farthest off you could have been to him, and then your blood had been the dearer by I know how much an ounce.

AUTOLYCUS [aside] Very wisely, puppies.

SHEPHERD Well, let us to the king. There is that in this bundle will make him scratch his beard.

AUTOLYCUS [aside] I know not what impediment this complaint may be to the flight of my master.

CLOWN Pray heartily he be at the palace.

AUTOLYCUS [aside] Though I am not naturally honest, I am so sometimes by chance. Let me pocket up my pedlar's excrement. [Takes off his false beard.] How now, rustics, whither are you bound?

SHEPHERD To the palace, if it likes your worship.

AUTOLYCUS Your affairs, there, what, with whom, the condition of that bundle, the place of your dwelling, your names, your ages, of what having, breeding, and anything that is fitting to be known, discover.

CLOWN We are but plain fellows, sir.

AUTOLYCUS A lie! You are rough and hairy. Let me have no lying. It becomes none but tradesmen, and they often give us soldiers the lie; but we pay them for it with stamped coin, not stabbing steel; therefore they do not give us the lie.

CLOWN Your worship had like to have given us one, if you had not taken yourself with the manner.

SHEPHERD Are you a courtier, if it likes you, sir?

AUTOLYCUS Whether it likes me or no, I am a courtier. See you not the air of the Court in these enfoldings? Has not my gait in it the measure of the Court? Receives not your nose Court-odor from me? Reflect I not on your baseness, Court-contempt? Think you, because I insinuate, or tease from you your business, I am therefore no courtier? I am courtier head to foot, and one that will either push on or pluck back your business there. Whereupon I command you to open your affair.

SHEPHERD My business, sir, is to the king.

AUTOLYCUS What advocate have you to him?

SHEPHERD I know not, if it likes you.

CLOWN Advocate's the court-word for a pheasant. Say you have none.

SHEPHERD None, sir. I have no pheasant, cock nor hen.

AUTOLYCUS
  How blessèd are we that are not simple men!
  Yet nature might have made me as these are;
  Therefore I will not disdain.

CLOWN This cannot be but a great courtier.

SHEPHERD His garments are rich, but he wears them not handsomely.

CLOWN He seems to be the more noble in being fantastical. A great man, I'll warrant. I know by the picking of his teeth.

AUTOLYCUS The bundle there? What's in the bundle? Wherefore that box?

SHEPHERD Sir, there lie such secrets in this bundle and box, which none must know but the king, and which he shall know within this hour if I may come to the speech of him.

AUTOLYCUS Age, you have lost your labor.

SHEPHERD Why, sir?

AUTOLYCUS The king is not at the palace. He is gone aboard a new ship to purge melancholy and air himself; for, if you are capable of things serious, you must know the king is full of grief.

SHEPHERD So 'tis said, sir—about his son, that should have married a shepherd's daughter.

AUTOLYCUS If that shepherd is not in custody, let him fly. The curses he shall have, the tortures he shall feel, will break the back of man, the heart of monster.

CLOWN Think you so, sir?

AUTOLYCUS Not he alone shall suffer what wit can make heavy and vengeance bitter; but those that are germane to him, though removed fifty times, shall all come under the hangman—which, though it is great pity, yet it is necessary. An old sheep-whistling rogue, a ram-tender, to offer to have his daughter come into grace! Some say he shall be stoned, but that death is too soft for him, say I. Draw our throne into a sheep-cote! All deaths are too few, the sharpest too easy.

CLOWN Has the old man ever a son, sir, do you hear, if it likes you, sir?

AUTOLYCUS He has a son, who shall be flayed alive; then anointed over with honey, set on the head of a wasp's nest; then stand till he is three quarters and a dram dead; then recovered again with aqua-vitae or some other hot infusion. Then, raw as he is, and in the hottest day prognostication proclaims, shall he be set against a brick-wall, the sun looking with a southward eye upon him, where it is to behold him with flies blown to death. But what talk we of these traitorly rascals, whose miseries are to be smiled at, their offenses being so capital? Tell me, for you seem to be honest plain men, what you have to the king. Being something gently considered, I'll bring you where he is aboard, tender your persons to his presence, whisper him in your behalfs; and if it is in man besides the king to effect your suits, here is man shall do it.

CLOWN He seems to be of great authority. Close with him, give him gold; and though authority is a stubborn bear, yet he is oft led by the nose with gold. Show the inside of your purse to the outside of his hand, and no more ado. Remember 'stoned,' and 'flayed alive.'

SHEPHERD If it pleases you, sir, to undertake the business for us, here is that gold I have. I'll make it as much more and leave this young man in pawn till I bring it you.

AUTOLYCUS After I have done what I promised?

SHEPHERD Ay, sir.

AUTOLYCUS Well, give me the moiety. Are you a party in this business?

CLOWN In some sort, sir. But though my case is a pitiful one, I hope I shall not be flayed out of it.

AUTOLYCUS O, that's the case of the shepherd's son. Hang him, he'll be made an example.

CLOWN Comfort, good comfort! We must to the king and show our strange sights. He must know it is none of your daughter nor my sister; we are gone else. Sir, I will give you as much as this old man does when the business is performed, and remain, as he says, your pawn till it is brought you.

AUTOLYCUS I will trust you. Walk before toward the seaside. Go on the right hand. I will but look upon the hedge and follow you.

CLOWN We are blest in this man, as I may say, even blest.

SHEPHERD Let's before as he bids us. He was provided to
  do us good.   *Exeunt Shepherd and Clown.*
AUTOLYCUS If I had a mind to be honest, I see Fortune
  would not suffer me; she drops booties in my mouth. I
  am courted now with a double occasion, gold and a
  means to do the prince my master good, which who
  knows how that may turn back to my advancement? I
  will bring these two moles, these blind ones, aboard
  him. If he thinks it fit to shore them again and that the
  complaint they have to the king concerns him nothing,
  let him call me rogue for being so far officious; for I am
  proof against that title and what shame else belongs to
  it. To him will I present them; there may be matter in it.
                                                    Exit.

Act V

SCENE I
Sicilia. Leontes' palace.

Enter Leontes, Cleomenes, Dion, Paulina, Servants.

CLEOMENES
Sir, you have done enough, and have performed
A saint-like sorrow. No fault could you make
Which you have not redeemed—indeed, paid down
More penitence than done trespass. At the last,
Do as the heavens have done, forget your evil;
With them forgive yourself.

LEONTES   While I remember
Her and her virtues, I cannot forget
My blemishes in them, and so still think of
The wrong I did myself, which was so much
That heirless it has made my kingdom and
Destroyed the sweetest companion ever man
Bred his hopes out of.

PAULINA .   True, too true, my lord.
If one by one you wedded all the world,
Or from the all that are took something good
To make a perfect woman, she you killed
Would be unparalleled.

LEONTES   I think so. Killed?
She I killed? I did so, but you strike me
Sorely to say I did. It is as bitter
Upon your tongue as in my thought. Now, good now,
Say so but seldom.

617

CLEOMENES   Not at all, good lady.
  You might have spoken a thousand things that would
  Have done the time more benefit and graced
  Your kindness better.
PAULINA   You are one of those
  Would have him wed again.
DION   If you would not so,
  You pity not the state nor the remembrance
  Of his most sovereign name, consider little
  What dangers, by his highness' fail of issue,
  May drop upon his kingdom and devour
  Uncertain lookers-on. What were more holy
  Than to rejoice the former queen is well?
  What holier than, for royalty's repair,
  For present comfort and for future good,
  To bless the bed of majesty again
  With a sweet fellow to it?
PAULINA   There is none worthy,
  Respecting her that's gone. Besides, the gods
  Will have fulfilled their secret purposes;
  For has not the divine Apollo said,
  Is it not the tenor of his oracle,
  That King Leontes shall not have an heir
  Till his lost child is found? Which that it shall
  Is all as monstrous to our human reason
  As my Antigonus to break his grave
  And come again to me, who, on my life,
  Did perish with the infant. It is your counsel
  My lord should to the heavens be contrary,
  Oppose against their wills.

        [*To Leontes.*]

        Care not for issue;
  The crown will find an heir. Great Alexander

Left his to the worthiest; so his successor
Was like to be the best.
LEONTES   Good Paulina,
Who have the memory of Hermione,
I know, in honor, O that ever I
Had squared me to your counsel! Then even now
I might have looked upon my queen's full eyes,
Have taken treasure from her lips—
PAULINA   And left them
More rich for what they yielded.
LEONTES   You speak truth.
No more such wives; therefore, no wife! One worse,
And better used, would make her sainted spirit
Again possess her corpse, and on this stage,
Where we offend as now, appear soul-vexed,
And begin, 'Why to me?'
PAULINA   Had she such power,
She had just cause.
LEONTES   She had, and would incense me
To murder her I married.
PAULINA   I should so.
Were I the ghost that walked, I'd bid you mark
Her eye, and tell me for what dull part in it
You chose her. Then I'd shriek, that even your ears
Should rift to hear me, and the words that followed
Should be 'Remember mine.'
LEONTES   Stars, stars,
And all eyes else dead coals! Fear you no wife;
I'll have no wife, Paulina.
PAULINA   Will you swear
Never to marry but by my free leave?
LEONTES
Never, Paulina, so be blest my spirit.
PAULINA
Then, good my lords, bear witness to his oath.

CLEOMENES
    You tempt him overmuch.
PAULINA   Unless another,
    As like Hermione as is her picture,
    Affronts his eye.
CLEOMENES   Good madam—
PAULINA   I have done.
    Yet, if my lord will marry—if you will, sir,
    No remedy but you will—give me the office
    To choose you a queen. She shall not be so young
    As was your former, but she shall be such
    As, walked your first queen's ghost, it should take joy
    To see her in your arms.
LEONTES   My true Paulina,
    We shall not marry till you bid us.
PAULINA   That
    Shall be when your first queen is again in breath.
    Never till then.

                    Enter a Servant.

SERVANT
    One that gives out himself Prince Florizel,
    Son of Polixenes, with his princess—she
    The fairest I have yet beheld—desires access
    To your high presence.
LEONTES   What with him? He comes not
    Like to his father's greatness. His approach,
    So out of circumstance and sudden, tells us
    It is not a visitation framed, but forced
    By need and accident. What train?
SERVANT   But few,
    And those but mean.
LEONTES   His princess, say you, with him?

SERVANT
    Ay, the most peerless piece of earth, I think,
    That ever the sun shone bright on.
PAULINA   O Hermione.
    As every present time does boast itself
    Above a better gone, so must your grave
    Give way to what's seen now. Sir, you yourself
    Have said and written so, but your writing now
    Is colder than that theme. She had not been,
    And was not to be equalled—thus your verse
    Flowed with her beauty once. 'Tis shrewdly ebbed
    To say you have seen a better.
SERVANT   Pardon, madam.
    The one I have almost forgotten—your pardon;
    The other, when she has obtained your eye,
    Will have your tongue too. This is a creature,
    Would she begin a sect, might quench the zeal
    Of all professors else, make proselytes
    Of whom she but bid follow.
PAULINA   How? not women?
SERVANT
    Women will love her that she is a woman
    More worth than any man; men, that she is
    The rarest of all women.
LEONTES   Go, Cleomenes.
    Yourself, assisted with your honored friends,
    Bring them to our embracement.
                    Exit Cleomenes with others.
                    Still, it is strange
    He thus should steal upon us.
PAULINA   Had our prince,
    Jewel of children, seen this hour, he had paired
    Well with this lord. There was not full a month
    Between their births.

LEONTES   Pray, no more; cease. You know
   He dies to me again when talked of. Sure,
   When I shall see this gentleman, your speeches
   Will bring me to consider that which may
   Unfurnish me of reason. They are come.

   Enter Florizel, Perdita, Cleomenes, and others.

   Your mother was most true to wedlock, prince,
   For she did print your royal father off,
   Conceiving you. Were I but twenty-one,
   Your father's image is so hit in you,
   His very air, that I should call you brother,
   As I did him, and speak of something wildly
   By us performed before. Most dearly welcome!
   And your fair princess—goddess! O, alas!
   I lost a couple that between heaven and earth
   Might thus have stood begetting wonder as
   You, gracious couple, do. And then I lost—
   All my own folly—the society,
   Amity too, of your brave father, whom,
   Though bearing misery, I desire on my life
   Once more to look on him.
FLORIZEL   By his command
   Have I here touched Sicilia, and from him
   Give you all greetings that a king, at friend,
   Can send his brother; and, but infirmity
   Which waits upon worn times has something seized
   His wished ability, he had himself
   The lands and waters between your throne and his
   Measured to look upon you, whom he loves—
   He bade me say so—more than all the sceptres
   And those that bear them living.
LEONTES   O my brother,
   Good gentleman, the wrongs I have done you stir
   Afresh within me, and these your offices,

So rarely kind, are as interpreters
Of my behindhand slackness. Welcome hither,
As is the spring to the earth. And has he too
Exposed this paragon to the fearful usage,
At least ungentle, of the dreadful Neptune,
To greet a man not worth her pains, much less
The adventure of her person?
FLORIZEL   Good my lord,
  She came from Libya.
LEONTES   Where the warlike Smalus,
  That noble honored lord, is feared and loved?
FLORIZEL
  Most royal sir, from thence, from him, whose daughter
  His tears proclaimed his, parting with her. Thence,
  A prosperous south-wind friendly, we have crossed,
  To execute the charge my father gave me
  For visiting your highness. My best train
  I have from your Sicilian shores dismissed,
  Who for Bohemia bend, to signify
  Not only my fortune in Libya, sir,
  But my arrival and my wife's in safety
  Here where we are.
LEONTES   The blessèd gods
  Purge all infection from our air while you
  Do climate here! You have a holy father,
  A graceful gentleman, against whose person,
  So sacred as it is, I have done sin,
  For which the heavens, taking angry note,
  Have left me issueless; and your father's blest,
  As he from heaven merits it, with you,
  Worthy his goodness. What might I have been,
  Might I a son and daughter now have looked on,
  Such goodly things as you?

                    Enter a Lord.

LORD   Most noble sir,
  That which I shall report will bear no credit,
  Were not the proof so nigh. Please you, great sir,
  Bohemia greets you from himself by me,
  Desires you to attach his son, who has—
  His dignity and duty both cast off—
  Fled from his father, from his hopes, and with
  A shepherd's daughter.
LEONTES   Where's Bohemia? Speak.
LORD
  Here in your city. I now came from him.
  I speak amazedly, and it becomes
  My marvel and my message. To your Court
  While he was hastening—in the chase, it seems,
  Of this fair couple—meets he on the way
  The father of this seeming lady and
  Her brother, having both their country quitted
  With this young prince.
FLORIZEL   Camillo has betrayed me,
  Whose honor and whose honesty till now
  Endured all weathers.
LORD   Lay it so to his charge.
  He is with the king your father.
LEONTES   Who? Camillo?
LORD
  Camillo, sir. I spoke with him, who now
  Has these poor men in question. Never saw I
  Wretches so quake. They kneel, they kiss the earth,
  Forswear themselves as often as they speak.
  Bohemia stops his ears, and threatens them
  With divers deaths in death.
PERDITA   O my poor father!
  The heaven sets spies upon us, will not have
  Our contract celebrated.
LEONTES   You are married?

FLORIZEL
   We are not, sir, nor are we likely to be.
   The stars, I see, will kiss the valleys first;
   The odds for high and low are alike.
LEONTES   My lord,
   Is this the daughter of a king?
FLORIZEL   She is
   When once she is my wife.
LEONTES
   That 'once,' I see by your good father's speed,
   Will come on very slowly. I am sorry,
   Most sorry, you have broken from his liking
   Where you were tied in duty, and as sorry
   Your choice is not so rich in worth as beauty,
   That you might well enjoy her.
FLORIZEL   Dear, look up.
   Though Fortune, visible an enemy,
   Should chase us with my father, power no jot
   Has she to change our loves. Beseech you, sir,
   Remember since you owed no more to time
   Than I do now. With thought of such affections,
   Step forth my advocate. At your request
   My father will grant precious things as trifles.
LEONTES
   Would he do so, I'd beg your precious mistress,
   Which he counts but a trifle.
PAULINA   Sir, my liege,
   Your eye has too much youth in it. Not a month
   Before your queen died, she was more worth such gazes
   Than what you look on now.
LEONTES   I thought of her
   Even in these looks I made. [to Florizel] But your
      petition
   Is yet unanswered. I will to your father.
   Your honor not overthrown by your desires,
   I am friend to them and you. Upon which errand

I now go toward him; therefore follow me
And mark what way I make. Come, good my lord.

Exeunt.

SCENE II
Before Leontes' palace.

Enter Autolycus and a Gentleman.

AUTOLYCUS Beseech you, sir, were you present at this
relation?

FIRST GENTLEMAN I was by at the opening of the bundle,
heard the old shepherd deliver the manner how he
found it; whereupon, after a little amazedness, we were
all commanded out of the chamber. Only this I thought
I heard the shepherd say, he found the child.

AUTOLYCUS I would most gladly know the issue of it.

FIRST GENTLEMAN I make a broken delivery of the
business; but the changes I perceived in the king and
Camillo were very notes of admiration. They seemed
almost, with staring on one another, to tear the cases of
their eyes. There was speech in their dumbness, language
in their very gesture. They looked as they had heard of a
world ransomed, or one destroyed. A notable passion of
wonder appeared in them. But the wisest beholder, that
knew no more but seeing, could not say if the importance
were joy or sorrow; but in the extremity of the one, it
must needs be.

Enter another Gentleman.

Here comes a gentleman that haply knows more. The
news, Rogero?

SECOND GENTLEMAN Nothing but bonfires. The oracle
is fulfilled; the king's daughter is found. Such a deal of

wonder is broken out within this hour that balladmakers
cannot be able to express it.

Enter another Gentleman.

Here comes the Lady Paulina's steward; he can deliver
you more. How goes it now, sir? This news which is
called true is so like an old tale that the verity of it is in
strong suspicion. Has the king found his heir?

THIRD GENTLEMAN Most true, if ever truth were pregnant
  by circumstance. That which you hear you will swear
  you see, there is such unity in the proofs. The mantle of
  Queen Hermione's, her jewel about the neck of it, the
  letters of Antigonus found with it, which they know to
  be his hand; the majesty of the creature in resemblance
  of the mother, the affection of nobleness which nature
  shows above her breeding, and many other evidences
  proclaim her with all certainty to be the king's daughter.
  Did you see the meeting of the two kings?

SECOND GENTLEMAN No.

THIRD GENTLEMAN Then have you lost a sight which
  was to be seen, cannot be spoken of. There might you
  have beheld one joy crown another, so and in such
  manner that it seemed sorrow wept to take leave of
  them, for their joy waded in tears. There was casting up
  of eyes, holding up of hands, with countenance of such
  distraction that they were to be known by garment, not
  by features. Our king, being ready to leap out of himself
  for joy of his found daughter, as if that joy were now
  become a loss, cries, 'O, your mother, your mother!'
  then asks Bohemia forgiveness; then embraces his son-in-
  law; then again worries he his daughter with enfolding
  her. Now he thanks the old shepherd, who stands by
  like a weather-bitten conduit of many kings' reigns. I
  never heard of such another encounter, which lames
  report to follow it and undoes description to do it.

SECOND GENTLEMAN What, pray you, became of Antigonus, that carried hence the child?

THIRD GENTLEMAN Like an old tale still, which will have matter to rehearse, though credit be asleep and not an ear open. He was torn to pieces by a bear. This avouches the shepherd's son, who has not only his innocence, which seems much, to justify him, but a handkerchief and rings of his that Paulina knows.

FIRST GENTLEMAN What became of his bark and his followers?

THIRD GENTLEMAN Wrecked the same instant of their master's death and in the view of the shepherd; so that all the instruments which aided to expose the child were even then lost when it was found. But O, the noble combat that between joy and sorrow was fought in Paulina! She had one eye declined for the loss of her husband, another elevated that the oracle was fulfilled. She lifted the princess from the earth, and so locks her in embracing as if she would pin her to her heart that she might no more be in danger of losing.

FIRST GENTLEMAN The dignity of this act was worth the audience of kings and princes, for by such was it acted.

THIRD GENTLEMAN One of the prettiest touches of all, and that which angled for my eyes, caught the water though not the fish, was when, at the relation of the queen's death, with the manner how she came to it bravely confessed and lamented by the king, how attentiveness wounded his daughter. Till, from one sign of dolor to another, she did, with an 'Alas,' I would fain say, bleed tears, for I am sure my heart wept blood. Who was most marble there changed color; some swooned, all sorrowed. If all the world could have seen it, the woe had been universal.

FIRST GENTLEMAN Are they returned to the court?

THIRD GENTLEMAN No. The princess, hearing of her mother's statue, which is in the keeping of Paulina—a piece many years in doing and now newly performed by that rare Italian master, Julio Romano; who, had he himself eternity and could put breath into his work, would beguile Nature of her custom, so perfectly he is her ape. He so near to Hermione has done Hermione that they say one would speak to her and stand in hope of answer. Thither with all greediness of affection are they gone, and there they intend to sup.

SECOND GENTLEMAN I thought she had some great matter there in hand, for she has privately twice or thrice a day, ever since the death of Hermione, visited that removed house. Shall we thither and with our company piece the rejoicing?

FIRST GENTLEMAN Who would be thence that has the benefit of access? Every wink of an eye some new grace will be born. Our absence makes us unthrifty to our knowledge. Let's along.   *Exeunt Gentlemen.*

AUTOLYCUS Now, had I not the dash of my former life in me would preferment drop on my head. I brought the old man and his son aboard the prince, told him I heard them talk of a bundle and I know not what. But he at that time, over-fond of the shepherd's daughter—so he then took her to be—who began to be much seasick, and himself little better, extremity of weather continuing, this mystery remained undiscovered. But it is all one to me; for had I been the finder out of this secret, it would not have relished among my other discredits.

Enter Shepherd and Clown.

Here come those I have done good to against my will, and already appearing in the blossoms of their fortune.

SHEPHERD Come, boy. I am past more children, but your sons and daughters will be all gentlemen born.

CLOWN You are well met, sir. You denied to fight with me this other day, because I was no gentleman born. See

you these clothes? Say you see them not and think me
still no gentleman born! You were best say these robes
are not gentlemen born. Give me the lie, do, and try
whether I am not now a gentleman born.

AUTOLYCUS I know you are now, sir, a gentleman born.

CLOWN Ay, and have been so any time these four hours.

SHEPHERD And so have I, boy.

CLOWN So you have. But I was a gentleman born before
my father, for the king's son took me by the hand and
called me brother; and then the two kings called my
father brother; and then the prince my brother and the
princess my sister called my father father. And so we
wept, and there were the first gentleman-like tears that
ever we shed.

SHEPHERD We may live, son, to shed many more.

CLOWN Ay, or else it were hard luck, being in so
preposterous estate as we are.

AUTOLYCUS I humbly beseech you, sir, to pardon me all
the faults I have committed to your worship and to give
me your good report to the prince my master.

SHEPHERD Pray, son, do, for we must be gentle now we are
gentlemen.

CLOWN You will amend your life?

AUTOLYCUS Ay, if it likes your good worship.

CLOWN Give me your hand. I will swear to the prince you
are as honest a true fellow as any is in Bohemia.

SHEPHERD You may say it, but not swear it.

CLOWN Not swear it, now I am a gentleman? Let boors
and franklins say it, I'll swear it.

SHEPHERD How if it is false, son?

CLOWN If it is never so false, a true gentleman may swear
it in the behalf of his friend. And I'll swear to the prince
you are a tall fellow of your hands and that you will not
be drunk. But I know you are no tall fellow of your
hands and that you will be drunk. But I'll swear it, and
I would you would be a tall fellow of your hands.

AUTOLYCUS I will prove so, sir, to my power.

CLOWN Ay, by any means prove a tall fellow. If I do not
    wonder how you dare venture to be drunk, not being a
    tall fellow, trust me not. Hark! The kings and the
    princes, our kindred, are going to see the queen's picture.
    Come, follow us. We'll be your good masters.

Exeunt.

SCENE III
Paulina's house.

Enter Leontes, Polixenes, Florizel, Perdita, Camillo,
Paulina, Lords, and Attendants.

LEONTES
    O grave and good Paulina, the great comfort
    That I have had of you!

PAULINA   What, sovereign sir,
    I did not well, I meant well. All my services
    You have paid home. But that you have vouchsafed,
    With your crowned brother and these your contracted
    Heirs of your kingdoms, my poor house to visit,
    It is a surplus of your grace which never
    My life may last to answer.

LEONTES   O Paulina,
    We honor you with trouble. But we came
    To see the statue of our queen. Your gallery
    Have we passed through, not without much content
    In many singularities; but we saw not
    That which my daughter came to look upon,
    The statue of her mother.

PAULINA   As she lived peerless,
    So her dead likeness, I do well believe,
    Excels whatever yet you looked upon
    Or hand of man has done. Therefore I keep it

Lonely, apart. But here it is. Prepare
To see the life as lively mocked as ever
Still sleep mocked death. Behold, and say it is well.

Paulina reveals Hermione standing like a statue.

I like your silence; it the more shows off
Your wonder. But yet speak; first, you, my liege.
Comes it not something near?
LEONTES   Her natural posture!
Chide me, dear stone, that I may say indeed
You are Hermione; or rather, you are she
In your not chiding, for she was as tender
As infancy and grace. But yet, Paulina,
Hermione was not so much wrinkled, nothing
So aged as this seems.
POLIXENES   O, not by much.
PAULINA
So much the more our carver's excellence,
Which lets go by some sixteen years and makes her
As if she lived now.
LEONTES   As now she might have done,
So much to my good comfort, as it is
Now piercing to my soul. O, thus she stood,
Even with such life of majesty—warm life,
As now it coldly stands—when first I wooed her!
I am ashamed. Does not the stone rebuke me
For being more stone than it? O royal piece,
There's magic in your majesty, which has
My evils conjured to remembrance and
From your admiring daughter took the spirit,
Standing like stone with you.
PERDITA   And give me leave,
And do not say it is superstition, that
I kneel and then implore her blessing. Lady,

Dear queen, that ended when I but began,
Give me that hand of yours to kiss.
PAULINA   O, patience!
The statue is but newly fixed, the color's
Not dry.
CAMILLO
My lord, your sorrow was too sore laid on,
Which sixteen winters cannot blow away,
So many summers dry. Scarce any joy
Did ever so long live; no sorrow
But killed itself much sooner.
POLIXENES   Dear my brother,
Let him that was the cause of this have power
To take off so much grief from you as he
Will piece up in himself.
PAULINA   Indeed, my lord,
If I had thought the sight of my poor image
Would thus have wrought you—for the stone is mine—
I'd not have shown it.
LEONTES   Do not draw the curtain.
PAULINA
No longer shall you gaze on it, lest your fancy
May think anon it moves.
LEONTES   Let be, let be.
Would I were dead, but that, I think, already—
What was he that did make it? See, my lord,
Would you not deem it breathed? and that those veins
Did verily bear blood?
POLIXENES   Masterly done.
The very life seems warm upon her lip.
LEONTES
The fixture of her eye has motion in it,
As we are mocked with art.
PAULINA   I'll draw the curtain.
My lord is almost so far transported that
He will think anon it lives.

LEONTES   O sweet Paulina,
  Make me to think so twenty years together!
  No settled senses of the world can match
  The pleasure of that madness. Let it alone.
PAULINA
  I am sorry, sir, I have thus far stirred you; but
  I could afflict you farther.
LEONTES   Do, Paulina,
  For this affliction has a taste as sweet
  As any cordial comfort. Still it seems
  There is an air comes from her. What fine chisel
  Could ever yet cut breath? Let no man mock me,
  For I will kiss her.
PAULINA   Good my lord, forbear.
  The ruddiness upon her lip is wet;
  You'll mar it if you kiss it, stain your own
  With oily painting. Shall I draw the curtain?
LEONTES
  No, not these twenty years.
PERDITA   So long could I
  Stand by, a looker on.
PAULINA   Either forbear,
  Quit presently the chapel, or resolve you
  For more amazement. If you can behold it,
  I'll make the statue move indeed, descend
  And take you by the hand. But then you'll think—
  Which I protest against—I am assisted
  By wicked powers.
LEONTES   What you can make her do,
  I am content to look on; what to speak,
  I am content to hear, for it is as easy
  To make her speak as move.
PAULINA   It is required
  You do awake your faith. Then all stand still;
  Or those that think it is unlawful business
  I am about, let them depart.

LEONTES   Proceed.
  No foot shall stir.
PAULINA   Music! Awake her, strike!

                 [Music.]

  It is time; descend; be stone no more; approach;
  Strike all that look upon with marvel. Come,
  I'll fill your grave up. Stir, nay, come away;
  Bequeath to death your numbness, for from him
  Dear life redeems you. You perceive she stirs.

          Hermione comes down.

  Start not; her actions shall be holy as
  You hear my spell is lawful. Do not shun her
  Until you see her die 'again, for then
  You kill her doubly. Nay, present your hand.
  When she was young you wooed her; now in age
  Is she become the suitor?
LEONTES   O, she is warm!
  If this is magic, let it be an art
  Lawful as eating.
POLIXENES   She embraces him.
CAMILLO
  She hangs about his neck.
  If she pertains to life, let her speak too.
POLIXENES
  Ay, and make it manifest where she has lived,
  Or how stolen from the dead.
PAULINA   That she is living,
  Were it but told you should be hooted at
  Like an old tale; but it appears she lives,
  Though yet she speaks not. Mark a little while.
  Please you to interpose, fair madam. Kneel

And pray your mother's blessing. Turn, good lady;
Our Perdita is found.

HERMIONE   You gods, look down,
And from your sacred vials pour your graces
Upon my daughter's head! Tell me, my own,
Where have you been preserved? where lived? how found
Your father's Court? For you shall hear that I,
Knowing by Paulina that the oracle
Gave hope you were in being, have preserved
Myself to see the issue.

PAULINA   There's time enough for that,
Lest they desire upon this push to trouble
Your joys with like relation. Go together,
You precious winners all; your exultation
Partake to every one. I, an old turtle-dove
Will wing me to some withered bough and there
My mate, that's never to be found again,
Lament till I am lost.

LEONTES   O, peace, Paulina!
You should a husband take by my consent,
As I by yours a wife. This is a match,
And made between us by vows. You have found mine;
But how, is to be questioned, for I saw her,
As I thought, dead, and have in vain said many
A prayer upon her grave. I'll not seek far—
For him, I partly know his mind—to find you
An honorable husband. Come, Camillo,
And take her by the hand, whose worth and honesty
Are richly noted and here justified
By us, a pair of kings. Let's from this place.
What! look upon my brother. Both your pardons,
That ever I put between your holy looks
My ill suspicion. This your son-in-law
And son unto the king, whom heavens directing,
Is troth-plight to your daughter. Good Paulina,
Lead us from hence, where we may leisurely

Each one demand and answer to his part
Performed in this wide gap of time, since first
We were dissevered. Hastily lead away.   *Exeunt.*